AN EPISODE OF
JEWISH ROMANTICISM

SUNY series in Judaica:
Hermeneutics, Mysticism, and Religion

Michael Fishbane, Robert Goldenberg,
and Elliot Wolfson, Editors

AN EPISODE OF
JEWISH ROMANTICISM

Franz Rosenzweig's *The Star of Redemption*

ERNEST RUBINSTEIN

State University of New York Press

Published by
State University of New York Press, Albany

For information, address State University of New York
Press, State University Plaza, Albany, N.Y., 12246

Production by Diane Ganeles
Marketing by Nancy Farrell

Library of Congress Cataloging-in-Publication Data

Rubinstein, Ernest.
    An episode of Jewish romanticism : Franz Rosenzweig's The star of
redemption / Ernest Rubinstein.
        p.   cm. — (SUNY series in Judaica)
    Includes index.
    ISBN 0–7914–4275–6 (hc. : alk. paper). — ISBN 0–7914–4276–4 (pbk.
: alk. paper)
    1. Rosenzweig, Franz, 1886–1929.   Stern der Erlösung.
2. Romanticism—Religious aspects—Judaism.   3. Baeck, Leo,
1873–1956.   Romantische Religion.   4. Schelling, Friedrich Wilhelm
Joseph von, 1775–1854.   Philosophie der Kunst.   I. Title.
II. Series.
BM565.R613   1999
296.3—dc21   99–17920
                                                                  CIP

10 9 8 7 6 5 4 3 2 1

For Paul,
my classicist companion
on life's way

If love be blind, it best agrees with night.

—Shakespeare,
The Tragedy of Romeo and Juliet
act 3, scene 2, lines 9–10

Contents

Abbreviations

The three major texts discussed within this study are cited according to the following abbreviations:

PA   Friedrich Schelling, *The Philosophy of Art*, ed. and trans. Douglas W. Stott (Minneapolis: University of Minnesota Press, 1989).

RR   Leo Baeck, "Romantic Religion," in *Judaism and Christianity*, trans. Walter Kaufmann (Cleveland and New York: World Publishing Co., 1958; Philadelphia: Jewish Publication Society of America, 1958).

SR   Franz Rosenzweig, *The Star of Redemption*, trans. William W. Hallo (Notre Dame, Indianapolis: University of Notre Dame Press, 1985).

Preface

A visitor to Germany today will find only fragmentary remains of the old, pre-Holocaust German-Jewish culture. The Jews living in Germany today do not, for the most part, descend from the flourishing Jewish communities of 1920s Berlin or Frankfurt. Still, through the monuments, memorials, and restored synagogues of 1990s Germany, it is possible to reexperience a piece of the old German-Jewish sensibility. It hovers above the partially restored New Synagogue on Oranienburger Strasse in Berlin, once the second largest synagogue in the world, whose portico accommodated passage of two different sizes of carriage; and above the Westend Synagogue in Frankfurt, whose interior recalls popular images of ancient Egyptian or Assyrian temples. In the Westend Synagogue, the brilliant colors of the walls, shading up climactically into the deep blue of the dome, suggest a German romantic fantasy: an inverted cave, whose quietening depths have been raised up to the place of a canopy. German romanticism and Judaism together shape the space of this synagogue, as much as they shaped the thought of Franz Rosenzweig, who lies buried not far from it, in the city's Jewish cemetery.

That at least is the burden of this study: to uncover the traces of German romanticism in Rosenzweig's now classic text of Jewish theology, *The Star of Redemption*. The reading offered here is suggested by Rosenzweig's simultaneous location in the Jewish-religious and German philosophical and literary traditions. Because even the specifically German romantic sensibility ranges so widely, two texts are brought to bear to focus it quite specifically: Leo Baeck's essay "Romantic Religion," and Friedrich Schelling's *The Philosophy of Art*. The two texts are of different types: the first, a polemical description of an amalgam of characteristics Baeck names romantic religion; the second, an instance of early German romantic writing, though it contains as well its own characterizations of romanticism. The Baeck and Schelling texts are natural choices for lenses through which to read Rosenzweig's romanticism. Baeck and Rosenzweig were cordially acquainted contemporaries, both schooled in the classical philosophical and literary texts of German culture, both communally engaged German Jews. Schelling, who early on in his career belonged to the Jena circle of German romantics, exercised, by both scholarly consensus and Rosenzweig's own admission, a significant influence, through his later works, on *The Star of Redemption*. The Schelling text also serves to test the accuracy of Baeck's overtly polemical study of romanticism. Between Baeck's text and Schelling's, and Baeck's as tested against Schelling's, we obtain a dual standard of romanticism, each half of which limits and corrects the other, through which to read Rosenzweig's work.

This study first appeared as a dissertation submitted to the Religion Department of Northwestern University. I would like to thank my advisor, Manfred Vogel, of the Religion Department, for sharing with me his critical appreciation of Rosenzweig and the complex intellectual history from which he descends, and three members of the German Department, Geza von Molnar, Peter Fenves, and Helmut Mueller-Sievers, who, while serving as guides to Kant and Hegel, at the same time fashioned between them a model of intellectual community. I also want to thank Nancy Ellegate, Acquiring Editor at State University of New York Press, and Diane Ganeles, Senior Production Editor, for guiding the manuscript through the several stages of publication, and the anonymous readers who recommended the manuscript for publication.

Acknowledgments

For permission to include copyright material in this volume, acknowledgment is gratefully made to the following publishers:

Jewish Publication Society: for excerpts from "Romantic Religion," from *Judaism and Christianity*, by Leo Baeck, copyright 1958 by The Jewish Publication Society of America.

Simon & Schuster and A. P. Watt Ltd: for two lines from "Among School Children," by W. B. Yeats, from *The Poems of W. B. Yeats: A New Edition*, edited by Richard J. Finnerman, copyright 1928 by Macmillan Publishing Company; copyright renewed 1956 by Georgia Yeats. Permission from A. P. Watt Ltd., for markets outside the United States, the Philippines, and Canada, is on behalf of Michael Yeats.

University of Minnesota: for excerpts from *The Philosophy of Art*, by Friedrich Schelling, translated and with an introduction by Douglas W. Stott, copyright 1989 by the Regents of the University of Minnesota.

University of Notre Dame Press: for excerpts from *The Star of Redemption*, by Franz Rosenzweig, translated by William Hallo, copyright 1985 by the University of Notre Dame Press.

CHAPTER 1

Introduction

Judaism and Romanticism

Franz Rosenzweig (1886–1929) lived through two of the most extreme periods of modern German history: World War I and the Weimar Republic. Even in a national history beset by extremes, these two relatively short time spans stand out, the first for the cataclysmic destruction that occurred during it, and the second, which immediately followed, for the creative brilliance of its cultural life. Students of modern German history must confront the alternatively terrible and sublime reality of contradiction. It should therefore come as no surprise that, in the case of the relatively small part of that history we propose to study here, namely Rosenzweig's *The Star of Redemption*, prima facie contradictions in the secondary literature assault us from the start. One writer calls Rosenzweig "one of the most sublime manifestations of the greatness and religious genius of our [i.e., the Jewish] people."[1] Another tells us that "Rosenzweig yachol leheichashev bedin lenetsigah shel haromantikah betechuma shel hayahadut"[2] (Rosenzweig may justly be considered a representative of romanticism within the context of Judaism). And a third pronounces that romanticism belongs to "ways of thought out of sympathy with Judaism."[3] How can a sublime representation of Judaism manifest in a current of thought out of sympathy with Judaism?

Perhaps this could only happen among what Hannah Arendt called that "altogether unique phenomenon" of German Jewry.[4] It has been said of romanticism that, next to the Reformation, no other cultural movement has had so profound and definitive an impact on

1

Germany's spiritual identity.[5] At the same time, students of Jewish diaspora history have noted the particular fervor with which German Jews especially, among all the different nationalities of European Jewry, sought to appropriate their host culture. A notable instance is Hermann Cohen, whose essay, "Deutschtum und Judentum," boldly declares the points of identity between these two thought-worlds.[6] Jacques Derrida calls this essay a "strange text . . . whose extravagance, indeed delirium," reflects what even Cohen himself might admit was a "psyche which is itself a reflexive delirium."[7] One cannot read Gershom Scholem's own reflections "On the Social Psychology of the Jews in Germany: 1900–1933" without feeling quite wrenchingly the force of Derrida's interpretation. Scholem depicts a self-delusive community, "strangely smitten with blindness," whose understanding of its own mission was to disappear as a distinct community.[8] Scholem implies that the German Jews purchased their German identity at the terribly high price of their own self-division and even self-sacrifice. But if German identity was romantic, then self-divisive and vanishing movements were not the price of it; they were that identity, itself.

But then, what was German romanticism? "The bewildering plethora of heterogeneous concepts, attitudes and images associated with the romantic,"[9] is so great that "one may easily begin to doubt whether there was such a 'movement' at all."[10] In a scattered sampling of recent articles from the cultural review sections of the *New York Times*, romanticism is associated with despondency, madness, escape and vampires.[11] But German romanticism in particular is typically confined to a family of ideas that flourished in Germany at the end of the eighteenth and beginning of the nineteenth centuries. By one reckoning, these years extend from 1796 to 1830, and are divided into stages: 1796–1804 was the period of early German romanticism; 1804–1815, the middle period; and 1815–1830 the late period.[12] If we confine ourselves still further to the early period, then romanticism becomes the ideas of a small group of people writing over a few years, and consisting minimally of the Schlegel brothers, Schleiermacher, Novalis, Tieck and Schelling[13]—the so-called Jena romantics, or *Fruehromantiker*.

The secondary literature on these writers and their romantic friends is vast; even a cursory review of it is beyond the scope of this slight introduction. But what must, from the start, impress any student of religion, is the patently religious character of the early German romantics. If this were not already obvious from Schleiermacher's important place among them, from works of their circle bearing such titles as *Effusions of an Art-Loving Friar*,[14] or from Lacoue-Labarthe's and Nancy's index to key concepts—such as Christianity, God, mysticism, religion—in Schlegel's works,[15] it could be gleaned by reading what one critic has called "the supreme creation of German romanticism,"[16] namely Novalis' *Heinrich von Ofterdingen*.[17] Despite Friedrich Schlegel's later conversion to Catholicism, the identification some critics make between Christianity and romanticism,[18] and Novalis' own "Christendom oder Europa,"[19] which pleads for a revival of the church universal, the religion that shows through the works of the early romantics is not normative or institutional Christianity. Some critics have preferred to distinguish a distinctive "romantic religion,"[20] or at least a "romantic view of religion."[21] Most would find in this religion a preoccupation with the idea of the infinite,[22] and an acute feeling for the interrelatedness of things. It is particularly over seeming opposites that the romantics find connections,[23] as of part to whole,[24] nature to history, death to life, past to future.[25] A configuration of linked oppositions constitute *das Ganze*, or the whole.[26] But these two pillars of romantic religion, the infinite and the whole, are themselves an opposition, since the whole implies a closure or self-enclosure, that the unbounded infinite disrupts. That, in building its structure of ideas, romantic religion simultaneously illustrates them, is the first of its vanishing movements, performed here on the space between form and content.

The space does not entirely vanish. Where opposition occurs as a content of romantic religion, as a belief in the relations that span opposites, the space between the opposites is closed over in the whole. But where opposition occurs as the form of romantic religion, in the space between the opposed doctrines of the infinite and the whole, the space is not completely closed. And here romantic religion performs another movement characteristic of it. It will not choose between the systematizable whole and the system-bursting infinite, but unsettlingly hovers between them. "It is equally fatal for the mind to have a system and to have none," says Schlegel. "It will simply have to decide to combine the two."[27]

If the simultaneity of opposites is a darkness to human understanding, then, says romantic religion, so much the worse for the understanding. The understanding, as Kant presented it, was the categorizing component of human reason, which actively determined the objectivity of what would otherwise be blind, sensual intuition. Where the understanding fails to combine opposites, feeling and the imagination succeed. According to Schlegel's famous phrase, the romantic was "was uns einen sentimentalen Stoff in einer phantastischen Form darstellt"[28] (what represents an emotive subject matter in a fantastic, or imaginative, form). A sentimental subject matter is a content of feeling; a fantastic form is one that the imagination "can raise . . . again and again to a higher power . . . in an endless succession of mirrors."[29]

The endlessness of the succession of mirrors itself mirrors what we posited as the first pillar of romanticism, namely the lure of the infinite. Schlegel here implicitly identifies the infinite with form. If the other originary concept in our construction of romantic religion, namely the whole, can be taken for content, then Schlegel's remarks reinterpret the opposition between the infinite and the whole as one between form and content. And if, by illustrating opposition in its very self-construction, romanticism reduces the distinction between form and content, it now reaffirms the distance between them by relating them, analogously, with the overtly oppositional infinite and whole. The instated distance inverts or reverses the vanishing one, as though the two were reflections in a mirror. And this, after vanishing and hovering, is the third characteristically romantic movement, namely inversion or mirroring.

The three movements are interrelated. The reflection of an object in a pool of water mirrors its object, but only as a hovering illusion that any disturbance to the pond's quiet surface will cause to vanish. If these movements are applied to the infinite and the whole, the religious mechanics of romanticism becomes clear. Romantic religion sanctifies a vision of the whole. But the whole is infinitely mirrored throughout its parts. The whole is the object and the myriad of particulars, its hovering reflections. The attuned romantic who disturbs the reflections causes them to vanish, at least momentarily, before the soteric vision of the whole.

The disturbance that reveals the reflections for the hovering concealments they are is, principally, art. Art structures reflection. By itself reflecting particular things, it mirrors what the particular things themselves reflect, namely the whole. Art is the organon of romantic religion, as prayer is of institutional religion, in the sense of being the means of passage from premise (in the world of particulars) to conclusion (in visionary wholeness). Indeed, the art-loving friar specifically compares art appreciation to prayer. Schleiermacher hoped that the religiously insensate might be brought to religious feeling through art, and Schlegel, who pictured the arts disconsolate on Mount Parnassus, ever since the departure of Apollo, offered them in Christianity a new religion to serve. Theodore Ziolkowski rightly notes that romantics did not so much substitute art for religion, as propose to fulfill religion by means of art.[30]

Under the aegis of art, the last pieces of romantic religion fall into place. These are self-consciousness and irony on the one hand, freedom and individuality on the other. Irony is a product of romantic hovering. The romantic's resolution of the tension between opposites is to hover between them. The constant awareness that any declared stance is balanced by its opposite, and, most especially, any stance of completion, by the breach of the infinite, is romantic irony. Irony keeps romantic religion from becoming too self-serious. The infinite punctures holes in self-satisfied visions of the whole, and returns any romantic who thought to forget himself there, to the self-conscious awareness of his own finitude. Romantic art, strung as it is between finite content and infinite form, is ineluctably ironic, and wishes to string its viewers between a similar opposition of finite self and consciousness of self raised "again and again to a higher power." To accomplish his revelatory feats, however, both the artist and viewer must not be trammeled by custom or convention. The romantic suspicion of the laws of categorial thinking, which obstinately insist on their so Aristotelian -$(p \text{ \& } \text{-}p)$, negatively mirrors the romantic's indulgence of the category-defying individual and his freedom.

If we can take irony, self-consciousness, individuality and freedom as mere implications of the ideas that preceded them in our construction of romantic religion, then that religion comprises in the main: a form, a content, three movements and an organon. (The form is the infinite, the content is the whole, the movements are vanishing, hovering, and mirroring, and the organon is art.) If a religion so constructed seems little different from a recipe for stew, that only goes to confirm how much this religion tastes of romanticism, which loves simultaneously to illustrate the ironies it describes.

With its subject heading, "Jewish Wit and Humor," the Library of Congress, responsible for cataloging, ideally, all books published in the United States, lends its most unironic but considerable authoritative weight to the idea of a distinctively Jewish brand of humor.[31] It has been called an ironical humor. And if it is, then the Jewish sensibility might seem highly receptive to romanticism. And yet, a writer on Gustav Mahler who, by asking whether that composer was "German romantic or Jewish satirist," implies that these are disjunctively opposed, observes that "it would be hard to imagine a Jew as a whole-hearted romantic."[32] His claim might be assessed from two different angles: the theological, and the historical.

Judaism foils any straightforward comparison with romantic religion by coming in so many shapes. If Arthur Lovejoy insisted that romanticism could only be discussed in the plural,[33] it is Jacob Neusner who repeatedly insists that Judaism is really Judaisms.[34] And yet, insofar as Judaism is, as it is sometimes called, a moral monotheism, it must resist almost all the principal traits of romantic religion. Monotheism does not aspire to a vision of the whole but, to the extent that it is visionary at all, of God. And God is quite pointedly distinguished from the whole, insofar as this includes the particulars of the world. This God is not infinitely mirrored in the world, but primarily in only one distinct part of it, which is thereby raised above the rest of it, namely the human. Neither vanishing nor hovering are characteristic movements of moral monotheism, but rather obedience is, to the divine commands. The aptly named *luftmensh*, from the Yiddish, meaning air-person, who inclines to vanish or hover in the midst of the world's concretions, is simply a figure of fun, never of normative behavior. Indeed, individuality as such, even of the saintly type, raises suspicions in the so communally oriented daily life of traditional Judaism.[35] The freedom that Judaism commends is for the sake of obedience, not the untrammeled unfoldings of art. If any one organon furthers the Jewish movement from finite soul to God, it is prayer, understood in the broadest sense as ritual observance, study, and good deeds.

The one clear point of affinity between Jewish and romantic religion is the idea of the infinite. Both religions agree that the infinite imposes limitations on human understanding, though romanticism makes more than Judaism does of the resulting darkness. The multiple literatures of Judaism—the biblical, rabbinic, philosophical, and mystical—all insist on the infinity of God. This tenet is popularly expressed in the liturgy, in proclamations of God's oneness and incomparability, and in day-to-day ways of circumventing the specific naming of God. The only style of Judaism that would stretch this one affinity into a broad congruence with romantic religion is the mystical; and it would do so precisely by compromising the otherwise so relentless monotheism in the direction of pantheism. Indeed, the congruences between German romanticism and kabbalah have been noted,[36] as has the romantic nature of mysticism generally.[37]

The turn to history at first blush seems to offer more promise of meeting between Jew and romantic. Writers on Jewish history single out several periods that reflect what they characterize as romantic tendencies in the surrounding culture. Ralph Marcus finds a "romantic political bent" showing equally in the utopian literature of ancient Hellenism, and in the apocalyptic literature of the ancient Jews, and additionally deems "romantic types" those Jews who were drawn to Zoroastrianism, dualism, angelology, and eschatological speculation.[38] In the Middle Ages, it is sometimes Judah Halevi who is singled out for romantic, on account of the so atypical (for the time) antirationalism he advanced. In modern times, romantic interest in the past is said to have fueled the rise of *Wissenschaft des Judentums*,[39] and two such polar opposites as Martin Buber and Samson Raphael Hirsch are thought to have sprung from the same German romantic ground.[40] The nineteenth century thinker, Joseph Wolf, is shown indebted to the "romantic notions" of Schleiermacher;[41] and several modern German-Jewish movements, Habonim and "Blau Weis", to the romantic teachings of the German Volkish movement.[42]

Of course, across these diverse attributions of romantic tendencies to Jewish thinkers and movements, no one meaning of romanticism prevails. The term conveys a diversity of traits: escapist longings for the ideal; nostalgic love of the past; antirationalism; mysticism; nationalism. Certainly all of these have marked important periods of Jewish history. But what seems unbridgably to divide Judaism from historical romanticism in general is the antisemitism commonly associated with its specific German expression. There is indeed ample ground for respecting this divide. Even apart from such sweeping claims as Heine's that "hatred of the Jews begins with the Romantic school,"[43] the antipathy of some German romantics towards the Jewish people is well documented. In a formidable study of middle romanticism, Guenter Oesterle examines the antisemitism of Clemens Brentano, Achim von Arnim, Adam Mueller, and their friends in the Deutsche christliche Tischgesellschaft.[44] At the same time, it must be respected that the early romantics— Schelling, Novalis, Schleiermacher—do not evince the same harsh animus. As Oesterle observes, it would flatly contradict Schleiermacher's *Geselligkeitsideal*, Schlegel's posited need of the complementary "other" (*der Fremde*) for self-fulfillment,[45] to say nothing of the whole tenor of the "progressive universal poetry,"[46] to exclude Jews from literary society. And of course, they were not excluded, but were, through the salon life that flourished at the beginning of the nineteenth century in Germany, at its very center. The antisemitism to be found in Schleiermacher, Novalis and Schelling is the standard European kind, dating back to the church fathers, that burdens Judaism with the role of superseded harbinger of Christianity,[47] although Novalis, commenting on the dispersion of the Jews, is more

struck in at least one passage by the reconciled opposition of East
and West it illustrates, than by any "lesson" it might teach about the
rejection of Christianity, and the late Schelling reproves Christians
for their neglect of Hebrew Scripture and praises the acuity of Jewish listeners at his lectures.[48]

It is perhaps of merely coincidental interest that two important
middle romantics, the Grimm brothers, did much of their work in
Kassel, Rosenzweig's birthplace, and that what one writer has called
the romantically motivated "Second Emancipation" of the Jews
began with Nathan Adler (1741–1800) in Frankfurt, Rosenzweig's
burial place.[49] For Otto Poeggeler, Rosenzweig had distinctly "romantic tendencies" that were related to his translation of Judah
Halevi's poems, and his late appreciation of Hoelderlin.[50] So far as
Halevi is concerned, Dorit Orgad goes so far as to interpret *The Star
of Redemption* as the rational-poetic outcome of a centuries-span-
ning dialog between Rosenzweig and that rational antirationalist of
the Middle Ages.[51] If the romantic line can be stretched from Rosenzweig to as far back as Halevi, perhaps it is less of a stretch to Pascal
and Kierkegaard.[52] To the extent that the existentialists descend
from the romantics, especially on the issue of feeling, these proto-ex-
istentialists may be taken for at least spiritual kin of the romantics,
and of Rosenzweig, too. But the most interesting "romantic" precedent of all may be Hoelderlin. Though Rosenzweig himself acknowledges his debt to that poet,[53] it is Scholem who linked the two most
memorably by prefacing his essay, "Franz Rosenzweig and his book
The Star of Redemption," with an extensive quotation from Hoelderlin's poem, "Patmos".[54] The verses describe a multiple vanishing of
life, beauty, and speech in which nonetheless a consummating end is
reached. The German Jews as a body wanted too much to vanish.
But vanishing is never a proper goal. The goallessly attained end
does not vanish in its end but leaves a living trace. *The Star of Redemption* is part of Rosenzweig's trace.

Romanticism and Idealism

If Judaism and romanticism are already, themselves, too plural-
istic to admit of easy comparison, idealism, at least in its absolute
German form, confines itself to a few works of, principally, three
philosophers: Fichte, Hegel, and Schelling. Like romanticism, ideal-

ism was relatively short-lived, and as Germany's reigning philosophical system, died with Hegel in 1831. Nonetheless, in its time it exercised great influence beyond the bounds of philosophy, and continued to do so even afterwards through the multiple and ongoing responses to it.

Rosenzweig is one of several German Jewish thinkers who lived under Hegel's spell. Though after writing his dissertation on Hegel's political theory, Rosenzweig grew to reject Hegel's idealism, he continues to write in response to it, even up through *The Star of Redemption*. In the early pages of that work, in a short section titled "Hegel," Rosenzweig discusses the resolution Hegelian dialectic effected between the claims of reason and faith. But Hegel is an unnamed presence in many other places throughout the work, as the index references under "Hegel," at the back of both the Notre Dame and Suhrkamp editions of the book, to pages on which the name does not specifically appear suggest. Part of the problem of interpreting the romantic features of the *Star* is determining their relation to the idealist ones. Romanticism and idealism are complexly interrelated. The early romantics, especially Novalis, built on Fichtean idealism. Schelling's esthetics borrows heavily from the Schlegels. But Hegel, according to one of the now classic works on German romanticism, *The Literary Absolute*, wrote largely in "opposition to the romantic gesture."[55]

In some ways, idealism and romanticism are simply different projects. Idealism's is largely epistemological: it rose in answer to what were perceived as troubling limitations and incompletions in Kant's theory of knowledge. It sought simultaneously to overcome all theoretical restrictions on human knowledge and to systematize the whole of it. Romanticism, by contrast, was in the main an esthetic movement, concerned with philology, criticism, and art history.[56] What blurs the bounds between them is that early German romanticism was theoretical and, in constructing its theory of literature, inevitably epistemological; while idealism just as inevitably included within its comprehensive reach the philosophical foundations of art. Any adequate account of these mutual trespassings and subsumings is out of the question here; we must confine ourselves to their bearing on a romantic interpretation of *The Star of Redemption*.

Idealism, like romanticism, generates a noninstitutional religion of its own. Rosenzweig himself specifically names the theoretical entity of "idealist religion,"[57] but others, too, have commented on the "religious self-consciousness of idealism."[58] As in all monistic religions, the central passage in idealist religion is from mistaken beliefs in the ultimacy of separation to knowledge of the one, undifferentiable unity. Perhaps the most significant tracing of this passage occurs in Hegel's very variously interpreted *Phenomenology of Spirit*. A tradition of religious readings of this work, some of which explicitly claim it for Christianity, continues into the twentieth century, but even the casual reader (if Hegel may be read casually) of its opening pages must be struck by the religious tone of the text. Spirit, the Absolute, and indeed God are the principal player(s) in Hegel's prefatory words. If, to all these terms, Hegel himself prefers "the Subject," that only shows how much God's principal business is knowing. *The Phenomenology of Spirit* follows what ultimately shows itself for the divine consciousness as it moves from its simplest claims to know something to its final awareness that what it knows absolutely, without any residue of an outstanding unknown, is simply itself. Hegel presumes to follow this process without importing any "of our own bright ideas." But this essentially epistemological journey becomes religious when the reader, far from importing ideas into it, is himself imported into it, so that what began with his private opening of the text ends in convergence with the traced consciousness' own divine and absolute self-knowledge. The organon of this passage is dialectic, a movement of reasoning that Hegel characterizes as the "transition of one opposite into its opposite." It is the very limitations of language that fuel the dialectical process, for no sooner has a description of the purportedly known been offered than it shows itself to apply to the very opposite of what was intended. The first such dialectical passage occurs over the word "this," used by consciousness to denote in the simplest way whatever sensation it is immediately having. For consciousness soon wakens to the fact that "this" not only fails to reach that specific sensation, but applies indiscriminately to any sensation it might have. A term employed to reach a particular winds up reaching, in precise reversal of intention, a universal. For Hegel, this inversive quality of language is "divine," for the simple reason that it leads both consciousness and reader to the ultimate awareness of its/their monistic allness. That ultimate awareness dawns at the point where language finally rests on, or indeed in, the object for which it reaches.[59]

It well serves the religious nature of Hegelian idealism that that resting point lies so very far from the originary "this." For as Hegel traces the repetitive course of dialectical inversion, consciousness pretty much traverses the whole of purported knowledge, leaving the fused consciousness/reader at the end with an organic vision of all there is to know. That the religious claims of such historical religions as Judaism and Christianity are mere, albeit late, stages on the dialectical course, points up how much idealist religion is indeed, as Rosenzweig suggests, an entity in and unto itself. If it has historical precedents, they are probably the religiophilosophical traditions of self-sufficiency, whose God is closer to Aristotle's or Spinoza's, than to the Bible's, and whose spokesmen include Kant who, in his famous essay, "What is Enlightenment?," pleaded for reason's self-sufficiency in religious matters, and entitlement to release from all "self-incurred tutelage."[60]

It is on this point of reason's self-sufficiency to its religious task of embracing the whole, that idealist and romantic religion may be most instructively and differentiably compared. For otherwise, the two religions are very similar: we encounter in idealism the same movements that characterize romanticism—the hoverings, vanishings, and mirrorings. Consciousness hovers when for a time it indecisively wavers between what it means and what it says until, having chosen, it momentarily collapses the distinction between the two. But the distinction has no sooner collapsed than it emerges again in a new guise; until, at the end of many repetitions of the same process, consciousness gazes restfully into what finally shows itself to it as the identically opposite mirror-image object of its own subjectivity. Certainly the two collapsed distinctions, between art and criticism (within romanticism), and between subject and object (within idealism), follow the same movement of two becoming one over a mirroring divide. We find in idealist religion the same longing for wholeness that romanticism shows, and, if we include under the rubric of idealist religion, the sixth chapter of Schelling's *System of Transcendental Idealism*, we can say that, like romantic religion, it is also able to take art for the organon of its progress[61] (though Hegel does not).

The "minute" difference between idealism and romanticism, say Lacoue-Labarthe and Nancy, is over the issue of "a supplementary complexity, hesitating, hovering, or *schweben*, to use a word that these [romantic] texts are immoderately fond of."[62] It is not the mere act of hovering that divides them since, after all, the idealist hovers too, but a "supplementary" hovering that occurs in romanticism over and above idealism's. Nor is the division over whether philosophy or art ultimately resolves the hovering, since the idealist Schelling already decides in favor of art, but whether the hovering ever wholly resolves at all. The same fundamental division appears over the issue of the infinite. We took the intractability of the infinite, its never wholly appeasable disruptions of the whole, for the first defining mark of romantic religion. Romantic religion hovers irresolutely between the infinite and the whole. The role of the infinite in

Hegelian dialectic is to be the "beyond"[63] that appears over the horizon of every claim to know that consciousness makes, except for the very last one. For where, in that last claim to knowledge, consciousness finally indicates its own act of indicating, all distance between subject and object has vanished without residue.

It was the romantic's claim that "there is nothing in philosophy that can provide the subject with access to itself."[64] The infinity of the Hegelian subject can never be its own circumscribed object. Rather, the infinite can only be presented to consciousness in an indirect way, through an "exergue," Lacoue-Labarthe's and Nancy's term for that which stands outside a thing as simultaneously its end and completion. This is precisely the role the concrete artwork plays to the infinite or, indeed, that romanticism would claim to play to idealism. The exergue hovers between self-instatement and vanishing before the infinite. It exists precisely to vanish before what disrupts it or, as Lacoue-Labarthe and Nancy put it, it is in its "not being there" that it is.[65] The exergue occupies that paradoxical space just on the other side of the infinite, like the never-reached limit on the infinitely decreasing space between a hyperbola and its asymptote. Idealism presumes to guide the curve of the hyperbola to its limit; romanticism hovers between the last-attained point of the curve, after which there is always another, and the line marking the limit the curve never touches. From a romantic point of view, idealism's claim is indeed hyperbole; the true completion of the idealist movement is the romantic's infinitely hovering postponement of completion.

The difference between romanticism and idealism is thus not merely minute, but actually infinitesimal. And yet even so great a smallness will help us differentiate the romanticism from the idealism within the *Star*. For we must not be misled by Rosenzweig's overt rejections of idealism. The existentialism associated with Rosenzweig has been traced back, alternatively, to both romanticism and idealism.[66] Much of what is romantic about the *Star* is also idealist. We shall be on special lookout for the differentiably romantic note.

Rosenzweig and Baeck

Both Franz Rosenzweig and Leo Baeck participated actively in Jewish communal life during the tempestuous years of the Weimar Republic—Rosenzweig as head of the Freies Juedisches Lehrhaus in

Frankfurt, and Baeck as rabbi in Berlin. Both were philosophically minded Jews steeped in German culture, sharing a common teacher in Hermann Cohen, and a common, concerned interest in Christian history and thought. In the secondary literature, they are sometimes grouped with Martin Buber as German Jewry's principal intellectual spokesmen during the years of the Weimar Republic. But, though Baeck and Rosenzweig were cordially acquainted—it was Baeck who carried out Rabbi Nehemiah Nobel's plan of titling Rosenzweig *morenu*, "our teacher" in the rabbinic tradition, a title that appears on Rosenzweig's tombstone, and who insisted that his Bnai Brith lodge buy 7,000 copies of the Buber-Rosenzweig Pentateuch translation[67]—and though the two wrote appreciatively of each other,[68] there can be no doubt that Rosenzweig enjoyed a closer relation to Buber.[69] It is not just their interpretations of Judaism that are more similar, or that they were more intimately connected by their shared, long-term project of translating the Bible into German, but their respective vocations were closer. Baeck was a professional rabbi; Buber and Rosenzweig were not. Buber was a university professor; but even this was too professionally compromising for Rosenzweig, who wanted the Lehrhaus he founded for educating adult Jews to be "non-specialist, non-rabbinical, non-polemical, non-apologetic," for its "personal features" would otherwise suffer;[70] as though the personal and rabbinical or the institutional of any kind were irremediably opposed. The *Freies* of Freies Juedisches Lehrhaus implied, in part, a spirit of free (nonapologetic) inquiry. Nonetheless, it should be noted that, despite the difference of vocation, Baeck did teach at Rosenzweig's Lehrhaus where, according to Glatzer, he "made a deep impression."[71]

It is probably on the issue of polemics that Baeck and Rosenzweig are so far separated that the very conjunction of their names rings incongruously, so much so that very little work comparing them can be found in the secondary literature.[72] If Rosenzweig was overtly antipolemical, Baeck's appreciative biographer, Albert Friedlander, concedes that an exhaustive survey of his subject's works "in the end identifies them with the literature of apologetics."[73] The gap between rabbinic and lay vocation no doubt informs these opposed evaluations of apologetics. That which seeks to be instituted, such as a structure of religious authority, may well require apologetic defense. Still, Rosenzweig was by no means as unsympathetic towards clerical office as was, say, Kierkegaard or even the less virulently anticlerical Kant. Though in his review of E. B. Cohn's book, *Judentum: Ein Aufruf an die Zeit*, he severely critiques the genre of the sermon,[74] he held the Frankfurt rabbi, Nehemiah Nobel, in very high esteem.

In 1923, in an essay entitled "Apologetic Thinking," Rosenzweig reviewed two contemporary apologetic works: Max Brod's *Paganism, Christianity, Judaism*, and the second edition of Baeck's *Essence of Judaism*. By way of preface and conclusion to the reviews proper, Rosenzweig considers the nature of apologetics generally. It is in contrast to dogmatic theology that Rosenzweig is able, quite unexpectedly, to present apologetic thinking in a sympathetic light. Judaism is blocked from developing any equivalent of Christian dogmatics by the peculiar resistance one of its central beliefs shows to dogmatic articulation, namely the chosenness of the Jewish people. Chosenness is a presupposition of conscious Jewish existence that, directly and propositionally formulated, in isolation, can only be denied. So it is not formulated as an isolated proposition at all, but is always embedded in liturgical, narrative or mystical contexts (almost never, Rosenzweig points out quite interestingly, in philosophical ones). By contrast, there are never enough discrete proclamations of Christianity's central Christological teaching. It is precisely by shared acceptance of a dogmatically formulable teaching that Christian community builds; while Jewish community rests on a presupposition, stored protectedly for the most part beneath self-awareness.[75]

If Judaism does not formulate its own teachings to itself, it can and does articulate them for others. But the stimulus must come from without it. If the charge against it comes from philosophers, that the Bible is too anthropomorphic in its speech about God, Judaism can respond, with Philo and Maimonides, that the biblical pictures are allegorical figures; if the charge comes from Christians that Jews are too insular, the response comes from Mendelssohn that Jewish teachings are in fact universal. Because apologetics responds as the occasion demands, it is "occasional" thinking. And this kind of recorded thinking, by its unsystematic and timely nature, both refreshes and charms, even centuries after the occasions that stimulated it have passed.[76]

Apologetics is stimulated from without, but its movement is entirely from within. It proceeds by deflecting from the inwardness it defends all threats and attacks from without. According to Rosenzweig's epistemology, which we shall consider in the course of our study, such a movement can never issue in knowledge. Knowledge, as we shall see, is always a projection backwards from relation. It shows itself as the presupposition of relation. But the movement of apologetics is precisely to deny relation, to negate the other that comes from without. Rosenzweig understands that, in the course of history, such self-defensive action is necessary. But one can have no illusion that it issues in anything more than self-defense. It does not yield self-knowledge, nor any insight into one's own individuality. On the contrary, the self-enclosed subject of apologetic defense patterns himself after the universal prototype of the human as such, which is the isolated, self-affirming self. Rosenzweig observes about the apologist, in a passage reminiscent of Hegel's reflection on the divine nature of language that, "although meaning himself, he speaks about man, about all men."[77] Self-knowledge admits into its realm a vulnerability that is foreign to apologetics. For the relationality that enables self-knowledge discloses an affectable self. What is known in self-knowledge incorporatingly receives, rather than deflects, movements from without, which help definitively to shape the self. So self-knowledge is not a matter of self-defense, but of suffering in the most literal sense, and of "the ultimate suffering of knowledge."[78]

After Baeck read Rosenzweig's review essay, he wrote to Rosenzweig asking whether, in the end, all philosophical thought was not apologetic. Was not all philosophical reflection, from Plato to Kant and Hegel, in defense of a goal? Baeck's subsumption of the whole history of philosophy under apologetics recalls Rosenzweig's corresponding judgment on the same history, that it was a continuum of presumptuous claims for monism (SR 12). Rosenzweig might well have agreed with Baeck about philosophy and added—so much the worse for philosophy. Instead, he develops the implication in Baeck's question, that apologetics is in fact so much the normal way of thinking that there seems no alternative to it. The alternative there is, namely the open-ended subjection of self to movements from without that condition actual self-knowledge, is too perilous ("lebensgefaehrlich") for everyday life. Rosenzweig admits that his review essay should have closed by qualifying the availability of self-knowledge, and credits Baeck with seeing the missing qualification written there, at the end, in "sympathetischer Druckerschwarze," i.e., invisible ink.[79]

Rosenzweig assigns the perils of self-knowledge to the decidedly unordinary liturgical context of prayer and repentance. Only there are the perils bearable. His reference to the "Buss- und Bettaegliches"[80] recalls the phenomenological analysis of sin and repentance that occurs in Hermann Cohen's *Religion of Reason out of the Sources of Judaism*, which Rosenzweig knew well and taught at the Lehrhaus.[81] Cohen understood the distinct individuality of the I to

be born in its very awareness of having sinned.[82] What defines the I
in this situation is the judgment it receives as coming from without,
and that uniquely fixes it. Self-knowledge, in effect, precisely reverses the movement of apologetics.

Certainly the occasional quality that, for Rosenzweig, characterizes all apologetic thought, qualifies much of Baeck's work, too.
The Essence of Judaism was written in response to Harnack's dis-
missive and subordinating judgment on Judaism in the *Essence of
Christianity*. If Rosenzweig was tempted by Christianity for his personal, spiritual life and remained, even after his return to Judaism,
a sympathetic interpreter of it, Baeck, the liberal rabbi and cham-
pion of Judaism in a largely Christian culture, found in Christianity
an unremitting occasion for defensive critiques. There is an irony in
that. One of Baeck's polemical categories was what he called romantic religion. But the occasional quality of much of his own work links
it to the modern genre of the essay, that reflective string of fragmentary looks at diverse subjects—precisely the genre that, according to
Lacoue-Labarthe and Nancy, foretells the romantic movement of the
early 1800s.[83]

Baeck and Schelling

In 1922, Baeck published an essay entitled "Romantic Religion."
It was half of a projected, but never completed, study on "Classical
and Romantic Religion." The essay illustrates Baeck's apologetic
stance. Albert Friedlander calls it, perhaps unfairly, the "sharpest
polemic possible."[84] In chapter two, we shall consider what Baeck
means by romantic religion. Suffice it here to note that, in attacking
it, Baeck was following a tradition of antiromantic polemics that was
already established in Germany. The first documented uses of the
word *romantisch*, applied by seventeenth century writers to the re-
ality-stretching sagas and legends of the Middle Ages, already carried a negative connotation.[85] By the end of the eighteenth century,
the romantic had come to be seen as a distinct literary category,
about which writers like Schiller and Jean Paul could unpejoratively
theorize. It was, however, in the Schlegel brothers that the category
found its most ardent theorists. For them, the romantic was a literary category in two senses, chronological and typological. Chrono-
logically, it referred to the "modern" literature of the Middle Ages

and after, especially Cervantes and Shakespeare, as opposed to the "classical" literature of antiquity. Typologically, it referred to certain marks of literary structure, composition and style—neatly summarized in Schlegel's formula, "sentimental material in fantastic form"—that came to clearest expression in the novel. August Schlegel, especially, pondered the typology of the classical and the romantic, calling it the "most essential" distinction for the interpretation of art. The classical for him was characterized by possession, harmony, completion in the present; the romantic, by division, incompletion, and longing for the past or future.

Already in the early nineteenth century, the designation *Romantiker* was applied pejoratively to proponents of the modern literary style. Parodies appeared of the group today sometimes known as the middle romantics: Brentano, Achim von Arnim, J. Goerres, and F. Creuzer. Hegel inadvertently contributed to the antiromantic polemic when, identifying the romantic with the largely medieval and Christian art of inwardness, he deemed it the highest expression of self-alienated subjectivity. Out of Kierkegaard's work, the romantic was identified with irresponsible longing for an appearance of self-dissolution, and out of Nietzsche's, with a symptom of cultural decadence. The polemic continued into the twentieth century. In his book *Political Romanticism*, Carl Schmitt characterized the romantic as "subjective occasionalism," i.e., undifferentiating acceptance of whatever could be turned to ironic or esthetic account, and deplored its vagueness and "dreadful confusion."[86]

Friedlander understands Schmitt's book to form part of the background to Baeck's.[87] Schmitt may be especially visible behind Baeck's comments on the Lutheran churches, which, according to Baeck, entered into irresponsible partnerships with the state.[88] But Baeck would have stretched Schmitt's own understanding of the romantic, which was exclusively esthetic and nonreligious.[89] A work that lies closer to Baeck's is Fritz Strich's *German Classicism and Romanticism*. Subtitled, "Completion or Infinity," the book assigns the classical to peacefulness, closure, organism, clarity, and the realizing powers of art; and the romantic to infinity, movement, openness, darkness and unrealizable ideas. For Strich, this typology results from the fundamental spiritual drive towards immortality, manifesting alternatively in terms of perfection or infinity, and applies to all areas of human culture, including religion. When the romantic manifests in religion, one of the forms it takes is Christianity.[90]

The understanding of the romantic as a category that subsumes Christianity is, as we shall see, Baeck's also. It is just because

Baeck's essay is locatable in a tradition of thinking about romanticism that, despite its polemical tone, it can be taken to represent a common understanding of romantic ideas. For his essay, "Romantic Religion," Baeck draws from the critical tradition of German writing on romanticism, as well as from the history of Christian thought. Paradoxically, these two sources for his essay infect it with the very romanticism he decries, since the two strands of the literary and the religious do not always harmonize, but divisively betray their distinct and to some extent opposed origins.

From the circle of the early romantics, Baeck names in his essay three of his sources: Schleiermacher, Novalis, and Schlegel. He does not name Schelling. And yet, Baeck wrote about Rosenzweig's essay, "The Oldest System-Program of German Idealism," which treats largely of Schelling, that it greatly influenced his understanding of romantic psychology.[91] Schelling might well prefer to influence from a concealed and unnamed station. On the other hand, the unnaming of Schelling in an essay on romantic religion may reflect an ambiguous position that philosopher holds in the history of romanticism. Schelling was associated with the romantics for only a short period of his life. *The Philosophy of Art*, written between 1802 and 1803, belongs to the end of this association, after the Jena group had begun to disperse. Still, Schelling himself expresses a debt to August Schlegel for the "empirical" examples of art that *The Philosophy of Art* illustratively employs.[92] Reciprocally, *The Philosophy of Art* is taken for a major influence in the German romantic movement.[93] "Schleiermacher was especially impressed by the early Schelling;"[94] and well he might have been, given their shared esteem for the religious import of art. On the other hand, Schelling "remains in many respects an 'outsider' of romanticism *stricto sensu*."[95] One respect in which he may differ from Schlegel and Novalis is that he seems, in *The Philosophy of Art*, finally to close the gap between infinity and finitude.[96] We shall explore, in chapter three, the extent to which this is true. But some would maintain, with Carl Schmitt, that any systematic philosophy is, by its very nature, opposed to romanticism.[97]

We do not wish to dispute over names. Schelling was certainly a systematic philosopher. But there is ample precedent in the secondary literature for distinguishing a particular type of systematizing as romantic philosophy, and for taking Schelling as one of its chief exemplars. Rosenzweig himself acknowledges that Schelling was "der Philosoph der Romantiker," and that he was so by virtue of the philosophy of art he conceived in the first years of the nineteenth century.[98] For Rosenzweig, the question is not over Schelling's romanticism, but over the major directions of influence between him and the other Jena romantics.[99] But even Lacoue-Labarthe and Nancy, who otherwise qualify Schelling's romantic credentials, allow for "'philosophical romanticism'" (albeit only in quotation marks).[100] Others quite openly concede that "romanticism was not only a literary, but also very consciously a philosophical movement."[101] Indeed, some sources go so far as to subsume all of philosophical idealism under "philosophical romanticism;"[102] Husserl, for example, took even the "anti-romantic" Hegel for a romantic philosopher.[103]

Schelling himself would be delighted to think he could simultaneously occupy two opposed positions, one within and one outside of romanticism. But let us recall Schlegel's famous pronouncement that "it is equally fatal for the mind to have a system and to have none. It will simply have to decide to combine the two."[104] Our interpretation of *The Philosophy of Art* is that it does precisely that. It will erect a kind of metasystem that carves out spaces for nonsystem. In his polemic against romanticism, Baeck was probably right to omit Schelling's name. The systematized nonsystem too easily passes for a rigorously distinguishing classicism. But by blurrily hovering above typological boundaries, Schelling shows himself all the more romantic.

Schelling and Rosenzweig

The influence of the late Schelling on Rosenzweig's *The Star of Redemption* has received ample attention in the secondary literature.[105] Rosenzweig himself thought of Schelling as his "patron saint,"[106] and distinguished him sharply from the other two builders of idealist systems, Fichte and Hegel. But if the patronage is as real as Rosenzweig claims, it does not show itself in any abundance of overt references to Schelling's work. Xavier Tilliette observes that Rosenzweig wrote much more about, and with explicit reference to, Hegel than Schelling; and that the latter's discernible influence is largely "diffuse, atmospherique, poetique."[107] Schelling is differentiable from Hegel and Fichte on several grounds, including, among others, the degree of change his thinking underwent over time, and the supreme importance he assigned, at different stages of thinking, to nature, art, and mythology. Rosenzweig cites Fichte's dictum that a person's philosophy depends on what sort of person he is;[108] and it may offer insights into Rosenzweig's own person that so far-ranging and changing a thinker as Schelling caught his imagination over the so focusedly will- and *Geist*-oriented idealist alternatives.

The temptation is to say that Schelling appealed to Rosenzweig because, of the three idealists, he was the only one to break so decisively with idealism, just as Rosenzweig did, and to begin to articulate a new way of thinking that, instead of equating thought with being, acknowledged its own dependence on a prior thought-resistance. But Rosenzweig was writing about Schelling already in 1914, three years before the so-called "Urzelle der *Stern der Erloesung*," where he first formulates, in a letter to Rudolf Ehrenberg, the philosophical importance of breaking with idealism. And the Schelling he wrote about so early on was precisely the young, idealist Schelling.

In 1914, while pursuing research for his doctoral study of Hegel, Rosenzweig came across a manuscript in Hegel's hand that he named "The Oldest System-Program of German Idealism." In a lengthy study of the manuscript, which examines it from orthographic, historical, and conceptual vantage points, he concludes that it is a copy of an original that Schelling wrote sometime between January and July 1796.[109] This hypothesis has been contested. Scholarship is still not agreed on the author of this work.[110] But the manuscript, which is available in print both in German and in English translation,[111] is of less interest here for its actual author, than for the occasion it provides Rosenzweig to write about Schelling with evident sympathy, and not a little feeling for the pathos of unfulfilled promise that seemed to haunt this longest-lived of the idealists. As Rosenzweig's own commentary on the manuscript has not been translated into English, a synopsis is provided here.

The commentary is divided into eight parts. In the first, Rosenzweig presents the case that the manuscript is written in Hegel's hand and, with reference to scholarship on Hegel orthography, dates it to sometime between April 29 and August 1796. Part two is a transcript of the manuscript. In the third part, Rosenzweig argues, on grounds of the tidiness of the work and several careless errors it contains, that it is a copy, but also, on stylistic, tonal, and philosophical grounds, that Hegel is not the author. Rather, the one proto-idealist writer of the time, of whom the rash projections of the manuscript are characteristic, is Schelling.

Part four is the heart of the commentary. Here, Rosenzweig divides the manuscript into five sections which, as the commentary proceeds, he refers to as the logico-metaphysics, the nature philosophy, the ethics, the teaching on art, and the religious philosophy, or mythology. He successively analyzes each part. The analysis proceeds by locating the ideas of each section in relation to the known Schelling works of the mid to late 1790s, primarily, but not exclusively, *Of the I as a Principle of Philosophy* (1795) and *The Philosophical Letters Concerning Dogmatism and Criticism* (1795). The metaphysical part of the manuscript concludes with the claim that "simultaneously with the free, self-conscious being there emerges an entire world—from out of nothing—the only true and conceivable creation out of nothing."[112] Rosenzweig locates this claim in a progression of ideas he traces from *Of the I* to the *General Overview of the New Philosophical Literature* (1796-1797). Rosenzweig downplays Fichte's influence on the Schelling of this period, and accentuates Kant's. But the I of *Of the I* breaks with both Kant and Fichte. This I was an absolute being, conceived after the pattern of Spinoza's substance, and Schelling's presentation of it has, says Rosenzweig, mystical and irrational overtones. However, by the time of the *Philosophical Letters*, the I has become an active will, practical and creative. Rosenzweig understands this change of view about the I as indicative of a problem that was becoming increasingly pressing for Schelling, namely "wie das Absolute aus sich selbst herausgehen und eine Welt sich entgegensetzen kann"[113] (how the Absolute can step out of itself and set against itself a world). In *The General Overview*, the act of will is presented as the highest condition of self-consciousness, which is itself the one synthetic act that creates freely out of nothing, and in relation to which everything else, including our own system of sensual presentations, is analytic. By subsuming the sensual representations that, for Kant, were simply given and that had constituted the content of the categories of theoretical philosophy, under the free act of self-consciousness, so that the free consciousness is cast as producer of its own only seemingly given representations, Schelling effects the synthesis of theoretical and practical philosophy that had eluded Kant. The free self of the System-Program that simultaneously creates out of its own self-consciousness and, what amounts to the same thing, out of nothing, resembles the primal, synthetic act of the Schellingian self.

The nature philosophy of the System-Program centers, for Rosenzweig, on the claim that, for the new physics "philosophy provides the ideas and experience the data."[114] Once again, Rosenzweig traces an evolution in Schelling's thought, this time from the Fichtean view that nature is comprehensible only as the domain in which the infinite will exercises itself, to an enhanced respect for nature itself, quite apart from any contexts it provides for moral self-realization. Newly dignified along with nature is the sensual experience that constitutes its content. When Schelling claims that nature is, in Rosenzweig's words, "das Anwendungsgebiet der theoretischen Philosophie"[115] (the domain of application of theoretical philosophy), he means to lift theoretical philosophy out from under its subordination to moral philosophy—the subordination Kant and Fichte had decreed for it—and fashion for it a new and independent integrity, alongside nature. Nature is invested, teleologically, and in opposition to Kant, with its own purposed progression "von der toten Materie zum lebendigen Geist"[116] (from dead matter to living spirit). Theoretical philosophy elucidates for nature its own rise to living consciousness.

The third section of the System-Program, on ethics, polemicizes against institutional religion and against the state, which will eventually disappear in subordination to a higher idea. Rosenzweig finds the same antistatist tendencies in Of the I and in the New Deduction of Natural Law (1796). Schelling demotes Kant's picture of a cosmopolitan constitution for world peace to the place of a mere condition for the complete cessation of statehood as such. The history of the state is to be perfected in its vanishing. The Philosophical Letters are as adamant in rejecting dogmatic religion, and in calling for humanity to find within itself what it previously sought outside.

In the fourth section of the System-Program, beauty is deemed the higher unity of truth and goodness, and esthetic acts, the highest acts of reason. Rosenzweig traces Schelling's fascination with art to one half of a two-part solution to Kant's problem of a common root for theoretical and practical philosophy. The Critique of Judgment hinted that the common root might be the natural organism and beauty. Schelling's famous claim for art, that it is the organon of philosophy, first appears in the System of Transcendental Idealism of 1800.[117] But Rosenzweig finds premonitions of this claim already in the Philosophical Letters of 1795, and in the treatises Schelling finished in the winter of 1796–1797: such claims as that esthetics is entrance to the whole of philosophy, and that the philosophical spirit can only be clarified in esthetics, which joins theoretical and practical philosophy together.

The last section of the System-Program calls for a new mythology of reason which, by sensualizing philosophy, and philosophizing myth, will unite philosophers and their non-philosophical neighbors together in one new religion. A similar call is sounded in the System of Transcendental Idealism,[118] but Rosenzweig dates Schelling's interest in myth to as far back as 1793, when he wrote On Myths, Sayings, Philosophemes of the Ancient World. Rosenzweig traces from there onward some reversals in Schelling's stance towards myth: first, that it is to be superseded by enlightenment; then, that it is to be preserved, but interpreted and communicated for the benefit of all; finally, that a new mythology will be demanded, but in a formulation that will baffle those unworthy of it and initiate those able to receive it into a new philosophy. Rosenzweig downplays the esotericism into which Schelling had grown by 1796, and which is so discordant with the optimistic universalism of the System-Program, and attributes it to Schelling's passing irritation over some negative reviews of his work.[119]

In the fifth section of his commentary, Rosenzweig considers the form of the manuscript and tries to date Schelling's original. Rosenzweig takes the manuscript for a fragment, the main body and conclusion of a piece whose preface is missing. It was possibly a letter, or an enclosure accompanying a letter, sent either to one or several friends. The Hegel copy sets a latest date of July 1796. Based on content analyses of *Of the I* and the *Philosophical Letters*, compared with the System-Program, and of a letter dated January 22, 1796, where Schelling describes himself undertaking the very project the System-Program proclaims, Rosenzweig concludes that Schelling wrote the program sometime between January and July 1796.

The sixth section reads as a defense of Schelling's philosophical integrity. Rosenzweig argues that the seemingly disparate stages of Schelling's thought, the nature philosophy, the esthetics, the mythology, form an organic whole that unfolded quite logically over time. In the System-Program, Schelling "die Mannigfaltigen Kraefte seines goettlichen Diebs-, Erfinders- und Virtuosenwesens gleichzeitig in einer kecken Tat offenbart" (reveals the manifold strengths of his divine thieving, inventing, and virtuosity, simultaneously in one bold act). By contrast, Rosenzweig also observes in this section that Schelling never did unite all the parts of his thought into a single system, much as he had hoped to, but "er ist sein Leben lang Praetendent geblieben, . . . das Wunderkind, das, alles versprechend, vieles haltend, doch nie zu der letzten resoluten Einfachheit des Mannes kommt, sondern in einem gewissen Sinne sein Leben lang bleibt, was es zu Anfang war: ein geniales Kind" (he remained his whole life a pretender, . . . the *Wunderkind*, who, promising all, bearing much, yet never comes to the last, resolved simplicity of the man, but in a certain sense remains his whole life long what he was from the start: a genial child).[120]

In the seventh section, Rosenzweig looks to Hegel, Hoelderlin and the early romantics for possible influences on Schelling. Here the defense is of Schelling's originality. For by the dating Rosenzweig has assigned the System-Program, he takes Schelling to have preceded Hoelderlin and the early romantics in expressing ideas that were common to them all, e.g., that poetry completes philosophy and religion. Hegel, on the other hand, was preoccupied with different problems in 1796, largely historical ones, that led him almost unconsciously to the systematic projects that would occupy him in later years.

In the last section, Rosenzweig analyzes the idealist project to found a system. What distinguishes German idealism from its ancient Greek counterpart is that it sought the union of truth and reality, i.e., it sought to extract the content of reality out of the sheer form of truth. "Die Einheit des gesamten Seins nicht etwa bloss auszusprechen, sondern sie irgendwie durch Verknuepfung mit dem seienden zu bestimmen, ist seitdem Aufgabe aller Philosophie geblieben" (Not merely to express the unity of all being but somehow to determine it through a tie to becoming has since remained a task of all philosophy). Schelling's idealism was "aus dem Begriff der Absoluten Tat den ganzen philosophischen Kosmos entstehen zu lassen" (to let the whole philosophical cosmos originate out of the concept of the absolute act), which origination was understood as the counterpart in becoming to Spinoza's absolute being. At first, Schelling incorporated into his view of system that it could never be completed. The point of the system-ideal was to stimulate the act towards completing it which, only while it is still exercised, offers scope for the thinker's freedom. Rosenzweig understands this Fichtean idea to have been expressed in the first two words of the manuscript, "eine Ethik," which he takes, not for the end of a sentence whose beginning is lost, but for the title of the System-Program itself. Schelling had indeed understood himself to be formulating "ein Gegenstueck zu Spinozas Ethik" (a counterpart to Spinoza's ethics). But as Schelling grew away from Fichte, the idea of the completed system grew more compelling. Nearly a decade before the *Phenomenology of Spirit*, Schelling "hat . . . den Begriff des 'Geistes,' der zugleich Subjekt und Objekt der Philosophie ist, gefasst" (conceived the concept of the "spirit" that is simultaneously subject and object of philosophy), and which, by proceeding out of itself in becoming, is able to return to itself in being. But it was Hegel, not Schelling, who, by building a dialectic around this concept, "jene Einheit des philosophischen Systems vollzogen hat" (perfected the unity of that philosophical system). Schelling himself would abandon idealism; but the task of coordinating being and becoming remained. For Rosenzweig, Schelling never diverted from this self-understanding of his task. The irony is that he came closest to completing it in a System-Program that, by its very form, postponed completion.[121]

Rosenzweig delighted in the unexpected inversion. In the last year of his life, he read a report of a public discussion between Ernst Cassirer and Martin Heidegger. He was so struck by the play of inversion in this debate—between Cassirer, the seeming heir of Cohen's thought, and Heidegger, the true heir, who only seemed to defy what would be expected of one who held, as he did, Cohen's chair in philosophy at Marburg—that he titled his reflections on it, "Vertauschte Fronten,"[122] which might be translated, Reversed Positions. But then, if Fichte was right about philosophical preferences, that they are rooted in personality, Rosenzweig's affection for Schelling is only to be expected, for none of the idealists, and very few philosophers from any period, offer as much appearance of inverting or reversing positions as Schelling does. Indeed, there is so much appearance of reversal, between the competing claims to preeminence of nature, art, and mythology, or of thought, action, and being, that it can become a positive task, which Rosenzweig takes up, to show that the idea of a string of mutually contradicting Schellingian reversals must itself be reversed, that from start to finish of Schelling's philosophical life, a unified intellectual project unfolds. Schelling illustrates Rosenzweig's concept of love, according to which it acts by inviting the other's act. Schelling invites his philosophical descendants to systematize his thought in a way, for example, that Hegel does not. One accepts the perfect system or rejects it; one does not continue in its project. It is Schelling, not Hegel, who left a task that may be taken up again even, as Rosenzweig says, today.[123] If Heidegger was, at most, only a seeming reversal of Cohen, so is Rosenzweig, despite his anti-idealist protests, visibly continuing in Schelling's line.

Synopsis of The Star of Redemption

Relatively brief, critical overviews of *The Star of Redemption* are available in any number of secondary sources.[124] Of these, perhaps Norbert Samuelson's is most helpful for highlighting the systematic nature of the work. But the *Star* can also be read as a collection of essays or even short fragments on a broad range of philosophical, religious, and esthetic topics. The poetic tone of the work, and its idiosyncratic use of language,[125] defy simple, summary presentation. The synopsis that follows introduces the basic structure of the book and some of its key structural terms.

The Star of Redemption was published in 1921. It is deeply imbedded in 150 years of German philosophical and literary history and is scarcely comprehensible apart from it. Its structural model, however, is visible even on the surface, through the part, book, and section titles. One commentator has suggested that the structural model is art,[126] but the *Star* could also be taken to be patterned after an organism, that repeats the whole of itself in its parts.

The work is divided into three parts, each of which is divided into three books. Each part begins with an introduction, and concludes with a transition to the next part. (The transition of the last part understands itself to be out of the book entirely and into life.) Part two, titled "The Course," is both the physical and conceptual center of the book. The other two parts are defined in terms of it. The course is the movement of meetings that, for Rosenzweig, constitute reality or the cosmos. What meets in reality are three conceptually separable, but in reality related, elements: God, human, and world. The first part of the *Star*, titled "The Elements," presents each of these three in their conceptual isolation. They must first be so presented before they can be understood to meet. But the separations are articulated purely for the sake of the cosmic meetings. So this first part, in its simultaneous priority and subordination to the second, is also titled "The Protocosmos."

The third part offers a vision of the three elements in their relationships of cosmic meeting. It does so in terms of the liturgical cycles of Judaism and Christianity, but also, climactically, in terms of a divine vantage point that surpasses these in a vision of the single, absolute truth. Human life is necessarily perspectival. So while we can momentarily glimpse the absolute truth, we cannot abidingly inhabit it. The point of the visions of the *Star*'s third part is to return us to the lived meetings of the second. Like the first part, the third also takes its name, Hypercosmos, from the second. Like Protocosmos, this name implies a simultaneous surpassing of and subordination to the cosmos.

The three books of part two are titled, in succession, Creation, Revelation, and Redemption. But these titles also expand, macrocosmically, out of part two into the whole of the book. The preliminary conceptualizations of part one constitute a creation; the meetings of part two, revelation; and the vision of part three, redemption. The titles also contract, microcosmically, into the confines of single books, especially the first and second books of part three, which analyze the Jewish and Christian liturgical cycles in terms of creation, revelation, and redemption.

The definition of cosmic reality as movements of meeting takes its significance from a heritage of idealism that it rejects. Idealism has no place for meetings of separable elements, and understands reality after an ancient monistic model: the real is the one. Parts of the *Star* can only be understood against the backdrop of idealism. Idealism is not uniformly rejected. The forms of its conceptual movements have a place in the protocosmos, where the three elements are reasoned into three separate isolations; but also in the philosophy of art that accompanies the passage from part one to three. The esthetics of the *Star* is, perhaps, a prime example of a part of it that can be read in relative isolation from the rest.[127] In addition, the *Star* contains political theory, history of philosophy, philosophy of language, comparative religious analysis (these sections are very tendentious) and literary criticism (mostly of biblical passages but also, indirectly, of Goethe).

Rosenzweig understood the *Star* as a system of philosophy.[128] It has, however, been read as a testament of Rosenzweig's own Jewish religious life[129] as it evolved against the challenges of philosophy, art, and Christianity. Insofar as this reading pushes the *Star* into apologetics, Rosenzweig himself would probably reject it. The Jewish tone he admits the book to have follows, he implies, from his own inescapably Jewish perspective, and not from any apologetic stance towards Judaism.[130] But what shows just as naturally and unapologetically from behind Rosenzweig's work is a romantic sensibility, noticeably different from the Jewish in some respects, that was first self-consciously articulated in Germany at the end of the eighteenth century. It is as an expression of romantic religious sensibility that we shall undertake to interpret the *Star*.

CHAPTER 2

🍂

A Reading of
The Star of Redemption
through "Romantic Religion"

Introduction

A common publication year of 1921 might seem the only affinity between Franz Rosenzweig's *The Star of Redemption* and the second edition of Leo Baeck's *Essence of Judaism*. When Rosenzweig reviewed the *Essence of Judaism*, in "Apologetic Thinking," published two years later, he critiqued all apologetic thought, of which the *Essence of Judaism* is an instance, on grounds that, in its relentless defense of essence, it missed the wholeness of the human self. Human beings are both inwardness of essence and outwardness of relational bonds. The point is made somewhat differently in "The New Thinking," where Rosenzweig sharply contrasts dialogical, relation-bound speech thinking to the "attitude made up of attack and defense." Rosenzweig certainly views his own *The Star of Redemption* as nonapologetic thought, perhaps indeed as the only non-apologetic treatment of Judaism and Christianity. He might claim this distinction for the *Star* on grounds that it proceeds by weaving the whole human self, both essence and relations, first into a revelatory and redemptive partnership with God and world respectively, and then into the concrete life of Jew and Christian.[1]

In the same review essay, "Apologetic Thinking," Rosenzweig briefly refers to Baeck's "Romantic Religion." Here, the relation between Baeck and Rosenzweig is more complex. For in a letter of

March 4, 1923, Baeck expresses his deep debt to Rosenzweig's commentary on "Das aelteste Systemprogramm des deutschen Idealismus," ("The Oldest System Program of German Idealism") published in 1917, for his own understanding of romantic psychology.[2] That debt may be somewhat hyperbolically expressed, since it is not easy to trace the influence of that early Rosenzweig essay, a work of finely focused and meticulous scholarship, on Baeck's much broader brush strokes in "Romantic Religion." Still, if a natural affinity occurs anywhere between Baeck and Rosenzweig, it may be through "Romantic Religion." Rosenzweig's brief comment on this essay is not quite just. He implies that "romantic" functions in that essay as an abstraction of Christianity.[3] This is not how Baeck himself presents the term. Rather, the romantic is a "characteristic form" (RR 195) in its own right much larger than Christianity. Among non-Christian forms of romanticism, Baeck includes stoicism, gnosticism, the ancient mystery cults, neoplatonism, Buddhism, and "modern romanticism," by which he means 19th century German literary romanticism (RR 197, 250, 264, 280). From this hybrid itemization, it is clear that romanticism takes not only religious forms, but philosophical and literary ones as well. Christianity itself is, through Paul, a combination of Judaism and ancient Hellenistic romanticism (RR 284). Romanticism is less a pale abstraction of Christianity than a driving force that moves it (RR 198), though only imperfectly, since Christianity in several of its forms, namely the "real Gospel," Calvinists, Baptists, and the side of the Catholic Church that emphasizes works (RR 253, 261, 286, 289), is distinctly nonromantic. Baeck concedes that romanticism infests even his prototype of classical religion, which is Judaism, as for example in the ancient intertestamental literature (RR 260). But it is not necessary to go back so far in Jewish history to find what Baeck calls "episodes of Jewish romanticism" (RR 214). Rosenzweig himself may well supply what was in Baeck's own time a living example.

If "Romantic Religion" is yet another instance of apologetic thinking, then the essence it implicitly defends is classicism. Rosenzweig fears that the typical apologist will show the living vibrancy of only his own religion, and portray the opponent's at a disadvantage from the start, by its very form, as a cold abstraction of ideas.[4] But in Baeck's case, Rosenzweig's fear is surely unfounded. Baeck's portrayal of romanticism draws from a rich abundance of sources. This is undoubtedly part of the reason so many Baeck scholars esteem so highly an essay that might otherwise be dismissed as mere polemics.[5] If anything, it is the ideal of classicism that comes through somewhat abstractly, for it serves largely as the preferred foil to romanticism.

We can tell from "Romantic Religion" that the religious classicist is an effortful sort who exults in struggle and who follows the Kantian call to the infinite ethical task. The Baeckian classical religionist is devoted to "this idea of becoming, of the never-quite-finished, of the directed ascent" (RR 217). But Baeck does not illustrate the classical ideal as richly as he does its romantic counterpart. This is hardly surprising. Baeck had already illustrated classicism profusely enough, in both form and content, in the *Essence of Judaism*. Even Rosenzweig subsumes that work under the larger rubric of authentic classicism.[6] But here a dissonance sounds in Baeck's and Rosenzweig's respective views of the classical. In "The New Thinking," Rosenzweig identifies "die Klassizitaet des klassischen Altertums,"[7] (the classicicity of classical antiquity) with the isolated self-enclosure of the three elements of experience—God, human, world—as they appear in the first part of his *The Star of Redemption*. It is just the seeming finish of their elementarity that is classical. And in "Apologetic Thinking," he implies that it is precisely the serene finish of the *Essence of Judaism* that expresses its classicicity. Its form shows nothing of its surely turbulent origins in Baeck's indignant response to Harnack's depiction of Judaism in the *Essence of Christianity*. All we see is a calm dialectic of pure ideas, compressing "a variety of material into a narrow compass."[8] But this is hardly a picture of the open-ended striving of Baeckian classicism.

Baeck precisely reverses what one might deduce from Rosenzweig's "Aelteste Systemprogramm" about the division of the finished and the open-ended between the classical and the romantic. If Schelling is the representative romantic philosopher, then it is romanticism that refuses to be constrained by any sort of finish. For, as Rosenzweig explains it, quoting the very early Schelling, the philosopher who completes a system becomes its instrument and is no longer creative.[9] For Baeck, on the contrary, it is just the romantic who cannot abide the robust air of the unfinished; he must have closure, enclosure, and completion. Baeck matches the form of his "Romantic Religion" to his understanding of its content. Just as Christianity, in all its romanticism, is a "self-enclosed system," (RR 240) so is "Romantic Religion." Baeck presents an inexorable romantic logic that leads, dialectically, from ideas of freedom, individuality and experience, to compulsion, authoritarianism, and tradition. These pairs of opposites constitute the "closed system" of romanticism (RR 247), and of Baeck's own essay.

Now Baeck's view of romanticism can be turned back on Rosenzweig. For one reading of *The Star of Redemption* is of a progressive movement away from chaos into closure and fixity. The goal of the book is to construct the fixed figure of the six-pointed star of redemption out of, first, a chaos of unrelated elements, and then a chaos of unfixed relations. Had Rosenzweig left us midway through his book, the star he had constructed might as easily have been a star of creation or revelation. It becomes the star of redemption because, by the end of the second part of the book, the element of God, which constitutes one tip of the star, and which hitherto had rotated helplessly with the other two elements, world and human, is fixed at the top. The bane of possibility, of the frightful "perhaps," at which Rosenzweig throughout his book has been relentlessly chipping away, is finally reduced to nothing. There is simply one orientation for the star—the one in which God reigns over human and world, even to the point of having no more world or human confront him at all. And that is the divine meaning of redemption.

From Baeck's point of view, that Rosenzweig's star is indeed of redemption, and not of creation or revelation, already hopelessly marks it for romanticism. Creation determines the value structure of classicism (RR 212); romantic faith in general, and Christianity in particular, is faith in redemption (RR 261, 276). Around this central idea, the dialectic of romanticism slowly builds. "Redemption is the fact of salvation which has been consummated in man" (RR 276). Redemption is an experience of consummation. It is a consummation coming miraculously from beyond the will, and passively received (RR 277–278, 204). Indeed, in one formulation, redemption is precisely a deliverance from the will (RR 205), though in other formulations, from original guilt, from ethics, or the whole of the harsh world (RR 196, 240, 203). As consummation, it is an experience of "everything," of an All that stands opposed to nothing (RR 200, 283). In this experience, the human is fundamentally changed, "made godlike and eternal" (RR 276). As experience, however, redemption is fleeting. It does not belong to the stable world of reality. The experience must be renewed in a succession of nows (RR 200, 202). Its transience generates an anxiety (RR 283, 284) of alternatively raised and dashed expectations that draws to romanticism its celebrated imagery of darkness, night and suffering. It also turns the romantic in on himself and his longings for renewed consummation. The self-centeredness of romanticism is projected onto God, who is conceived as seeking his own redemption (RR 281). In the end, the romantic cannot bear the burden of longing for a redemption he cannot control. Various stabilizing substitutes for the experience of consummation emerge: preeminent among these is the sacrament, an institutionalized miracle that saves (RR 223, 225). Knowledge, too, supplants experience as the bearer of salvation (RR 205) and, as against experience, presents itself as a permanent possession. This possession is dogma and its guardian is the priest. Part of dogma are doctrines of determinism and election that effectively secure the romantic's place in a permanent haven. By a paradoxical inversion, spontaneously received experience has ossified into a rigid authoritarian structure (the church) (RR 278, 236). The reality-supplanting experience of consummation has itself been supplanted by a structure that excludes all private redemptive experience. The pathos of religious romanticism is that, in seeking to preserve itself, it overturns its own constitutive ideals.

In his commentary on "Das aelteste Systemprogramm," Rosenzweig alludes only briefly to the German romantic movement. If this essay did significantly influence Baeck in his writing of "Romantic Religion," it may not have been through its actual content. Indeed, as we have already seen, on at least one crucial point—the attainment of closure—Baeck expressly claims for the romantic just what Rosenzweig denies of Schelling. But if not in its content, then something in the form, style, or tone of Rosenzweig's essay must have impressed Baeck as romantic; in which case, the delineations of "Romantic Religion" owe less to Schelling seen through Rosenzweig's eyes, than to Rosenzweig himself. Then it is not so surprising if "Romantic Religion," held up to *The Star of Redemption*, reflects Rosenzweig back to himself, as in a mirror. It is a distorting mirror. For Baeck's simplifying and dichotomous essay can never hope accurately to reflect all the many and complex images in Rosenzweig's *Star*. Still, the distortions might tell a partial truth, which is better than, by virtue of being much unread, telling none at all—a fate that falls to books like the *Star* that, by telling too much in too short a space, are, as Spinoza said of excellent things, "as difficult as they are rare."[10]

If the *Star* is a rare and difficult book, a reading of it through Baeck might bring it more within our reach. And then a more accurately focusing lens, such as Schelling supplies, can be brought to bear. "Romantic Religion" shows its propaedeutic usefulness to a reading of the *Star* already in its first few pages. Baeck takes the apostle Paul for the first of a long line of Christian romantics. His thesis is that Paul combined the Jewish hope in a future messiah, a distinctly classical idea, with the belief in the dying and rising god of the mystery cults, those exotic exemplars of ancient pagan romanticism. After a few introductory paragraphs, it is Baeck's comments on Paul that open the specifics of his essay. But it is striking how well, with a few minor changes (indicated in the sequel by brackets) the specifics of his comments apply to Rosenzweig as well. If Asia Minor supplied the context for Paul's synthesis of Judaism and ancient pagan romanticism, modern Germany was the backdrop against which Rosenzweig harmonized Judaism with paganism's modern romantic equivalent, namely Christianity:

> Paul [or, alternatively, Rosenzweig] was, like all romantics, not so much a creator of ideas as a connector of ideas. . . . He knew how to fuse the magic of the universal [or, in Rosenzweig's case: Christian] mysteries with the tradition of revelation of the secrecy-wrapped Jewish wisdom. Thus he gave the ancient [modern] romanticism a new and superior power—a power taken from Judaism. . . .

> In Paul's [Rosenzweig's] own soul, this union in which romantic and Jewish elements were to be combined, had prevailed after a period of transition. Subjectively, this union represented the story of his struggles which became the story of his life. The images of his homeland, Asia Minor [Germany], had early revealed to him the one element, romanticism [Christianity]; the parental home and the years of his studies had presented him with the other, the Jewish one. . . .Thus the promises and wisdom . . . from paganism [Christianity] and from Judaism entered into his unrest and doubts which pulled him hither and thither, looking and listening far and wide, in his craving for the certainty of truth. . . .

> Finally he had perceived an answer. It was a victorious and liberating answer to his mind because it did not merely grant a coming, a promised day, something yet to be, but a redemption which was fulfilled even then—as it were, a Now. This answer became for him the end which meant everything because it contained everything. . . . Alongside the one God before whom the gods of the pagans were to vanish, it [here Baeck means Christianity; he is speaking for Paul, but he could also be speaking for Rosenzweig, who saw paganism's promise realized in Judaism and Christianity together] now placed the one redeemer, the one savior [for Rosenzweig the one God] before whom the saviors of the nations could sink out of sight. . . .Thus he experienced it: paganism with its deepest aspirations and thoughts was led to

Judaism; and Judaism, with its revelation and truth, was bestowed on the pagans, too. . . .

He saw the hitherto divided world unified. In the messianic certainty of Judaism he now recognized the goal toward which the seeking and erring of the pagans had, in the depth of truth, always aspired; and in that which the pagans had wanted but not known, he now grasped the content and answer which was spoken, which was promised to Judaism. Judaism and paganism had now become one for him. . . . And now the pagans . . . could comprehend the mystery which had since ancient times been present among them as their precious possession. Judaism and paganism were now reconciled, brought together in romanticism. (RR 199–202)

Like Paul, Rosenzweig too was a connector of ideas. Indeed, part two of the *Star*, its central part, centers on connections, or, as Rosenzweig puts it in "The New Thinking," on the relational work of the little word "and."[11] Part three of the *Star* draws Christianity and Judaism together as complementary opposites. Judaism is the inward-turning religion that cherishes its own "secrets," and Christianity the outwardly turned one that takes power from Judaism as it victoriously supplants all pagan competitors. Part three of the *Star* sets Judaism and Christianity as present preludes to a future certainty of truth. Though redemption is future, it is experienced proleptically in the present. The redemption of the future may be glimpsed in the present as a final reconstitution of the collapsed idealist All, an end where everything is contained in God. Paganism is represented in the *Star* by the protocosmic elements of part one. As the *Star* moves into parts two and three, these elements are recast first as presuppositions of creation, revelation and redemption in general, and then of Judaism and Christianity in particular. Rosenzweig provocatively connects the redeemed "hypercosmos" that futurely succeeds all creation, revelation, and worldly redemption, with the protocosmic preludes to those same relations. In that sense, "paganism" appears as presupposition of "hypercosmic" Judaism, and Judaism as guarantor of paganism's own meaning and sense. But these reworked quotations are a mere whetting of the appetite for a reading of Rosenzweig as Baeckian romantic. As each concept emerges, let us trace its counterpart in *The Star of Redemption*. Then we will have offered as complete a reading as possible of Rosenzweig through the lens of Baeckian romanticism.

Romantic Redemption

"Everything in romanticism leads back to subjective experience" (RR 220). So experience is the heart concept of romanticism. The experience Baeck has in mind is extreme. It is a subjective response of ecstasy, of immersion, to an objective "taste of infinity" (RR 190, 204). The subjective response is further analyzable into the concepts of feeling and passivity. Here Baeck draws self-admittedly on Schleiermacher (RR 204). The passivity, in turn, bifurcates into a positive notion of miracle purely received and a negative one of suffering and sin darkly endured.

Baeck tells us relatively little about the objective content of the romantic's infinity. That he characterizes it sensually, with Schleiermacher, as a "taste," already compromises its objectivity. But Baeck does not in any case consider the possibility of objective romantic experience. Romantic experience is all feeling, "feeling is supposed to mean everything" (RR 290), and so is, by implication, noncognitive. Here Baeck may show a debt to Kant, who marked off pleasure and displeasure from all other features of any given presentation, by their absolute inability ever to be elements of cognition.[12] Cognition occurs through concepts, never through feelings. Kant's esthetic theory rests in part on a relation between feeling and cognition that in turn presupposes a formal boundary between them. But Baeck holds the Kantian line on feeling and cognition to a very different purpose. It can be no accidental choice of words on Baeck's part when he says "the capacity for feeling defines the dimensions and the limits of romanticism" (RR 195). Kant had claimed for critique the capacity to define the dimensions (volume) and limits of reason.[13] Baeck's choice of words evokes an analogy—feeling is to romanticism what critique is to reason—that lets devolve upon feeling all the reality-delimiting powers of the Kantian critique. And we do indeed read that, for romanticism, the world is not the conceptual determination of sensual intuition, as Kant would have it, but "an experience to be felt" (RR 191). Reality is simply moods.

Of course, the critique of reason, in Kant, was an activity of reason itself; all the more ironic then is the implicit analogy with feeling, when feeling is so wholly passive. Baeck expresses this quite neatly in German through a suggestive wordplay on *leben* and *Erlebnis*: "Der Mensch lebt nicht, sondern er wird erlebt, und was ihm bleibt is bloss . . . das Erlebnis."[14] Life passes into experience through the passive form, *gelebt*. And the *Erlebnis* is, again with Schleiermacher, simply the "feeling of absolute dependence," (RR 192) or, in Baeck's own formulation, "the mood . . . of one who knows himself to be wholly an object" (RR 204). Baeck again suggests, through his choice of words, the Kantian foil to romanticism: the romantic's existence is exultingly "heteronomous," (RR 205, 222) as opposed to the autonomy of the Kantian ideal. When Hegel summarily dismissed the view of cognition as an instrument of knowing,[15] he may have had in mind what the whole of the Kantian program presupposes, namely that reason can be, theoretically, the autonomous instrument of its own self-critique and, practically, the arbiter among possible objects of the autonomous will. But romantic instrumentality is wholly "will-less" (RR 192). If, for Kant, reason was the instrument of our own theoretical knowing and moral behaving, for romanticism, inversely, we are ourselves instruments of another and higher knowing and behaving (RR 208). We are the objects of God's activity (RR 204). Baeck notes, with barely concealed disgust, that the romantic's only activity is "self-congratulation" on his "state of grace" (RR 211).

The grace-fullness of the central romantic experience is its simultaneous blissfulness and heteronomy. Not only the will-lessness, but also the happiness of the experience is absolute. The absoluteness of the bliss owes to its identification with "the one and only meaning and purpose of existence" (RR 282). To describe so great a happiness, the romantic reaches for stronger, more colorful terms, like "voluptuous" (RR 191), but, finally, the union of this happiness with its absolute heteronomy, demands no less a term than miracle. Religion, says Baeck, speaking for St. Paul, "is to be exhausted by the miraculous experience" (RR 249, 227).

The concept of miracle serves as a bridge, back from the subjective component of the central experience of romanticism, which is the romantic's first focus, to the objective. On the one hand, the very fluidity of feelings, their unclearly demarcated boundaries, predispose them to register the "quasi-miraculous" (RR 193). But, on the other hand, the religious romantic's miraculous experience is quite simply and objectively of God (RR 224). So, despite the noncognitive character of feeling, romantic religious experience is still noetic. The implication is that there is a nonconceptual knowledge disclosed through feeling. In one passage, Baeck virtually identifies the romantic's emotive experience of "seizure" with romanticism's ideas of revelation and ultimate truth (RR 210). Truth is simply the living experience of romanticism (RR 206).

These four ideas—experience, feeling, passivity and miracle—are the central pillars of Baeckian romanticism. At one time or another throughout his essay, Baeck identifies each as, if not the heart, then at least an inevitable concomitant, of romanticism.[16] There is no inconsistency here. What Baeck means to describe is all four at once: an emotive and miraculous experience of dependence. This characterization of romantic religion has a curious parallel in *The Star of Redemption*, where Rosenzweig briefly presents the features of "idealistic religion" (SR 193–194). What is in part so curious is the phrase itself. It occurs as a subsection heading in the chapter on creation, but not within the body of the text, oddly disconfirming Rosenzweig's claim in "The New Thinking" that the word "Religion" does not at all (*ueberhaupt*) occur in the *Star*.[17] For surely there is no more obvious place for a word to occur than in a section title. Idealist religion is predicated on the idealist philosophical concept of generation, *Erzeugung*. Generation is a necessary implication of idealist self-positing. The infinite self, in positing and so limiting itself as object, so surpasses itself as subject that part of it remains closed to its own self-awareness. Generation is what results as the infinite self follows a sequence of logical moves that brings what it knows escapes its awareness, within its awareness. Part of what is generated in the process is a multiplicity of finite conscious selves. And one of these finite selves may reconstruct for itself, in reverse, the sequence of generative acts that ultimately issued in it. Following the steps back to their origin in the self-positing of the infinite self, the finite self accomplishes its highest submission: idealist religion's goal of merging or disappearing in the "ultimate form," i.e., the infinite act of self-positing (SR 143). Generation and submission are the inverse movements, from universal to particular in the first case, from particular to universal in the second, that together "close the idealist world into a whole" (SR 142). Rosenzweig himself notes the parallel in this to emanation theory, a central doctrine of neoplatonism, which Baeck in turn deemed one of the ancient pagan forms of romantic religion. But Rosenzweig emphatically rejects idealist religion; and if it is indeed in parallel with romantic religion, then it would seem that, far from illustrating the romantic sensibility, he joins Baeck in shunning it.

The term "romantic" hardly ever occurs in the *Star*. But even if romantic religion were simply idealist religion more accessibly expressed, Rosenzweig's avowed rejection of it would be no proof that he truly disowned it. The consensus among Rosenzweig scholars is that, for all his protestations against idealism, his religiophilosophical work is very much its child. But Baeckian romantic religion and Rosenzweigian idealist religion are not, in any case, the same. The foundational concept of idealist religion, namely generation, is actively logical and derives ultimately from the idealist mathematical equation of self-positing, $A=A$. It is neither experiential nor emotive, and certainly not miraculous. Where romantic and idealist religion overlap is in their shared estimation of passivity. The infinite self of idealism is a paragon of activity; but the finite selves, whose logical reconstructions of their own generation issue in their own disappearance do illustrate an ideal of passivity. Rosenzweig emphasizes the final surrender of volition that the finite self makes in its inverse work of reconstructive logic. It no longer wills its own acts, but rather the "supreme personality's" act of self-positing (SR 144). Here is the idealist analog to Baeckian romantic will-lessness.

But that leaves three romantic ideas that Rosenzweig does not reject—experience, feeling, and miracle. And these ideas, far from being banished from the *Star* in romantic disgrace, occupy very central places within it. A crucial difference between Baeck's and Rosenzweig's understanding of these ideas is, however, that while for Baeck they virtually define the romantic idea of redemption, which is romanticism's central religious category, for Rosenzweig they are much more definitively allied with revelation and creation. To read Rozenzweig as Baeckian romantic is to uncover within his thoughts on creation and revelation, the relation of experience, feeling, and miracle to redemption; which obliges, in turn, an exploration of the relation, in the *Star*, of redemption to revelation and creation.

The task of applying Baeck's categories of romanticism to the idea of redemption in the *Star* is complicated by the several meanings Rosenzweig assigns that idea. Here are three statements about redemption in the *Star* couched in the form of definitions: (1) "Redemption is never other than the growing of eternity into the living" (SR 369); (2) "What is redemption other than that the I learns to say thou to the he?" (SR 274); (3) "What is redemption if not the concord between revelation and creation?" (SR 314).

The third definition points most directly to the bearing of creation and revelation on redemption. But the first two hint at the broad range of categories that redemption subsumes. It is, on the one hand, to be expressed in terms of time, and, on the other, in terms of the elements of reality—God, human, world. For what is eternity if not the transcendence of time, and what is the "I" if not the human, one of the three protocosmic elements? What all three definitions share is a predicate composed of a relation—between eternity and the living, I and thou, or revelation and creation. The first of these relations could be more abstractly expressed as between eternity and the present; and the second, as between human and human. But redemption does not stop with these relations. It applies, beyond eternity and the present, to the other tenses of time—past and future—and beyond interrelated humans, to the other elements of reality—God and world. Indeed, if Rosenzweig's section titles are any guide, the primary redemption is of the world—for it is only redemption in this sense that names a book of the *Star*, the third one of part two.

Of all three elements of reality, it is only the world whose essence is not yet established. It is true that, in the reciprocal act of creation between God and world, God actively affirms the categories or kinds of things in the world. These worldly kinds are universals— but, insofar as they are many and mutually limiting, they are also particulars. And the particular is always subject to death or destruction.[18] So, the worldly kinds, as *particular* universals, press for a force to sustain them, which God supplies. But this does not yet establish the whole world. For as one of Rosenzweig's mentors, Hermann Cohen, observed in his later work, the universal never speaks to the individual as individual.[19] God's providential care for the particular *universals* leaves the singular individual subsumed by them untouched. But the world wants providential care for all of itself, including the singulars. We, who have philosophized on the world's behalf, "sought . . . a substance of the world beneath the phenomena of its existence. . . . We sought an infinite, standing by itself" (SR 223). It is the old desideratum of every monism, that each individual be safely enclosed within the embrace of the All.

One consequence of Rosenzweig's break with idealist monism, is that creation is incomplete. It is incomplete in the sense that the worldly singulars have not yet been touched by God's providence; but also in the sense that it omits from its dialogue the third element of reality, namely the human. And now one of the perfect matchings so typical of the *Star*, and so reminiscent of its idealist roots, occurs: the human, in a second dialogue with the world, completes both the trio of elements to be involved with creation, and the affirmation of the world so far only partially supplied. For the focus of the human in its dialogue with the world is precisely the singular that God ignores. It is this focus that defines redemption, as it applies to the world.

As Rosenzweig puts it, the Aught, i.e., the individual placeholder within a worldly kind, becomes "unique, subjective, substantival through the power of the deed" (SR 229). The infinite substance sought is simply the interconnection in a single whole of all the individually redeemed aughts. A redeemed aught of the world is unique, as opposed to a mere instance of a kind, and, whether human, animal or mineral, it becomes subjective in a sense it was not before. The deed which accomplishes this feat is the human's—"learning to say thou to the he," as the second definition of redemption phrases it. Redemption is the human's act in God's stead (SR 267), the completion of the worldly work of creation.

But the human can only perform this act because God has "freed" him for it (SR 267). God does not perform the worldly redemptive act but stands behind it (SR 241). It is in this sense that, if we take eternity for God and follow the first definition of redemption, eternity's growth among the living is redemption. But what is the concord between creation and revelation that, according to the third definition, constitutes redemption? The answer is bound up with the state from which God has "freed" the human so that he can behave redemptively.

At the heart of Rosenzweigian revelation stands the concept of love. The love is of God for the human. As redemption is the relation between world and human, so revelation is the relation between God and human. Revelation in this sense occurs at the center of the *Star*, the middle book of the central part. It is just here that feeling plays its most important role for Rosenzweig. For the beloved human's state exhibits some of the hallmarks of the Baeckian romantic. He is "immersed in God's loving glance" (SR 206) to which he has acquiesced and surrendered (SR 251), gives himself over to "a feeling of dependence and of being securely sheltered" in a private "bliss of the soul" (SR 168, 206). Just as feeling constitutes reality for the Baeckian romantic, the beloved soul in Rosenzweig only first awakens to his own being (or reality) through being loved (SR 182). This awakening is more sensual than cognitive. What was merely a rock (of selfish self-enclosure) now flowers; what was senseless now senses (SR 169). As for the intellect, the divine love "forges fetters" around it (SR 381).

The logic of divine love obliges this silencing of the intellect. For no descriptive claim can carry the immediacy of love. A description of love already distances it, consigns it to a known past, and so destroys it (SR 179). The only language that can hope to carry love without destroying it must perform it in its very speaking. "All true statements about love must be words from its own mouth, borne by the I" (SR 202). The only form performative language can take to carry love is the simple command "Love me!" There is no distance in that utterance between love and the speech that expresses it. Rosenzweig, reflecting on the Song of Songs, notes that prenineteenth century commentators knew that, though it was a sheer earthly love lyric, "the distinction between immanence and transcendence disappears in language" (SR 199). It is not that the divine love is one thing, transcending human experience, and its expression, immanent in experience, another. The reality of divine love is identical with its expression in the command to love. Where love is expressed in the imperative to love, the distinction between language, immanent to human experience, and that which, transcending it, is expressed there, disappears. Language performs the love in the very act of commanding it.

The beloved soul that receives this command rests in the "serene glow" of affirming it (SR 171). The Rosenzweigian beloved is the Baeckian romantic given over blissfully to his redemption. But the beloved in Rosenzweig has not yet entered into redemption. He has only just scaled the peak of revelation in preparation for the next move, which is out into the world.

Redemption effects a concord between creation and revelation in this sense: revelation guarantees a blissful but self-enclosed dialog of two. Outside this enclosure, the created world continues to reel in its incompleteness. The divine love has transformed the elemental, isolated human being into beloved soul. The freedom revelation confers is from the former isolation. Now redemption comes to carry what the human has received from God over to the rest of the world. "The reveille sounds for God's revelation to man, its echo reverberates into [the] It of the world" (SR 260).

It is the human who causes the echo to resound. The primary reason for this is that the beloved state proves unsatisfactory to the beloved himself, as indeed it will to the Baeckian romantic. It is unsatisfactory because it hovers groundlessly above the created order, to which the beloved human, as instance of a worldly kind, still belongs. "The I longs for orientation" in the world outside its revelatory inner order (SR 187). It wants its "duo-solitude" to find expression among the multitude (SR 203). So strong is the longing that the state of being loved and the imperative to love become virtually identified (SR 259).

Here, then, is how Baeckian romantic feeling bears on Rosenzweig's concept of worldly redemption: as presupposition. Rosenzweig emphasizes that only the beloved of God can love the world (SR 215). Rosenzweig allows that in passing to redemptive act, the soul retains an internal awareness of its beloved state (SR 204). But worldly redemption proper is too active in tone easily to accommodate romantic feeling. The hallmark in passivity of romantic feeling appears prominently again only in two historical expressions of redemption, both of them in differing degrees flawed. These expressions occur in Asian religion and Christianity. In the "Metaethics" section of the first part of the *Star*, Rosenzweig discusses Buddhism and Confucianism as complementary foils to ancient Greek views of the human. Indeed, the first redemption to enter the *Star* is Buddhist. But it is premature redemption. The trouble with it is that it cannot sustain the tensed opposition between the defiant freedom of human will and stasis of human character that will come, respectively, to underlie the human parts in revelation and the true redemption. Buddhism represents an abortive resolution of that elemental human tension by wholly renouncing the will. Since the character that remains is unwilled, it has no staying power and properly sinks back into nothing, the Buddhist desideratum, before it has known any life. This protoredemptive "immersion into the Nought" has for its counterpart the Chinese sage. His tack precisely reverses the Buddhist's. The sage wholly renounces character for the sake of will. A will which has nothing beyond itself to will, now that the beyond of character is gone, wills nothing. And an objectless will is reduced to moments of pure feeling. Detached from any enduring self, these feelings are fleeting and impersonal. It is just that quality of feeling that the great lyric poets of the East aspire to capture in their spare structures of words. The Baeckian romantic, who longs to linger in a high insubstantiality of feeling, would find profitable reading in their poems.

Rosenzweig rejects these romantic mock redemptions. They forfeit their chance at the true redemption. Here he speaks with Baeck, who classed Buddhism with the nonChristian romanticisms, rather than in unwitting illustration of what Baeck critiqued. When romantic feeling rises once more to prominence, in the last book of the last part of the *Star*, Rosenzweig's tone towards it is more ambiguous. For there he is speaking of Christianity, no mere mirror of passive feeling, but in partnership with Judaism, half the picture of the one historically fixed figure of the true redemption.

Both Baeck and Rosenzweig offer typologies of Christianity. For Baeck, the important distinction within Christianity is between its normative romantic form, represented by Paul, Augustine, and Luther, and its marginal, classical form, represented by the Synoptic gospels, Calvinism, and the Baptist churches. It is only romantic Christianity, admittedly the most of Christianity, that luxuriates in feeling. On this point, Rosenzweig goes farther than Baeck. For according to Rosenzweig's typology, which follows the historical divisions of Eastern Orthodox, Roman Catholic, and Protestant, *all* of Christianity is sorely tempted to take feeling as its final end.

For Rosenzweig, Christianity, unlike Buddhism or Taoism, understands that redemption is of the world and not of the private self. The world Rosenzweig means in this context is paganism. But to redeem the world, Christianity must to some extent conform to the world. The pagan world rests on a complex of three dualities that Rosenzweig describes in the first part of the *Star*. The dualities are within the pagan views of God, human and world. The pagan divine divides between an infinite essence and the power that affirms it. God actualizes through his power all that he infinitely is. As infinite, God cannot be confronted by anything that he does not self-incorporatingly divinize. Applied to the relation between God and world, this axiom of divine omnivorousness elevates all God touches to godly status. Trees, rivers, and human beings become divine. To speak to this pagan spread of the divine over God and world, Christianity must mirror it. And so it does with its doctrine of God the Father and God the Son. The Father is the transcendent divine; the Son, the incarnate ("enworlded") divine. Finding itself mirrored in Christianity, paganism loses any capacity to distinguish itself from Christianity, and comes to understand itself as an expression of the distinction between Father and Son. But the price of this power of conversion for Christianity is bifurcation. While there is still redemptive work to do, Christianity must bifurcate. It places all its hope for unification in its doctrine of the Spirit. At the close of the worldly work of redemption, that third person of the Trinity will have led the bifurcated God to unity. In anticipation of that hoped-for time, the Christian is tempted to idolize the Spirit, and to forget that God has any orientation to the world at all, either transcendent or immanent. This is the specific temptation of Eastern Orthodoxy, which historically inclines to mystical otherworldliness. The Spirit becomes a refuge in which the Christian finds respite from this still unredeemed world. But as there is no reality of fully realized redemption to fill this refuge, the mere feeling of refuge fills it instead. The hallmarks of romantic feeling surface once more. The Christian succumbs to an "immersion" in feeling, a "complete losing [of] oneself in the individual emotion" (SR 413). Here is a mysticism oriented towards the Holy Spirit that, like the fleeting moments of Taoist feeling, leads nowhere beyond itself: the feeling is the end (SR 412).

The Buddhist and Taoist are optings off the way to full pagan humanity. That humanity divides between the stasis of fixed character and the ever-renewed surgings of individual will. A Greek tragedy like *Antigone* can be read in these terms. Christianity conforms to this division through its own bifurcation of the human ideal into priest and saint. The priest is the fixed, institution-backed character; the saint, the spontaneous, ever newly surging will. Here it is the person of Jesus Christ, both priest and saint, who holds out the promise that this tension will one day resolve. In anticipatory longing for that resolution, the Christian is tempted to idolize, through Christ, the human ideal. This is the specific temptation of Protestant Christianity, which has historically inclined, in its pietistic forms, to inward applications of perfectionist ideals. The refuge here is in "the still corner of longing" (SR 400) for human perfection, while God and the world wait outside for the human's redemptive act. This is an individualistic mysticism whose rapture is to dwell on a Christ whose perfections have not yet been humanly realized.

The pagan world was a dualism of essential categories and the individual phenomena that filled them. Christianity conforms to this division with its teaching of the two kingdoms. To the pagan's categorial world of concepts and ideas, the Christian holds up the spiritual world; and against the world of individual phenomena, he places the all too worldliness of politics and conflict. Now the pagan distinction between essence and individual is subsumed under the Christian contrast between church and world. Once again, paganism, confronted by Christianity, finds itself transformed into a mirror of Christian bifurcation. Christianity does not leave the bifurcation standing, but offers hope of final healing. Here, the healing takes the form of a future worldly peace. Now the temptation is to take the picture of that future world for the whole object of longing. The future kingdom that unites spiritual and worldly world in one, absorbs the divine and human into itself and leaves nothing outside. This is the specific temptation of the Catholic Church, which, when it appropriated the Roman legal codes and ritual of state, embarked on its still incomplete task of divinizing the world. This final form of anti-redemptive Christian mysticism is pantheistic; the two worlds collapsed into one leave nothing to redeem. In a world still unredeemed, the refuge here is the momentary impulse of the love for redeeming it. For that impulse, when taken as its own end, becomes effectively deaf to the cries of the real world and the commands of its creator God.

Because Christianity's office is to redeem the bifurcated pagan world, it cannot itself know anything but bifurcation until "the fullness of the pagans has dissolved" (SR 401). Where Christianity is faithful to its office, it pushes the perfection of God, human and world forward to a future it does not know in its own life. Where it succumbs to the temptation to know redemption, it becomes romantic in Baeck's sense. The redemption it presumes to know is all feeling, all longing or moment of love, for there is no other present reality to constitute it. The images that evoke the feeling—the spiritual God, the divine human, the pantheistic world—are powerful enough to do so only because they are distortedly extreme. Each image presumes to be the culmination of perfection, when it is, in fact, only one-third of perfection's picture. The real God, human and world are, in the world's redemption, configured in mutual relationships, not dissolved into one of the three. This is why Rosenzweig calls the Christian distortions of God, human and world endpoints. They do not interconnect as they should but, like the raptures of feeling they elicit, end in themselves.

The Christian distortions inadvertently concede the victory to paganism after all. For, in the pagan order it was also true that a self-enclosed God, human and world each presumed to be the whole (SR 84). Baeck could only applaud this analysis of Christianity. As amalgam of Judaism and pagan romanticism, Christianity is indeed ever signing itself over to its pagan roots. Rosenzweig's critique of Protestantism would draw special praise from Baeck, who could apply it to all of romantic religion. "The romantic always needs a person to worship" (RR 259).[20] The connoisseur of feeling savors his ideal all the more the higher above him it rises. And so he relishes the sweet self-abasement that, like the declining end of a seesaw, raises the ideal at the opposite end to its maximum height. Baeck's use of Schlegel's "over-holy" (RR 258) for the romantic's admired human ideal fits Rosenzweig's analysis nicely; for "over-" has just the connotation of degenerative excess that Rosenzweig wants for his Protestant mystic's devotions.

And yet even in excess, Christian emotion is not ineffectual from the standpoint of redemption. And for that reason Rosenzweig forgives its much more readily than, say, Taoist emotion. For a Christian missionary bearing even distorted ideals to the pagan mind, bears a structure that, undistortedly understood, truly figures redemption. The pagan who hears and accepts the Christian message at last has words for the creation, revelation, and redemption that he hitherto only darkly and unknowingly experienced. Here Rosenzweig and Baeck must part. For in Rosenzweig's view, emotional excess is no essential part of Christianity, but a mere temptation. It is Judaism, the world-removed structure of a living redemption, that testifies to Christians how much their own worldly redemptive work still falls short of completion. The faithful Christian thanks the Jew for this testimony: Christianity "is not permitted to anticipate redemption emotionally" (SR 414) and so keeps clear of the romantic path Baeck lays out for him.

It would not oversimplify to say that, for Baeck, feeling is the content of romantic experience. The passive and miraculous aspects of that experience pertain more to its form. But it would vastly oversimplify Rosenzweig's concept of experience to reduce it to feeling. In "The New Thinking," Rosenzweig assigns experience to the whole second part of the *Star*.[21] So experience embraces creation, revelation, and redemption. It does so almost by definition. Experience is always of and within relations. (The word "and" is "the basic word of all experience."[22]) And creation, revelation and redemption are the three relations to emerge out of the elementary facts of reality—God, human, and world. A relation for Rosenzweig always connects two logically separable endpoints.[23] Consequently, experience in Rosenzweig's sense cannot have self-contained moments of feeling for its whole content.

But even Rosenzweig's vocabulary of experience moves beyond feeling. His preferred term for experience is *Erfahrung*, as opposed to Baeck's *Erlebnis*. Baeck's term is associated with the punning transformation of life into being-lived that we earlier noted, and so with the passivity that helps define romantic feeling. While Rosenzweig's *Erfahrung* is as multifaceted as the dictionary definition of the word, and more so. It connotes both what is actively known through experience and what is passively undergone to the point of suffering. Rosenzweig presses the concept to an oxymoronic limit when he insists that the best name for his new thinking is "absolute empiricism,"[24] or, as even more paradoxically phrased by one commentator, "speculative empiricism."[25] Rosenzweig implies that what is absolute about his empiricism is its refusal to claim to know of God and world anything more than experience teaches it.[26] Experience marks an absolute limit. But it is no ordinary empiricism that can so coolly juxtapose God and world as comparable experiential categories; although it is no more extraordinary than a concept of experience that turns on the theological ideas of creation, revelation, and redemption.

There are at least two senses in which Rosenzweig can reduce his concept of experience to revelation alone. "Creation" is a term Rosenzweig applies to the three unrelated elements, God human world, of the first part of the *Star*. Creation so applied is "primeval creation," or "arch-createdness" (SR 111, 261). He also applies "redemption" to the whole of the third part of the *Star*, which aims to figure the temporally coursing movements of the second part in the fixed structures of Judaism, Christianity, and eternal truth (SR 417, 419). In these senses of creation and redemption, "revelation" applies to the whole of the second part, and becomes identical in meaning with experience. But the organically constructed *Star*, now reproduces the same three categories, microcosmically as it were, in the second part itself. So reproduced, their meanings change. There is a "revelation of creation" and a "revelation of redemption" (SR 110). The ambiguity of the genitive is instructive. On the one hand, creation and redemption belong to revelation as types of it. All revelation takes the form of relation. Creation is revelatory relation between God and world, redemption the relation between human and world, and revelation the one between God and human. Rosenzweig signals the layers of ambiguity here by designating *this* creation, "created creation" (SR 111), as opposed to primeval creation, and *this* revelation, the "second" revelation (SR 161), as opposed to created creation (which is the first revelation). But revelation also belongs to creation and redemption as their experiential origin. Revelation here applies simply to the relation between God and human. This is the love relation that the human experiences with God. Rosenzweig uses "experience" more narrowly here, for what is wholly present. Creation and the completed redemption, as past and future respectively, are not experienced in this sense. We only experience them through revelation, as its ground and consequence. We already encountered the consequential relation between revelation and redemption. Creation now emerges out of revelation as its presupposition or ground. For the human's assent to God's love command elicits an affirming acknowledgment from God: "thou art mine." In Rosenzweig's typology of grammatical forms, the declarative or narrative is always oriented towards the past. Declarative speech is the grammatical form of conceptual knowledge. God's acknowledgment, insofar as it is knowledge, retrospectively projects some past point of the beginning of his relation with humanity. That fixes revelation, backwardly, in the known world of creation, just as redemption projects revelation, forward, into the anticipated world of universal community (SR 183).

Experience, then, in its broadest sense coincides with all three relations between God, human, and world, and in the narrower sense pertains to the pure presentness of the God-human relationship alone. In the broader sense, experience is defined over against a creation that is wholly conceptual (part one of the *Star*) and a redemption that ultimately transcends both concepts and experience (part three of the *Star*). In the narrower sense, experience is defined over against a creation and a redemption that are themselves types of revelation, and that are only experienced obliquely through the God-human relation.

If we examine any one of the three relations that experience broadly denotes, we will find complex inversions and meetings of active movements and passive states. One observer sees in the "tridimensionality" of Rosenzweigian experience an anti-idealist envaluing of multiplicity, contingency and openness, and dual components of cognition and belief.[27] Experience here so bursts the Baeckian romantic mold, that even that redemptive one-third of it, broadly conceived, can hardly illustrate the experiential redemption of a feeling-consumed Baeckian romanticism. And yet two strands from the narrower sense of experience in Rosenzweig—its sheer presentness, and its way of occurring at Yom Kippur—do mirror Baeckian romantic experience.

Part of what made romantic redemptive experience so blissful, according to Baeck, was that it concentrated all of what was most desirable in a wholly accessible Now (RR 206). The romantic would not postpone any higher satisfaction to some future time. What the romantic experiences in this Now costs no effort because it is entirely given. It is a state of perfect rest. In the Rosenzweigian analog to this state, which occurs as revelation rather than as redemption, the beloved, too, enjoys a blissful repose. But this repose is the very opposite of a momentary Now. The finite self meets the divine love sent it with a "serene diffusion" of pride (SR 167). The pride has the nature of an essential attribute, not a momentary surge. It is the pride of one who is so wholly at rest that he "allows himself to be borne" (SR 168); a pride that Rosenzweig sees merging into humility, though Baeck might call it mere dependence. It was in part the passivity of this feeling-state that allowed us to judge it romantic in Baeck's sense.

Where momentariness occurs in revelation is at the opposite endpoint of the God-human relation—in God's loving act. Here is where Rosenzweig asks of language a way to convey sheer presentness, and finds his answer in the form of the imperative: "the presentness of experience is only satisfied by the form of command" (SR 186). Here, too, is the "love me" command of God we have already encountered, but can now appreciate from the standpoint of its "wholly pure and unprepared-for present tense" (SR 177). Rosenzweig's grammatico-phenomenological analysis of this command shows his debt to the old idealist desideratum of a knowing in which all sub-

ject-object distance has disappeared. Quite early in the *Star*, he
notes that "in the present the thing presented disappears behind the
gesture of presenting" (SR 46). But it is in the passages on love, some
of the most lyrical in the book, that Rosenzweig struggles from various angles for an adequate formulation of the distance that disappears in love. Love is "audible at the instant of its birth," "is
completely fulfilled in the moment in which it exists," is "devoted
only to the individual present moment" (SR 177, 164, 163). Audibility, fulfillment, and devotion here all designate expressive acts identical with what they express. The distance vanished is between the
thing-in-itself of love and its expression, the same vanishing Hegel
sought for spirit in his *Phenomenology*. By this vanishing, love is
constricted to the infinitesimal "space" that constitutes the very idea
of the pure present, in which no distance separates a beginning from
an end. Rosenzweig, applying this idea to the love-command, calls it
a "unity of consciousness, expression, and expectation of fulfillment"
(SR 177). Such a love is "veritable" (SR 165), because its confirmation is its audible expression. Here an analog appears to romantic
experience in Baeck's sense, where a whole, the whole of what is desired, is concentrated into the moment. For divine love is an outward
expression of God's inward essence, which Rosenzweig characterizes, in Greek mythological terms, as a fatedness or destiny. The
whole constricted into the single moment of love is "all the weight of
[that] destiny" (SR 160). But by this same constricting, the moment
of love is volatile: confined to the space of a moment, it perishes as
soon as it begins. Love is inherently unstable, and faithless, having
nothing within it to extend it through time (SR 163, 162). Its only
continuity is successiveness, an ongoing repetition of Now-moments.

It is precisely the stabilizing component of the human self, experienced as a willingness to be borne, that in the very act of receiving divine love, assures its continuity. For the self is constant in its
humble/proud receptivity to being borne. It is the divine love that
bears it, in ever new moments of "ever first love" (SR 160).

From the standpoint of romantic feeling, revelation was the mere
presupposition of redemption in the *Star*. For it did not seem that the
passive being-borne of the beloved translated over into the redemptive
act itself. But, from the standpoint of momentary presentness, an aspect of redemptive romantic experience, according to Baeck, the translation does occur. For the human's redemptive act towards the world
mirrors God's revelatory act towards the human. Both loves are momentary and successively new (SR 215). But where God's revelatory
love passes in a succession of moments from one human to the next

(SR 163), human redemptive love, limited at each moment to its literal neighbor, passes successively through all the world. If God's love constricted a whole of destiny to a single moment, redemptive human love finds in its neighbor a constricted representative of all the world (SR 218). The identity of divine love with its expression in the love-command finds its analog in the blindness of human redemptive love. It is blind in the sense that its action precedes its direction. It does not first recognize an object outside itself which it proceeds to reach. It has reached the object before it knew where it was going, before an object apart from it could even declare itself to it. Here is the mirror of the vanished distance in divine love (SR 269), that constitutes its momentariness. The literal neighbor is inevitably so close that he may be touched without being seen. Unseeing love feels its way, or as Rosenzweig puts it, is "led only by feeling" (SR 267).

With this language, Rosenzweig seems of his own to reach back to romanticism, quite without our promptings. And he does indeed cite the romantic theologian Schleiermacher as the author of "the theology of the new epoch" (SR 107), with which all subsequent theology (including Rosenzweig's own) must come to terms (SR 100). Schleiermacher, the theologian of feeling, saved Christianity from the erosions of historicism, by regrounding religion, out of the past, into the present. His theology "zealously guarded the pure presentness of experience" (SR 107), from any incursions deriving from doubts about the historical Jesus. At most, a tie was allowed between present experience and, with a bow to Enlightenment teachings, a distant future when the ethical implications of religious experience would be realized (SR 100). But Rosenzweig does not endorse this view which, except for its ethical implications, nicely illustrates Baeckian romanticism. Schleiermacher's view completely undermines the concept of miracle so central to the relation between creation and revelation.[28] But the relation between redemption and revelation is also different for Rosenzweig. Rosenzweig's redemptive experience reaches back to feeling not for content, as in Schleiermacher, but for form, if the form of a thing, following Hegel, is its movement. The passive feeling of belovedness in revelation passes, with redemption, into a love that moves feelingly to its neighbor. Let us take Rosenzweig seriously when he says all modern theology must come to terms with Schleiermacher. Then it is as though Rosenzweig's understanding of the relation between revelation and redemption builds on romantic redemptive experience by dividing from each other two of its component parts. That experience is at once momentary presentness and passive feeling. Rosenzweig reallocates the passive feeling to the recipient of revelation, and the momentary presentness, converted from passivity to sheer act, to the agent of redemption. But if this re-allocation is too abstract, the third part of the *Star* obligingly fills in some detail, though with a striking twist. The Christian there appears as the worldly agent of redemption and the Jew as the world-removed recipient, not merely of revelation, and here is the twist, but of redemption, too. So we read that Christianity makes of the present a stationary epoch, the moment writ large, extending from the time of Christ to the second coming (SR 338). Within this present, the church sends out its missions, and its temporal-secular festivals that entice the nations' life into the church's. The church acts on redemption's behalf, but does not experience it. Its premier liturgical acts memorialize and relive the founding event of Christian revelation. It is Judaism that shapes a liturgical life that beckons redemption into lived experience. All Jewish liturgy builds up to the actual experience of redemption that occurs on Yom Kippur. And this experience is a paragon of Baeckian romanticism: eternity "is actually there . . . holding every individual close in its strong grasp" (SR 325); the "we" of the praying congregation on that day "can be nothing less than . . . mankind itself" (SR 325). Here are the characteristic marks of being-borne, and of constricting the complete whole into the part. It is, in the end, just a foretaste of redemption, since Yom Kippur is hardly over before Sukkot has neutralized it by commemorating a redemptive stage in Israel's own history (SR 328). The high point of redemption can only be experienced from out of a context of weekly and seasonally repeated experiences of creation, revelation and lesser redemptions. That is the conditionality of Yom Kippur. Redemption in Judaism is not the epoch-making present of Christianity, but a future only fleetingly experienced in the now. Still, Yom Kippur wins back for redemption the experience of blissful wholeness and embrace that was ceded to revelation. Here Rosenzweig is unqualifiededly a child of romanticism.

It is just such a concentrated experience of wholeness, folding the human in its embrace, that the romantic calls a miracle. It is miraculous in its heteronomy, coming from beyond the human will, and in the completeness of its fulfillment of all human longing. And so Rosenzweig seems set up to illustrate this third defining feature of Baeckian romanticism. But in the few pages explicitly devoted to Yom Kippur, the term "miracle" does not once occur. Where it does occur, and very centrally, is as a bridge concept between creation and revelation. So once again, as in the case of feeling, a feature of romantic redemption is shifted back, in Rosenzweig, to revelation.

Rosenzweig refers to "the experienced miracle of revelation" (SR 182–183). Such a phrase lends another nuance to the paradoxical philosophy of "absolute empiricism." The experience of revelation is experience itself; the miracle is that experience occurs at all. Such a view is not so surprising, when experience and revelation have been virtually identified. The romantic, of course, will not deem all experience miraculous, but just his heights of bliss. And if Rosenzweig meant by the miracle of revelation, just the God-human relation, his use of "miracle" could be judged romantic. But in fact, creation is miracle too (SR 108, 208). And now, recalling Rosenzweig's critique of Schleiermacher, we have left romantic miracle, since it was from all past tense, including creation, that romanticism zealously guarded its present experience. And so Rosenzweig's meaning of miracle must be different from the romantic's.

> For . . . erstwhile humanity . . . miracle was based on . . . its having been predicted, not on its deviation from the course of nature as this had previously been fixed by law. Miracle is substantially a "sign." (SR 95)

A miracle is sign that something predicted has come to pass. This is no fulfillment of scientific prediction. The miracle is still nonrational, in the sense that no law or reasoning compels the passage from prediction to sign. It is rather that two matched halves of a whole are seen together as a whole, when they could as easily have been separated by a divide as great as that between existence and nonexistence. It is the matching that makes the miracle. For Rosenzweig, revelation is a miracle because it is so perfectly matched to creation. In this context, creation refers to the prereal domain of the three protocosmic elements, God, human, and world; and revelation, to the real world of relations between them.

The manner of matching between the relations and the elements is inversion. Inversion is, in its own right, a favorite maneuver in the romanticism Baeck considers, but it is still several steps ahead of us in his dialectic, so we will not consider Rosenzweig's analog to it here. Suffice it for now to note that the disparity between romantic and Rosenzweigian miracle may not be so great as at first appears. A romantic might well reinterpret his experience along Rosenzweig's lines as the matching of a singular need to its fulfillment. The need could not compel the fulfillment, but by its shape— its dissatisfaction with all finitude—it might be seen to have predicted it, once the fulfilling wholeness was actually experienced.

This points to a more important congruence between the two meanings of miracle: both are bridge concepts between subjectivity and objectivity. In Baeck's use of the term on the romantic's behalf, "miracle" hovers between the heightened feelings that constitute the subjective experience and the "truth" of the wholeness to which they refer. For Rosenzweig, miracle is the bridge across which the very disciplines of "objective" philosophy and "subjective" theology send back and forth their mutual supports. The problem of theology, ever since Schleiermacher, was that the experience of feeling it made so central had no ground or warrant. It was pure subjectivity, without any claim to be taken seriously by anyone who had not already surrendered to it. Theology undercut itself when it severed its experience from any potentially doubt-inspiring ground in the objective world.[29] Philosophy, on the other hand, ever since Feuerbach's critique of Hegel, was saddled with structures of concepts that had no application to reality. Hegel's bold attempt in the *Phenomenology* to trace the identification of thought with being fails, says Feuerbach, because thought in that work never leaves its own domain in the first place. It begins not with sense-certainty, as it claims to, but with the idea of sense-certainty, and so cannot presume by the end to have subsumed the being of sense under thought.[30] Rosenzweig adds that philosophy can never be content with a systematic account of a mere part of the world—the conceptual part. It wants the whole. But its concepts cannot colonize the being of sense for its own. It stands helpless before the real world, gazing into a "bottomless abyss" (SR 104) of resistance to mere ideas.

For Rosenzweig, the needs of philosophy and theology are perfectly matched, and so poised to illustrate between them the reality of miracles. Rosenzweig, who praised Kant as personally the greatest of all philosophers for acknowledging, in defiance of philosophy itself, that human freedom was simply a miracle,[31] might have invoked him here as well. For, in imitation of another famous Kantian claim, it might be said that philosophy is empty and theology is blind. The mutual need of concepts for objects is the Kantian miracle that anticipates Rosenzweig's. But all philosophy of the Hegelian type must first surrender its claim to know the truth through concepts alone. It must content itself to know that part of the truth which is creation alone; and not here the creation-relation between God and world, but the primeval creation of the self-enclosed concepts of God, human and world, where no relation, and so no revelation, even presumes to be. This creation is primeval because it is recessed back before the real creation, and its partners in revelation, ever came to be. What makes for the recession is that the conceptual world of primeval creation anticipates theology's world of subjective revelatory experience. Creation is the "point from which philosophy can begin to reconstruct the whole edifice of theology" (SR 103); and conversely, the point through which philosophy must pass for its relevance to the real world. That is the miraculous relation between them. The manner of the reconstructing and the realizing of relevance is, once again inversion, which we have already once teased into appearance before its proper time. Suffice it here to note the bearing of miracle on redemption. In Rosenzweig's scheme, congregational prayer holds the place between revelation and redemption that miracle does between creation and revelation, i.e., the place of the bridge between the two relations (SR 294). But these two bridges are not unrelated. The passage from revelation to redemption presupposes the grounding of revelation in creation. There would be no aching to extend the private bliss of the God-human relation to all the world, if the human were not too bound to the world for it to be excluded from his relation with God. Revelation is anchored to the primeval world of God, human and world as miraculous sign of its fulfilled prediction. And when Rosenzweig says that the "miracle of revelation . . . demands its completion in a further miracle which has not yet happened" (SR 184), he implies that redemption is miracle, too. Still, it is not the primary miracle. And we must conclude that miracle, like feeling, is shifted back in Rosenzweig from a content of redemption, as in Baeckian romanticism, to a presupposition of it.

The experience, feeling and miracle of Baeckian romantic redemption all find analogs in *The Star of Redemption*. Passivity was also a defining mark of romantic redemption. The passivity of romantic religion seemed to find an echo in the submission idealist religion enjoined of the finite to the infinite. And in rejecting idealist submission, Rosenzweig might seem to have been rejecting passivity as such. But now we can see how misleading that appearance is. The dominant tone of idealism is much more active than passive. The infinite self is itself an act of self-positing; indeed, when idealism paid its respects to its famous precursor in philosophical monism, Baruch Spinoza, it at the same time saw its advance over him in the activity it located at the heart of "substance." Idealism was Spinozism enlivened to self-consciousness.[32] The finite self submits to the infinite, only to join the one grand act of self-positing.

One early form of protest against Hegelian idealism was to newly envalue passivity. Rosenzweig, who credited Feuerbach with anticipating his "new thinking,"[33] might have credited him here too. For

Feuerbach undercut the epistemological dependence in idealism of knowing on acting; it is on self-limitation, not self-positing, that knowledge depends. Thinking itself is a "form of receptivity"[34] led by feeling.[35] And the principal feeling that assures the objective knowledge of another is love.[36] We have already seen some of the alliances of passivity with feeling, love and knowledge in the *Star*. The beloved soul who hears God's command is "wholly receptive" (SR 176) in its bliss. God's love responds much more to the deficiencies and recessions (*Maengel*) in the soul than to the presumed excellencies (*Vorzuege*) there. The active love that emerges from the beloved state is passive in the sense that it grasps at no expectation of success (SR 176). It does not control or calculate, but illustrates "the standard of romantic aimlessness" that Baeck took for one expression of romantic passivity (RR 241). The Jewish liturgical structure that figures the beloved soul, but translated expansively out from revelation to redemption, is just that—a quiescent structure, as opposed to the "going, doing, becoming" of Christianity—and something passively born into, rather than actively decided upon (SR 354). Finally, through the miracle, passivity appears as well as a condition of knowledge. Human knowledge comes into being as the past of experience (or revelation). That past already exists predictively in philosophy; the experience is present in theology. The matching of the two is the miracle that no human can will, but can merely behold in wonder.[37]

For all that, the passivity Rosenzweig implicitly endorses may be too impure for Baeckian romanticism. Passivity as Baeck presents it in the romantic is the unalloyed article, "purely receptive," precluding all activity (RR 249). It is helpless, weary, and slothful (RR 192, 212). This is not Rosenzweig's passivity, or even Feuerbach's, whose notion of self-limitation already connotes activity. All the passivities in the *Star* considered previously have active dimensions. Rosenzweig notes that "being loved is after all [only] apparently a purely passive attribute" (SR 170). The passivity is simply the surface of a surging free will that has emerged towards God as serenity (SR 167, 170). It is not that the human falls passive before God; but that he produces his own passivity from out of himself, which is then matched to the concentrated moments of sheer love activity from God. In that sense the soul must "unlock itself" to divine love (SR 177). This self-made passive soul "allows itself" to be loved (SR 169). The active dimension of redemptive love that emerges from the beloved needs no comment, except to note that even it is not sheer act, but is, in part, forcibly elicited by the world's own need of it (SR 228)—a "passively attracting" feature of the world already protocosmically anticipated by the "need for application" to individuals its static categories have (SR 44). As for Judaism, it requires its active complement in Christianity or it could never seriously believe in a universal redemption. Finally, the miracle itself would never be if the human did not participate in it. Knowledge itself is simply a reflection of three miraculous matchings that occur between the joint passivities and activities of God, human, and world.

Baeck's own picture of passivity may be more of an alloy than he lets on. For if it is truly weary, and not simply helpless and slothful, then something has been wearing it down; which implies an assertion of resistance that, even if it is finally overcome, cannot have been wholly passive. If Baeck's passivity is inadvertently tainted with activity, and so unintentionally more faithful to the life of passivity than a mere caricature would be, then, once again, as in the case of experience and miracle, Rosenzweig is closer to Baeckian romanticism than might at first appear. But, in the end, Baeck's statements on passivity do read like caricature. Schlegel may have said that "'sleep is the highest degree of genius'," as Baeck quotes him, but this is hardly to be interpreted, in Baeck's manner, as a show of preference for passive dreaming over active working (RR 212). Schlegel, who said many other things about genius besides, among which was that it was "organic spirit,"[38] may well have found in dreams organic models for artistic works, in which case the dream is, contra Baeck, a kind of working in its own right. Baeck, of course, was not out to produce sympathetic interpretations of Schlegel; but, more to the point, neither was his chief concern to caricature the romantics. The concealed purpose of Baeck's essay is to defend classicism against the foil of romanticism, of which passivity is a defining feature. Baeck presents a caricatured extreme of passivity just so that he can judge it all the more harshly. And the harsh judgments are concealed praise for what he deemed romantic religion's sorest lack; namely, ethics.

Romantic Anti-Ethics

It might surprise readers of Baeck that he devotes so little attention to what is sometimes taken for romanticism's central concept, namely that of individuality. Rosenzweig, for example, deems the idea of a "lebendig wirkende 'Individualitaet'" (actively effective

individuality) the definitive "Einsicht der Romantik" (insight of romanticism).[39] In fact, Baeck subsumes the romantic notion of the individual under the larger category of feeling. Feelings define and
distinguish the romantic self. Romantic individuality is simply an
excess of attention to one's own feelings. Here the romantic resembles the idealist, for whom the act of self-consciousness constitutes
the self. But Baeck himself seems aware of how poorly this notion of
individuality bears up under the closer scrutiny of feelings. Feelings
are too fluid and adaptable to stamp a personality with any characteristic marks (RR 193). Besides, the romantic hope for the self is not
that it definitively exist but that it sink down and drown (RR 192).
The romantic notion of individuality, on Baeck's account, simply self-
destructs.

This ending of romantic individuality reveals more of Baeck's
own apologetic needs than of any actual romanticism. Romanticism
has no rights to the idea of individuality because they have already
been claimed by classicism. Individuality is a function of obedience
to the moral law. Duty and demand, not feelings, are the mirror in
which the individual self appears (RR 194).[40]

Baeck's religiophilosophical descent is from Kant through Hermann Cohen, who was his teacher. It is no surprise, than, that ethics
is so much the touchstone of religious worthiness in his thought. For
Baeck, absence of ethics in romanticism is the dark shadow cast by
the ideas it affirms: feeling, experience, miracle, and passivity. A single quote neatly illustrates:

> Everything that is characteristic of romanticism makes a
> united front against the idea of a moral law. All its multifar-
> ious tendencies coalesce in this opposition. Justice is to be
> reduced to a mere feeling and experience; the good deed is ef-
> fected not by human will and action but by divine grace; man
> himself is a mere object and not a personality; and the con-
> ception of the finished dominates everything (RR 269–270).

The concept of the finished corresponds here to the wholeness en-
capsulated in romantic experience. The objectness of the human is
his passivity. The good deed effected is the miracle. And feeling
heads the list of the multifarious tendencies. Romanticism and
ethics are not always simply opposed in Baeck's account. Sometimes
romanticism simply wants to distance ethics and to remain amoral
(RR 192, 278). Other times it wants to supplant or subordinate it
(RR 250, 248) and so border on the immoral, as Baeck implies when

he notes that indifference to wrong is "more romantic than intolerance, for it is more passive" (RR 275). So, for example, experience can float blissfully above all ethical tasks (RR 193), positively contradict those tasks (RR 212), or make them over into an aspect of itself (RR 265). Miracle, for its part, is so staunchly opposed to ethics that the two "cannot be reconciled" (RR 249); while feeling, by borrowing from ethics the ideas of autonomy and validity to justify itself (RR 190, 198), goes farthest, of all the components of romanticism, to supplant ethics.

Ethics is, of course, the Kantian, classical way to redemption. But such redemption is always merely envisioned: it belongs to the future. Indeed, the future redemption cannot be envisioned without heeding the command to work towards it (RR 193). Romanticism, which rejects the moral command, must also reject a future redemption. And it may express this rejection by envaluing the past (RR 193). That already seems to contradict Rosenzweig's own observation on romantic theology, that it deliberately cut itself off from the past. But the past there meant the potential disconfirmations of religion that historical research might unfold. The past of Baeckian romanticism is not the object of disciplined research but of empathic and lyrical retellings (RR 194). It is nonserious and poses no threat to the only serious tense of romantic psychology, the present.

We now begin to uncover, through the contrast with classicism, a set of "negative" signs of romantic tendencies. Feeling, experience, miracle and passivity are essential traits of romantic religion. Together they constitute romantic redemption. But romanticism is sensitive to the charges ethics levels against its view of redemption, and adopts additional traits to meet them. One of these is affection for a lyricized past. This affection is meant to counter the future-oriented demands of ethics which, taken seriously, would undermine romantic redemption in the present. It is not an unintelligent ploy, given the division sometimes cited in the history of religions between utopian future redemptions and those of the past golden age. For apologetic purposes, romanticism endorses the golden age.

Baeck develops two additional apologetic features of romanticism, which both arise from the challenge of ethics: enthusiasm and casuisty. These are instances of romantic subsumings of ethics (RR 256, 269) and both protect the central redemptive experience from moralistic underminings. Enthusiasm elevates an idea of the good hopelessly beyond reach. From a position far below, the romantic can admire, adore, and even yearn for the ideal without having to acknowledge any obligation towards it (RR 258). If obligations are required for behavior in the world, they are developed casuistically, without any organic grounding in ethical command. Casuistic rules allow a calculated, negotiated passage through the world (RR 267), leaving the core of redemptive life fixed in present experience. Baeck implies that ethics inevitably launches romanticism on a path through enthusiasm and casuistry. Casuistry "has always belonged to romantic faith" (RR 268) and, as the "precipitate of exuberance" (RR 267), that is, of enthusiasm, which is unable to chart a way through the world, it comes last in this two-termed sequence of ethics substitutes.

Here then is another quadrivium of romantic features—amorality, nostalgia, enthusiasm, and casuistry. These are not essential features, but fall on romanticism as the shadow cast by its rejection of the moral command. How do these appear in the *Star*?

Of the 460 subtitles in Rosenzweig's *Star*, not a single one is named for ethics. The third book of the first part is indeed about metaethics, but this is precisely the absence of ethics, at least as understood in the Kantian tradition. Rosenzweig seems almost to tempt the term "romantic" into his book when he writes about metaethics that "one must acknowledge the otherworldliness of the new enquiry as against everything which the concept of ethics hitherto solely meant" (SR 11). What ethics hitherto solely meant was the identification of the autonomous finite will with the universal moral law. Rosenzweig allows, as Baeck implied, that the moral command presumes to both address and affirm the autonomy of the individual, and so to constitute the human as a personality, rather than as a mere object. But the necessity for the universal formulation of the moral law, which is the first expression of the categorical imperative, just as focibly denies the uniqueness of the individual person. Hermann Cohen's acknowledgment of and answer to this problem attracted Rosenzweig immensely: certain individually experienced human burdens, such as sickness, sin, and death (as opposed to social poverty, for instance), do not admit of ethics' universalizing solutions. An address needs to reach the individual in her aloneness before these burdens can be eased, and it is precisely religion's purpose to supply it.[41] Cohen's ethics grounded religion without swallowing it. But Rosenzweig's religion stands on a foundation that is indeed amoral: metaethical otherworldliness.

Rosenzweig's concept of metaethics is defined against the culmination of Kantian thought in Hegelian idealism. That idealism aspired to a monism that quite jubilantly effaces all distinction. Rosenzweig's objection to this, in which he hardly differed from

Baeckian classicism, was that it simply was not true. Distinction is real, as death surely teaches. But where Rosenzweig differs sharply from Baeck is his sense that the movement towards monism already began in the subsumption of the individual under the Kantian moral law. The mistake of monism needed to be uprooted at its ethical beginnings. Metaethics provides an alternative origin for human uniqueness and personality that bypasses the moral law and universalizing agents of any kind. Metaethics conceives the human as pure finitude (SR 69). Indeed, the object of metaethical thought is a human reality from which all subsuming and relating universals, all infinites, have been abstracted. Such a human is metaethical because, so deprived of all relations, and so impoverished, it sinks back beneath reality into a sort of conceptual prelude to any living, ethically engaged human being we really know. What there remains to see of this abstracted human is, precisely, nothing. But that paradox need not concern us now. What matters here are three things: (1) Rosenzweig develops an understanding of human uniqueness and personality from out of this nothing; (2) the human uniqueness becomes an essential building block in the particular relations of revelation and redemption; and (3) all this occurs without any need of ethics.

If the idea of metaethics awakens in the casual reader a hope for moral guidance, which is now dashed, he might turn to part two of the *Star*, which shows the reality of redeeming human love. But Rosenzweig warns us early on against expecting any ethics in the book's later parts. What the *Star* does offer, he implies in the same preliminary metaethical subsection, is a life-view; while ethics is inevitably a world-view. It is world view because only the world contains the universals under which humans can be subsumed. What part three presents is two alternative configurations, the Jewish and the Christian, of the living reality of relations shown in part two between God, human, and world. But none of these relations are ethical in the Kantian sense.[42] None are subsumings of particulars under universals, but rather simply meetings between particulars and universals. World-views and life-views appear to do the same work, namely guide the life of individual human beings, but they do so on such different grounds as to be mutually exclusive. In the second part of the *Star*, we do indeed read that "the individual moral deed as such is really valueless" (SR 172), a scandal of a claim to any good moralist. The claim comes in a discussion of Islam, whose religiomoral deeds win merit for their agents in the sight of God, while for the truly beloved soul, in Rosenzweig's view, all affirmation of itself owes to God's initiative alone. As for the beloved soul turned agent of its own redeeming love, neither is there any ethics here. The ethical act is purposive and pointed towards a goal, if only towards the end-in-itself of all human being. But redeeming love, as we saw in connection with romantic passivity, is precisely goalless, "off guard and unpremeditated" (SR 269). Redemptive acts simply do not belong to ethics.

The amorality of the *Star* hardly expresses any discernible wish to protect religious experience from intrusive moral commands. But it may well illustrate the subsumption of ethics under religion that the occasion of religious experience in the *Star* is itself a divine command. Baeck himself comes closer to Rosenzweig when he concedes that romanticism has a point "against that activism which would take care of and execute everything" (RR 290). That is just the problem, Rosenzweig might say: even the distinct act, under ethics' sway, is finally delivered up to the nondiscriminating sum of everything (SR 210).

Rosenzweig clearly inverts the Kantian implications for individuality of the moral law. Far from establishing individuality, subsumption under the moral law effaces it. On the other hand, he has hardly yet endorsed Baeck's account of the alternative romantic view. Metaethical individuality is defined not by feeling but by finitude. Whatever feelings move the human being who stares out at us from the metaethical ground are frozen and masked. And yet a self formed by feelings does arise in response to the metaethical self. Rosenzweig does not abandon the metaethical self to bare abstraction. He translates it into the silent, self-enclosed heroes of classical Greek tragedy. These heroes are emotionally rigid and unmoved (SR 81). But the spectator who watches them is roused to terror and compassion, as Aristotle had already theorized. And these "same emotions at once move inward and turn him too into a self-enclosed self" (SR 81). These emotions inwardly fix the viewer's attention, which, wholly self-directed, inspires "the feeling of one's own self" (SR 81). Baeck himself could not have offered an account of the self's origins more faithful to the romantic ideal.

Baeck's characterization of romantic nostalgia recalls the line from an English novel, "I seem to like the idea of anything old."[43] In fact, for a time, Rosenzweig took the past much more seriously than this. His early academic turn away from medicine was towards history and philosophy, and his dissertation, *Hegel and the State*, was written under the direction of the German historian, Friedrich Meinecke. Meinecke himself propounded a historicism that set ages of history and their "great personalities" in organic relation: history was to study the radiation outward of the ideas of great individuals into the whole of their age. Meinecke saw his view as, at least partially, a legacy of German romanticism.[44] And historicism as Meinecke holds it certainly illustrates Baeck's idea that romantic history is empathic. Meinecke cites Herder for coining the word *Einfuehlung*,[45] and this is what the historian is to bring to the personalities he studies. The difficulty is that, as Meinecke also notes, such an historicism is inevitably relativistic.[46] And he struggled against this, as one commentator observes, by insisting that, through the study of many expressions of great personality, some "glimpse of the absolute" must show.[47] But it is difficult to see why. And unless that difficulty is resolved, historicism seems to illustrate that other feature of Baeckian romantic history, as well, namely its lack of seriousness. It poses no threats to any philosophical or religious truths, because it contributes nothing to the objective understanding of reality.

It was just this problem of seriousness that Rosenzweig came to feel acutely. Rosenzweig, like Feuerbach before him, was greatly exercised by the distance between reality and the idea of it. All academic scholarship was inherently unserious because, confined to ideas, it could never bridge the gap to reality.[48] But a double burden of unseriousness fell on history, which, in addition, ever since the Great War, lost all rights to any claims to guide a tentative and faltering humanity into a better state. Rosenzweig added a preface and concluding note to the final version of his dissertation, published in 1920, in which he implies that any hopes of recovering the idea of the Hegelian state, after the *Realpolitik* of Bismarck had supplanted it so thoroughly, burned up with most of the rest of Germany during the war.[49] He concludes:

> Wenn der Bau einer Welt zusammenkracht, werden auch die Gedanken, die ihn erdachten, werden auch die Traeume, die ihn durchwebten, unter dem Einsturz begraben.[50] (If the structure of a world crashes, then the thoughts that devised it and the dreams that wove through it are buried under the remains.)

Avineri is right to note the elegiac tone.[51] If Rosenzweig is mourning for the broken promise of the past, the tribute he thus indirectly pays it may be romantic in Baeck's sense. But no such elegies carry over into the *Star*. Rosenzweig's vengeance on the so cruelly disappointing past is to freeze it into a "thing-like stillness" (SR 131). Inverting the open-ended relativism of historicism, Rosenzweig closes the past off into objectivity. Far from eliciting feeling or empathy, the past is the tense of objective knowledge. It is so in two senses. The elements of the protocosmos constitute a past that is ever prior to the revealed world of relations. The late Schelling would call it the eternal past. It is the world of objective but empty concepts that philosophy takes for its province, and that, serving as ground to theology, yields knowledge in the miracle. But the past is also the tense of revealed creation, the relation between God and the world. Within experience, which is always present, the relata of creation appear in the past imperfect, as having-created, in the case of God, and having-been-created, in the case of the world (SR 132); which is to say that, from the standpoint of the present, creation is experienced as presupposition. Here is the warrant for descriptive claims about reality. As Hegel taught about language that seeks to describe present sensation, it invariably reaches what is only just passed. For the utterance that presumes to carry an intention to its sense object takes time; and in that time, the intended object has fallen into the past. That might cause some never to speak; but reality enables descriptive speech by presenting to humans, along with its presentness, its presupposition in the past. We have descriptive knowledge because the past is present in presupposition.

The past functions for Rosenzweig in an austerely epistemological way. If we seek in Rosenzweig an analog to Baeckian romantic nostalgia, we must turn to the future. Here, present human speech is not declarative but interrogative; its mood is the subjunctive wish, intensifying to a cry (SR 185). The cry is for the world's redemption, which the future holds in hiding. But if the past is present in presupposition, the future is so in expectation: "the future is experienced soley in expectation" (SR 219). To have any reality, i.e., any location in the present, the future must be anticipated (SR 234). The analogy between presupposed past and anticipated future carries over to creation. The past creation, presuppositionally experienced in the present, is the created world: the future redemption, anticipatedly experienced in the present, is the redeemed world. The redeemed world is the perfecting complement of the created world. Redeeming love moves towards it blindly; this object of wishful cry is no object of knowledge. Charles Dickens was quite right to picture the ghost of Christmas future a shrouded being whose face we cannot see. But if unseen in the present, how is redemption experienced there?

The future is experienced in the present as eternity. The concept of eternity, like that of pure love, is predicated on the idea of a vanishing. In the command to love, the distance between the act of love and its expression vanishes. Here, the distance to be erased is between present and future. But here, unlike in the case of love, the distance is only virtually erased. Eternity is experienced in the moment before the erasure, in the space between the present and the last moment the future extends to the present before it cedes it to the present entirely. "Eternity is a future which, without ceasing to be future, is nonetheless present" (SR 224). Such a moment cannot simply be the present; but neither can it be the last prepresent moment of the future—for that is still future. It must occur in the infinitesimal space between them, where the future vanishes into the present. Eternity is this vanishing. Eternity is to express a moment "that must begin at the very moment that it vanishes" (SR 289). It is a paradoxical idea, though one not new with Rosenzweig. Hegel had pondered the paradoxical results of vanishings between form and content. A succession of such vanishings finally issues in absolute knowledge. In Rosenzweig's case, the issue is a moment that infinitely reissues itself (SR 289). For if this moment begins, it must have vanished; if it has vanished, it must begin. The pauseless play between beginning and vanishing is the experience of eternity.

Now there can be no doubt that, in Rosenzweig's future, we have struck the romantic chord. For an ever-renewed vanishing is a type of hovering, an oscillating preference for the in-between of two. Here is another translation of romantic unseriousness—the refusal to decide. Baeck calls it romanticism's experience of *das Schwebende*.[52] And suddenly in the midst of redemption, in the last book of the last part of the *Star*, we learn that, in all our seemingly concrete experience, so miraculously grounded in the past, we are ourselves *Schwebenden*[53] between the past and the future; as though these endpoints are, after all, the location of the final seriousness, and we the vanishing moments who are strung between.

It is precisely the office of the Jews to hover vanishingly. Christians hover too, but not vanishingly. The future enters their present, and eternalizes it, but their own attention is not on the vanishing. They accept the eternalization of the moment, so as to stretch it out into a way through the world. From their perch in the long liminal present, they busy themselves redemptively with the passing temporal order that they accompany. But they do not live in the eternity that supports them. Only the Jews do (SR 370). It is in the context of Jewish liturgy that Rosenzweig concretizes the abstract idea of hovering. The unit of the week, on which the liturgy builds, figures the vanishing moment of eternity by beginning again at the end. The figuring repeats at the level of the month, but most especially the year, which closes and rebegins through the course of the high holy days. Yom Kippur, standing "at the boundary between two years, which signifies eternity" (SR 325) is the high point of experienced redemption that we have already once encountered. But the Jewish people anticipates throughout the whole course of their year the realized future of Yom Kippur, and to that extent never ceases to experience eternity. The Christian both lives in (*lebt*) and experiences (*erlebt*) the between separating future from past. And now comes Rosenzweig's own play on *lebt* and *erlebt*, with respect to the Jewish people, but to opposite effect of Baeck's. "So erlebt es [das ewige Volk] das Zwischen nicht, obwohl es doch natuerlich, wirklich natuerlich, darin lebt."[54] The Jewish people inhabits the Between through "natural propagation." The chain of propagation is its own figure of eternity (SR 299), which accounts for the emphasized *natuerlich*. But unlike the Christians, the Jews do not stretch the Between out over the whole present; they live instead for the ever-recurring vanishing of future into present: they live in and for eternity.

Rosenzweig's distinction between the Jewish and Christian relations to eternity might be restated in terms of the old idealist preoccupation with form and content. Hegel distinguishes between the movements consciousness undergoes on its way to absolute knowledge, and the content of its awareness at any given moment of movement. Except for the endpoint of absolute knowledge, consciousness' awareness of its own movements always follows their actual execution. That is, while executing the movements, it is unaware of them. Only in absolute knowledge do execution and awareness coincide. The movements of consciousness are its form, the objects of its awareness, its content. In absolute knowledge, form and content are one. Otherwise stated as the union of thought and being, this is precisely the idealism that Rosenzweig fights throughout the *Star*. But idealist structures sometimes show through incongruously from behind Rosenzweig's lyricism, and, once uncovered, may go far to clarify what is lyrically obscured. The vanishing of the future into the present is a movement. The movement's issue is an eternalized present. Rosenzweig is anti-idealist enough to separate the movement of the vanishing from its issue, contra Hegel, who would ultimately unite them. The separation invites the application of a bifurcated consciousness, one that attends to the movement, and one to the issue. Jews attend to the movement and Christians to the issue.

Since the experience of eternity is precisely of the movement, Jews experience eternity. Christians forfeit that for the issue, which, as a stable (unmoving) content, supports them for their work in the world.

Romantic feeling is a temptation to Christianity that it properly rejects for its work in the world. Romantic redemption of the present moment is an experience of Judaism that it properly affirms for its eternal life. Romantic longings for the past are irrelevant here, but it is not as though they wholly disappear. They are reflected into a future that, contra Baeck, issues no commands, since the tense of commands is always the present. The unseriousness of nostalgia, which vanishes before it can issue in any act, is mirrored in momentary anticipations of the future, which, in a succession of vanishings, constitute eternity. The Jewish people, "always somewhere between the temporal and the holy" (SR 304) are, once again, the paragon romantics.

Enthusiasm, understood as worshipful projections of ideas above and beyond any hope of realization, has already appeared once in our study of the *Star*. Here is the excess of feeling that particularly tempts Protestant Christianity into a type of Christolatry, where both God the creator and any obligations to his creation, are forgotten. What is normal Christianity for Baeck is, for Rosenzweig, aberration within Christianity. But the question remains whether the *Star* itself is not a work of enthusiasm. Passages in it have certainly been called "rhapsodic,"[55] and Gershom Scholem once pointed to the uncomprehending enthusiasm with which early readers of the book first received it.[56] Baeck notes that one form of enthusiasm is "sentimental pathos" (RR 256). While the rigorously systematic *Star* is never sentimental—at least not in the sense Baeck probably intends, of being uncritically indulgent of feeling—it is often pathic. The connotations of this word, from its Greek origins, are suffering, experience and emotion. Experience permeates the center of the *Star*, and emotion crowns the revelatory peaks. (The suffering is yet to come.) For Baeck, a pathos so disconnected from the urgings of the moral law is at sea in the world. Casuistry, an artificial and nonuniversal construct of rules for survival, becomes its worldly guide. The closest analog to this in the *Star* is the Jewish law when incorrectly taken as the world (SR 407). At the emotional peak of revelation, the Jew receives the love command. The Jewish liturgy structures a life that is continuously turned towards the source of the command, but that expands, phenomenologically, on Yom Kippur to include the whole world in a foretaste of its redemption. A Jewish temptation is to ignore the distance separating the world from the liturgical structures during the rest of the year, and to force those structures on a world that is unprepared to receive them. So unnatural a fitting is akin to casusitry, which has cut action's organic tie to the moral law. In an unexpected turn, mysticism will save the Jew from this temptation. But the question remains whether the *Star* is not itself casuistic in parts. Casuistry, for Baeck, is the advance guard of enthusiasm, cutting it a way through the world. Schleiermacher, that watershed of modern theology for Rosenzweig, with whom all subsequent theology must come to terms, exemplifies for Baeck the synthesis of enthusiasm and casuistry (RR 256). And at least one commentator has noted in the *Star*, alongside the pathos there, an "imperious aggressiveness,"[57] tearing through the traditional categories of Jewish theology and—perhaps—reshaping them to fit its elegantly systematic three-part structure. Then, from a Baeckian standpoint, Rosenzweig stands accused with Schleiermacher of the same romantic synthesis of pathos and artificial force.

Romantic Darkness

In the early pages of his essay, Baeck notes the romantic fondness for "twilight and the moonlit night, the quiet, flickering hours" (RR 191). Twilight, the between of day and night, images in temporal terms the romantic idea of hovering. But the moonlit night is a considerable advance into darkness and must figure a different idea. Baeck explicitly connects the image to dream and illusion, but he might have endowed it, more seriously, with the whole weight of the romantic investment in the nonrational, the resistance to reason. The four defining marks of romanticism already point this way—even passivity, which opposes what, ever since Kant, was a very active and determining reason. A set of secondary characteristics of romanticism begins to emerge, which might be grouped under the broad figure of darkness. But the darkness is not simply nonrationality. The miraculous and emotive experience of dependence is, by its very nature, momentary. Its inevitable passing is the great romantic grief.

Perhaps even more than feeling or miracle, passivity opens onto the darkness of unreason. Of course, pagan, neoplatonic romanticism already connected passivity to darkness through matter. (Baeck, too, links romantic passivity to matter.) The passive, giving-way of self in romantic feeling stands "immune against doubt and rational examination" (RR 209). But Baeck paints an oddly self-divided picture of the romantic nonrational. On the one had, the romantic who confronts an opposition to reason is inclined to take it for the finished truth (RR 207), as though its very unreasonableness were its recommendation. But on the other hand, the romantic cannot accept the overtures of unreason at face value, but must make them over into something else. So, says Baeck, the profferings of "the hidden darkness of the unconscious" (RR 208) are interpreted as revelation—as though the unconscious itself were, like the Magwitch of the famous Dickens novel, too frightful a benefactor. The more striking illustration is in Baeck's analysis of romantic freedom. Freedom, which in the late Schelling served as essence to a ground of darkness, is, in the romantics, completely divorced from will. The spontaneously moving will, presumably reason's greatest adversary and so a prime candidate for romantic tributes, is, instead, identified with sin (RR 244). Freedom is not of the will, but *from* the will (RR 248). Freedom is reinterpreted as release from sin by grace. Of course, Baeck has Martin Luther in mind, that arch Protestant romantic. For Luther, as for Paul, sin was a bondage that held humans captive. There was no humanly willed release from it; instead, that freeing came by divine grace. But by taking Luther for his guide here, Baeck forgoes a perfect opportunity to accuse romanticism of irrational willfulness. It is as though Baeck's polemic had tripped him up. He would like to uncover the unreason of romanticism. On the other hand, he wants to show its poverty of will to respond to law. He denies himself the chance of the one polemic—against irrational willfulness—to preserve the integrity of the other—against the lack of will entirely. But the outcome is a picture of relative moderation in romantic unreasonableness. The romantics limit their acceptance of a potentially more frightening form of the nonrational, the arbitrary will, by converting it via the ambivalent concept of freedom, into the more congenial one of received grace. Surely this is about as rational as sublimation gets. But of course grace, the end-product of this ploy, is a suprarational concept, too. Baeck himself will not exclude the nonrational from religion entirely. Calling it mystery, he understands it to "give birth" (RR 210) to important features of religious life.[58] The romantic error is to take this basis for the end.

The unreason of romanticism extends further, into a curiously contradictory attitude towards contradiction. On the one hand, romanticism sharply distinguishes opposing concepts, even to the point of founding dualisms. Romanticism begins in "man with his contradictions" (RR 194). (Even the great Christian romantics themselves were self-divided between their doctrines and their characters.)[59] And it ends by positing dual worlds of sin and justice, devil and savior. Baeck explains that the poles of these dualisms reciprocally necessitate each other. Grounded in romantic passivity, the Christian cannot redeem himself. The devil serves to hold in unredemption what the savior comes to redeem. Original sin assures a passive sinfulness from which a passively received grace supplies the release (RR 246–247). Poised passively in the middle of the two active poles, the human soul can take on movement only through their agency.

Of course, reciprocally implying oppositions may be taken as contradictory ends of a single whole. And then the boundary between the ends is in danger of collapsing. Thus emerges romanticism's other stance towards distinctions: it wants to efface them. The merging into one of two seeming opposites, enthusiasm and casuistry, was already an example. But romanticism will take the same approach to appearance and reality, knowledge and illusion, even all and nothing (RR 191, 192, 196). It wants everything subsumed under a totality (RR 205, 215). It weaves a web of relations that leaves nothing unconnected. Its embrace of feeling and rejection of ethics already indicate this. For feeling can "enter into everything," while ethics "sets limits" (RR 193, 255–256).

Baeck will not decide on the romantic's behalf between sharp opposition and blurry synthesis. Perhaps this opposition is, itself, to blur in a hovering refusal to choose. The upshot is, in any case, an unreal world. The unreality is not, for romanticism, an unfortunate consequence of its views on contradiction, but a point of proclamation. Romanticism is, precisely, "'sentimental material in phantastic form,'" as Schlegel, quoted by Baeck, puts it (RR 189). However Schlegel himself may have meant those words, Baeck takes them to indicate a presentation of feelings without regard for the distinction between appearance and reality. All four of the defining features of romanticism lead into this view. Feeling does, obviously. But Baeck suggests that experience, divorced from the moral command, becomes a "floating sphere" (RR 195) that indifferently accommodates the illusory and veridical. Law-bound life, which maintains that distinction, is forfeited for living experience—*leben* for *Erlebnis* (RR 193, 197). Energy that might have stimulated acts, is rerouted in passive romanticism towards the "union of phantasy and emotion" (RR 259). Reality, figured again by the moral command, is replaced by "the miracle of salvation" (RR 193). But now, in illustration of that very contradiction between defining and effacing contradiction, romanticism reaches over to reality and claims it for its own. The feelings which represented a positive aversion to reality (RR 239) are transformed into reality itself (RR 191). Baeck does well to claim for romanticism the "poetry of transition" (RR 194).

A world that is all transition of things to their opposites is a cognitive darkness, for it has no place for the distinctions cognition presupposes. Nothing can be taken seriously. In particular, suffering cannot. And yet the momentariness of romantic experience, its inability to sustain, can only lead to an earnest pessimism (RR 209). On the one hand, romantic suffering is itself a dream (RR 191), and the dreamer at liberty to "enjoy his wounds and the streaming blood of his heart" (RR 190). On the other hand, romantic resignation to the wiles of grace yields a salvation that first passes through a genuine despair (RR 283). Perhaps there are two kinds of romantic: the religious one, of Pauline-Lutheran descent, who genuinely despairs, and the artistic one, who enjoys his suffering from an ironical distance. Or perhaps all romantics, fated in any case to suffer, take their suffering self-reflectively, and thereby convert it into joy.

If so, Baeck has severed the romantic from the object of his dependence and closed him off within himself. If romanticism makes itself the object of its own experience, it becomes self-intoxicated (RR 190). It revels in its experience of itself, feeds on itself, finds itself in its own self-contained feeling (RR 194, 266). But then, has not the romantic become the self-reflective agent of his own redemption, in blatant denial of the passivity ideal? Here again, the strands of Baeck's polemic intersect at cross purposes. Romantic phantasy, which denies the real world only to convert it into its own image, issues ultimately in self-enclosure. The romantic surrenders to his image in the mirror (RR 194). The ideal for which he pines is simply "the artifact of his own feelings" (RR 259). The romantic may not himself be aware of how creatively active he is, but Baeck, who studies him, certainly must be. If romantic passivity is a sham, Baeck's polemic against it must take a different turn, more towards its dishonesty. But here again, the double strain within romanticism of the Christian and the literary is Baeck's cover. Baeck grants to the Christian hermit his private relation with God (RR 279). Seen against the demands of the moral law, even a private enclosure of two is egoism enough. Egoism is construed, not as perfect self-enclosure, but as a self-centered thirst for redemption (RR 211, 212, 278) that genuinely involves God. The egoism is even projected onto God as his quest for his own redemption (RR 281). The world is left to fend for itself (RR 275). And as Baeck's measure of self-transcendence is action in the world, he can critique romanticism simultaneously for its utter egoism[60] and perfect passivity.

One of the most striking images in the *Star* is of the two midnights. For Rosenzweig, units of time are figures of eternity because they begin again at their end. The transition point from end to beginning figures the moment that must vanish to begin, i.e., the moment of eternity in the movement from future to present. Rosenzweig reads one of the temporal units, namely the day, onto the whole of his book. If eternity is the "tense" of cosmic redemption, no wonder the book is named for redemption, and not the revelation that so clearly centers it. The day of the book is strung between two midnights, the first of the protocosmos, the second of the hypercosmos. Images of darkness and night appear frequently in the first part of the *Star*. All the elements there begin in the "night of the positive" (SR 83, 87).[61] The subheading of the last section of the first book, "Twilight of the gods," refers not just to the imminent end of the gods' self-enclosure, but to the darkness of the world they inhabit. Human defiance, too, is a "night" (SR 171)[62] and night is the origin of the phenomena filling the metalogic world (SR 45). The whole protocosmic realm is shrouded in darkness (SR 16).

But of course, the romantic night that Baeck presents is moonlit. Rosenzweig fashions a startling image in the *Star*'s third part that may correspond. The second midnight of the redeemed hypercosmos is "all light," a darkness of "eternal stellar clarity" (SR 254, 417); it surpasses both cognition and experience (SR 391), and surely belongs to what Scholem calls Rosenzweig's "mystical astronomy."[63] Rosenzweig implies that the vision of the second midnight is the Yom Kippur worshipper's alone (SR 391) and that the darkness of this light owes to the fact that it conceals the face of the redeeming God (SR 382). The image recalls a picture from the late Schelling, of the God who reveals himself without ceasing to be concealed;[64] a picture that, in turn owes much to the idealist concept of expression. In his *Phenomenology of Spirit*, Hegel first presented his dialectic of expression in the chapter on force and the understanding. The dialectic turns on the distinction between force and its expression. On the level of practical science, there is no distinction there, and it is part of the point of this chapter to show why. Language separates force from its expression, but dialectic transcends the difference and unites the two in one. While Rosenzweig's love resembles Hegel's force by collapsing expression into essence, the God of Rosenzweig will not conform to the Hegelian model. Schelling, and Rosenzweig after him, who both ultimately rejected idealist dialectic, want to grant the divine that expresses itself an unknowable transcendence over its expression, while still allowing a relative knowledge of it through the expression, much like the relation between God and his attributes in Spinoza. The revelation that conceals is the moonlit night.

But now the glow of this darkening light extends back through the *Star* to its protocosmic beginnings. There, the protocosmic God appears symbolized by the equation, $A=A$. This equation of identity descends from the old idealist equation of self-positing, $I=I$. But Rosenzweig's equation is not a self-positing. It is the identification within God of a universal essence and an infinite power, both grounded equally in a common source. The equation $A=A$ is the product of a movement of reason. The reasoning proceeds from a positing of the negation of the idea of God. The right-sided A stands for the infinite essence of God, which reason reaches by denying the negation of God; the left-sided A stands for the infinite power of God, which reason reaches by denying of the essence all it is not. Because the divine essence and power are derived from the same original negation, they are equatable. Reason's last movement in the protocosmic deduction of God is to equate the divine essence and power. The final equation of God, $A=A$, is a product of reasoning movements. Sitting quietly on the page, this equation of identity conceals its descent from motion; it conceals its status as a product. It must do so if it is truly to symbolize God. For the symbol of God, like the attributes of Spinozan substance, must be perceived as original and self-satisfied (SR 33). Like the face of the redeeming God, concealed in the bright light of the *last* midnight, the "vital figure" of the protocosmic God is concealed in the static equation of the first (SR 33).

Even parts of the cosmic day, strung between the two midnights, are cast in darkness. For the world of preredeemed creation, which is the morning after the first midnight, is also a "nocturnal realm," a "gloom of infinity," that seems to stretch out endlessly through the "night of the future" (SR 163, 185, 293). When revelation enters upon creation, it brings, once again, the moonlit night. For the God who reveals himself in love, by that very act, conceals the essence that grounds the love. The closeness of the love necessarily silences any predicative, essence-determining claims that the beloved might make about his lover (SR 381). And so we encounter the darkening moonlight of the romantics, converted, to be sure, into starlight, all throughout Rosenzweig's book.

But all this darkness by no means merges into a single uniform black. Baeck's divisions of the dark fairly neatly apply to Rosenzweig's, too. There is cognitive darkness, moral darkness, emotive darkness, and a fourth that, though crucially important to Rosenzweig, is barely distinguished from ecstasy in the Baeckian romantic, for it is simply an extreme of the romantically privileged passivity: the existential darkness of death.

For Rosenzweig, philosophical idealism is in fact a shadowland (SR 146). But by presuming to leave nothing inaccessible to reason, it affects to eliminate all cognitive darkness (SR 144). And so it becomes the chief foil of Rosenzweig's starlit romanticism. Here what opens onto the nonrational is no garden-variety passivity, but the most final of all negations of human activity, death itself. The Baeckian romantic, at least in Nietzschean dress, gladly dies the death of drowning in the waves of the world (RR 197).[65] If this romantic turns idealist, the waves of the world, which constitute the whole, become Philosophy and its all-consuming reason. And so it is against the backdrop of the world that Rosenzweig develops his critique of reason. The idealist claimed that the world, or being, was the same as reason. Only a death made reasonable can be subsumed under the identification of reason with being. Otherwise, it is simply nothing, and justly sport for the Baeckian romantic; a mere means to abdication of responsibility (SR 414). But Rosenzweig teases out the paradoxical presupposition of the identification of reason with being, that in some sense they are not the same, otherwise there could be no two to identify as one (SR 13). And once a separation between reason and being is admitted, no bridge can connect them. As Feuerbach observed, in line with Hegel's thoughts on the limits of the language of sense-certainty, reason can never of its own efforts reach the real world. Lacking identification with being, reason must content itself with application to a world it receives as inexplicably given, i.e., as denial of reason (SR 43).

And now death takes back the sting that reason had presumed to extract from it, and joins the prereasoned, or metalogic, world in the further dismantling of reason. The death that is unreason is not simply nothing, but something (SR 4). Inverting the revelation that conceals, death is the concealment that, we cannot quite say reveals, but better perhaps, obtrudes. "Death," the second word of the *Star*, obtrudes before cognition and philosophy receive their first mention. Death is the nothing in defiance of which human character defines itself before any character-conferring philosophical-moral law is even brought to bear. Rosenzweig, who has already once claimed Kant for his philosophical forbear, does so again now (SR 21).[66] For the Kantian thing-in-itself, which is a limit to knowledge, takes two forms: the human and the worldly. By that dual nonknowledge, and a third, common "mysterious root" (SR 21) of them—which Rosenzweig identifies with the "metaphysical Nought of knowledge" (SR 21), i.e., the divine Nought—Kant showed that he, too, understood how multiple nothings are something.

But Kant critiqued reason from another angle, too. He traced the issue of reason's dialectic in three objectless ideas—soul, world, and God—that could never, themselves, be objects of knowledge. Impetuous idealism could not refrain from supplying an artificial content to these objectless ideas, and so missed the content that in their emptiness they already had. For what the three Kantian ideas showed was that the "Nought" is threefold. Kant may have meant this for the conclusion of his critique. But a threefold Nought is also a perfect beginning. For, insofar as it is threefold, it is not sheer nothing; the distinctiveness of the three from each other is already something. "The Nought is not Nothing, it is Aught" (SR 5). And so like death itself, the three ideas—God, human, world—are concealments that obtrude, "irrational objects" (SR 19). Here is the first midnight and the first appearance in the *Star* of cognitive darkness.

In Baeck's analysis, romanticism cannot assimilate freedom in the fullness of its challenge to reason and subordinates it instead to a corollary of grace. For Rosenzweig, human freedom emerges out of the cognitive darkness. But Rosenzweig already has a means of taming the freedom that stops short of its transformation into grace. The human is only one of three elements; its freedom is necessarily limited by the other two. What is more, of the three elements, the human is the only one that emerges from the darkness a pure and perfect finitude. Both God and world contain elements of infinity. It is a tribute to the power of death that the human character that emerges in denial of it is defiance. For it is only the stronger, and in this case the one who is fated to win, that one defies. The tragic man is the pagan Everyman who wills his own finitude in the face of death's looming nothing. This is his freedom. By identifying with a human essence that is already finite, human freedom submits itself to finitude before any romantic transformations are even required. The submission is at a price. There is suffering in the "peculiar darkness" (SR 78) of the tragic human's life. His self-willing is self-enclosed. He receives uncomprehendingly the events destined for him from beyond the limits of his finitude.

So the first cognitive darkness of the *Star* embraces as well its first emotive darkness. It is the darkness of self-enclosed suffering (not yet sin or guilt). The self-enclosed Baeckian romantic seemed to suffer unseriously, ironically. There is nothing unserious in the tone of Rosenzweig's words about the tragic human. Still, like the romantic's, his is also a playful suffering, in the sense that it really occurs only in plays—prototypically in the tragic dramas of ancient Greece. For Rosenzweig, no living human ever knows in his real life the silent unrelatedness of Agamemnon or Oedipus. A third limit on the finite human freedom of the protocosmos is that it simply is not real.

Suddenly we seem on the verge of reality-denying romantic fantasy. But in fact, what Rosenzweig proceeds to supply is reality. The protocosmos is no free-floating fantasy, but presupposition to reality (SR 88). The darkness of human defiance is realized in the love of the nearest worldly neighbor. What in self-enclosure acted defiantly, in negation of a nothing, now acts positively, in affirmation of a something. The self-enclosed human willed his own finitude. The self-disclosed human wills blindly to affirm what he hardly knows, except that it is outside himself. Self-conscious self-enclosure, turned inside out into self-disclosure, is blind love.

The blindness of love was its passivity; but its blindness is so much more obviously its darkness. The love which touches its object prior to any seeing, then moves on to the next, never sees at all. It seems to act as though content to lavish itself on whatever stands near; but in fact, it could not pour itself out so wholly in each successive moment, if it did not presuppose a growing order to the world (SR 241). For if love thought it spent itself on an intractable chaos, it would despair and cease. But love has no time for consciousness of the world's growing order, and so its worldly awareness must be unconscious. At the same time, when love speaks, as in the Song of Songs, its words are more than words, but love itself. For love's word, which is always the command, bridges the divide between language and reality. The word's sensuality—its spokenness and audibility—carries the "divine supersense" (SR 201) of the love it expresses, rather like the revelation that still conceals. It is as though love, which moves in cognitive darkness, is surrounded by it as well—from below, in its worldly unconsciousness, from above, in the sense of its words that surpasses all language.

The loving human bears this resemblance to the tragic human—they are both fundamentally blind. Of the two, the tragic human seems nearer the Baeckian romantic, who is also self-enclosed. But the Baeckian romantic was also too troubled by freedom to let it stand, and transformed it into grace. Has not the loving human done this too? For his love of the neighbor follows on a serene belovedness that is itself the inversion of his darkly protocosmic freedom (SR 213). And if the Baeckian romantic simply exchanged one form of darkness for another, so has the loving human. For he cannot love except from his state of belovedness; and he cannot be beloved, except at the price of sin, nor can the creation he loves stand, except at the price of death.

The tragic human suffers, but not from any sense of sin. To sin is to miss the mark, and one cannot have missed the mark if there is no orientation to supply the distinction between a hit and a miss. And the self-enclosed human, lacking all relation, also lacks orientation. The beloved human inverts the tragic human's self-enclosure. The moment of inversion is simultaneous with the receipt of God's love. It is the love bursting in from outside that awakens shame for the former self-enclosure. Only from the standpoint of revelation is the prior self-centeredness revealed as sin. But the priority is present even in the moment of love, just as, for Rosenzweig generally, the past that grounds the present is experienced through the present. If, in the moment of love received, the sin is acknowledged as present, then the whole of it submerges into the past, since acknowledgments, like all descriptions, always historicize the present, and the feeling of shame is lifted (SR 180–181). But the moment of shame is inescapable.

What Rosenzweig has offered is a phenomenology of forgiveness. What is forgiven is not, with the Baeckian romantic, simply freedom, but self-enclosure—the freely willed finitude of one's own self. Rosenzweig puts it otherwise in a brief comment on the Psalms: "in revelation, the soul . . . surrenders its individuality so that it might be forgiven its individuality" (SR 251). One might just as well say that in revelation, the self is forgiven its creatureliness and lifted out of mortality. For a peculiar logic connects individuality, creation, and death.

Creation is a meeting of God and world. The world meets God with its distinctive universals, its categories filled with individual instances. As distinctive, these universals are prey to extinction, and need to be sustained. God meets the world with a universally sustaining providence, i.e., one that acts on universals. What the world needs and God offers constitute the meeting of creation. It is the mortality implicit in the distinctive that draws out God's providential care. So the distinctive as such is the focus of creation. The individuals within a distinct category of living thing instance the category so long as they live. It is at the moment of death that they take on a distinctiveness of their own, apart from their category. For a moment before they return to the all of nature, they persist beyond the requirements of the distinctive universal. For Rosenzweig, the human who has done the work of eros, already begins the journey to death. Here is where the self is formed, as over against the individual instance of a category. The self is what persists in the face of nothing. Its persistence climaxes at the moment of death, when it no longer even instances its former worldly kind. Here it is pure self-enclosure, the distinctive beyond the grasp of the universal.[67] Death is the maximal reach of the distinctiveness that focuses creation. As the ultimate self-enclosure, whatever enters into it requires forgiveness. And this is what the love as strong as death provides.

The tragic human self on the way to its death is arrested by revelation. In the moment of revelation, it acknowledges the sin of its self-enclosure. The self-enclosure encloses it on both sides—from behind, in the protocosmic self from which it has just emerged, and from in front, in the death that, as creature, it awaits. In revelatory love, both forms of sin are forgiven, and the enclosed self lifted out of creation. But apart from sin and death, no forgiving love can occur.

The human self, having emerged from the protocosmos and passed through the portals of sin and death, now stands at the center of the *Star*. This is the book of revelation. The protocosmos was no reality at all; sin and death are real, but are now submerged in the created past. What sort of reality does the beloved soul now see from its secure perch in revelation?

The reality of revelation is, as we know, relational. The flight into selfishness is away from reality, as much for Rosenzweig as for Baeck, though for Rosenzweig the master of this escape is much more idealist than romantic (SR 355). For Rosenzweig, reality is defined against the chaos of possibility. The real is the ordered. And order can only arise from orientations taken towards a fixed point. The revelatory meeting of God and human, which occurs at the center of the *Star*, supplies the fixed point. From here, reality extends backward and forward according to the orientation taken towards revelation—backward into creation, if the orientation is presuppositional; forward into redemption, if the orientation is anticipatory.

For Baeck, the opposite of the selfishness that denies reality is the moral obedience that obliges relations. For Rosenzweig, the opposite of selfishness is relation itself. Rosenzweig's reality, though anti-egoistic, is romantic by the immediately defining role it assigns relationality. Connection and transition are the romantic's tools of trade (RR 194, 199). It is precisely the romantic connection of opposites that undermines distinction and ultimately reality itself.

Even a cursory overview of the *Star*'s subheadings suggests the importance of transition to this book. "Transition," "Threshold," and "Gate" are the concluding segments of parts one through three respectively. Romantic relation hovers indecisively between the sharp distinction of opposites and the blurry transition of each into the other. Rosenzweig was too much Hegel's heir to rest content with that kind of darkness. Hegel himself had contemptuously dismissed the romantic (Schellingian) "night in which all cows are black."[68] Rosenzweig, like Hegel, constructs a rigorous dialectic that allows for clearly distinguished opposites to come into relation. Each of the protocosmic elements is constructed from two conceptual movements, an affirmation and a negation, performed on a content that itself resists conceptualization. The affirmation issues in a static essence, which is either universal or particular, and the negation in a movement, oriented towards the essence, which is either infinite or finite. Universal and particular, infinite and finite, are oppositions of content. In any given pairing of essence and movement, one member of the pair is active and the other passive. These are oppositions of form. The pairings are equations in which essence and movement are identified, as, for example, finite, passive essence of character with finite, active motion of will, in the case of human being.

The oppositional vocabulary of form and content, the lesser oppositions subsumed therein, and the algebraic equations abstracted therefrom, are all the inheritance of idealism. The constructs of the protocosmos are deeply indebted to it. But Rosenzweig departs from idealism in a romantically significant way. Hegelian dialectic aims ultimately to eliminate opposition. The night of black cows is objectionable not because it effaces all distinction, but because it has not properly and rigorously developed the effacement over a naturally logical course. But the oppositions constructing the protocosmic elements are not effaced. They are held together in equations that symbolize a relation in which the partners, though identified, are still distinguishable. More than merely distinguishable, they become really distinguished in the succeeding part of the *Star*. The reality of revelation is simply the emergence and regrouping of the protocosmic oppositions, as for example, of universal divine essence with finite human will, to constitute the "second revelation." Rosenzweig's unsubsuming meetings of opposites are an anti-idealist's translation into logic of the romantic hovering between posited oppositions and their demise.

Has Rosenzweig's idealism-indebted clarity banished the darkness of the romantic world? Not quite. In one of his few explicit references to early German romanticism, Rosenzweig invokes the notion of a world-soul and opposes it to the world-generating spirit of Hegelian idealism. He specifically cites the early Schelling's "romantic philosophy of nature" (SR 45) and Novalis, the author of *Hymns to the Night*. The world soul of the early romantics opposes the world-generating spirit of idealism by containing its life within itself. It is no mere product of a generative Reason. What is more, the world is ensouled from its very protocosmic beginnings on. The protocosmic world is a construct of logical categories and chaotic, unnamed individuals. The individuals are alive with a movement that has no direction; the categories are alive with a need for application. It is as though Kant's duo of concept and object had come undone, and truly empty concepts ache to reconnect with truly blind objects. The structure of categories, heir of the ancient Greek logos, is spiritual, in the idealist sense, in that it is forceful, or at least "passively attracting" (SR 44). But it is soulful (romantic?) in its receptivity, its ache to receive rather than create. The chaos of individuals that "hurtle" into the categories, are embraced, as though by kabbalistic vessels, and named (SR 46).

But this ensouled world is as dark as the human that exists by its side, though unknown to it, in the protocosmos. The passively active logic of this world is prior to the all-illuminating, because all-generating, logic of idealist spirit. The logos of the protocosmic world, unlike the idealist spirit, is in the dark about itself. It has applicability but no explicability. It does not generate itself, but emerges, just like human character, from the affirmation of the opposite of a resistance to reason.

In creation, the categories receive the support they internally lack. The support comes not from reason but from the universal power of God. The vessels that protocosmically received a chaos of individuals, press out in creation to be received under the "wings of a Being such as would endow [them] with stability and veracity" (SR 121). This would seem an advance into the light. Even the first creation story of Genesis brings on the light quite early on. Rosenzweig tells us, in what sounds like a blanket dismissal of the Baeckian romantic, that "the world is neither shadow nor dream nor picture" (SR 133). It is alive with reality. Reality is supplied by direction. The protocosmic categories confer direction on chaotic individuals but are, in and of themselves, empty. But the kinds of living things, which emerge in creation as organisms, do possess direction, and so reality. They are not only self-directed towards their own preservation; God providentially preserves them for the sake of the world's own organic order. The world follows the lines of growth with which divine providence has endowed it (SR 267). And this organicity is everywhere, "not only [in] living beings, but also [in] institutions, communities, feelings, things, works" (SR 222).

As the ensouled world emerges, wholly alive, into creation, it advances precipitously, despite Rosenzweig's protests, into the romantic dream world, at least to the extent that one distinction, that between animate and inanimate, the living and the dead, disappears from view. And now, as though responding to the romantic's siren call, the world Rosenzweig describes does indeed revert into darkness. For the death that climaxes individuality proves to be the "capstone" of creation as a whole (SR 156). Creation purchases its knowability at the price of a perpetual past tense (SR 103). The life of creation, if it is not to burst the bounds of knowledge, must progress out of the past no further than the present perfect. It must carry within it the marks of its own completion. The reality that stamps all life with the inevitability of completion is death.

It is in that sense that creation is a "nocturnal realm." What God creates is ultimately the dead (SR 381). The problem of the world is that it "is created as phenomenon long before it is redeemed for its essence" (SR 219). The world as phenomenon is its individuals, its instances of kinds of things. Divine providence supports the kinds but not the instances. For the world to be redeemed for its essence, "it must become alive as a whole" (SR 223) in both kind and instance. The world presses its instances forward to receive their own affirmation. It does so with the same passively attracting force that the protocosmic categories exerted over the primordial chaos of individuals (SR 228). And what the world attracts to it is the redemptive human love we have already encountered. This is the love that affirms the nearest neighbor. The redemption of the world is the match seemingly by design, and so, miraculously, of blind love to forceful need.

The instance of a kind, redeemed by love, is eternalized (SR 241). It becomes "unique, subjective, substantival" (SR 235). Its individuality is no longer defined within and against its kind (SR 241). It is individualized beyond the seeming maximum of created death. Death does in a sense predict eternal life. For life could not be complete in death unless in death it somehow still remained. And now words begin to fail. For the onset of redemption is the approach of the moment that must end to begin. In such a moment, there is no space even for the words of command.

Standing on the edge of the last revealed darkness before the onset of redemption, the beloved soul confronts a vast expanse of world. Everything that instances a created kind asks to be redeemed. So not just human beings, but the "branches, twigs, leaves, blossoms," and "seas and rivers" of creation are included (SR 240, 232). What beckons is nothing less than a "supernatural community, wholly personal in its experience yet wholly worldly in its existence" (SR 204). But such a community cannot be experienced in an instant. In a companion piece to the *Star*, Rosenzweig explicitly distances animistic pantheisms that fraternalize "forest and bush"[69] at no cost of redemptive love. Like the absolute of Hegelian knowledge, the supernatural community only comes at a price.

It is tempting not to pay it. Redemptive love is grounded in revealed belovedness. But the human need not continuously receive the revelation. Indeed, Rosenzweig endorses the theodicy of the hidden God, who ensures the freedom of human good will by denying both spur and visible reward (SR 266). The human who seeks restoration to revelation from outside it is tempted by sinful and fanatical prayers. The sinful prayer reverts to self-enclosure. Whatever it beseeches for itself, has already been surpassed and so granted overflowingly, in divine revelation. The sinner simulates the self-enclosure that revelation submerged in the past. The fanatic, on the other hand, would force the future. He wants the supernatural community before its time has come. So he leaves unfinished the one work he can complete, the redemption of the nearest neighbor. The sinful and fanatical prayers are abuses of freedom, the last points of darkness in the cosmic day of revelation.

That day is relatively bright by Baeckian romantic standards. Thanks to the rigors of an opposition-preserving dialectic, the distinction between reality and unreality has remained intact. The divide between them is the point of turning from self-enclosed protocosmos, to reciprocally revealing God, human, and world. Life, so far from being banished, suffuses the whole of creation. It does not transpose to dream, but to the still deeper reality of death, which, contra the playful ecstasy of the romantics, is very serious indeed. No moral law stirs the beloved soul to act, but the dark ground of defiance, inversely expressed as love in the real world of revelatory meeting, moves outward to a world that actively receives it. Neither does soul merge with world, nor world with God, nor soul with God.

The soul does not merge with God. But a third temptation of the soul, apart from those of sin and fanaticism, is not to part from God at all. This is the way of the mystic. The mystic's offense is to linger too long in revelation, to the denial of redemption (SR 208, 274). By this lingering, the mystic merges with the Baeckian romantic. He longs to vanish in the love he receives (SR 211) as the romantic would drown in the waves of the world. Like the romantic, he ultimately flees the world by denying its reality. He severs creation from God (SR 208). He takes God's relation to be only with himself, so that the distinction collapses between reality and the dreams of his private ecstasy (SR 202). In the ultimate Baeckian indictment, he is reduced to the passive role of "vessel of his own experienced ecstasies" (SR 208).

Rosenzweig's harshness on the mystic may mask a secret, but uncomfortable, affinity with him. In the last paragraph of "Die Urzelle des Stern" (Germ Cell of the Star), Rosenzweig confesses his astonishment over the role he has just discovered for mysticism, mediating between philosophy and theology, and proposes to study their etymological amalgam, theosophy.[70] He very likely means by mysticism there the miraculous meeting of God and human, or revelation in the strictest sense. And that would suggest a good mysticism that passes, and a bad one that lingers. It is not so surprising then, that Rosenzweig finds in Jewish mysticism a mediator between Judaism's tendency to self-enclosure and its universalistic mission. Self-enclosure is always the philosophical inheritance; relation—which climaxes in universalism—the theological. The self-enclosing Jewish law, mystically interpreted, is a figure of the universal creation; the self-enclosed Jewish people harbors only an exiled God, according to the mysticism of the Shekhina, and so points to the need for a redemption beyond the Jews alone. Finally, according to kabbalah, Jewish observance of the law restores the self-exiled God to unity. In all three cases, the self-enclosed particular expands via mysticism into relation with a larger whole, just as, via miracle, self-enclosed philosophy transforms to relational theology (SR 408–411).

But now, Rosenzweig himself sounds much closer to the Baeckian romantic. It is striking that what Baeck takes for an egoistic excess of romantic religion, namely the teaching that God must redeem himself, becomes so central to the third part of the *Star*. Rosenzweig already introduces this teaching in the last book of the second part. The teaching seems to surface there with a gasp, as though fully conscious of the hushed incredulity it must provoke (SR 230, 238, 272). But Rosenzweig prepares the way for it by broadening the scope of redemption. At first it seems the world that is redeemed. But soon redemption includes the soul as well. The beloved soul's loving act redeems it from its mystic seclusion with God (SR 235). By its very act of love, it incorporates itself in the community of redemption it aches to know (SR 232–235, 251). It only appears the next logical step for God to undergo a redemption, too.

And yet there is still a jump from redemption of soul to that of God. Rosenzweig notes as early as the first part of the *Star*, that the human doubles as worldly kind and free, transworldly self. In the protocosmic equations, the B of the world's $B=A$, is the same as the right-handed B of the self's $B=B$, both are aimless distinctives (SR 65–66). This is Rosenzweig's transformation of Kant's claim that the human is a "'citizen of two worlds'" (SR 70). So it is not such a stretch of redemption to apply it, reflexively, to the redeeming soul itself. But how could God, a protocosmic equation of infinites, $A=A$, who, once revealed, does not directly redeem either soul or world, require redemption himself?

Here we stand under "the blinding midnight sun of the consummated redemption" (SR 238). It is the starlit darkness of the second midnight. Part of the darkness is the very counterintuitivity of the self-redeeming God. It is a notion that from the Jewish perspective is mystical indeed, finding its fullest expression in kabbalah. Rosenzweig has already told us that the God of redemption is beyond both cognition and experience. Language, which is the speech of revelation and hence of experience, has no role here. The speaking human is reduced to silence (SR 383). But Rosenzweig, in the company of all good mystics, will not be silent. He will stretch language as far as he can to follow the shape of the self-redeeming God. One such stretch is in the direction of human and world. These two are engaged in reciprocal redemption of each other. What happens when the redemption is done? We should expect something as startlingly unexpected as the event that, within creation, completes life—which was death. We seek the x in the analogy, death/created life as x/redeemed life. Rosenzweig points to the value of our variable when he says that God's redemption "is the eternal deed in which he frees himself from having anything confront him that is not himself" (SR 383). The idea within theisms of extra-divine reality has troubled many a thinker, and some, like Spinoza, have found themselves pushed by it towards pantheism. The complete God is simply all. Rosenzweig, who has rejected pantheism from the start, does not clearly reject it at the end (SR 395, 258). But it is less that God is all than that the all ceases to be anything but God. If the ceasing is anything like death, it is an intensification, not an extinction, of what came before. What comes before the ceasing of all but God is the all of God, human, and world. But this all, from the very start of the *Star*, has been shattered. There is never one perspective on it, but always many. True, each of the protocosmic elements in their self-enclosures presumes to exhaust the all. But we who live from within revelation, know what a mistake that is. But then, it is not as though we are any better off. The self-disclosure of the elements actually doubles the number of possible perspectives on the all, since each of the elements emerges twice a partner in relation, once with each of the other two. So radical is the perspectivism here that the relations appear from each of their respective poles opposite to the way they appear from the other. From God's side, creation is ever-renewed, from the world's side, stably growing; revelation is momentary for God, enduring for the soul, as redemption is, respectively, for soul and world. But even this characterization of perspectivism is perspectival. Its perspective is the beloved soul's, the only perspective Rosenzweig and his readers can hold while occupied with his book. Within the history of religions, the beloved soul has figured these six perspectives in two ways, the Jewish and the Christian. So, from the protocosmic opening of three, to the end of the beloved soul's experiential reach, the perspectives have increased fourfold. Where then is the truth in all these perspectives? It is inevitably only partial. What would the intensification of truth be, then, but the end of partiality, i.e., the end of perspectives. This is what Rosenzweig calls the eternal truth. It is God's perspective on the all, which comes to all other perspectives as death comes to life. It stands asymptotically beyond the beloved soul's reach, for to reach it is to cease. But what sort of ceasing would this be? If it is truly in parallel with creation's death, which opens onto revelatory life, then there must begin on the other side of it an intensification of what came before, only on a previously inconceivable level. But to this far point, Rosenzweig will not venture with words.

Where he has ventured is straight into the arms of the Baeckian romantic. For the blinding light of the second midnight must take its place with all romantic ecstasies of self-annihilation. True, Rosenzweig will not linger here. He figures God's perspective on the all with a face that, returning our gaze, shows us ourselves, the beloved soul, looking out on what we already know through revelation. But the second midnight points back even further all the way to the protocosmic first. The two midnights are endpoints of the same cosmic day. Rosenzweig chose the day to figure the passage through his book because, like all temporal figures of eternity, it ends where it begins. It is the same stroke of midnight for both. Darkness is the beginning and the end.

Romantic Inversion

The romantic himself is troubled by the darkness of his world. The root of the trouble lies in the very nature of romantic redemption. Of its four defining features, it is only passivity that subsumes the other three. Feeling, experience (*Erlebnis*), and miracle are all by nature passively received. No other selection of three from the group is necessarily characterized by the fourth. So it was passivity, the group spokesman, that first opened onto the cognitive darkness. It is the very uncontrollability of romantic redemption that leaves its devotee prey to unredemption. Nothing guarantees it will endure. It becomes a desideratum of romantic sensibility to stretch the emotive and miraculous experience of dependence out permanently over time. The very endeavor is self-contradictory. What is willfully stretched is no longer sheer miraculous gift. But the romantic finds paradoxical means to this self-contradictory end. The means is inversion. A given quality is potentially, then actually, its opposite, without ceasing to be what it was at first. We have already encountered illustrations: the revelation that conceals, the light that darkens. But to generate these instances the romantic needs a method that converts things to their opposites without sacrificing their original identity. The method will convert passive receipt to passive endeavor, the phenomenon of fleeting to the fleetingly enduring.

Hegel, the archenemy of romantic unrigor, proves an unlikely friend to this romantic quest. For chapter three of the *Phenomenology of Spirit*, on force and the understanding, presents an entire world of inversions. Here the romantic may find the precise kind of thing he seeks: black whiteness, northerly souths, honored dishonorables, positive negatives in abundance. It is significant that the Hegelian inverted world spans physical, psychological, and moral properties, for the darkness the romantic wants to invert is variously shaded ontologically, emotively, and ethically. What is more, the inverted world is the product of a repeatable method, an organon, namely dialectic. At the point of the dialectic where the inverted world appears, consciousness is struggling to conceive pure change. It is an old philosophical conundrum how the same can be different. Previous solutions, based on a substance/attribute distinction, always proved unsatisfactory, though Hegel generously incorporates these formulations on the dialectic way. It is through the paradoxical concept of force that consciousness hits upon pure change. For the concept of force seems intuitively divisible into the thing of force itself, and its active expressions. Consciousness holds the two apart, the in-itself of force and its expression, only to discover that it cannot consistently designate either of them the true force. For no sooner does it mean by force, the expression of force, then it commits itself to holding the thing expressed as force instead. For what does an expression of force express, but force? While if what force expresses is force, then alternatively the expression of force, qua expression, steals the same designation away. For how can something express force except by itself being force? Force seems to be a concept that enfolds in one a simultaneity of opposites. And this is just what pure change is. The inverted world is the world of pure change. What more congenial home could there be for the Baeckian romantic poets of transition?[71]

But alas the inverted world is only a weigh station on the dialectical course and no true home. It vanishes the moment it appears, in semblance of the pure change it seems to express. The rigors of dialectic are not in any case to the Baeckian romantic taste. Baeck himself presents a multitude of romantic inversions. All of the modes of romantic passivity, namely feeling, miracle, and experience, undergo inversion. Feeling becomes dogma (RR 234, 267) miracle becomes sacrament (RR 221), experience becomes clerical performance (RR 230). These are all movements from the uncontrollable to the controlled. Baeck does not present on the romantic's behalf any common method by which these transformations occur, but implies they are implicit in romantic redemption itself. So, for example, orthodoxy, an expression of dogma, is "grounded in this faith [i.e., romantic faith] from the beginning" (RR 236). A key romantic inversion is the very concept itself of a ground. The ground contains, incipiently, all that is dependent on it; so much so that the dependence is reciprocal. The end is already contained in the beginning before the beginning even emerges, or, as Baeck puts it, "the answer precedes every question, and every result comes before the task" (RR 206). It is not so much a case of having and eating the same cake, but of having it before it is baked, so that no problems in the baking can possibly arise. By romantic inversion, the permanent and controlled is already groundingly present in the fleetingly received, and so need not be effortfully sought. The miraculous experience of dependence unfolds from deep within its ground a miraculous permanence of, to use a Hegelian term, solicitability.[72]

Though no precise organon of inversion appears in Baeck's account of romanticism, he does present what might be more modestly called the romantic sleight of hand: this is self-consciousness. We have already encountered it as a part of Baeckian romantic self-enclosure. In a move that borders on severing the romantic from his dependence, Baeck, as we saw, reduced the romantic's ideal to an "artifact of his own feeling." Here the relevancy is the artifactual status of the ideal. A feeling can leave an artifact, but cannot actually be an artifact. The two are so different as almost to seem opposed. Baeck sharpens the image of the opposition when he shows the romantic personality "admiring himself in the mirror of introspection" (RR 194), presumably via an artifactual ideal. Nature is often such a self-reflective ideal for the romantics (RR 260). An object and its mirror image are indeed opposed, frontward to backward, as appears when a written word is held up to a mirror. An object and its reflection in the mirror together make a visual image of Hegelian pure change, a simultaneity of opposites in the self-same. Here is a simpler means than dialectic of converting a thing to its opposite.

That what a person admires in his mirror-image is simultaneously the same and opposite of himself offers ample scope for play, as Lewis Carroll showed in *Through the Looking Glass*. But the particular sort of play for which it especially sets the stage is irony. Baeck commented on romantic "self-congratulation" (RR 211). The romantic heteronomous ideal may indeed be to "pass away in the roaring ocean of the world" (RR 192), but not without enough awareness of the passing to be able to congratulate oneself on it; in which case, how complete, how wholly ecstatic is the passing? The romantic who self-reflexively enjoys his suffering is behaving ironically. And the suffering is thereby converted to its opposite while remaining itself. For Baeck, this is one of the definitive moves of romantic liberal Protestantism. The classically conceived Christian gospels, full of their charge to moral acts, are converted into New Testament handbooks that leave actual Christian life at liberty to move in precisely opposite directions. Since the handbook has captured the ideal of poverty, the sermon is freed to expound the satisfactions of wealth. It is as though the handbook is the mirror, and the image the gospels cast in it, the self-satisfied opposite of the biblical verses' intent. It is, for Baeck, "the triumph of romantic irony over the ideal" (RR 264).

The play of irony in this process is itself a play on words. It is the play or room for movement in the space between the thing and its self-same opposite; but it is also a comic drama. Play in English, as *Spiel* in German, carries both meanings. And Baeck calls the "handbook holiness" of certain styles of Christian piety a "romantic comedy" (RR 264). The charge is not as derisive as it sounds, for it points to the artistry in all ironic play. The comedy proceeds by taking the gospel as "pure literature" (RR 262). Aesthetics and irony are associatively linked in Baeck's account (RR 290–291). If self-consciousness is the romantic sleight of hand by which things are simultaneously their opposites, irony and art are the chief forms of its expression. Here Baeck means chiefly the literary arts, the "dazzling poetry and gloomy prose" (RR 290) of Christianity, but also the "artistry of concepts" (RR 265, 266) of the early German romantics. Language functions ironically as a game, in which "superlatives" are played against each other in a style "agitated, excited, overheated, intoxicated" (RR 190).

It is clear how mimetic art plays perfectly to the needs of romantic self-consciousness. Self-portraiture and autobiography may be the clearest examples. But if feeling is reality, then the artist's reality may be reflected in almost anything she creates. Feeling here functions connectively between self-consciousness, irony, art and the very essence of romantic redemption. Just as feeling is fluid enough to mean everything, so the play of romantic irony, like the Kantian esthetic idea, invites an infinity of interpretations (RR 265). What disturbs Baeck about art, romantically understood, is that, like feeling itself, it ceases to refer to anything beyond itself and becomes its own end. Baeck traces this idea to the romantic Luther, for whom the word "does not merely mean something, but it is something" (RR 225). It is a short, secularized step from there to a view Baeck would identify with romantic religion, namely that reality may be identified with self-contained language and subsumed under art. We return to the cognitive dark, where to all the other effaced distinctions, we can now add that between poetry and life (RR 191).

Baeck suggested that the ideal was an artifact in which the romantic admired himself. But how much more concrete and obliging is the esthetic artifact, which can be seen or heard at will. It was Plato who first remarked on the mediating role beauty played between the ideal world and the world of sense.[73] It is precisely such a mediator the romantic seeks. He wants the volitionally inaccessible ideal to be permanently present to him. Surely there is no more universally permanent part of human functioning than the five senses. Whatever is ever accessible through these is for all intents and purposes permanent. Art is romantic religion's most natural ally.

If revelation is the content that centers the *Star*, then inversion is its centering form. Here Rosenzweig follows the spirit, if not the letter, of Hegel. The inverted world was the climactic content of a progressive sequence of inverse forms. For Hegel, the form of a thing is the movement in consciousness that generates it.[74] Consciousness is set in motion by its quest for knowledge. *The Phenomenology of Spirit* is phenomenological in its observation of this motion. It presumed to describe nothing more than the natural movements themselves, and the products that issue from them. Long before the inverted world comes on the scene, consciousness has been reversing its direction of attention from itself to its seeming objects, in hopes of at last hitting on a point of genuine knowledge. These reversals of attention shape the forms of consciousness.

For Rosenzweig, inversion is the movement, or Hegelian form, that issues in the content of revelation. But unlike Hegel, Rosenzweig does not observe the movements of a single consciousness. The single consciousness has shattered into three elements that confront consciousness as unassimilable resistances. Protocosmic reasoning is indeed, like idealist dialectic, a tracing of natural thought courses, or *Gedankengegangen*, but these are mere conceptual reactions to a threefold being that exceeds conceptual grasp. They cannot themselves generate being or entertain hopes of uniting with it. But the miraculous fact is that if these thought-courses, once complete, are inverted, they serve as viable elucidations of the reality we actually experience. Nothing obliges the inversion, except the suitability of what results to the reality of experience. If the inversion occurs, it is not because thought necessitates it, but because, retrospectively, from the standpoint of reality, it is presupposed.

In Hegelian dialectic, the relata of relations are identified; in Rosenzweig, revelatory relations are identified with protocosmic movements, but the relata themselves remain distinct. Rosenzweig rejects Hegelian dialectic as the organon of inversion, because it presupposes an identity of consciousness with its objects that is simply not justified. But for a very similar reason, he must also reject the organon of romantic self-consciousness. Self-consciousness functions in the *Star* as a result of inversion, not as a means of it. The self-enclosure that romantic self-consciousness preservingly presupposes, is overcome in Rosenzweig's revelatory inversions. Self-consciousness occurs in the between of the relationships connecting God, human, and world. Only after an other is received as other, does self-consciousness occur.[75] But if the organon of Rosenzweigian inversion is not precisely Hegelian, or romantic, what is it?

It is simply the miracle we have already once encountered, and that flavors Rosenzweig's thought so much more romantically than idealistically. But of course, to the extent that a formal organon stands to a content as Aristotelian logic does to thought, a miracle is scarcely more of an organon than self-consciousness is. They are both movements that simply happen, like everything romanticism holds most dear. It is just that the romantic movement happens *within* self-enclosures, and Rosenzweig's between them.

Even this is not strictly true. Inversion happens within the protocosmic self-enclosures as well. But it is just here, where Rosenzweig would seem even more romantic, that he becomes most idealistic. The self-enclosures of the protocosmos are no moonstruck poets of self-absorption. They are silent, algebraically constructed concepts that, even by Rosenzweig's admission, constitute one of the most difficult parts of the *Star*.[76] Part of their unlikely provenance is Hermann Cohen's neo-Kantian and profoundly idealist logic of origins. Nowhere else in the *Star* is its peculiar mixture of pathos and rigor[77] so touchingly exposed.

The elements themselves are founded on an algebraic image of nonknowledge: the equation of variables, $y=x$. Even Fichte, whose *Science of Knowledge* is no stroll through the finite world of concrete images, embarks on the epistemological way with an equation of envalued variables, $A=A$, which soon becomes $I=I$.[78] This concession to the concrete is not available to Rosenzweig, for whom $I=I$ could stand in for simply one of the elemental facts of reality. The fact of three facts, God, human, and world, requires the most general equation to be stated in terms of unvalued variables, which will then receive the A's and B's (symbolizing universality and particularity, respectively) that, differently arranged, make up the distinct threesome. At this stage, idealist monism cannot even picture inversion algebraically, because it has only the one letter A, or I, to work with. But for Rosenzweig, death has severed the conceptual link between subject and object, or subject and predicate, that underlay idealist monism. What is more, the subject of the old idealist claims has been reduced to a threefold resistance to conceptual graspability. We hardly know whereof we speak, in speaking of such a subject, until we can definitively differentiate it. Differentiation is the role of predicates. So if x stands for subject, and y for predicate, then in reasoning about resistances to reason, the predicate comes first. Hence the inverse equation that begins the protocosmic thought courses.

Rosenzweig's mock-idealist reasonings do, in the case of the human, take on an authentically idealist ring. A definitive credo of German idealism was that the self is its self-consciousness. How can what is not yet constituted be conscious of itself? Such a paradoxical self occurs in the vanishing space between a being so active there is scarcely anything left of it merely to be, and pure action itself. The pure act here is thinking. Kant may have shown that there is no self-consistent idea of a substantival self, but he by no means precluded the possibility of a purely active one. Indeed, he pointed in that direction with his original synthetic unity of apperception. In the midst of Rosenzweig's protocosmic reasonings, we learn that human self-consciousness is the same as the human self (SR 68). The human self is the defiantly willed affirmation of its finite character against the nothing, typified by death, that lies outside it. Nathan Rotenstreich observes that self-consciousness is unique to the protocosmic human, for it does not occur definitively in protocosmic world or God.[79] The essences of God and world are infinite, so the predicative affirmations of them stumble on no limits that startle the divine or worldly wholes into self-awareness.

But protocosmic self-consciousness is not yet inversion. It would be, on the Hegelian dialectic course, but on Rosenzweig's, the defiant will and finite character that together constitute human being do not, either of them, become the other. Rather, both originate separately and with equal primordiality from the same human resistance to reason. The movements from which they issue, one affirming, and the other negating, are indeed opposing, but do not wholly merge. Instead, they meet in self-enclosed relationship.

Within the generalized protocosmic equation, $y=x$, the finite character takes the letter B, for *Besonderes*, and occupies the x position. The finite will takes the same letter, B, and occupies y. Though the equation $y=x$ reads from left to right, it is the right hand side that is first filled. The essence, x, is not yet defined, but its place must be held by something before the active predication, y, can begin the defining process. One of the first things to invert in revelation is precisely this order. Whereas the predicative follows the essential protocosmically, it precedes the essential in revealed reality. This is another way of saying that while relation is protocosmically subordinated to essence, in reality relation is primary. The reversal of order is important to the sequence in which creation, revelation and redemption unfold. A sequence of these is determined by the fact that revelation presupposes creation and anticipates redemption. As Rosenzweig notes in "The New Thinking," while the books of part one of the *Star* may have occurred in any order, the books of part two are sequentially determined.[80] The correct order is predicted by the inverse unfolding of the dual constituents of essence and predicate within each of the protocosmic elements. In the human being, finite will, which was protocosmically second, is realistically first. The relation to which emerged will contributes is revelation. Finite character, which was protocosmically first, is realistically second. The relation to which it contributes is redemption. So by the inverse order of the emerged human constituents, revelation is fixed prior to redemption in human experience. Similarly, the divine essence that was protocosmically first is realistically second. The relation it partially constitutes is revelation. The divine power that was protocosmically second is realistically first. The relation it partially constitutes is creation. So creation is fixed prior to revelation. Only the world breaks the expected reversal of order. Its protocosmically prior essence does indeed emerge first into revelation, and its predicative individuality only second. Only by this repetition of the protocosmic order, can the world experience its creation before its redemption. For the emerged essence of the world, the first in reality, belongs to creation, and its individuality belongs to redemption.

Because inversion is expected, Rosenzweig calls the world's failure to invert a "peculiar inversion" (SR 420). The peculiar inversion is intimately related to the fact that of all the elements, only the world emerges into reality essentially incomplete. The perfect inversions of God and human create mirror-image reflections of themselves. The sequence of emergence their constitutive parts follow across the divide between protocosmos and reality is *EP/PE*, where *E* is essence and *P* is predicate. How do these perfect mirror-image reflections bear on the essential completeness of revealed God and human?

The answer lies in the presuppositional relation that obtains between reality and protocosmos. The problem of philosophical presupposition is the second to enter the *Star*, directly after death. The two are connected by philosophy's presumption to presuppose nothing. But, says Rosenzweig, death is the preeminent nothing for human beings, so philosophy by rights should begin with death, as indeed Rosenzweig's does. But since death is only one of three nothings, its distinctiveness from the others makes it something—so philosophy is not presuppositionless after all. If presupposition is inescapable, the task for philosophy is to choose its presuppositions well. Good presuppositions lead towards reality by predicting it. And how do conceptual presuppositions predict reality? They predict reality by means of the romantic sleight of hand, the mirror-image.

It is important to note how much, in the midst of a dialectic so heavily freighted with the Hegelian past, it is a romantic notion that here navigates the gulf between presupposition and reality. Hegelian dialectic would actually generate reality. The mirror-image only softly and silently tells of its coming. The presupposition would contain all of reality within itself, according to both Baeckian romantic wish and Rosenzweig's own claims about the protocosmos.[81] But it must contain it inversely. For what fulfills a prediction must precisely copy it except in relation to reality. The prediction is the empty space precisely shaped for the sign in reality that fills it. Prediction and sign are together an instance of romantic opposition in the self-same. God and human, emerged into reality, have perfect mirror images of themselves in the protocosmos. And so the protocosmos predicted their reality perfectly. Hegel might say, they are tested by their essence and pass. But the world is confronted with a peculiar "perversion" (SR 221) of itself when it looks into the mirror of the reality/protocosmos divide. It sees its uninverted self. It would be as though a person looking into a mirror saw the back instead of the front of his face. What it sees does not complement but simply duplicates itself. So the protocosmic picture does not predict the world's reality. For the prediction to occur, the individuality of the world would have to know its redemption before the categories of the world knew their creation. But now, in a triple inversion, Rosenzweig suggests that is indeed so. The world is not wholly created until it is redeemed. Creation is in process. The mirror-image occurs for the world after all, but only in the consummated redemption. The crack that breaks the mirror now, and prevents the inverted image, is precisely the unredemption of the worldly reality we know.

But then Rosenzweig has not employed romantic inversion to romantic effect. It is almost as though the two perfect inversions of God and human serve merely to accentuate how painfully perverse the world's failure of inversion is. We must wait until eternity to know it; whereas the whole point of romantic inversion is to secure redemption now. Rosenzweig's inversions may not serve the purpose of the present, but they do secure the three relations of creation, revelation, and redemption, in a striking image of eternity. The sequences of inversion may be tabulated as follows:

Table 1
The Perversity of the World

	Protocosmos	Reality	Revelatory Relations
God	*E P*	*P E*	Creation Revelation
Human	*E P*	*P E*	Revelation Redemption
World	*E P*	*E P*	Creation Redemption

line of sequential order ➤

E is essence and *P* is predicate. In the world of reality, only the world's components fail to invert. If they had inverted, the sequences of revelatory relations, read as lines in a book from top to bottom, would create a larger sequence that ended with its beginning. But the movement that begins with its end is precisely the temporal image of eternity. The chart extended through to the hypercosmos would generate that image. For then at last the world's components switch. But in eternity, as we have already seen, the human and worldly perspectives vanish. The perfected world is only for God to know.

Or so it would seem. The hypercosmic end of the *Star* bears a highly suggestive resemblance to the end of Frank Baum's famous tale, *The Wizard of Oz*. If Baum's story can be taken as religious myth,[82] perhaps *The Star of Redemption* can be read as children's story. Rosenzweig, who found something of the eternal child in Schelling,[83] may be so mirrored in this earlier writer that the same could be said of himself. Certainly the closing image of the book, the star that becomes the speaking face, is fantastic enough for the pyrotechnics of the famous wizard. The closing figure of the *Star* represents the truth above all perspectives. It is the truth that God eternally knows. What functions here as mirror is not God himself, Rosenzweig is careful to say, but God's truth (SR 423); i.e., the absolute truth God knows. The starlike face is patterned after a human face. But it truly mirrors the human reality only when it speaks. For the human as beloved soul is only born in revelation, whose medium is language. What the face speaks are the very words, love me!, that constitute the beloved soul and establish it in the real world of revelation. That is, the truth God knows and whose image we see in the face, directs us back to the very constitution of the beloved soul, that is, to our own selves. It is a bit like the wizard's gifts to the pilgrims of a clearer vision of what is already theirs. Both the star-face and the wizard point back to beginnings, or, to speak romantically, the finish is contained in the start. Rosenzweig indicates as much with his last two section headings: "The Last," followed by "The First."

If romantic irony is the play on opposites contained in the selfsame, then this climactic end-beginning is ironic too. Like the pilgrims of Oz, Rosenzweig's readers are set on a course that moves climactically towards redemption; and then at the point of climax, moves back startlingly to the beginning (SR 392). The return to the beginning, here, means not a rereading of the book, but in what is perhaps the *Star*'s final irony, the laying it aside. The book is written to move its readers into the very life its central part struggles to reach with words. The typography itself, funneling to a finish, suggests the vanishing of the written word and beginning of the spoken. Rosenzweig implied about his book that, like all creations, it is fundamentally past,[84] and served at most as presupposition to the realities of living, spoken life.

If the tone of the *Star* is set by its rigor and pathos, then irony is hardly its keynote, unless the pathic rigor is itself ironic. Certainly the *Star* sparkles with enough instances of such oxymorons. All of the inverse transitions from protocosmos to revelation issue in them: God's "serene vitality" (SR 116) and the world's "unessential essence" (SR 120) are the products of inversion that yield creation; the fated momentariness of divine love (SR 160) joins with the soul's proud humility (SR 167–168) in revelation; and the essential moments of human love (SR 214) with the eternal coming (SR 224) or vital endurance (SR 223) of the world in redemption. There are ambiguities, such as the double meaning of revelation, and points of self-conscious awareness, where Rosenzweig reflects on his book from within his book (SR 109)—all of which contain within them the self-identical opposites on which irony builds. But Rosenzweig does not exploit these identifications of opposites ironically or playfully. Instead, they are all allowed to frame, by their extremeness, the central point that Rosenzweig wishes to make about language in part two of the *Star*, namely that it is, itself, thinking. The collapse of distinction between speech and thought is the core idea of the core book on revelation. It is the signal achievement of the love me command, uniting thought with its expression in the precise present, and fanning out from there narratively into the past, chorally into the future. All of language is contained in these three tenses.

In "The New Thinking," Rosenzweig credits Feuerbach with discovering the method of speech-thinking.[85] Here he may be too generous. Feuerbach certainly struggled with the relation between language and thought. Hegel had shown how, at the level of sense-certainty, language could never reach its intended object—it pointed rather to the opposite of what it actually spoke, to the universal when it meant the particular.[86] But it was just such inversions between intention and act that provoked consciousness on to the final and adequate meeting of thought and being, or subject and object. Feuerbach accepted the terms of the Hegelian dichotomy between thought and being, but, because he would not advance with Hegel any further than sense-certainty, he cut himself off from their final dialectical meeting. All reality began and finished in sense. Thought was real only to the extent that it could be understood as sensible through the "refined senses."[87] Language hovered uncomfortably between the two realms, more obviously sensual than thought, but failing fully to partake of the reality of sense. In the end, it served merely to stimulate the separate sensing of thoughts in individual consciousnesses, not to bear thoughts communicatively between them.

Perhaps Rosenzweig felt more indebted to the communicative and reality-establishing function Feuerbach assigned to love. Such a role for love might indeed have anticipated a new philosophy of the future, as Feuerbach sought to found in his seminal work, but not necessarily the new thinking that Rosenzweig advanced. In the new thinking, language actually bears the love, is the love, that for Feuerbach can only be stimulated by words and that remains ultimately without linguistic expression.

In a self-reflective passage in the *Star*, Rosenzweig notes that language is its center-piece (SR 174). Baeck had claimed the same about Lutheran romanticism, for which the word did not merely mediate but was itself salvation. Over the course of time, the Lutheran word may have been secularized—divorced from its divine source and left groundless—but it remained as miraculously given. For Rosenzweig, the givenness of language does not necessarily imply a speaker of it. In the mystery of language, the agent of the word's spokenness is the word itself (SR 237). What was so disturbing to idealism about language, namely that it "resounds in man without apparent reason" (SR 145) was just its attraction for the Baeckian romantic. For Rosenzweig, God is no more the exclusive creator of language than he is of revelation. Language, the organon of revelation (SR 110) is the means by which the meetings of revelation occur. Language is foretold in the algebraic symbols of the protocosmos, a kind of protolanguage, just as the revelatory meetings are. So language is to reason, or thought, as revelation is to the protocosmos. Rosenzweig solves Feuerbach's problem of the distance between language and thought by casting them as self-identical inverse opposites (SR 110).

The mechanics of the inversion is complex. Reason has two choices with regard to any object it faces—to affirm or deny it. Protocosmic reasoning consists of three sequences of affirmation and denial. Each of the sequences begins with a distinctive resistance to reason, and concludes with a thought-construct, based on the resistance, of God, human, or world. The aim of the reasonings is conceptually to derive something from nothing. Neither of the logical movements performed on a nothing yields anything; not affirmation, because a nothing affirmed is still nothing; but not negation either, for a nothing denied is a chaos. The directions away from nothing, fanning out radially around it, are infinite. And chaos is no advance over nothing. So each of the three reasonings begins with an affirmation of the opposite of the nothing with which it starts. The opposite of a distinctive "no-thing" is not a chaos but the bounds of the thing itself. This is the conceptual essence of the thing which we have already once indicated by E. But the concept of the essence is not fixed until it is explicitly distinguished from other essences. The function of distinguishing is the role of the second logical movement to proceed from the originary nothing, namely the negation. This is the predicate already once encountered and symbolized by P. The negation of the original nothing is no longer chaotic, but takes its direction from the essence whose opposite it negates. Depending as it does on the essence, the logical movement that produces the predicate must succeed that which indicates the essence. It we symbolize the affirming movement by A, and the negating by N, the order of their emergence in all three sequences of protocosmic reasoning is $A\,N$. But now, just as the sequence of the movements inverts, in the passage to revelation, so do their logical values. The negating movement emerges in revelation under a positive sign, and the affirming movement under a negative sign. The negating movement within God, for example, becomes his affirmation of the created kinds of the world; while the affirming movement within God becomes the ever momentary need of human affirmation, expressed in the "love me" command. The protocosmic essence resulted from a logically affirming movement, and the predicate from a negating one. If the logical values invert along with the sequences, then in the order $E\,P\,P\,E$, the second P is affirmative, and the second E, negative, in precise reversal of the values E and P held in the protocosmos.

For Rosenzweig, what corresponds to the affirming predicate and the negated essence of revelation are certain words. These are the words which, in the first case, can only be affirming, and, in the second, can only be negating. The only ever affirming word is the predicate adjective. And the most affirming of these is simply, "good." Beginning with this, Rosenzweig identifies all the other parts of speech by their relation to it. The language which results is that of subject-predicate assertions, the language of the narrative past. The only ever negating word is simply "I." It is ever negating in the sense that it can never but refer to an individual that is always "otherwise" from all else. The language of the pure "I" is all essence; it can take no predicates that would subsume it under an adjectival category and consign it to the past. The pure I, unencumbered by predicates, needs a way of speaking in the pure present. And this way, as we have seen, is to speak imperatively. The imperative speaker who is never subsumed under a category is simply the God of the love command. Once the mute affirmation of the protocosmos has become the predicative "good," and the negation has become the essential "I," there still remains the equal sign of the protocosmic equation to find linguistic expression. That expression would connect the predicative "good" with the essential "I." But God who, once revealed, never merely asserts anything about himself, much less that he is good, cannot be the speaker of the implied predicative claim; neither can the human alone, for to speak of the God who loves him in his solitude already distances God; but neither can the world alone utter the claim, for it yet lacks cause so to praise God, who has created it unredeemed. The speakers of the claim must be two: human and world together. The redeeming human has already turned from the private receipt of divine love to its active expression, and so can afford to, indeed must, distance the private relation with God. The world, for its part, receives its redemption from God through the human, and so through the human is empowered to praise the divine. World and human together speak the collective language of praise, which is the language of the ever-coming redemption. The tense of this language is implicitly future. The claim "God is good" is wholly true only when the whole world has been humanly redeemed.

Of the three tenses of language, past, present, and future, only the first two result from pure inversions of logical movements. The exception of redemptive language corresponds to the exception of redemption itself. Redemption is the inversion of the world that has not yet happened. Redemptive language speaks in the moment of eternity, whose end must vanish to begin. Rather than inverting a prior conceptual sequence, redemptive language presumptuously inverts a posterior sequence composed of an ending and all that precedes. But language in this inversive moment is scarcely language anymore. It neither describes the past nor expresses the present. It lingers as an echo of what has already happened. For the cohortative prayer of praise between human and world has already effected the unison that redemptive language anticipates. If redemptive language is quintessentially future, then its utterance robs it of its very essence. Like the protocosmic speech of the tragic hero, it becomes a kind of silence. Here the Jews are prototypically silent. For their language, as a holy language, is really not meant for interhuman communication. It is a gestural language, whose word "forgets itself," and "perishes" in the answer it receives even before it speaks (SR 372).

Language that moves into redemption is fulfilled in its own perishing. Such a climax to the linguistic inversion of thought reaches back beyond inversion and all its attendant irony to the very essence of Baeckian romanticism itself. It was part of the bright darkness of the romantic mood, and already an inversive reaching for endurance beyond the moment, to exult in its own passing. The drama of language is precipitously Wagnerian. The "Bayreuth stage" is one of the public Christian festivals of redemption (SR 372). For the gods too move climactically and triumphantly into their own end. But of course, even after the gods have perished, the artwork that repeats the perishing remains to be performed over and over again. Art is not quite that redemptive in Rosenzweig. But it does function in the service of redemption.

The Baeckian romantic loved art for instating in permanence the passing redemptive moment. Art was a principal means of effecting the conversion of the passing to the permanent. Rosenzweig recognizes a kindred stance towards art in idealism. When idealism begins dimly to sense that no true passage leads from ideas to reality, it looks to art to assuage its doubts. Kant had already pointed to the provocative congruence of natural organism with the moral ends that practical reason knows via the moral law, and deduced therefrom a morally instructive function for the clearly amoral beauties of nature.[88] But Kant refrained from inferring from the congruence any divinely teleological source of it. For (Schellingian) idealism, art supplied the explanatory basis of the congruence. Art is the unconsciously produced product of consciousness. It thereby shows the organic structure of the purposefully created thing, while withholding from creative consciousness the knowledge of its own authorship. Art confronts both the creator and the appreciative consciousness with the same seeming "purpose without a purpose" that Kant found in the beauty of natural organisms. Idealist esthetics linked abstract, generative consciousness reassuringly to the sensual world, just as romantic esthetics reassured its devotees of redemptive permanence within the vagaries of life.

But just as Rosenzweig rejected idealist religion, so he rejects idealist esthetics. Art does not secure thought in reality. That is the role of revelation, whose organon is language. But art does bear on the inverse passage of thought to language. Art, like the algebraic symbols of the protocosmos, stands to language as prediction. It is almost as though Rosenzweig appropriates Kant's puzzle of the "purpose without a purpose"[89] and solves it through inversion. Art is not the solution, as idealism taught, but one pole of the inversion that is. Art is language without speech. It effects a common response to itself in a gathering of spectators, while leaving them incommunicado (SR 81). It suggests communication without supplying it. At the other pole of the inversion, in revelation, where speech actually occurs, the promise of communication that art supplied is fulfilled. Art scarcely knows what or even that it is predicting. Its predictive role becomes clear only when the sign to its prediction, namely language, has appeared. Its oxymoronic status owes to its relation of inverse identity with language.

But art is not content with its predictive role, alongside thought, harbingering revelation. It wants to claim for itself, too, the role of redeemer. Here is where idealist religion becomes more patently romantic. Since the human is the agent of art, art's presumption to redeem is equivalent to the subordination of divine and worldly to human being (SR 421); while the *Star* wants to conclude with the unambiguous subordination of all being to God. The *Star* registers the ambitions of art from quite early on, and begins countering them already in the first part. Art predicts the real world but is not in itself real. The shared responses it evokes in its spectators are merely moments; they do not connect up out of their self-enclosures into enduring relations. The Baeckian romantic's inversion fails because the moments of esthetic appreciation are not enduring. All attempts to make them so are at the expense of the real world, not on its behalf. A breakthrough to the real would issue in relations, while art is always self-contained (SR 60). The painting on exhibit creates an unshared space of its own (SR 355); the musical composition performed momentarily substitutes its own self-contained time for the world's (SR 360); and poetry surpasses them both in its pretensions, for in its highest purity it would enclose both space and time within the pages of a book (SR 371). The seeker of redemption who follows the lead of any of these arts sets himself up for the profound disappointment that settles on him who steps out of esthetic experience into the world of real but unredeemed relations. It is only in discussing the redemptive lure of art that Rosenzweig's tone takes on the polemical virulence of Baeck's, as though here lay his own, personal temptations: the lovers of art and music absolve themselves of any care for the world (SR 360); they dream themselves into oblivion (SR 360); their whole esthetic stance is delusion and disease (SR 354, 360).

But art need not be delusory. When it escapes from the hands of the self-enclosed connoisseur into the arms of the public, it becomes a part of the real world (SR 244). Art that educates, indeed recreates its spectators, is finally relational and so real (SR 244). From disease and delusion, it becomes "precious inner possession and treasure of the soul" (SR 248). The particular bearing of art on real life is the consolation it provides for suffering. The artwork consoles not by explaining suffering but by structuring it for the viewer. For Rosenzweig, all art structures "the ever-present poverty and deficiency of existence" (SR 376) and so is fundamentally tragic. But it does so in a way that simultaneously affords pleasure. In one of his few references to romanticism in the *Star*, Rosenzweig observes that art's tragic contents are presented in the form of "romantic-ironic levity" (SR 376). The comment recalls Baeck's on the romantic whose suffering is converted through self-consciousness into joy. This ironic-inversive power of art takes connoisseurship as close as it can come to a true redemptive function. Indeed, art here challenges the redemptive power of the cross, which also structures suffering. The difference is that because the consolations of art are never for more than individuals, they never fully console. Rather like the beloved soul whose joy in love is troubled by the sufferings of the world it senses outside, so the consoled viewer of art aches for a consolation that breaks through the bounds of his own self. This the cross does indeed provide. For the consolation of the cross restructures whoever receives it in the vast community of the Christianly consoled (SR 377–378).

It would seem that art, like language, perishes in the fulfillment of its own redemptive promise. The cross casts in shadow all the lesser consolations that anticipate it. But the cross is a visible symbol and can itself be fashioned artistically. Inverting the pure arts of connoisseurship, the arts of the church are applied. Rosenzweig traces the movement of the Christian arts from the promise to the fulfillment of the redeemed community. The architecture of the church establishes a shared space with a fixed orientation towards the altar. In the clear demarcation of direction, heavenward and earthward, towards Jerusalem and towards the world, a real space is created, not only within the church but, projectively, outside (SR 356). Even if a congregation does not yet fill it, the single room of the church predicts a unity to come (SR 357). The choral singing of the assembled congregation is already a fulfillment of the promised unity. The Christian hymns are a spoken music in which individuals speak in a common voice (SR 362). The spatiality of architecture and the temporality of music unite in the third Christian art, which is poetry. The poetic image joins spatial perception and temporal feeling in one. For Rosenzweig, the ultimate expression of this union is no longer linguistic but gestural. Its artistic form is dance, which originally was no spectator art but wholly participatory. The distinction between artist and observer that still obtained within church architecture, and to a lesser extent, within Christian music, is completely effaced within that liturgical descendant of primal dance, the ritual gesture. "Wherever man expresses himself wholly in gesture, there the space separating man from man falls away in a 'wonderfully still' empathy" (SR 372).

That, of course, is the redeemed community. At least in the formation of its Christian version, art functions in a uniquely necessary way. The arts of redemption culminate in silence. The silence is already foretold in the stillness of the unoccupied church building. The choral speech of the congregants, the first fulfillment of the promised unity, silences the private, personal word (SR 362). And the poetic gesture of the ritual, coming full circle in imitation of the architecture, silences all speech, but without sacrificing the realized community first effected through choral song. Language, having served as organon of revelation, surrenders any place it might have had in redemption. It already experienced its height in the revelatory divine command. If it lingers on into redemption, that can only be to anticipate the still higher unity of silence that will succeed. The distance that revelatory language effaced was between love and its expression; the distance that redemptive silence overcomes is between all humans and the world. But language cannot serve to frame its own perishing, for then it would not have wholly perished. It is art that fills this role on language's behalf. The silent, ritual gesture of the liturgical arts is the linguistically blank trace that language has perished in its goal.

Romantic Completion

It was Nietzsche who said of idealism that it was never refuted but simply froze to death.[90] Baeck would not care to have been anticipated by Nietzsche, but his comment on dogma, that it is simply frozen feeling (RR 234), seems to have been. The freezings of idealism and romanticism are curiously inverse. Idealism freezes from want of feeling and romanticism from excess. Feeling can only be preserved at the cost of its spontaneity. The preservation process converts a vital emotion to frozen dogma. Dogma is propositional assertion. It is rational form without rational ground. It is by lacking rational ground that it can translate emotion; and by having rational form that it can obtain for the translated emotion a continuous existence. For however fleetingly available the redemptive moment is to feeling, the assertion of rational form is ever open to the intellect's solicitation. Feeling acquires continuity in its dogmatic form, but only by sacrificing the immunity it formerly enjoyed to rational doubt. Feeling masquerading as proposition must submit, in company with all other propositions, to the tests of credibility. And this it is loath to do. So it changes the meaning of truth (RR 237). Truth becomes confession (RR 238). There is to be no "brutal" (RR 239) striving for knowledge of either the theoretical or practical type, and no submission to epistemological judgment. The act of confession is itself the verification of the confessed. The dogmatic inversion of feeling yields a complex of dogmatic ideas for a faith that had wanted to drown (RR 235). In the end, it is intellect that drowns,[91] and feeling that is preserved, artificially, in intellectual form.

But except for passivity, which is already a protractable state, all the essentials of romanticism must undergo inversions if they wish to endure. The miracle becomes sacrament (the sacrament is the "ever-present miracle" (RR 225)). What was unpredictably received becomes a repeatable possession (RR 221). But sacraments require officials to repeatedly perform them. And these are the priests of the romantic church. The experience that was formerly individual and private is now made over to the priest. Romantic experience becomes the clerical office (RR 230) of the priests, the divine office of the monks (RR 224). The laity is left its merely "adequate piety" (RR 232) of dependence on the perfect piety of experienced officials. Such lay experience as remains takes the form, primarily, of obedience (RR 230).

The church becomes the arbiter of salvation. The division within it between clergy and laity is reflected outwardly into a division between itself and the rest of the world. The redeemed are separated from the unredeemed (John 14:6), even to the point, at least in some non-Christian romanticisms, of a "racial scholasticism" that channels election through the "dark abysses of the blood" (RR 207). What seem like virtues in outsiders are interpreted as vices (RR 273). Exclusivity passes into intolerance (RR 274). For Baeck, "it becomes increasingly manifest how romanticism leads on all its paths to the compulsion of authority" (RR 251). Whatever individualism might have been implicit in the religion of feeling is ultimately sacrificed to institutional authority. Missions at first charitably motivated become egoistic extensions of power (RR 228). Incipiently authoritarian, the romantic church soon allies with secular powers. Here Baeck has Luther in mind and the state churches founded in his name. By this natural alliance, the passive inward faith of romanticism acquires an outward prop, while the state is enabled to patronize a religion that poses no challenge (RR 233). The Protestant state churches are only too happy to consign the moral good works that might be expected of them to the offices of the state (RR 251).

All these inverse movements of romantic religion towards compulsive authority simply repeat the originary transformation of feeling into dogma. It is only the aristocrats of romanticism, its artists and ironists (RR 290-291), who escape the descent into authoritarianism. For where art fails, as it must for the common mass, permanently to instate the redemptive moment, authoritarianism fills the breach. Art and authority are the two alternative ends of romantic inversion. Together they close the self-enclosed system (RR 240) of romantic religion. For Baeck, given the essence of romantic redemption, it is possible to "prove and derive everything from that" (RR 240). Here the form of romanticism matches its content. The romantic love of the past is a longing for rest[92] and completion. Art and the self-enclosed system are the romantic's final rest.

What corresponds in the *Star* to the romantic transition from feeling to fixed dogma is the passage from relativity to configured truth. Both transitions are movements from instability and chaos to order and stasis. Here the romantic and idealist heritages mingle. Romanticism acknowledges the chaotic unpredictability of feeling and ultimately seeks order. Idealism's starting point was not feeling but the self-positing consciousness. Its movement was from defective to absolute truth. Rosenzweig borrows from idealism its epistemological bent and from romanticism its sensitivity to chaos. The originary chaos for Rosenzweig is not emotive but epistemological. It is the unordered relationships of the three protocosmic elements.

The transitional section from the first to second parts of the *Star* is subtitled "The Chaos of the Elements." The backdrop to this chaos is the shattered All of absolute idealism. It was the idealist premise that all of reality was generated out of a single self-positing consciousness. Rosenzweig followed Feuerbach and the other postidealists in denying logical passage from thought to being. But Feuerbach,

who unraveled the idea of God into a mere mirror of the human subject who projectively imagined it, simply replaced one monism with
another. Instead of founding reality in God, it was now founded in
human being. What separates Rosenzweig from other postidealists is
his insistence on three foundational elements of reality, none of which
are reducible to the others. The shattering of the All is the establishing of three.

But the foundational elements of reality are, after all, merely
foundations. They are not, themselves, reality. Rosenzweig has already defined reality as relational orientation: a situation in which
above and below, before and after are clearly distinguishable. Not
simply order but reality itself is the opposite of chaos. Part of what
makes the elements elementary is that each stands in self-enclosed
unitariness apart from the others. Rosenzweig so constructs each of
them that no passage leads from one to the other. Each might presume to be the only element, and has in fact done so (SR 84–85). The
vying for ontological primacy of three, each of which has as much, or
little, claim to that status as the others, is just the chaos Rosenzweig
means. The philosophical observer of the contest has no reason to
prefer any one of the three to the others.

At least he has no rational, objective reason to show a preference. The privileged "we" of Hegelian philosophical observation
watched an all-generating consciousness proceed to absolute knowledge, at which point all distinction between observer and observed
vanished. The post-Hegelian philosopher who no longer recognizes a
single, all-generating consciousness might well distinguish his own
consciousness as unique and unassimilable, as Kierkegaard did with
reference to personal sin (SR 7). But ultimately this move culminates in Nietzsche's recognition that the human self is more fundamental than its philosophy, and determines its philosophy according
to need or predilection.[93] The chaos of the elements becomes the relativity of philosophies, or more disturbingly expressed, of the object
of philosophy's love—the truth.

For Rosenzweig, a chaos of competing truths is no more a resting point than a chaos of feeling is for the romantic. And for both, an
inverse movement lays chaos to rest. In Rosenzweig's case, the inversion is the passage from protocosmic foundation to revealed reality. For the outward-turnings of the elements towards each other
begin to establish fixed relation and orientation. These turnings do
not simply supersede chaos—they consign it to a status of permanent presuppositional possibility. From the standpoint of revelation,
chaos is a possibility that never reaches reality or, as Rosenzweig

says, the doctrine of creation—which is subsumed under revelation—"contains the denial of chaos" (SR 138).

The passage from protocosmos to reality corresponds to that from philosophy to theology. And there is some resemblance here to the romantic transition from feeling to dogma. For both theology and dogma are matters of belief. But by theology, Rosenzweig does not mean assent to declarative statements. Theology is the subjective, experientially based narrative, imperative, and choral language of, respectively, creation, revelation and redemption. Ideally, Rosenzweig would emerge from the pages of his book and successively tell his readers a story, command them to love, and join them in common praise of God. Practically, what he does instead is to interpret three biblical passages that are, respectively, in the narrative, imperative, and choral modes.[94] Theology is indeed the word of God, but a word spoken in three different voices. And all of them are grounded in the private, subjective experience of belief.

Philosophy, for its part, could resign itself to relativity. But after some 2,500 years of philosophical presumption to objectivity, only an ironist of Nietzsche's rank could transpose resignation into a bold and free-spirited new philosophical style. But irony does not set the tone of the *Star*. Its mood is pathos, conformed to the rigors of a system. The principal channel of pathos in the *Star* is its experiential theology; and of rigor, its algebraic philosophy. Rosenzweig took his cue for the distinctive role of philosophy from the late Schelling. Schelling conceived a distinction between positive and negative philosophy.[95] The distinction rested on his postidealist denial of passage from thought to reality. On either side of this divide, philosophy had work to do. On the side of reality, its function was primarily historical, to trace the concrete expressions of reality in the great historic mythologies. On the side of thought, philosophy's role was purely conceptual. Conceptual philosophy is negative in that it cannot of its own reach reality. But its conceptual constructions, held up to reality, may successfully mirror it. The mirroring of reality in a thought construct that does not presume to extend beyond itself is a little like the Kantian natural purpose without a purpose. It suggests design and even miracle.

For Rosenzweig, all philosophy is negative. It inversely images a reality that is as startled as it is by the inverse correspondence. For neither presumes to cast the other as image. Rather, each moves independently of the other into the inverse correspondence, like two reciprocally mimicking mimes who pretend a mirror divides them. But unlike the mimes, philosophy and theology in inverse relation each rectify a failing from which they suffer apart. Theology's failure is its experiential subjectivity; philosophy's, its relativistic objectivity. In concert, the two produce experiential objectivity, i.e., experience in which there is before and after, above and below, or at least, before and after. The inversions of the elements fix creation, revelation, and redemption in a sequential order. But above and below are as yet undetermined.

The figure of the star of redemption is determined by the elements in their relationships. The endpoints of the upright triangle are the elements, and of the inverted triangle, the relations. But nothing prevents the star from rotating on its points, letting now God, now world, now human assume the ascendancy. Towards the end of the second part of the book, the star is fixed with God ascendant. Rosenzweig advances two reasons for this. The first is simply that, since "we have recognized God as creator and revealer," we have established "beyond every Perhaps that God is above."[96] Stephane Moses takes Rosenzweig to mean that of all three elements, God is the only one "that is defined as absolutely active."[97] God creates, reveals, and redeems. The human does indeed redeem, as well, but is also a passive recipient of revelation, while the world passively receives both creation and redemption. Rosenzweig himself presents this reason in a summary and passing way. He does not spell out God's ascendancy in terms of absolute activity. If he does not, it is probably because it is not strictly true. God's love is passive in its unstable, ever-recurring death and renewal, and it looks to the human response to it for endurance. Indeed, the inversions of the elements succeed only if each element presents to the other two taken together both a passive and an active face. As though Rosenzweig were not satisfied with this account of God's ascendancy, he adds a second and more complex reason for it, which he presents as the "real" one. He says, speaking of God, that the

> direct equivalence of assurance and fulfillment of eternity is not valid for the other "elements"; it is this indeed which makes them the "others" and God the One. It is, in fact, the real reason that, for us, God is "above" in the hierarchy and world and man are eternally subordinated to him in rank.[98]

The distinction Rosenzweig makes here between God and the other elements rests on what he earlier called the perversion of the world—the failure of its constituent part to emerge in inverse order to that in which they protocosmically converged. As a result of this perversion, the relation of redemption is incomplete. The world receives the assurance of eternity through the human's loving stance towards it, but, by the finitude of human efforts, is as yet denied the fulfillment. Both world and human, who is also part of the world, suffer from the separation between assurance and fulfillment of redemption. But God is not directly involved in the redemption relation. So he does not experience or suffer from the separation between promise and fulfillment. And this is what fixes God above the world and human in the figure of the star.

What God does experience we only briefly glimpse in the *Star*'s last part. It is the face that directs us back to our own charge to love and redeem. So our vision of God's truth, in which we cannot live, leads back to the partial truth, in which we can (SR 393). The notion that truth is more importantly lived than known harks back to the confessional truth of the Baeckian romantic. The religious confession is not so much a description as an act of commitment. For Rosenzweig, the importance of a truth is measured by the amount of life that must be devoted to it.[99] Rosenzweig secures the stellar symbol of truth in a single orientation that disposes of chaos once and for all, and then, anticlimactically, returns his readers to an experientially verified perspectivism that seems little advance over the old Nietzschean relativism. But the advance is here: there are only two perspectives from which to live the truth, Judaism and Christianity. These two liturgical structures embody the narrative, imperative and choral language of reality. One who lives these faiths rehearses in regular cycles the reality of creation, revelation, and redemption.

Baeck focused on the Christian sacraments as the final, instated product of the romantic inversion of miracle. For Rosenzweig, it is the entire cyclic structure of both the Christian and Jewish liturgies that instate the otherwise unstatable core experience of divine revelation. But Rosenzweig emphasizes much more than Baeck does how much the liturgical structures open up again onto the experiences that first gave rise to them. The blessed bread and wine of the ordinary Sabbath is to taste as it did to the first harvesters and gatherers (SR 312); the Passover celebrant is to count himself among the Jews just delivered from pharaoh; the Yom Kippur worshipper is to see "in memory the Temple service of old" (SR 323–324). The legal prescriptions for these festivals externalize a "living moment" of relation with God into "custom concluded once and for all" (SR 333). The finality of "once and for all" speaks straight to romantic longing. Rosenzweig goes even further to satisfy it when he allows, in accord with romantic presupposition, that all of Israel's "further destinies are prefigured in its origins" (SR 318). The Jewish festivals unfold organically out of the Sabbath, the festival of creation that prefigures the revelatory significance of the pilgrimage festivals, and the redemptive significance of the high holy days. The fixing of the star of redemption results, by Rosenzweig's own admission, in an inevitable hierarchy. The Jewish festivals, which play out the star's symbolic meaning, are correspondingly weighted towards the climactic festival of redemption, Yom Kippur. But Rosenzweig constantly resists the direction in which Baeck would take a liturgical hierarchy, namely towards compulsion and authority. Perhaps the reason Rosenzweig's highly structured liturgical theology could be appropriated by a modern Jewish sourcebook as antiauthoritarian as the *Jewish Catalog*[100] is that even as he is building the once and for all liturgical structure, he is simultaneously pulling it down. At all the levels of the festivals, a democratizing movement works to efface structure: at the Sabbath level, by including all (not just Jews) in its rest; at Passover, in the unaccustomed status there accorded children (SR 318), and most especially at Yom Kippur, whose imagery of nakedness, humility, and death effects a virtual stripping of all claims to superior status of any kind (SR 325, 327).

But as though not content to undermine the particular expressions of liturgical structure within Judaism, Rosenzweig sets the whole liturgy within a larger antistructural context. He does so by a threefold denial of the elements that typically constitute a people: land, language, and law. The whole of the Jewish liturgy is embraced within the radical antistructure of this sweeping renunciation. If Rosenzweig, at his system's end, moves so far from the possessive authoritarianism of the Baeckian romantic, it is only because, in imitation of the cyclic movements he likes so much to describe, he has himself returned to the Baeckian romantic beginnings. Perhaps Rosenzweig never sounds quite so essentially romantic as when he is describing the Jewish people. Here is the preinversive romanticism of longing without possessing (SR 300), of disharmony with the times (SR 302), and of the radical denial of history's seriousness (SR 304). Here also is the self-enclosed redemption that the romantic wished unpossessively to possess. The Jewish people, far from allying with national powers, stands in permanent judgment of their faulty efforts to mold a secular redemption (SR 332–335). It stands entirely outside the time of temporal states.

In what is perhaps the most sublime inversion of all, the Jewish people experiences what Rosenzweig calls "the inversion of the

Between" (SR 420). The Jewish liturgical structure moves climactically to the imaged redemption of Yom Kippur. Because the Jewish people always anticipates redemption, it always inhabits it as well (SR 328). For the redemptive moment occurs precisely in the anticipatory space between the nearest future moment and the present. But by inhabiting a redemption that has not yet universally occurred, it inverts the sequence of beginning and end. The redemptive end is made the beginning of Jewish life. In that inversion, the temporal between vanishes, and the people "places itself outside of time" (SR 420).

The Baeckian romantic longed for an enduring redemptive moment. Such longing might find a surfeit of satisfaction in the inversion that supplants temporal endurance entirely, provided the romantic who feels it is Jewish. For only the Jewish people inverts the Between. And this people is a blood community (SR 299). It is precisely the "dark abysses of the blood," as Baeck would say, and a people cyclically renewed on their coursings, that constitute the base of instated redemptive experience. For a people defined by land eventually dies; only the blood base survives over conquest and exile.

Blood was already by Rosenzweig's time an image darkly tinged with ethnic ferocity.[101] Rosenzweig knew the philosophies of the Volk, and explicitly combated them in his "Atheistic Theology." It was precisely the temptation of atheistic theology, in one of its forms, to divinize the Volk.[102] Rosenzweig countered all Jewish tendencies in that direction by noting traditional Judaism's reluctance to formulate the doctrine of election as an obligatory dogma. The teaching of Jewish chosenness, though a presupposition of all Jewish life, is glaringly absent from the most famous Jewish formulation of faith, Maimonides' Thirteen Principles. It is virtually hidden even from the people itself, recessed back many layers beneath the surface levels of consciousness. Its life is in its work of binding the nation, where it functions presuppositionally to direct assertions about God, Law, or the Messiah. The chosenness doctrine is to Jewish thought what the protocosmos is to revelation: a state of being that resists thought, and can only be understood from the standpoint of the reality it grounds.[103] But what further distinguishes Rosenzweig's doctrine of Jewish election from mere racism is the place it holds in his system. The system's need of a biologically transmitted election is prior to the Jewish people's supply of it. The election is never its own end, but always subordinate. Like the Hegelian system, Rosenzweig's develops constructs to which historical realities are matched.

Thus the hero of ancient Greek tragedy was matched to protocosmic humanity. The matching of Jewish people to inhabitant of redemption could only take place if the people itself imaged eternity. But this they could do only if, like all such images, they began with their ending. They could not do that if their principal identity was in any static thing, like land, or linearly changing thing, like law or language. Only cyclic change images eternity. The descent of generations is an image of cyclic change. By defining itself by its generational continuity, i.e., its blood, the Jewish people can serve the system as inhabitant of redemption.

Its counterpart is the Christian church, which forfeits redeemed life for the sake of bearing it to the rest of the world. If, for Baeck, missionary activity was simply one expression among many of romantic authoritarianism, for Rosenzweig it constitutes the very essence of Christian being. The form of witnessing to Christian faith, namely proselytizing, is simultaneously its content (SR 342), just as the self-propagating Jewish people is part and parcel of the Jew's own faith. The eternity of the church consists of its infinite expandability, of the fact that for every x members of the church, where x is the number of members at any given time, $x+1$ members is always a possibility to be realized. The church is sustained by its unceasing commitment to that realization. It both believes in the $x+1$ as a faith-content, ever hovering before it on its way, and is determined by it to its proselytizing form of witness.

But Rosenzweig holds his Christian missionaries back from the imperialism into which Baeck virtually escorts them. He does so through an old idea, dating back to Joachim of Fiore (ca. 1132–1202), of the third Christian age. Joachim divided salvation history into three periods, named for the persons of the Trinity. In the last, or Spiritual period, the church would advance beyond the old ecclesiastical structures into a new freedom. Rosenzweig named the third Christian period of his own conceiving the Johannine,[104] after the fourth and most inward of the Gospel writers, but it shares with Joachim's an inspiritedness that obviates all need of structure. Johannine Christians exhibit the blind redemptive love that unpremeditatedly feels before its sees. And this love resists all imposition of authoritarian structure: "the Johannine church is amorphous and necessarily unestablished" (SR 285).

Like the Jewish liturgical structure, ensconced within a sweeping antistructure, the foundation stone of Christianity, namely its proselytizing, hovers within a vast unstructured expanse. The spatial image is less adequate than a temporal one: Christian time is an expansive present that stretches between the first and second comings of Christ. Beyond those endpoints are past and future. But within them, the Christian, like the Jew, is ever realizing eternity by anticipating it. Only his anticipations are not directed, with the Jew's, towards the endpoint of redemption, but to the next worldly $x+1$ who has not yet received words for the divine revelation. By its constant focus on the immediate future, the church loses sight of the distant one the Jew anticipates, and so of the final redemption altogether. That is the principal difference between the Jewish and Christian liturgical structures. The church's movement towards the next soul to be converted is a movement towards baptism. But baptism is the sacrament of Christian beginnings. So the expansion of the church is an ongoing repetition of beginnings, not anticipation of endings. From the point of baptism on, the Christian is guided through festivals of creation and revelation, in parallel with the Jew. But all these festivals are renewals of origins. Thus Sunday, the Christian festival of creation, falls on the first, not the last, day of the week. Christmas, Easter, and Pentecost, the Christian festivals of revelation, begin and conclude with beginnings. Christmas celebrates the beginning of the Christian revelation, and Pentecost the receipt of the Spirit that transforms the apostles into makers of new Christians. Christianity does not accompany Judaism on its advance to Yom Kippur with any parallel festival of redemption. Christianity's redemption festivals are secular; they celebrate the turning of the church from within its sacred space of music and poetry out into the secular world, as on the processional festival of Corpus Christi. But these redemptive festivals of the Christian calendar stand outside the sacred dates of the church year.

The Christian orientation towards beginnings seems flatly to contradict the romantic longing for ends, except that the baptismal beginning of Christian life, by Rosenzweig's account, subsumes all the rest of life (and so the end) within it (SR 374). The Christian is "co-opted" for redemption at the start; which mimics the romantic move to safely secure the end within the confines of the beginning. Indeed, the Christian could not proselytize except from the standpoint of the end he has personally known his whole Christian life long. Of all the revelation festivals, it is Easter that calls up the long-known end most forcefully to present experience. That end is the crucifixion. Perhaps Rosenzweig's Christianity is most romantic during the Easter season, when the full suffering of the cross is made most present to the Christian. Rosenzweig's Christ is much more of the cross than of the resurrection. This is why art, ever tragic, so rivals Christianity. "It is the cross, not the manger, that is always present for the Christian" (SR 365).

It is in the context of an origins-oriented *theologia crucis* that Rosenzweig sets those three pillars of the Baeckian romantic church—dogma, sacrament, priest. The Eucharistic meal, that for Baeck froze a miracle into a repeatable act, is for Rosenzweig the means by which the Christian may "confront the head full of blood and wounds, face to face, directly" (SR 365). Like the Jewish festivals that cyclically reawaken the experiences that gave rise to Passover, Shavuot and Sukkot, the Eucharist sets the Christian directly under the cross at Golgatha. The priest is not the authoritarian substitute for personal experience, but a "vessel of revelation" (SR 351) who, by his very garments, prescribed by the church, sacrifices his individuality, merges with the sacred space created by the church architecture (SR 357) and disappears before the worshipper's own eucharistic experience. As for dogma, it is no propositional assertion, descended from feeling, but the actual, suffering life of Christ, under whose dominion the Christian places his own (SR 277) by receiving the sacrificed body and blood.

At every step of his liturgical theology of Judaism and Christianity, Rosenzweig combats the incipient authoritarianism of ritual that Baeck as insistently underscores. Rosenzweig constructs anti-structural structures, a possibility that Baeck, for all his sensitivity to romantic inversion, does not consider. There is support for Rosenzweig's efforts from the possibly unexpected quarter of religious anthropology. It was Victor Turner who coined the term *liminal* for those states that occur "betwixt and between the positions assigned and arranged by law, custom, convention, and ceremonial."[105] Intimately related to liminality is *communitas*, Turner's term for the spontaneous community that arises out of liminal levelings of structure. Paradoxically, so structured a phenomenon as religious ritual becomes a bearer of liminality and communitas,[106] especially in modern cultures that so positively weigh material possession and status. Baeck took the monastic orders as Christian exemplars of the permanent instating of what Turner might call religious liminality. And Turner himself allows that complex societies may spawn enclosures of permanent communitas.[107] Like Baeck, he takes his favorite illustration from monasticism, in particular the Franciscan order. And so it is all the more striking that, for Rosenzweig, the paragon of evangelical poverty is not the church—whose applied arts and missions are, after all, costly and to some extent compromising—but the synagogue, whose magnificent renunciation of land, law, and language is symbolized in Christian art by a slightly bowed and blindfolded woman, holding a broken staff.

If Rosenzweig's Jewish people sports a monk's cowl, this is hardly the only inversion that the *Star* performs on Judaism and Christianity. The two religions are frequently related throughout the third part of the *Star* as inverse opposites. Christianity is a common way, Judaism a common structure (SR 354); Jews view the truth, Christians carry it (SR 416); Jews anticipate ends, Christians remember beginnings; the Jew is reborn at Sinai before his natural birth in the world, the Christian is born to the world before rebirth in Christ (SR 396). The inversions are no casual play. They are reflections of oppositions that Rosenzweig set up at the beginnings of the protocosmos, and that ultimately derive from the shattering of the idealist all. It was two routes that opened up from each component of the threefold nothing, because affirmation and denial exhaust the possible responses of reason to them. The legacy of two persists through the *Star* up until the end, passing through inversion, relation, and liturgical configuration. Only at junctures of eternity does the distance between two vanish, leaving one. So at the high point of the Jewish year, Jewish prostration before God makes room beside itself for the world (SR 373, 325)—from which, during the rest of the year, the people stands apart—since, at that moment, the self-reference of the people in its prayers includes the whole world. But the unity of the idealist All is never quite reestablished. The legacy of two, whose form always points back to the shattered All, asks for a content of two up to the very end. And this is what Judaism and Christianity together supply. Unlike the Hegelian "we," the Rosenzweigian Jew and Christian never unite with God, and so never see the absolute truth he sees. Hegel's *Phenomenology* promises from the beginning of its introduction a final union of knowledge's form and content. What blocks the fulfillment of our hope, says Hegel, is the mistaken view that the "light of truth" must reach us through a medium.[108] The *Phenomenology* promises that the distance between that particular duo, of the light of truth and its medium, will vanish before our very eyes. It is from this promise that Rosenzweig deliberately breaks. The Hegelian image of light persists into the *Star*, but broken in two. The star of redemption is the epistemological light, the Hegelian medium, by which reality is truly seen. But the light and the reality do not coincide. Jews gaze at the light itself, and Christians at what it illuminates. But neither sees the whole of the light and the illuminated. And so neither sees the whole of truth (SR 416).

Rosenzweig will not allow the *Star* to self-enclose peacefully in a Baeckian romantic structure. The hypercosmic liturgies of Judaism and Christianity do indeed reach back to the protocosmic beginnings of the work, raising hopes of a perfect self-enclosure. The protocosmos and hypercosmos are, like Judaism and Christianity themselves, inverse opposites. They are both silences, one from lack and the other from surpassing of words (SR 295). But they differ from Judaism and Christianity in that they function as boundaries of a third situated between them, namely the real world. And their relations to this reality are also identically inverse. The protocosmos foretells it; the hypercosmic face of God points back to it. A system rises up on inversions of two, but climaxes beyond itself in a reality that is not preeminently system, but speech. Rosenzweig presents the spoken by written means in the central part of the *Star*. But his closing words are the real invitation to leave the system behind for genuine speech.

That is undoubtedly the fullest realization of those antistructural structures Rosenzweig raised in the *Star*'s third part, i.e., the Jewish liturgy suspended in possessionlessness, the Christian one in blind directionlessness. The philosophical-religious structure is ultimately to be forgotten, even while it is being practiced, in the unselfconsciously lived experience of creation, revelation, and redemption.

Conclusions

Our own construction of romantic religion, gleaned from the secondary literature on German romanticism, comprised six principal ideas—the infinite, the whole, vanishing, hovering, mirroring, art—and four derivative ones—self-consciousness, irony, individuality, and freedom. Baeckian romantic religion incorporates all of these ideas except for the first and last, i.e., the infinite and freedom. Baeckian romantic religion effaces freedom under grace, and excludes the infinite on account of its opposition to the self-enclosed completion of the whole. Baeckian romantic religion resembles Hegelian idealist religion here, which subordinates individual freedom to the absolute's and resolves the infinite into the whole. But Baeckian romantic religion is indebted less to Hegel than to Kant for its take on infinity and freedom. The infinity of our constructed romantic religion was ontological; it limited human claims to grasp the whole of being. And the freedom was esthetic; it freed the creators and appreciators of art from the claims of convention. But Baeck understands the infinite and freedom in a moral sense, after Kant. What is infinite is the demand on the free moral will; or alternatively, it is the moral will that is infinite in its freedom (if not its power). Baeckian romanticism omits infinity and freedom because, in their moral senses, they are already claimed for Baeckian classical religion.

A romantic religion shorn of infinity is a little like a hero deprived of his nemesis. What remains is less complex than what built on a tensed opposition. A self-enclosed romanticism of rest mimics the infinity-sublating movement of idealism, minus the drama of the dialectic. Baeckian romanticism is a relatively simple affair. But it is just on account of their simplicity that the Baeckian romantic categories may be gratefully received as tools for interpreting the at times tortuously complex *The Star of Redemption*.

For all that, a reading of Rosenzweig through Baeck suggests a flirtatious dance. Baeck's simple romantic categories reach out for Rosenzweig's embrace, but never quite receive it. Then, after the Baeckian romantic has turned away, an idea of Rosenzweig's several layers deep unfolds a part of itself into the unsuccessful suitor's hand. Part of the distance between them owes to an intervening third, to which Rosenzweig in particular stands in vexed relation, namely philosophical idealism. While Rosenzweig's overt rejections of idealist contents point in romantic directions, his covert affinity with idealist forms lends his work a complexity that Baeck's straightforward categories cannot easily subsume. Rosenzweig does indeed dignify the category of the nonrational, but by means that are sometimes relentlessly rational, especially in the first part of the *Star*. And just where the rationality is most successfully aspiring to system, as in the last part, a leveling movement undercuts its achievement.

But one of Rosenzweig's departures from idealism may surpass all the rest for erecting semantic barriers to a straightforward Baeckian romanticism. This is the departure from atemporality. The move is not into any idealized romantic past. Rosenzweig may have found the life and customs of East European Jewry historically evocative,[109] but he indulges no sentimental historicism in the *Star*. Here he breaks with the incipiently romantic history of his early mentor, Friedrich Meinecke. Rosenzweig's precursor in tensed thinking is not an academic historian at all but that far-ranging philosopher of nature, art, freedom and myth, Friedrich Schelling. It was

Schelling who, in his late work, *Ages of the World*,[110] began a three-part treatment, never formally finished, of a synchronically conceived part, present, and future. These tenses do not proceed in a simple diachronic line. Rather, they denote epochs that nest in the present, presuppositionally in the case of the past, anticipatorily in the case of the future. Here is the first rejection of Baeckian romanticism that holds within it an acceptance. Baeckian romanticism centers on the category of redemption. But the constituents of romantic redemption—experience, feeling, miracle, passivity—apply only marginally to Rosenzweig's view of redemption. And so Rosenzweig appears to exceed the grasp of the Baeckian romantic categories. At the same time, Rosenzweig clearly speaks the Baeckian romantic's language, only in a different tense—the a-redemptive tense of revelation. Revelation, for Rosenzweig, is the miracle of experience that accommodates both feeling and passivity. That refraction of Baeck's categories of redemption through Rosenweig's categories of revelation conceals a genuine acceptance of the Baeckian romantic. For redemption is presuppositionally contained within revelation. Redemption is a "content of revelation" (SR 250) an unfolding of it. Redemption also "verifies" (SR 107) revelation as the price in human energy and life paid to realize it in the world. Insofar as this content and verification are foreseen in revelation, redemption is anticipatorily present there, just over the horizon of the received miracle of experience. Rosenzweig will not choose between a mutually exclusive classicism and romanticism, but takes one for the other's indispensable ground. True to his nonapologetic stance, he subverts the Baeckian polemic, and sets himself up to receive the label of at least partial Baeckian romantic.

But Rosenzweig will ally still more closely with Baeckian romanticism. For that very grounding of the classical in the romantic is itself a romantic move. Presuppositional grounding is itself the ground of the romantic organon, namely inversion. What is grounded inverts the ground; the mirrors of identical opposites that result constitute the wholes of prediction and sign, philosophy and theology, knowledge and belief, creation and revelation, Judaism and Christianity, that the *Star* is so fruitful in constructing. The constructed wholes verge on constituting a single, stellar system. And this is precisely where Baeck himself would lead it. For the romantic system should close over within itself. But here Rosenzweig will not follow. Those endpoints of Baeckian romanticism—dogma, sacrament, priest—are so mercilessly removed from the feeling, miracle, and experience that originally gave rise to them. Here Baeck's critique of romantic religion fails. For a true inversion preserves the ground in the grounded that inverts it. Otherwise there is no inversion but a mere succession of discrete opposites. Rosenzweig's inversions are true instances of their kind and what Baeck himself would have called romanticism if his polemic against it had not blinded him. It is only the frozen feeling of the false inversion that demands the coercive, authoritarian system. The true inversion, suspended on its own ground, has no need of artificially self-enclosed systems. And Rosenzweig does not supply one. He supplies only just enough to lead the intrepid reader back to where Baeck thought no romantic system would ever go—into life itself.

CHAPTER 3

A Reading of
The Philosophy of Art
against "Romantic Religion"

Introduction

A "philosophy of art" hardly seems an appropriate test case for
Baeck's theory of romantic religion. Art may claim to be an important
part of that theory, but never the whole. And yet Schelling might advance his own *The Philosophy of Art* as a valid test of Baeck's theory,
on grounds of a principle repeatedly stated in that work, that the part
of true or beautiful things undividedly contains the whole. Such advances aside, *The Philosophy of Art* has as much to say to a religious
sensibility as to an esthetic one. Once Schelling is situated in the circle of the early romantics, this comes as no surprise. In his *Speeches
on Religion*, Schleiermacher had raised the possibility of a meeting of
art and religion in a future *Kunstreligion*, a term that Novalis then
applied to what he took for Schleiermacher's own religion of love.
This occurred several years before a section entitled "The Religion of
Art" would appear in Hegel's *Phenomenology of Spirit*.[1]

Schelling locates Dante in "the holy of holies, where religion and
poesy are one" (PA 240), but he belongs there just as much himself.
Religion is the "poetic world" of art, and art, religion's "objective manifestation," so much so that "a scientific knowledge of art" is required
of all religious persons (PA 8). Schelling demands esthetic knowledge
of religious persons, but what he supplies is religious knowledge for
what is presumably an audience of esthetic persons. The first num-

bered principle of the first part of the book is about God, and the last sentence of the last part is about public worship. In between are extended sections on Greek mythology and Christianity, and scattered reflections on miracle and mysticism, on creation, revelation, and redemption. In an appendix to *The Philosophy of Art*, Schelling defines religion as a philosophical view of the world "that has become an unchangeable objective view of things."[2] Religion in this narrow sense reduces, for Schelling's purposes, to ancient Greek mythology and Christianity. These are objective in the sense that specific, formulable contents belong to them by definition. What they objectify is a philosophy that is defined less by specific contents than by a specific form— what in German idealism generally goes by the name of self-positing, but in *The Philosophy of Art*, by self-affirmation. This is the act of an absolute consciousness that, in *The Philosophy of Art*, Schelling explicitly calls God. When Schelling demands a knowledge of art of religious persons, he probably has in mind pious Christians. But the religious knowledge he supplies his esthetic readers is only tangentially a Christian knowledge. It is, rather, a knowledge of God as such, conceived as transcendent to religion in the narrow, objective sense. One might say that what Schelling offers his esthetic readers is a formal, philosophical religion that provides a framework for understanding both art and Christianity.

Schelling could demand a reciprocal awareness between this philosophical religion and art, as much as between Christianity and art, for scientific knowledge forges necessary links between all three. By scientific knowledge, he means philosophical construction. To construct an idea is to locate it in a product of relations generated by the absolute act of self-affirmation. German idealism foils easy entry by explaining itself in terms of the very concepts it presupposes. But once the absolute act of self-affirmation is understood as God's, even so abstract a rendering of Schellingian construction points to its beginning in God and, if art must be constructed, to art's divine descent.

For all the major expressions of German idealism, self-affirmation, or self-consciousness, is problematic. It is both the condition of a desirable self-knowledge and the expression of a painful self-division. The desideratum of idealism is a self-knowledge that surpasses self-division. In pursuit of that goal, consciousness generates products that must in turn become objects of its awareness if it is to attain a complete self-consciousness.

What Schelling's absolute consciousness generates in its quest for an undivided self-knowledge is, simply, the universe. The universe is a network of relations patterned after the single tripartite relation that divine self-affirmation presupposes, namely an act of affirming, of being affirmed and, since God must ultimately remain indivisible, of reuniting the two acts in one. This last act of reuniting, Schelling calls indifference.

One of the several tickets of entry to the difficult thought world of absolute idealism is the inversion of our customary way of relating action to being. For idealism, it is not being that acts, but acts that antecedently constitute being. If all acts are relations, between actor and acted-upon, then a more general formulation of what idealism presupposes is that relation precedes being. That presupposition is easier to understand if it is set in idealism's monistic framework. Monism already dispenses with any problem of being as such. To be is simply to be one. The problem is: how do distinguishable particulars come about? The first step to solving that problem is precisely to invert the customary view of beings as actors. What is one is itself the act of absolute self-affirmation. The indifference between the affirming and affirmed components of that act guarantees its oneness, and so its being.

The being of God may then be understood as the principal product of the absolute self-affirmation. But there are other products, too. Spinoza already formulated in his monism the idea that each of God's infinite attributes contains his essence. That was a way of preserving oneness over diversity. Schelling, too, observes the principle that God produces nothing that does not in turn reproduce his essence (PA 84). If the essence of God is his being, and his being is both the indifference between the affirming and affirmed components of his act of self-affirmation, and a product of that act, then reproduced within the components of the act the same divine essence must occur, i.e., the same indifference of acts of affirming and being affirmed. It is the reproduction of that triad of acts within each component of the triad that generates distinguishable particulars. But as these are ultimately subsumed under either the one absolute act of affirming, being affirmed, or reuniting in indifference, which are themselves, on account of indifference, all one, the ultimate oneness of being is not compromised.

Part of what philosophical construction reveals is that what we take for distinguishable particulars are, in fact, relational acts. Every distinguishable particular is either an act of affirming, of being affirmed, or of the indifference between the two. When Schelling demands of religious persons a scientific knowledge of art, he wants them to know where art falls in the network of relations embedded within the single absolute relation of divine self-affirmation. For knowing this is part of knowing God. It is no small feat of knowledge. It takes the whole length of *The Philosophy of Art* to accomplish it.

Of course, many other particulars besides art fall within the network of relations generated by the absolute self-affirmation. This includes all the subject matter of natural science, for instance, and the autonomous acts of ethics. Must not religious persons, then, know as much about natural science and ethics, as about art? If Schelling does not demand this of them, it may be because within the network of relations that constitute the universe, art enjoys a particularly intimate relation to the originary act of divine self-affirmation. Nature is the reproduction within reality of the divine act of being affirmed; ethics belongs to the reproduction within reality of the divine act of affirming. Art is the reproduction of divine indifference as an indifference between the real and ideal or, as may otherwise be stated, between nature and ethics, necessity and freedom. No philosophical descendant of Kant, which Schelling was, could fail to appreciate the grandeur of the role that thus falls to art. For it was a particular problem of Kant's to understand the relation between the synthetic necessities of the *Critique of Pure Reason* and the autonomously willed ethics of the *Critique of Practical Reason*. *The Philosophy of Art* comes, in part, to offer a definitive answer to Kant's problem: the seemingly separate provinces of nature and ethics, which together exhaust the real and ideal components of the universe, are united in art.

For Schelling, God, the universe, and art join in a trio that itself borders on indifference. Certainly Spinoza anticipated Schelling's claim that God and the universe are the same thing viewed under different perspectives. Schelling's formulation, that God is the universe viewed as identity, and the universe, God viewed as totality (PA 15), shows the intervention between Spinoza and Schelling of Kant, and his categories of quantity. The Kantian categories are, after all, that through which we not only view but determine sensual intuition. Schelling has simply (or, for the faithful Kantian, outrageously) applied two of them to the single object (or subject) of his monism.

The extension of the old Spinozistic monism into art is where Schelling clears new paths. Not only God and the universe, but the universe and art are two sides of the same thing. The real and ideal components of the universe repeat within art, objectified as the course of the formative arts in the first case, and the verbal arts in the second (PA 31). Reciprocally, the universe, taken as the indifference between its real and ideal components, offers up another relational node where art can show. The universe is itself "an absolute work of art" (PA 32). The indifference that manifests in music, painting, sculpture, and the varieties of poetry perfectly mirror the one great art-constituting indifference of the real and ideal components of the universe.

Where God has become universe, and the universe, art, there is scarcely any distance left between art and God. But the distance there is, Schelling negotiates very carefully. God and art are not simply two sides of the same thing. They cannot be, since God is the cause—immediate, absolute, and formal (PA 32, 83)—of art. Art is an objective representation of the divine creation (PA 31). Art is objective because it is impossible without sensual contents or objects, written, sounded, colored, or shaped. It is representational not because it expertly copies natural objects, for then, Schelling mordantly observes, the artist's task would be to create larvae, not art objects,[3] but because its forms reproduce the "forms of things as they are in God" (PA 102). Schelling's qualification of the forms of things suggests there is an alternative way for them to occur, outside of God. That way is precisely under a dedivinized natural perspective, i.e., the natural world as we perceive it when we either forget or deny its divine descent. By the forms of things, Schelling means, as Hegel would mean after him, the movements in consciousness that produce them. The forms of things as they are in God are the pure reproductions of the affirming, affirmed, and indifferently uniting movements that constitute the divine self-affirmation. The forms of things outside of God are the movements that determine their course—often towards suffering, always towards death or destruction—within nature solely, dissociated from God. Even to the atheist eye, nature reproduces the divine indifference at the level of the generic organism, but not at the level of individual organisms.[4] It is the role of art to make plain even to the mind untutored in philosophical construction that the divine indifference does indeed recur at the level of particulars, but only in the particulars of the art world, not the natural world.

Of the three divine movements or forms, the affirming and affirmed jointly constitute the act of separation. Even in Schelling's early work, but more so in the later, separation carries connotations of painful rending. In *The Philosophy of Art*, Schelling calls difference impure (PA 108), but in *Bruno*, a related work of the same time, it is "intrinsically and truly the sort of thing that ought not to exist."[5] Set against a backdrop of division, indifference shows as a healing movement. And it is precisely indifference that art takes up as its formal specialty. Philosophy, says Schelling, represents the whole of God to its students; art discloses to its scientific observers simply indifference as such (PA 29).

Schelling's idealism is not revelational in the biblical sense. There are no untoward breakthroughs of God in *The Philosophy of Art*. But the three component movements of the divine self-affirmation are suggestively akin to the more biblically relational acts that structure Rosenzweig's *The Star of Redemption*, namely creation, revelation, and redemption. "To be real," says Schelling, "is to be affirmed" (PA 23). The movement of being affirmed would correspond to the real world, or creation. The affirming movement, which is ideal, and is reproduced within the universe as knowledge and ethics, would correspond to revelation (a correspondence that would delight that Jewish neo-idealist, Hermann Cohen). And the balm of indifference would correspond to redemption. But now these correspondences suggest the first major test that Schelling makes of Baeck's theory. According to Baeck, redemption is the determining category of romantic religion. Let indifference be the Schellingian redemption. Then if *The Philosophy of Art* is *Kunstreligion*, and indifference is art's specialty, redemption is the central religious category of Schelling's book. Baeck's point is provisionally verified, at least in this one case of romantic religion.

The Baeckian romantic note does certainly sound many times in Schelling's work, especially at the climactic peaks of the ancient formative and verbal arts, in sculpture and tragedy respectively. A sculpted god "rests in the highest satisfaction" (PA 196); the tragic hero is "granted that absolute vision that is like the sun itself that finally bursts through dark storm clouds" (PA 87); and we, who behold the statue or the hero, are assured that reality does indeed attain the ideal. Art anticipates our own eternity and "paradise of life" (PA 243). What is more, it does so in the characteristically Baeckian romantic way—through inversion, rendering the infinite finite. Art is "the representation of the absolute within limitation without suspension of the absolute" (PA 45). Of the formative arts, sculpture accomplishes this in the highest degree (PA 201), but perhaps painting, when it takes historical themes, comes closest to satisfying the Baeckian romantic sensibility. An historical painting "is a moment eternalized empirically;" it projects outward the rest it has denied itself by virtue of the action it depicts, onto its viewer, and transports him into a state that is "in a sense, untouched by time, external to it" (PA 214). Could Baeck himself have arranged a more redemptive moment for one of his romantics?

But let us not assign Schelling prematurely to the Baeckian romantic ranks. If, in our introduction, we established Schelling's romantic credentials, and these opening remarks, now nearly concluded, to chapter three, have demonstrated that *The Philosophy of Art* is, among other things, a religious work, then we have successfully summoned a bona fide piece of romantic religion out of the German romantic past. It remains to test Baeck's theory systematically against our find. And as we have begun with redemption, let us proceed with it.

Redemption

Experience, the heart concept of Baeckian romantic religion, sustains a host of other concepts. For example, both the world and truth are reducible to experience (RR 191, 206). Experience itself flows into and enlivens the idea of being an object (RR 204). And experience serves better to define both life and rationality by standing so wholly opposed to them (RR 197, 209). These several reductions and oppositions locate experience centrally within a network of ideas, in which truth and the world occupy the positions of passive objects, and life and rationality the positions of subjective activities.

But this picture of ideas, overlaid *The Philosophy of Art*, produces some jarring dissonances, chiefly because Schelling's work assigns experience as such scarcely any role at all. Schelling does indeed describe individual experiences that resemble different aspects of the Baeckian romantic's redemptive elevation. That elevation was, in part, an experience of consummate rest. Such a rest, we have already seen, comes to the appreciative viewer of historical paintings. Apart from the genres of painting, among its forms, which include drawing and chiaroscuro, Schelling singles out chiaroscuro as "the one form of painting" that especially realizes its ideal nature, for chiaroscuro, hovering as it does between light and dark, produces in the viewer's "inner sense . . . a condition of indifference . . . that must be the truest and most genuine effect of all art" (PA 138). Creators of classical epic literature also know a "profound peace" (PA 138), by a logic akin to that relating historical picture to viewer: the action the epic poet sustains in his work excludes him entirely, and elevates him by contrast to a godlike rest (PA 216). An experience of godlikeness was a Baeckian romantic desideratum (RR 276). The Baeckian romantic redemption was an experience of totality or wholeness (RR 200, 223). And the effect of tragedy on the appreciative viewer is also an experience of at least inward wholeness, all divisive passion purged (PA 262). But for all these references to redemptive consummation, they by no means either center or climax *The Philosophy of Art*. It is rather a piece of the poignancy of these experientially redemptive passages that they occur so infrequently, relative to the whole work, and when they do, bound by a curiously ascetic restraint. They do not read as voluptuous indulgences or immersions, but rather like Schelling's own image of the sun, momentarily dispersing a cover of clouds, as brief relaxations of a taut logical line.

The logical tenor of the work owes to the fact that it is a construction, i.e., an arranging of ideas after a repeating formal pattern. Significantly, the idea of experience is not one of the ideas constructed. It is true that art enables an immediate viewing of the eternal in visible form. Schelling's term for the viewing is "schauen,"[6] the verbal base of *Anschauung*, the Kantian term for the intuitions of given phenomena that the Understanding, or *Verstand*, determinatively forms in experience proper. But what Schelling has in mind is no ordinary, empirical intuition in the Kantian sense, but an esthetic intuition that is too closely related to reason to ally easily with the so reason-resistant experience of Baeckian romanticism. Schelling takes great pains to exclude merely experiential, and so, for him, necessarily unreasoned, philosophical perspectives. Merely empirical rules cannot be admitted into any constructive enterprise (PA 280), indeed empiricism must be rigorously separated from "true scientific investigation" (PA 12). So actual practitioners of art, the supremely reposing poets of epic verse, for example, are quite useless to Schelling, even if they could be summoned for questioning from out of their ancient tombs. Practice does not guarantee understanding (PA 11).

But what further detracts from any climactic position the poet might claim for his redemptive repose is that Schelling is just as interested, if not more so, in the repose that inheres in artworks themselves, quite apart from their relations to creators and viewers. It is more art itself than the human experience of it that embodies the divine indifference. In sculpture, what reposes is the sculpted god himself. Schelling goes so far as to select from mythology the deities that particularly lend themselves to the plastic realization of indifference. (These are Jupiter, Minerva, Pluto, and Apollo (PA 43).) And within painting, portraiture reverses the direction of the projected rest, from the subject depicted onto the artwork itself (PA 147). (The viewer, by contrast, is to be moved by portraits and cannot regard the best of them without being moved, "ohne Bewegung,"[7] not becalmed.)

If the Baeckian romantic's redemptive experience is viewed under the aspect of its perfect repose, then what most closely corresponds to it in Schelling's system is not primarily an experience at all, but a form, namely the form of indifference. Human experience can exhibit this form, but is hardly its principal exemplar. It is indifference that makes the universe itself a work of art, and that joins necessary truth to free action in the creation of beauty. Experience plays no role in the construction of either truth or the universe. So much for the Baeckian romantic's reduction of truth and the world to human experience. But the original location of indifference is God himself. And once indifference is located in its divine origin, the transcendent abstractness of it contrasts all the more markedly with any Baeckian romantic experiences. The divine indifference is the interpenetrating movement of opposites that lifts God above any positive predications. Thus God is "neither conscious nor unconscious, neither free nor unfree" (PA 26). There is no difference in him between "the idea and the concrete" (PA 25), or "between actuality and possibility" (PA 33); so that, as a result, he is all he can be. A being that necessarily fulfills all its potentials is indescribable, because it cannot submit to the even merely possible changes that would admit it to a denominable category or class of things. It is "absolutely one, inseparable, indivisible" (PA 15). Schelling is speaking the old medieval and even older neoplatonic language of negative theology. There is hardly a more abstract, less experience-bound tradition in which to locate an idea. Even the form of the word "indifference" betrays its austere, negation-oriented provenance.

But indifference is not a mere restatement of the old negative theology. What brands it with the characteristic mark of German idealism is that it is a movement within consciousness. And with that German idealist reforming, this ancient negative ideal bows a bit earthward, if only enough dimly to differentiate within Baeckian romantic experience a kindred shape: the shape of feeling, which is, after all, from motion (emotion). The Baeckian romantic's redemptive experience is principally a feeling. How can the highest rest of indifference also be a movement?; because along with all other oppositions within God, the highest rest and highest activity are one in him (PA 153).

Baeckian romanticism also played with this paradox; the redemptive peak of romanticism was rest, but the broad sweep of romanticism's redemptive content was "tense feelings" (RR 190) as such, including the extreme and presumably unrestful states of both ecstasy and despair. The romantic, or at least the poetically gifted among them, does in a sense enjoy them both from what does indeed remain a restful state of ironic detachment. Feeling receives no such open-armed embrace in *The Philosophy of Art*, but it has this advantage over experience, that it is only partially dismissed. Schelling associates the expression of passionate feeling in ancient Greek drama with the beginning of its Euripidean decline (PA 262). Ancient Greek drama, which Schelling understands from a modern standpoint after Schiller's concept of the naive, is to betray no subjective investment of authorial feeling, and to provoke in the viewer no psychological intimacy with the writer (PA 92). On the other hand, this is precisely what modern drama should do. The modern, which Schelling understands after the Schillerian concept of the sentimental, is to present nothing but the author, feelingly objectified in his work (PA 92). The novel, which is the modern form of the ancient epic, both expresses passion and stimulates it in the reader (PA 232); while modern lyric poetry quite explicitly takes "subjective, individual momentary emotions" (PA 211) for its object.

These contrasting placements of feeling, definitively within the modern and outside the classical, owe to the opposing ways in which ancient and modern art realize indifference. Indifference is the interpenetrating movement of the affirming and affirmed components of the absolute act of self-affirmation. The affirmed, as the real and contentful, must have boundaries and so is necessarily finite. But the affirming, which must surpass the real in order to embrace it, is always boundary-breaking and so infinite. So indifference may also be understood as the active interpenetration of the finite and the infinite. But the penetration may be viewed from either of two perspectives: from the infinite towards the finite, or the finite towards the infinite. It is the indifference effected from the perspective of the infinite towards the finite that ancient art realizes; and the indifference effected from the perspective of the finite towards the infinite that modern art realizes. Where art moves from the finite to the infinite, it subjectifies. Modern art is subjectifying art. It takes objects, such as characters in a novel, and makes them over into subjects, into both the writer of the novel and its readers. A significant part of human subjectivity is emotion. That is why modern art is so much about the expression and stimulation of feeling.

Since for Schelling it is only modern art that reproduces indifference through feeling, only the modern artist and his audience are illustratively romantic in Baeck's sense. But Schelling himself would emerge from his book a Baeckian romantic only if he clearly pre-ferred the modern form of art to the ancient. It is true that one can-not designate the naive as such except from the standpoint of the sentimental (PA 97). The modern age, Schelling's own, is sentimen-tal, and one cannot but speak from the standpoint of one's age. But Schelling does not favor the feeling-orientedness of his own age.[8] If anything, he senses dangers in feeling: purely emotional responses to art are as "crude and uncultured" (PA 9) as any failure to respond to it with one's whole being. And here it becomes clear that, for Schelling, even the emotive appreciation of art is not, contra Baeck-ian romantic feeling, opposed to life and rationality. All appreciation of art presumes subjective activity (liveliness), not merely passivity; and activity of the understanding, not just feeling (PA 9).

Passivity was the third defining mark of the Baeckian romantic redemption. It was a characteristic longing to "pass away" (RR 192). If the indifference of opposites is the hallmark of Schellingian re-demption, it comes as no surprise that the redemptive moments of esthetic appreciation are "both active and passive, both swept away and reflective" (PA 10). The viewers of art who allow themselves to be completely dominated by the emotions it awakens in them, even to the point of "cleansing their soul," are succumbing to a "com-pletely passive and to that extent rather lowly pleasure" (PA 9). The higher pleasure, wherein indifference is attained, interprets the re-sponse through the "active perception and reconstruction of the work by the understanding" (PA 9). In this way, the indifference between finite and infinite that the artwork itself attains is reproduced in the viewer as the indifference between his passive response and active understanding of how the response was artistically effected.

But passivity, imitating feeling, has a deeper significance in the cleft it constitutes between, once again, the ancient and the modern. Only here the cleft is not so much between esthetic styles as between the mythologies that supply the contentful world of those styles. One respect in which Schelling seems more typically romantic than ide-alist is his lifelong interest in mythology. This interest appears early, but fully blossoms only quite late in his work. Within *The Philosophy of Art*, mythology is constructed in intimate proximity with art. It is, alternatively, the ground, condition, foundation, and content of art (PA 45, 52). It is able to be these things by virtue of yet another op-position, in addition to that between finite and infinite, that is indif-ferently embedded in the absolute act of self-affirmation. This is the opposition between real and ideal. Schelling has already once identi-fied the real with the affirmed; he also identifies the infinite with the ideal (PA 203). Hegel, critiquing the constructive method, faulted its analogical reductions of everything in the universe to a single pair of concepts.[9] But within the thought world of German idealism, affirming, infinite, and ideal do constitute a family of concepts united in opposition to affirmed, finite, real. If the generating principle of reality is an act in consciousness, then an ideal realm is posited from the start. The real is simply what holds the place of the object or content of that act. Of course, by indifference, the two are one.

By the Spinozan principle that nothing can follow from God that does not reproduce his whole essence within itself, an infinite series of divisions is generated within each half of the primal division between absolutely affirming and affirmed. If the absolutely affirming is the ideal, and the affirmed, the real, then within the ideal is reproduced a secondary division between the real and ideal, as well as their indifference. Ideas are an indifference of the real and ideal within the ideal. Ideas have this peculiarity: they are simultaneously bounded, because real, and infinite, because ideal. The concept of the bounded infinite was not new with Schelling. Fichte had understood the moral will as an ever-bursting of an ever-receding bound.[10] Schelling, however, understood this oxymoronic concept after the pattern of the Spinozan relation between God and his attributes. Compare Schelling's definition of ideas:

> Particular things, to the extent they are absolute in that particularity and thus to the extent they as particulars are simultaneously universes are called ideas (PA 34),

with a claim of Spinoza's about attributes:

> An attribute is that which the intellect perceives of a substance as constituting its essence, therefore it must be conceived through itself,[11]

reworded thus:

> Perceptions of substance, to the extent they are conceived through themselves and thus to the extent they, as perceptions of substance, are simultaneously infinite, are called attributes.[12]

The Schellingian ideas and divine self-affirmation are both absolute, just as the Spinozan substance and attributes are both conceived through themselves. "Conceived through itself" is not a poor translation of Schelling's "absolute." Schelling himself equates absolute with "within itself,"[13] (the other defining mark of Spinozan substance), which makes sense in a system where, from the start, all being takes place within a context of conceiving. An idea does not exhaust the universe, but encapsulates its infinity by being unlimited by any other idea—much the way colors are unlimited by numbers (as opposed to reds, which are limited by greens). Schellingian ideas also resemble the universals of the medieval realists as categories that can claim the status of individual existences, quite apart from any actual individuals that might instantiate them.

If ideas are an ideal indifference between real and ideal, then something must fill the place of the corresponding real indifference between real and ideal. And those are the gods of mythology. Gods are simply ideas "intuited objectively or concretely" (PA 17). That gods are realistic reproductions of ideal indifferences shows both Schelling's platonism, the idea as god, and the religious overtones of indifference. The gods, like the ideas, are both bounded and unbounded. But they attain the indifference between the two in a context of boundedness—the sensual, the material—just as artworks do. It is at this juncture that mythology appears as the condition and content of art. Mythology is the guarantee within Schelling's constructed universe that the sensual can attain to indifference. It holds the place, *in potentia*, of the point of real indifference between real and ideal until actual artworks are produced that realize the indifference. But it is a relation of logical, not temporal, priority that mythology has to art. Schelling himself sets poesy and mythology in analogical relation to form and matter (PA 45), which, understood after the ancient Greek and medieval conceptions of that relation, nicely captures the intimacy of the dependence—except that, contra Aristotle, the Schellingian mythological matter, in its identity with the ideas, does occur without artistic form. The gods, formed as objects within matter and figures within poetic language, are simultaneously those individual objects or figures and the point of indifference between the ideal and real realistically expressed. It is art's role to realize the gods that, in their sheer identity with the ideas, are only potentially present in a real way. Thus Homer, or the collective poets of the Iliad, were "reciting a poem that was already there, though perhaps not empirically" (PA 52).

A corollary of the fact that the gods of mythology appear in a real way is that they can turn against and resist their opposite, the purely ideal. The singular story of Prometheus shows the finite's capacity for rebellion against the infinite (PA 55). Schelling locates the cleft between ancient and modern mythology precisely at this point. It is no accident that all the illustrations of realized gods are from Greek mythology. Only ancient art follows the direction of mythology in its movement from ideal to real, or infinite to finite. Modern art reverses that direction, culminating in the infinite, which has no place for the "pure limitation" (PA 35)[14] of sensually realized gods. The infinite is beyond sense. It was Christianity that effected this reverse movement. It holds the place of mythology in the modern world. But by its central claim, the domain of the finite is effectively destroyed as the realization point of indifference. For God is incarnate for the purpose of nullifying the finite, offering it up on the cross, and exalting, instead, a finite-free infinite (PA 64). Christ, the last of the gods, destroyed the ancient realm of the gods (PA 64).

Christianity's movement from finite to infinite replaces ancient mythology with mysticism. All direct reaching for the infinite is mystical (PA 55), and "the essence of Christianity is mysticism" (PA 72). This would have been the end of art, too, if Christianity were not more than its ideas. But it is within the realm of Christian ideas that Schelling contrasts ancient and modern attitudes towards passivity. For the mystical goal is precisely that "unconditional surrender to the unfathomable" (PA 62)—Schelling's words—that Baeck located at the heart of romantic religion. The contrast between the pagan and Christian attitude towards the infinite (an occasion for the exercise of freedom in the first case, of surrender in the second) is, for Schelling, the definitive contrast between ancient mythology and Christian theology (PA 62).

And now Baeck and Schelling weave between them a curious pattern of harmonious and conflicting ideas. For Baeck contrasts the romantic and classical attitudes towards passivity in very similar terms. If the romantic was passive, the classical was active. Classical activity shows itself primarily in ethics, "a matter of work and achievement . . . and striving for the good" (RR 242). Ancient Greece offered the prototype of classical religion in its "traditional national religion" (RR 196), which Baeck contrasts with later romantic incursions of the Dionysian and Orphic. By the traditional, national religion, Baeck presumably had in mind, at least partially, the hero stories of Greek mythology. Here Schelling, if asked, might helpfully illustrate with one of his own favorite figures from that corpus, namely Prometheus. Is the classical religionist "directed towards others?" (RR 212). Then surely Prometheus, who, for the sake of human beings, risked Zeus' anger, illustrates the classical ideal.

Does the classicist fight and struggle? (RR 210). That becomes Prometheus' fate, in the face of the tormenting vulture. Prometheus does not simply act morally, in illustration of the Baeckian classical ideal; he is, says Schelling, "the archetype of morality that ancient mythology offers to us" (PA 55).

But even that phrasing begins to uncover a divergence between Baeck and Schelling. Prometheus stands out precisely because of "the total absence of any ethical concepts in mythology to the extent that they might concern the gods" (PA 55). By Prometheus' act, he becomes less a god than a symbol of moral humanity (PA 55). Baeck would not object to this refocusing of the ethical in the human, except that Schelling's account of classical ethics is directly at odds with his own. For Schelling, the highest moral act of the Greeks lies, in part, in the voluntary acceptance of afflictive finitude. That is why the gods can never be moral—except for Prometheus, they are never afflicted. Greek ethics is predicated not only on limitation, but subjugation. In the end, for Schelling, it is less Prometheus' just act, than the suffering he accepts on account of it, that transforms him into a symbol of the Greek moral ideal. This is a far cry from the ethics of active aspiration, of asymptotic approach of the moral ideal—the ethics of Baeckian classicism.

Schelling would agree with Baeck's claim that romanticism "destroyed the classical spirit of the Greeks" (RR 197) if, as probably both would allow, Christianity were substituted for romanticism. For it was after all Christ, on Schelling's view, who, by his self-sacrifice, also sacrificed up that necessary condition of classical mythology, the finitized infinite. But here again, their respective bases for the agreement diverge. For Baeck, romanticism can destroy but not create; its highest attainments are rediscoveries and restorations (RR 194), or connections between ideas already given (RR 199). This follows from romanticism's subordination of creation, as a value, to redemption. Romantic Christianity was nothing new, but a mere continuation of romantic strains that had already infested ancient Greece, mixed, to be sure, with elements from classical Judaism (RR 196, 200–202). In contrast, classicism seeks "to create the break where something new could be built" (RR 233). But it is precisely for Christianity that Schelling claims the capacity to break with the old and begin anew. Christ ends the era of the real and inaugurates that of the ideal (PA 64). Baeck and Schelling to some extent mourn the loss of the old, but for different reasons. If romantic Christianity, on Baeck's view, replaced ethics with religion (RR 250), then, on Schelling's, it replaced art with mysticism. As much as the ancient mystery cults undermined Greek ethics, on Baeck's account, they undermined mythology, on Schelling's (PA 64). Mysticism and art are as antithetical within Schelling's estheticism as romanticism and ethics are within Baeck's moralism—with the result that Schelling, far from exhibiting the Baeckian romantic's proneness to mystical immersions, subjects them to critique, albeit on esthetic, not moral, grounds.

What Schelling critiques in mysticism, and Baeck, in what he takes for Christianity in general, is the same willingness to surrender the finite completely to the infinite, to "pass away," as Baeck says, "in the roaring ocean of the world" (RR 192). Art requires the finite; it cannot exist in the sheer infinite. No pure passivity, whether of absolutely unresisting suffering (PA 64), or mystical dissolution can supply the limitations on which art builds. If mysticism is the essence of Christianity, then there can be no Christian art. But this is obviously untrue, despite the resistance to outward forms that some groups of Christians show, and Schelling himself allows that "Christianity creates the conditions for a complete and totally objective view of art" (PA 5). The reason for this is that Christian ideas, which are fundamentally mystical, do not exhaust the whole of Christianity. Christianity is also the church, a corporate and corporeal body whose bounded extension in history offers ample scope for art. And now comes a key Schellingian reversal of Baeckian romantic expectation: historical entities are acting ones, unlike the beings of nature divinized by the Greeks, which simply and restfully are. So the foundation for art laid by Christianity, in all its admitted romanticism, is essentially active, not passive. "The entire spirit of Christianity is that of action" (PA 65).

Of course, the Baeckian romantic in Christian guise is supremely passive. Perhaps there is no real disjunction here between Schelling and Baeck, for the activity Schelling ascribes to Christianity is less moral than liturgical. And liturgy Baeck will not deign to deem active. The premier liturgical act of Christianity is the Eucharist, which repeats the crucifixion and resurrection of Christ. This symbolic act is artistic because it successfully incorporates the infinite in the finite without loss of the finite—the bread and wine retain their natural forms even after supernaturally transfigured into body and blood. Baeck and Schelling agree that this sacrament constitutes a miracle,[15] that final defining mark of Baeckian romantic redemption. But here again, the grounds of their agreement diverge. For Baeck, miracles originate in the childhood of religion. Judaism spawned miracles in its early days but gradually "overcame" them, only to cede their centrality to Christianity (RR 227). In romantic religion, what counts as miracle is primarily subjective, a soteric experience of dependence, and not an outwardly observable breach of the natural (objective) order. Miracles only subjectively suspend the real world, as those who succumb to them withdraw ever more deeply into the privacy of feeling. The world itself is unaffected by romantic miracle, except to lose to self-enclosed feeling those who might otherwise have made positive contributions to the moral order.

Schelling also assigns miracle a central, indeed founding, role in Christianity (PA 69). But this role is far from child's play. A role for miracle arises at all only in consequence of a significant ontological change, namely a reversal of the direction in which indifference is effected. Christ is the dividing point between the ancient informing of the infinite in the finite, and the modern informing of the finite in the infinite. But if either of these movements is to count for childlike, it is the first. The finitized infinite of the ancient world allows for Greek art which, from the modern perspective, is naive (childlike) in its self-enclosed perfection and absence of self-consciousness. The modern movement of finite to infinite introduces a previously unknown division between these two halves of self-affirmation. For while the infinite can successfully condescend to finitude, the finite cannot attain to infinity except by losing itself (precisely the mystical goal). Where infinity is the goal, the finite loses its organic grounding (PA 69). It serves at best to indicate the infinite (PA 73) at the cost of itself, which translates esthetically as allegory. It is just in the modern world that division comes to constitute individuals (PA 73). The individual is the part of the whole that fails organically to repeat the whole (PA 34). The modern world comprises individuals divided from the infinite and from each other; it is the world of the broken and abandoned (PA 59, 235).

It is the modern world itself, not the private romantic consciousness, that creates a space for miracles. Miracle is the modern means of bridging the gap between the finite and infinite. It is the raising of finite to infinity without self-loss. This reverses the movement of mythology, but results in the same indifference. So Schelling can say that Christianity's historical miracles are its mythology (PA 69). Schelling is relatively uninterested in the subjective import of these miracles for modern believers; that would be mere mysticism. What concerns him is that they constitute points of indifference within his construction. If indifference is the Schellingian equivalent of redemption, then Schelling illustrates Baeckian romantic redemption by the role he assigns miracle in the modern world. But no one is necessarily experiencing these miracles. They are rather like the statues of saints that hold niches of distinction in grand cathedrals. So objectified, they lend his discussions of them that "austere spirit" (PA 247) that so characterizes Schelling's own much esteemed and quintessentially modern, Dante Alighieri.

It is the idealist tenor of Schelling's romanticism that accounts for its austerity. Schelling's idealism sets his system outside the experiential domain in which Baeck would place all romanticisms. For all that Schelling dismisses that one leading feature of Baeckian romantic redemption, his work does, perhaps surprisingly, incorporate all the other three, at least up to a point. It must be expected that what remains of feeling, passivity, and miracle, once experience has been abstracted out of them, is abstract indeed. They are all points in Schelling's construction, defined not by our loose conceptions of them, but by their constructive positionings. Feeling, passivity, and miracle all hold key positions within the expression of indifference under the aspect of the ideal. They are all components of the modern, what Schelling himself calls the romantic. Feeling is part of the motion that occurs in the very movement that defines the modern, from finite and individual to infinite and universal. It marks the beginnings of the movement in subjectivity. Passivity occurs climactically at the finish of the movement, in mysticism, where the finite reaches the infinite and vanishes. Miracle holds the place of indifference between these two, preserving the finite as finite within the infinite.

Neither feeling nor passivity receive the unqualified endorsements Baeck would have us expect from a romantic. Feeling is to be interpreted through the understanding; the final passivity of the mystic establishes the direction in which modern individuals are to move, but not their preferred goal. Even the church, according to Schelling, would not commend the mystic's goal to its faithful, if only because those who reach it escape the ecclesiastical embrace (PA 75).

Schelling has his own reasons for limiting the appeal of the mystic: mysticism precludes art. Conversely, esthetic considerations establish miracle as the one aspect of Baeckian romantic redemption that can be presented without caveat. Christianity's miracles are its mythology, and save it for art. But the question remains whether the category of salvation, or redemption, as such is as religiously significant to Schelling as a Baeckian analysis of romanticism would predict. Schelling devotes a great deal of attention to redemption's Baeckian classical rival for centering religious category, namely creation. That is hardly surprising in a philosophy of art. But he is concerned with more than artistic creativity alone. The artist's act and God's are the same (PA 85). They are both impartings of infinity to finitude. But creation so defined is simply the enacting of indifference, the Schellingian redemption. Creation and redemption are themselves fundamentally indifferent, whether performed by God or human. The very difference between God and human borders on disappearing in Schelling's monism, since the artist as creator is simply "an eternal concept in God" (PA 84). But if the centrality of redemption is so compromised, Baeck might say, it is only because of that characteristically romantic refusal to decide, so aptly illustrated by indifference itself. The most significant consequences of that carelessness are hardly for abstract philosophy, but for ethics. Indifference to ethics is the beginning of the romantic darkness.

Ethics

If Baeck is right that ethics sets limits (RR 256), then all monisms are morally problematic. For monisms maintain that, ultimately, there are no distinguishing limits. Nonetheless, ethics is one of the domains that Schelling does construct in his system. It occurs as the expression of the real under the larger aspect of the ideal. It is that free action which, indifferently united with necessary, theoretical knowledge, yields beauty. So while hardly the culmination of his system, it does hold a necessary place within it.

Schelling does not openly acknowledge any tension between monism and ethics. That is hardly surprising in light of his debt to Spinoza, author of one of philosophical history's most grandly monistic moral-metaphysical systems. Spinoza's solution to the problem of ethics-enabling limits was modes; Schelling's is the particular. The particular is a separation from the absolute self-affirmation. Particulars, in contrast to affirmations, are negations, privations, or limitations (PA 126, 142). In *The Philosophy of Art*, Schelling is relatively unconcerned with why these negations exist. For art, what matters is that they do. But in the roughly contemporary *Bruno*, Schelling explains that the world of particulars is the realization of the idea of difference.[16] And the idea of difference must be realized if indifference is to accomplish what Kant had started but left undone, namely to construct a knowledge without division between subject and object.

Knowledge must begin with the separation between subject and object, but it cannot end there, otherwise the subject's distance from the object introduces an element of doubt or even unknowability into the knowledge. In God's self-affirmation, the subject-object split is healed in an undivided self-knowledge. But the healing is predicated on a division that cannot exist in God. The world of particulars is, in effect, the location of the split within God, and the guarantee of the significance of his indifference. Schelling expresses this idea in *The Philosophy of Art* in the context of his esthetic typology. For instance, within the verbal arts, the epic displays a world of merely undifferentiated subject and object. Drama presupposes their difference and, through indifference, restores their unity. Only drama would contain the genuine particulars that allow for ethics.

So Schelling generates the particulars that ethics presupposes, only not for ethics' sake, but God's. Ethics is the tertiary domain that is to govern the behavior of the particulars that exist for the sake of God's indifference.

But now, as though reproducing the very idea of difference that particularity presupposes, the particular itself divides. There is the particular as such (*das Besondere*), the genuine part of the whole, and the individual (*das Individuum*), which merely divides from the whole. The particular imparts the whole by reproducing it. If the whole is the self-affirming absolute, then the particular, too, is absolute—an absolute, to speak oxymoronically, but monistically, after the pattern of Spinoza's multiattributed God. The particular reproduces the division within God, but also the indifference. The individual reproduces merely the division.

If the point of the world of particulars is to realize difference, then why should indifference occur there at all? On the one hand, Schelling himself feels the force of this question and replies that the indifferent particular is itself a miracle. But, on the other, does not the principle that God reproduces only the whole of himself bind Schelling to a world composed entirely of indifferent particulars, i.e., a perfect world? The difficulty is that the realization of all that God is requires that not all of him be realized; that is, for indifference to be realized within God, he must generate a world of unindifferentiated difference. As an essential of his own realization, this world is part of God; but as failing in indifference, it is apart from God. In *Bruno*, Schelling plays on the paradox, calling real God's indifference of real and ideal, and the differences of the "real" (divided) world, ideal.[17]

Baeck might charge that Schelling's attempt to generate particularity, or genuine difference, turns on word plays. In later years,

Schelling himself abandoned the notion of indifference. But in *The Philosophy of Art*, where he is concerned more with expression than explanations of particularity, he formulates two different ethical schemas based on the distinction between the particular proper and the individual. The distinction turns, once again, on the division between the ancient and the modern.

Ancient ethics is determined by the dominance of finitude in pre-Christian times. Indifference there is generated by the movement of the infinite towards the determining finite. The gods are the resultant locations of indifference. As indifferent, they are absolute, but as finitudes, they are particular. As particulars, they embody the absolute and suffer no lacks. And this transports the gods above ethics (PA 38). In this respect, they are like the natural forces with which they are associated. Indeed, nature is one translation of the finitude that sets the tone of ancient ethics. Schelling knows the moral critiques of the gods' behavior. But these critiques mistakenly judge them by a modern standard, as failing adequately to subsume the finite under the infinite. That is not the movement that generates gods and so not the one by which to judge them. As particulars, or absolute finitudes, they cannot fail by any applicable standard. Perhaps what Schelling means when he says, "immortality . . . expresses itself in the Homeric figures . . . as pure limitation" (PA 39) is that at most the nature of the gods as pure finitudes can be judged immoral, but not their particular behaviors within their finitudes. Strictly speaking, they do not act at all (PA 196), any more than any purely natural object does, because action requires a movement towards the outside of oneself, and the gods, as absolute finitudes, are completely self-enclosed.

But though the gods transcend ethics, they determine ethics for the humans of antiquity. In was the stance that Prometheus took towards the divine self-enclosure, of rebellion against it, that established the condition of ancient morality (PA 55). It is by rebelling against the gods that humans meet their own relative finitude, i.e., their own failure through their own natures to attain indifference between infinite and finite. Ancient human morality freely accepts the relative finitude which is brought to awareness by rebelling against its absolute counterpart. If Prometheus accomplished the act of rebellion for humans, once and for all, then to each human remained simply the decision to accept the limitation thus raised to consciousness. And by this moral act, humans do finally attain indifference. The indifference is one of necessity and freedom. If nature translates finitude, then the analogous translation of infinity is freedom. In ancient ethics, freedom is indifferently subordinated to nature, or necessity. In the absolute limitation of the gods, freedom and necessity are one in the Spinozistic sense that identifies freedom with willing the naturally necessary (PA 39). In the relative limitation of humanity, freedom and necessity are initially separate. Relative limitation is human necessity; the decision to accept it is freedom. Joined together, the two produce "the highest morality" of antiquity—"the recognition of the boundaries and limitations to which human beings are subject" (PA 55). Paradoxically, the human becomes particular like the gods (PA 89), through indifference, just when he accepts his essential difference from them.

Modern ethics is determined by the dominance of infinity since Christ. Indifference lies in the direction of infinity, towards which the finite moves. But modern ethics is plagued by a necessary disunion (PA 38); for the finite that attains the infinite vanishes. Modern ethics demands what, if achieved, undercuts itself. For once the finite, or limited, is gone, there is no role for ethics at all. So modern ethics must live in the separation it aches to bridge, if it is to live at all (PA 61). The ancient infinite was confined by the spatial finitude of nature. But the modern infinite, rather, subordinates nature. What outside nature can provide full scope for the infinite? It is time. Time is simply the form of informing the infinite into the finite, i.e., the contentless paradigm of infinite finitude (PA 109, 127). It offers a discreteness of finite points in infinite succession. And how does the infinite show itself contentfully in time?; through the free acts of history. Freedom translates infinity for modern ethics, as much as for ancient, but the nature subordinated to it, in modern times, is primarily human nature. Because finitude and infinity cannot attain indifference for modern ethics, human freedom invariably surpasses human nature, as St. Paul so neatly captured with his, "I can will what is right, but I cannot do it" (Rom 7:18). This is the separation that confines the modern human to mere individuality. Modern humanity, insofar as it is moral—and in precise reversal of ancient humanity—fails to reproduce indifference. But this in turn guarantees the preeminence of action and history for modern ethics. For if limitation and individuality are implicit in multiplicity, then Schelling agrees with Baeck when he writes, "action and history are found only where there is multiplicity" (PA 67).

The open-endedness of modern ethics, the fact that, unlike ancient ethics, it cannot attain completion, marks modern morality with a peculiar intensity. For Christianity, which shares with modern ethics the movement from finite to infinite, morality pervades the entire universe (PA 61). What is meant by the universe here, however, is not nature but history. Both modern culture in general and Christianity in particular view the universe as history (PA 59, 76). This history begins where classical mythology ends, namely with Rome (PA 60), and extends as yet indefinitely into the future. History repeats on a larger scale the infinity that also manifests in individual human acts. Its infinity is one of successive moments. This succession will finally attain completion when it is transformed into simultaneity (PA 74, 76, 77). And that will happen when history converges with nature in modernity's climactic indifference of finite and infinite, freedom and necessity. At that future point, history, ethics, and individuality all vanish into their completions.

Baeck critiqued romantic ethics on two grounds, that by reducing individuality to feeling, it inverted ethics, valorizing all-tolerant passivities that are, in fact, immoral; and that, having surrendered the law-full ground of ethics, it substituted for it either an authoritarian casuistry, or an ineffectual enthusiasm for ideals. Schelling, of course, does not reduce individuality to feeling, or uncritically valorize passivity. Insofar as he locates ethics in an organic system, he cannot be casuistic or enthusiastic in Baeck's sense, since casuistry and enthusiasm are, by definition, ethics-substitutes without organic ground. But Baeck does not completely miss the mark in Schelling's case. Feeling, passivity, and ineffectuality add up to a pathos that does indeed characterize the moral human of both antiquity and modernity. The moral human of antiquity is tragic. He attains his morality precisely by accepting the limit-enhancing consequences of deeds for which he is not responsible. Schelling rejects Aristotle's characterization of the tragic hero as one whose fall derives from an error of his own (PA 252). It is just by freely accepting the responsibility for necessary, not self-derived, acts that freedom and necessity become indifferent in antiquity. The pathos of modern ethics, on the other hand, owes to the unbridgable divide on which it is founded. It must live in its own self-division, which amounts to self-denial, or perish. Here is Faust's "eternal contradiction" (PA 276). It is curious how Baeck and Schelling apply the same Kantian ethics to very different ends to found a classical morality of limitless striving, in Baeck's case, and a modern morality of hopeless self-division, in Schelling's. The Schellingian modern is the Baeckian classicist regarded from the standpoint of the infinity he can never reach.

Schelling's dual ethical system of ancient and modern wreaks a havoc of inversions on the expectations of Baeckian romantic ethics. The Baeckian romantic takes his ethics outside of time and history into a hovering domain of feeling; but the morality of the timeless is, in Schelling's scheme, precisely the classicist's. The modern moralist, far from disregarding time, is immersed in it to the point of pain. His very location in Schelling's construction, under the dominance of the infinite that he can only approach by incessantly crashing through boundaries, sets him up for exertion and struggle, not Baeckian romantic repose. His is the great exercise of freedom (PA 241), by which he struggles for a grounding perspective within ever-expanding and so ever-undermining vistas. It is the classicist who rests in the limits he accepts. Far from preferring the past to the future, the modern Schellingian moralist depends on the future for his hope of final rest.

But then, it is not for Baeckian classical reasons that Schelling's modernist is so time-bound, or for Baeckian romantic reasons that Schelling's classicist is at rest. The Schellingian ancient has not escaped from time; he cannot have, since he has not yet known it. The dominance of the finite—nature, or necessity—in his world locates him primarily in space, not time. He is not so much timeless as onesidedly spatial. This is why the plastic arts dominate in antiquity over the verbal ones (PA 203). Conversely, the Schellingian modern, unlike the Baeckian classicist, does not look to the future as the issuing point of commands he rises to meet in the present. And here Schelling does draw nearer the Baeckian romantic. For the history in which the Schellingian modern is enmeshed is "a transition to an absolute condition" (PA 243), namely that indifference of the finite in the infinite that the ancient knew naturally in reverse. An ethics-supplanting rest is, after all, the future's final prize.

Darkness

At the center of Baeckian romantic darkness was an exaltation in the blurring of boundaries. Without distinction, there is no understanding. Kant had founded understanding on distinctions: between subject and object, phenomenon and noumenon, the groups of the twelve categories. Since Schelling's concept of indifference aspires to transcend the distinctions of the Kantian understanding, it appears to qualify as an image of Baeckian romantic darkness.

The idea of indifference presupposes opposition. Indifference is not simply unity, but the negation of a prior difference. Baeck noted a romantic preoccupation with opposites that are alternatively accentuated and wholly effaced. Certainly *The Philosophy of Art* offers up a panoply of seemingly diverse opposites. The very title of the book is one of them, as "anyone can see," since "the concept of a philosophy of art combines antithetical elements" (PA 13). Schelling explains that the opposites so combined are the real and the ideal. Philosophy's province is ideas, and art's is concrete, sensual realities. For Schelling, the contrast between the real and ideal is paradigmatic. This is the contrast that runs through all of poesy, philosophy, and religion, and that qualifies every idea, as well as the absolute as such (PA 57, 158). But it is simply the first among a host of suboppositions that are in precise analogy with it. The ideal is to the real as infinite to finite, freedom to necessity, history to nature, modernity to antiquity, philosophy to art. Opposition is made so universally pervasive just so that its overcoming in indifference can be all the more encompassing. "Regarding all these antitheses we must always keep in mind that they cease being antitheses when taken absolutely" (PA 91).

In an earlier work, the *System of Transcendental Idealism*, Schelling presented the idea of absolute opposition.[18] Such an idea is more obviously oxymoronic than the seemingly (to the philosophically untutored) simple notion of a philosophy of art. For absolute connotes unopposed. An absolute opposition must raise the dually and inimically posited to unity. And so it does. It can do so by virtue of its descent from the third Kantian category of relation, namely reciprocity. Each of two reciprocal concepts is defined by its opposition to the other. So they can only exist in pairs. Such are the Kantian concept and object. But because each member of the pair is opposed to the other, it moves to supplant it. It cannot succeed, or it would cease, itself, to be. So instead, the two exist in tensed proximity, in that space of vanishing that so captivated the idealists, between two and one. Indifference is what happens at the pole of unity in this space of vanishing. At the pole of duality occurs all of the real world we know. But it is not as though the vanishing occurs in any small, easily negotiated space. The dual of the real approaches the unity of the ideal across a space as vast as that which separates the hyperbola of geometry from its asymptote.

So does the string of Baeckian romantic concepts organically unfold, from opposition to the even more characteristically romantic *Schwebende*, that twilight concept of the in-between. In *The Philosophy of Art*, absolute opposition and its hovering mediations occur illustratively. The Faust character, for example, spans two opposite reactions to modernity's experience of necessarily frustrated longing for the infinite, namely succeeding, all-encompassing indulgences in first spiritual, then worldly excess (PA 277). But even God hovers ("schwebt"[19]) "above the ideas of truth, goodness and beauty as their common element" (PA 29). How all too typically romantic such a claim must seem to Baeck, for it shamelessly defers decision between truth, beauty, and goodness as reigning values, by effacing any distinction between them at all.

Schelling himself advances the Baeckian romantic unfolding into darkness. Of course, the effaced distinctions of indifference are dark to the understanding—lawless (PA 88), irrational (PA 166), "an absolute bottomless emptiness" (PA 36). For understanding presupposes division, and no divisions exist within the absolute itself (PA 36). But if the point of indifference is dark, no less so is the world of division outside it. Nature, that guarantor of the significance of God's indifference and, as such, "the locus of removal from God as true center" is itself an "eternal night" (PA 243). Phenomenal reality is the realm of "false, dark and confused conceptions" (PA 153). Here the darkness is presumably of difference that fails to vanish into the darkness of unity: two distinct darknesses, or two forlorn black cows of the Schellingian night?[20]

Schelling himself is not distressed by these boundary-blurrings. He coolly observes that "the complete removal of all limitation is either the complete negation of all form, or thorough-going mutual restriction, that is, reduction to nullity" (PA 40). If limits bestow form, then the extremes of limitation—no form, nothing but form—begin to resemble each other. For both are nothing to the understanding, the first from lack of distinction, the second from an over-determination that excludes commonality. For without commonality, there is no categorization, the definitive act of at least the Kantian understanding. To speak with Kant, it might be said that formlessness at one extreme of limitation is blind objects without concepts; and the overformed, at the other extreme, is empty concepts without objects. The understanding can operate under neither condition. For it, "the highest form. . . becomes formlessness, just as in other cases formlessness itself becomes form" (PA 91).

Schelling's other term for absolute formlessness is chaos (PA 88). Absolute chaos is also "night, obscurity" (PA 37). And this, too, as Baeck might predict, is equally untroubling to Schelling. For the formless chaos the understanding beholds when it attempts to gaze at any complete indifference is the means by which it, the understanding, finally surrenders to the powers of a higher Reason (PA

88)—the very Reason Kant critiqued and confined to heuristic roles in the *Critique of Pure Reason*. "Knowledge," says Schelling, quoting Schiller, "resolves to take 'incomprehensibility itself . . . as a principle of judgment'" (PA 88). And to this Baeck might reply, with the satisfaction of being proved right, that it is romanticism showing when "something opposed to reason . . . may be the truth" (RR 207).

If, in Baeckian romanticism, darkness triumphs over truth, death still more strikingly triumphs over life. The Baeckian romantic longed for death because it seemed a point of entry to the life of the larger whole. Schelling, too, plays with a sense in which death is higher life. His discussion occurs in the context of remarks on sculpture. Sculpture is constructed as the point of indifference, within the formative arts, of music and painting. If the finite is the infinite's goal in music, where the infinity of time is apportioned out into finite rhythms, and the infinite is the finite's goal in painting, where finite spatial forms evoke the ideas of what they depict, rather than any concrete reality, then sculpture attains an indifference of mutual informing between finite and infinite. Sculpture does not simply depict something ideal beyond itself; it *is* the ideal in finite form. Identifying the infinite with life and the finite with death, Schelling sees in sculpture a union of life and death (PA 193). Where infinity of life enters the deadness of a marble block in sculptural form, the issue is the peace of indifference (PA 198), available to the viewer without actually having died. That is, of course, the Baeckian romantic toying with death from a safe (and ironical) distance.

The Baeckian romantic's suffering is somewhat less ironic. For he does truly suffer over the passings of experienced redemption, at least until he instates these in permanent ecclesiastical forms. For Schelling, suffering is an inalienable part of human life, which mostly knows only the difference between real and ideal, and not their indifference. The nature of the suffering varies, depending on whether it occurs under the dominance of the real, as in antiquity, or the ideal, as in modernity. It was in contrast to the blessed life of the gods, those absolute particulars, that ancient humans knew their own lives to be "full of toil and discord and . . . subjected to illness and age" (PA 39). Such are the concrete sufferings of the noninfinite finite. Modernity's suffering, by contrast, shapes itself according to an infinity that wakens in the finite an unfulfillable longing, and self-perception of emptiness (PA 234). Schelling's judgment on modernity's "empty time seeking to be killed" (PA 234) is timely indeed. Both types of suffering figure centrally in the arts of their respective ages. The tragic hero of antiquity who attains indifference can only do so if he is first subjected to "the misfortune that physically casts down and destroys" (PA 89), what another modern writer aptly termed affliction.[21] He must accede to the "hard sight of necessity" (PA 89), to a guilt unavoidably imposed by fate (PA 255), for the free acceptance of these punishing confinements is precisely his indifference. The modern hero, by contrast, does not so much receive as generate his own suffering. He does so by his hopeless reaching for the infinite from his moorings in the finite. A classically modern work, *Don Quixote*, illustrates precisely this "struggle between the real and the ideal" (PA 234). The modern world is that of the individual disconnected from the whole, whose daily fare is "degeneration and collapse" (PA 73). The Christian mythology comes in answer to this state. Suffering is read onto its finitized god, a scandal to antiquity, so that by his voluntary acceptance of it he can, through his own self-negation, nullify the finite completely (PA 64).

In the context of his discussion of painting, Schelling invokes a dictum he has from Leonardo da Vinci: "do not fear the darkness of shadows" (PA 137). Baeck might say that, far from fearing them, Schelling luxuriates in them. For Schelling's account of the different shades of darkness (cognitive, emotive, existential, moral) comes closer to illustrating Baeckian romanticism than do his so nonexperiential musings on redemption, or his twofold accommodation of ethics. The difficulty with the dark is that, by that so irrepressible idea of indifference, it comes to pass for light. Painting is the art that most graphically illustrates this miracle, for, by color and contrast, and the magic of chiaroscuro, it allows, "negation to appear as reality, darkness as light" (PA 137). The concept of light is in fact constructed as the ideal whose real opposite, matter, together in indifference yield the organism (PA 119). But light comes closer to the center of indifference itself when Schelling calls it "the identity of all bodies" (PA 122). Light as the eventual goal of all form (PA 129) seems like the counterpart to chaos within the absolute; the pure determination that cannot be differentiated from the dark of absolute formlessness. In *Bruno*, the absolute is explicitly designated "pure light."[22]

Certainly the light of reason must seriously disturb the cognitive dark. Schelling's idealism, like all idealisms since Plato's, entrusts itself to reason. Kant had found in theoretical reason the source of much epistemological mischief. It was Kant who founded the distinction between the Understanding and Reason, that so exercised his successors. While the Understanding faithfully executed its humble determinings of sensual intuition, Reason, stringing out syllogisms in endless succession, presumed to arrive at the highest and most comprehensive of knowable objects—world, soul, and God. But the critique of Reason established that all objects are in sensible intuition, the last conceivable locale for the objects of these high ideas. And so these ideas cannot have objects after all. At best, they serve the Understanding as suggestive connective devises in its worldly researches among the objects of sensual intuition.

It was Kant's critique of pure, theoretical reason that challenged his idealist successors to find objects for reason's objectless ideas of world, soul, and God. Idealists and romantics acknowledged the achievements of the Understanding but were impatient with them. The Understanding could be no guide in spiritual matters, as the "shallow" teachings of the Enlightenment exposed not only for Schelling (PA 70), but also for his compatriot Novalis.[23] Here they had the French in mind, but Kant too, insofar as he confined intuition to space and time.

Idealism's break with Kant was to allow for nonsensual, or intellectual intuition, an activity of reason that grasped as unified objects what for Kant were mere placeholders for collections of sensual intuitions, syllogistically connected by repeated applications of the relational categories. Through intellectual intuition, human reason could know God directly. Further, intellectual intuition had this advantage over its sensual counterpart—the medium of its activity and of its objects is the same, namely consciousness. No unknowable noumenon need be posited to ground the object outside the knowing subject. Intellectual intuition secures its knowledge by erasing the subject-object divide entirely. So human knowledge of God soon shows itself to be God's self-knowledge.

Schelling follows this idealist thought path quite closely. He constructs reason as "the full reflected image of God" (PA 27), a puzzling claim that he helpfully elucidates by a kind of perspectivism. Schelling connects reason immediately to nature. In one of its products, namely the organism, nature moves towards indifference with reason (PA 84); but individual natural organisms are not perfect mutual informings of real and ideal. Only nature taken as a totality, as itself an organism, reproduces indifference. It is the indifference of God reproduced under the aspect of the real, or affirmed, pole of the absolute self-affirmation. Reason provides the perspective under which to see nature as an organic whole, rather than as a chaos of multiple, mutually conflicting individuals. In nature's organicity, all its distinct forms dissolve into one, a precise copy of the indifference achieved, within the absolute itself, of chaos and nullity. Reason is the name for the perspective under which the real world is perceived as an organic whole.

Reason is a perspective on nature, but it occurs within consciousness. Reasoning consciousness both perceives the totality of nature and itself, in its own act of perceiving, produces it. For reasoning consciousness' perception of nature is an intellectual intuition. It is a conscious act that is simultaneously the known object of its act. This accords with ancient teachings about the creative powers of the logos. And it comes as no surprise—the perspective on nature that always sees it whole is, after all, God's.

What invests idealist reason with mystical overtones is that its perspective on nature can also be the human's, in which case reason mediates an identity between God and human. The human being is constructed as the indifference of organism and reason (PA 84); it is the organism within nature that is capable of seeing the whole of nature organically. So understood, idealist reason shows its debt to Kant. For it was the Kantian reason that strove to embrace the whole of nature under a single, objective idea, and failed. Idealist reason is Kantian reason empowered to succeed.

Schelling's attitude towards reason is hardly the debunking one a Baeckian analysis of romanticism would expect of him. If anything, he inverts the Baeckian romantic stance and moves towards an elitism of reason. Now that reason is empowered objectively to know the real and ideal as one, Schelling is nearly contemptuous of those humans whose reason has not been exercised in that direction: they possess "neither philosophical nor poetic sensibility" (PA 35). But Schelling can so exalt reason precisely because of the quasimystical, supra-Kantian powers with which he has invested it. Does he thereby pay reason its highest tribute, in defiance of Baeckian romanticism, or convert it to its opposite, in illustration of the same?

In either case, reason in Schelling's hands is not what it is in Baeck's. Baeckian reason also descends from Kant, but from his practical, not his theoretical, philosophy. Reason is what discerns the moral law. Schelling's reason, made self-conscious in philosophy (PA 29), constructs.

Philosophy is reason's companion antidote to the cognitive dark. Schelling's claims for it are certainly grand:

> Philosophy is the basis of everything, encompasses everything, and extends its constructions to all potences and objects of knowledge. Only through it does one have access to the highest (PA 13).

Schelling calls philosophy the self-consciousness of reason. As self-conscious, reason reflects not only on its own object, which is nature, but on the opposing world that defines nature as real, namely the ideal. In this way, philosophy's extension is exhaustive.

If chaos could be tolerated in indifference with nullity, it has no place here. Schelling is disgusted by the "sheer quantity of philosophies" (PA 14) when in fact there is only one. From a philosophical perspective, multiplicity only occurs in what Schelling calls potences of the absolute. These are "ideal determinations" (PA 14, 281) of the absolute—determinations, in the sense of limited expressions of the absolute that nonetheless express it whole; ideal, in the sense of perspectival, i.e., visible as determinations only outside the one real point of indifference of all determinations. Potences are like the Spinozan attributes which, as what the (human) intellect perceives of substance, are more explicitly perspectival. But potences are independent of human intellectual perceiving. They are a necessary consequence of the self-divisive act of absolute consciousness in affirming itself. The connotation of "potential" is apt. They linger as shadows of the components of indifference, indifferently united in the absolute. They exist in the space of vanishing between the affirming and affirmed components of the absolute self-affirmation. The vanishing simultaneously guarantees the indifference of the absolute and the potence-constituting trace of difference.

The world of potences (the world we inhabit) is a vanishing breath. To encompass such a fleeting thing, which is philosophy's task, hardly seems worth the trouble. But the vanishing space of the potences is logical, not temporal. It necessarily and always exists. So it becomes a feat of some intellectual strength to span this vanishing space, which holds the trace of the difference we inhabit, and know the culminating indifference, only seemingly within easy reach. Philosophy's method of spanning the space is construction. The point of construction is to exhibit all recurrences of indifference or, as Schelling says, to exhibit "the suspension of antitheses" (PA 8). So all constructions presuppose at least three points: two for the antitheses and one for the indifference between them. The archetypal indifference is between the affirming and affirmed components of the absolute self-affirmation. And since the seeming parts of God must reproduce the whole of God, each point of the archetypal three-pointed construction contains embedded within it a reproduction of all three. New locations are thus generated that can receive new determinations. As these locations are necessary products of God's

self-affirmation, they are, in a sense, real prior to the determinations
that fill them. This is perhaps Schelling's justification for the claim
that "all that is possible is also real" (PA 54). The possible is the potential; the potential follows necessarily from the divine self-affirmation; all that so follows is real; therefore the possible is real, a
claim that Spinoza also made. Philosophy asserts that what a thing
or concept is, is its constructed location. In principle, philosophy
would not recognize the distinction between a constructed location
and the designation of a thing or concept that fills it. But we who inhabit the vanishing space of division, divided even from the philosophy that would save us, know only a multiplicity whose discrete
parts we naively and unphilosophically name. Now philosophy
comes to show us that what we call beauty or light or even ourselves
are actually locations of points in relation to each other and, ultimately, to the absolute self-affirmation. (How austere a spirit is
Dante, compared to the spirit of constructive philosophy?) Constructive philosophy provides a solution to the ancient Socratic problem of
how one can search for the definition of a term one has not somehow
already defined. Things have their eternal definitions in philosophical construction. We who know only multiplicity receive things dis-
lodged. Philosophy simply relocates them for us, like disconnected
puzzle pieces, back to where they so clearly fit.[24]

Now the same question addresses itself to philosophy that earlier addressed reason: are the molds of construction revelations or
concealments of our ordinary designations—do they enlighten reality, in defiance of Baeckian romanticism, or fantasize it, in illustration of the same? Schelling himself acknowledges the seductive
allure of concealment, which tantalizes modernity when, having allowed finite nature to retreat behind infinity, it takes nature up
again as a secret-bearing mystery (PA 77). Such a concealment, like
the concealments of art itself (PA 181), are partially revealed by
their very locatability within construction. Certainly for Schelling,
construction is revealing. But it is not only spirits as removed from
Schelling's as Baeck's is, who must receive Schellingian construction
as an order-crazed fantasy. Even Hegel, as we saw, had unkind remarks for this method.[25]

If Schelling were asked whether construction conceals or reveals
the real, he would very likely respond that the question conceals an
unjustified assumption, namely that the real is addressable apart
from the ideal. For "the ideal is the real and is much more real than
the so-called real itself" (PA 35). The so-called real is the reality that
presumes to exist without the ideal. In fact, real and ideal are con-

structed correlatively. Each can enjoy only so much ontological status as the other. They are both potences inhabiting the vanishing space between the separated components and completed indifference of God's self-affirmation. They together constitute a division that asymptotically approaches unity. Depending on the point at which they are seen, they are either separate, or have vanished into one. Schelling happily indulges the opportunities for play this perspectivism affords. *The Philosophy of Art*, echoing *Bruno*, calls the separation between the real and ideal itself ideal, and the union real (PA 14); and, alternatively, the separation real, and union ideal (PA 17–18). There can be word play just because real and ideal are the paradigm of self-identical inverse opposites that, according to Baeck, the romantic so loves playfully to exploit.

Inversion

In a recent commentary on *The Philosophy of Art*, Bernhard Barth locates at the center of the work two correlated ideas: prototype and reflex.[26] The German terms *Urbild* and *Gegenbild* point more directly to the opposition in the correlation. Schelling himself already in the introduction presents "the law of the universe which decrees that everything encompassed by it have its prototype or reflex in something else" (PA 5–6). Reflection is implicit in the act of absolute self-affirmation. That act comprises an infinite act of affirming, and a finite state of being affirmed. The two components are opposites, but simultaneously identical with the same absolute. By that shared identity with the absolute, they are also identical with each other. Their oppositional identity is reflected in their joint identity with the absolute. For that joint identity, too, is an opposition— of two with one. The act of absolute self-affirmation is a sort of hall of mirrors, the unitary absolute reflected in its dual potences, which are further reflected in each other.

It is precisely the oppositional nature of these identities that invites the language of reflection. In *Bruno*, the concepts of opposition, identity and reflection unite in the picture of the mirror image.[27] An object and its mirror image constitute two inverse opposites that are really one. In *The Philosophy of Art*, the two to first fill these roles are the absolute and its potences, then the two potences themselves in relation to each other, and finally the vast array of opposing determinations that are in analogy with the two potences. The inversions that unfold are multilayered and kaleidoscopic.

The real and ideal, a dual reflection of the single absolute, are the two potences. Schelling characterizes them in several ways: the ideal is infinite, the real is finite; the ideal is affirming, the real is affirmed. Since the potences, like the Spinozan attributes, repeat the absolute whole, each one additionally comprises reality, ideality, and what becomes the third potence, namely the indifference between the two. Indifference corresponds to the absolute identity of God. These repetitions offer up further scope for inversion. For a potence, as its etymological kinship with potentiality implies, always perspectively opposes, i.e., reflects as in a mirror, that of which it is a potence, just as the dualism of real and ideal is a perspective on the uniquely absolute. The potence of reality is determinatively real; so the collection of three that are potences to it are correspondingly ideal. Likewise, the potence of ideality is determinatively ideal; so the collection of three that are potences to it are correspondingly real.[28] To say the potence of reality is determinatively real is to say that of the three potences it subsumes, the real one must be that which is affirmed there. The role of affirming falls to the ideal. One could also say that in the real potence, the real is instated and passive, and the ideal instating or active. The real is seen, and the ideal, which acts, unseen. Now designations from unphilosophical speech are marshaled to fill the places of these abstract potences. Within the potence of the real, matter repeats the potentiality of the real. It is passive, instated, finite, revealed. Light repeats the potentiality of the ideal. It is active, instating, infinite, concealed. When light informs matter so that the two emerge indifferent, the result is the organism which, one might say, lives out both active and passive roles, has concealed and revealed parts, and instates itself.

A corresponding structure of abstractions unfolds from within the ideal potence, and another group of common language terms are marshaled to fill them. But the roles of affirming and affirmed, or infinite and finite, are reversed between the real and ideal. Within the ideal potence, the ideal is determinative, or affirmed. The role of affirming falls to the real. Here, the ideal is instated, passive, finite, and revealed. The real is instating, active, infinite, and concealed. Knowledge is the relative concretion that fills the role of the ideal here, and action, that of the real. The indifference of the two is art, which is simultaneously active and passive, revealed and concealed, and, like the organism, though less obviously so, self-instating. If, in addition, all the potences within ideality are oppositionally real, and all those of reality, oppositionally ideal, then what results are idealities of matter, light and organism; realities of knowledge, action, and art. This overlay of inversions matters primarily for the outcome of art, which emerges as the real potence of indifference within the ideal.

Baeck might respond to this display with the exclamation of a fictional ex-priest of minor renown, Reverend Shannon, of Tennessee Williams' *Night of the Iguana*, whose response to every untoward astonishment was the single word, "Fantastic!"[29] It is indeed a fantasy, by Schelling's own admission, but in a technical sense yet to unfold. But this construction of inversions is much less fantastic, in the ordinary sense, if it is contextualized by Kant. One of the now, in retrospect, doomed hopes of the German idealists was to unite in a single system all the diverse threads from the three Kantian critiques. If Kant separately exposed, in three distinct works, the conditions of theoretical and practical knowledge, and of esthetic judgment, then now was the time, in the introductory words of Schelling's *System of Transcendental Idealism*, for a "system of all knowledge."[30] The three Kantian critiques are visible behind the single Schellingian construction. What Schelling constructs as the tripartite real potence of the absolute is that same physical nature, the certain knowledge of which Kant secured for us in the first critique. Schelling would call natural philosophy the project he only sketchily completes in *The Philosophy of Art*, but more fully elsewhere, to uncover the full range of the unfolded potences within nature. Schellingian nature's climax in the indifference of the organism builds on Kant's own fascination in the third critique with that puzzling purpose without a purpose, so provocatively suggestive of beauty and goodness. Schelling will define all beauty as the indifference within the potences of the potences there microcosmically repeated. And in that way he systematizes Kant's intuitions about the relation between natural organism and beauty. What Schelling constructs as the tripartite ideal potence of the absolute are further developments on the Kantian understanding of the first critique, the moral will of the second, and the esthetics of the third. The finite knowledge of the ideal potence is the knowledge of the Understanding, its category-driven determinations of nature, minus the noumenal underpinnings. The action of the ideal potence is the moral will, whose noumenal Kantian hiddenness is here revealed as the real repetition in ideal infinity of the concealed light of nature and, ultimately, of the affirming potence of the absolute itself. Finally, the art of the ideal potence is the art of the third Kantian critique, only now revealed in the partnership with natural organism that Kant stopped short of exposing, because he lacked the principle of indifference that identifies the two across the real/ideal divide. Of course, what is missing in the construction is any affirmation of the old Kantian reason, so mercilessly (or ascetically) confined by the Transcendental Dialectic. That reason is excluded in Schelling for the same reason indifference is excluded in Kant. Indifference is intellectual intuition to the new reason, and outrageous presumption to the old.

For Baeck, romantic inversion was to hold in permanence that whose essence it was to pass. Schelling inverts for a different reason, to account for why difference and multiplicity, which by all prima facie monistic rights, ought not exist,[31] nonetheless do. But of course, transience, difference and multiplicity are not unrelated. Schelling undercuts the presupposition of transience when he confines difference to a space that, at least to the artist and philosopher, has always just vanished. But he does not thereby realize the Baeckian romantic hope of banishing all grief; the transient remains in its ever just vanished space. What he does realize is a hope much more disinterested, and much more indebted to Kant, that great and austere spirit other than Dante, namely a securing of knowledge. The knowledge secured is not even his own, but God's. For the whole unfolding of inversions follows on the one divine inversion needed for God's self-knowledge. That inversion is a "subject-objectifization" (PA 119). Kant began to objectify the subject when he empowered it with categories that determined its objects. Schelling simply completed the project when he recast the object as an externalization of the subject, whole. That becomes Schelling's definition of a relation that had been equally important to Spinoza's monism, namely expression. "Expression is in general the portrayal of inner substance by means of external elements" (PA 133), says Schelling in a picture that evokes images quite different from the cascading fountain of expression's medieval monistic cousin, neoplatonic emanation.[32] Medieval emanation and idealist expression are, of course, to different ends. Emanation is the consequence of ontological overfullness in God. Expression is the presupposition of knowledge in God. Unless God expresses himself as an object, he cannot know himself as a subject.

There is a paradox in the presuppositional character of God's self-knowledge. The presupposition seems to condition a being that is traditionally understood as unconditioned. God cannot lack self-knowledge; but in order to have it, he is compelled to act, when he ought to be free of all compulsions. Schelling solves this dilemma by identifying God precisely with his act of self-affirmation—"God is the immediate affirmation of himself" (PA 23). God is then understood as an act. If God is also being, that can only be understood as the indifference that follows the performance of the act; in which case, God's being is no longer conditioned by an act that compels his performance, but rather by God himself.

Baeck noted the romantic interest in the inverse logic of presupposition. As a means of securing redemption permanently in the present, the Baeckian romantic sought to contain ends in beginnings. What seems a mere presupposition of a goal turns out to contain the goal, complete, within itself. This, too, is inversion, now between the ordered pairs of first and last. God's own self-affirmation illustrates. Common sense would locate being prior to action. But then, to know himself, God seems compelled by his act of self-affirming. If, by the romantic logic of presupposition, God's being already contains his act at the start—indeed, prior to the start—then he is no longer compelled by the act, for he is the act itself.

God's relation to the potences, and theirs to each other, also follows the logic of presupposition. Common sense would have the divine act of self-division follow the constitution of the divine. But by the logic of presupposition, the divine self-division itself already constitutes the divine. The self-division comprises the affirming ideal and the affirmed real. The two are correlative and so mutually presupposing. By the logic of presupposition, each must contain the other in itself. And so they do. For each potence repeats within itself the whole triune body of potences, including its own opposite.

Thus the real potence, which is nature, subsumes the ideal as light; and the ideal potence subsumes the real as moral action. Reason provides the perspective on nature that sees its subsumed real and ideal potences, i.e., matter and light, united in the organism. Indeed, reason, whose act is intellectual intuition, simultaneously produces and sees the organism, both in multiple forms and as the totality of nature. If we ask after the perspective that does the same work for the world of ideas, we stumble at last on the domain of inversion that Baeck would deem reason's opposite, namely, fantasy. The analog to reason in the world of ideas is imagination. Where reason intellectually intuits, the imagination fantasizes. Both the intuitions and the fantasies are simultaneously acts of production and perceiving. But whereas reason, through intellectual intuition, produces and perceives nature as both multiple and unique organism, the imagination, through fantasy, produces and perceives the artwork both in multiple manifestation and as uniquely and comprehensively one.

That reason and the imagination are analogously related to the natural and ideal worlds, respectively, may either fantasize reason, in accord with Baeckian romanticism, or rationalize fantasy, in opposition to the same. In either case, fantasy in Schelling is no capricious exercise. Fantasy "forms into the particular the entire divinity of the universal" (PA 37). The magnitude of this achievement becomes clear when it is set in the context of its descent from Kant's transcendental dialectic. There, reason had sought particular objects for its most universal ideas of world, soul and God, and critique had denied it them. Now reason, in the guise of its identical inverse opposite, the imagination, does secure these objects in the form of artworks.

Nature, under the purview of reason, is a multiplicity formed into a totality. The world of ideas, under the imagination's sway, is a total universe formed into particulars. Schelling also called the fantastic world of the imagination an "absoluteness in limitation" (PA 37). This is the world we have already once encountered as that of the gods. If each god embodies the same universal, then each must be complete in itself and, at the same time, identical with all the others. Reason and the imagination operate in precise parallel here. Everything in their respective domains "is free and moves about in the same realm without crowding or chafing, for each is within itself equal to the whole" (PA 37).

Because reason and the imagination are identical inverse opposites, the distinction between their respective domains begins to blur, as Baeck would predict. Schelling says that the imagination "is the power whereby something ideal is simultaneously something real" (PA 32). But the real is simply nature, and reason's domain. Are the products of the imagination natural objects, then?; no, they are not, though they relate to natural objects, unsurprisingly, as identical inverse opposites. The sense in which artworks are real is different from the sense in which natural objects are real. Nature is the first, affirmed potence of the absolute, which is determinatively real; artworks are the potences of indifference within the second, affirming potence, which is determinatively ideal. All the potences within the ideal potence of the absolute are oppositionally real. It is in that, one might say mediate or reflected sense, that art objects are real.

Schelling's construction of art as an indifference of opposites carries some intuitive plausibility even for nonidealist reason. Schelling speaks more directly to this commoner reason in the *Sys-*

tem of Transcendental Idealism, whose closing chapter comes nearer the euphoria Baeck would expect of a romantic. There Schelling uncharacteristically appeals to the "testimony of all artists, that they are involuntarily driven to create their works and that in producing them they merely satisfy an irresistible urge of their own nature."[33] In satisfying an urge of his own nature, the artist, according to the Spinozan definition of freedom (which Schelling follows) is free.[34] So the opposition resolved in artistic activity is the old Kantian one between the naturally determined and free aspects of human being. In *The Philosophy of Art*, Schelling, taking the opposition between freedom and necessity as the "highest contrast" (PA 264) (not surprising for a Kantian), sets it in analogy with that between particular and universal (PA 78, 212), infinite and finite (PA 247), and defines art as their resolution (PA 30, 249).

That art resolves a tension that originates in (Kantian) philosophy, draws the philosopher and artist into intimate relation. In illustration of Bernhard Barth's point earlier cited, Schelling presents philosophy and art as "prototype and reflex for each other" (PA 6). The reflection is precisely that of the inverted mirror image. The philosopher sees in art "the inner essence of his own discipline as if in a magic and symbolic mirror" (PA 8). Here the philosopher resembles the absolute itself, which must see itself reflected in order to know itself. The inversion between philosophy and art is the same as that between the potences of the absolute, namely it occurs across the divide of the universal and the particular. Philosophy represents "the indifference of the universal and particular within the universal" (PA 45) and art, the identical indifference within the particular.

But the mirror art holds up to philosophy is more than a reflecting surface; it is magical and symbolic. Schelling understands the symbolic in relation to the schematic and allegorical, which analogically reproduce, in yet another instance, the relation between the universal and particular. When the universal moves to embody itself in the particular, the relation between the two is schematic. When the particular moves to efface itself in the universal, the relation between the two is allegorical. When the two movements so unite that the universal and particular mutually contain each other, without loss of either, the relation between them is symbolic. Symbolism reproduces indifference. A symbol does not simply mean what it symbolizes; it is what it symbolizes (PA 46). If art reflects philosophy symbolically, then the relation between them is intimate indeed. And this Schelling affirms. "Art enjoys the most immediate relationship to philosophy and distinguishes itself from it only by virtue of the determination of particularity or of the reflected nature of its images" (PA 29). As expected, the intimacy unfolds in a host of analogies. Philosophy is to art as ideal to real (PA 6), ideas to artworks (PA 11), ideas to gods (PA 42). The relation of part to whole in the organic objects of philosophy's study is identical to that in the works of artistic creation (PA 282). Indeed, so intimate is the symbolic relation between art and philosophy that the two will eventually pass into one (PA 226), even if for now the separation between them is bridged by the philosophy of art, which constructs the universe—philosophy's general ambition—"in the form of art" (PA 103).

Of course, art is simply one potence constructed within the whole of Schelling's philosophy. It is this fact that answers the potential objection to *The Philosophy of Art* as a test of Baeckian romanticism; the philosophy of art subsumes art under a broader religious (and romantic) philosophy. Or does it? A curious transition of tone informs Schelling's slightly earlier work, the *System of Transcendental Idealism*, when it passes from the Kantian-Fichtean reconstructions of parts one through five, to the final, brief, and more distinctly Schellingian philosophy of art of part six.[35] What was first a tortuously difficult, transcendental-genetic account of Kantian philosophy, becomes rhapsodic, a sort of doxology to art. Compared to what came before, this section is hymnal in its simplicity and patent religious vocabulary. It is indeed as "hymns" that several of Hoelderlin's and Novalis' poems are named.[36] Schelling himself also composed verse, and if part six of the *System of Transcendental Idealism* can be taken for poetry, then it could be argued, and has been,[37] that by the end of this work, Schelling has himself effected the transition from philosophy to art by organically capping his philosophical treatise with an artwork. When Schelling doffs the cap, two years later, in *The Philosophy of Art*, what now unfolds as the philosophical base to art is no longer a Kantian-Fichtean reconstruction, but his own philosophy of identity. Philosophy as grounding presupposition to art is, by the logic of presupposition, itself transposed to art. So the philosophical constructions of the first section of *The Philosophy of Art* constitute an artwork, too.

Now it can be understood in what sense these constructions are fantasy. They are informings of the infinite universe into the confines of words, if not quite a book. (It was Schelling's son who edited and published *The Philosophy of Art*, after Schelling's death.) It is the power to do just this and similar finitizings of the infinite that the imagination claims for itself, and that fantasy concretely executes. The result is the artwork, of which *The Philosophy of Art* must now present itself as an instance. Ultimately, neither philosophy nor art subsumes the other, because the two are one.

However, it was not as a fantastic mirror that Schelling related art to philosophy, but as a magical one. Schelling understands magic as "every effect that things have on one another solely through the medium of their concepts and not in a natural fashion" (PA 77). Art's mirror of philosophy is magical because it is not an effect of nature, but of Schelling's own unfolded construction of concepts. Without the construction, we cannot see, as Kant could not, the mirroring. But once our hazy notions of nature and art are fit into the places constructed for them, the mirroring is crystal clear. Magic is not submission of reality to illusion, but of illusion to reality. And so does Schelling tease Baeck once again with his ambiguous reality of fantasy.

For Baeck, inversive mirroring was the romantic's means of permanently securing redemption. For Schelling, inversive mirroring secures God's self-knowledge. But Schelling is not blind to the implications for human religious life of philosophy's reflex in art. Both philosophy and art offer intuitions of God. Philosophy does so through ideas, in every one of which we intuit eternity (PA 25). Art does so through visible and audible forms, in which we likewise view the eternal (PA 13). This twofold way to intuition of God comes as no surprise, since artworks are simply ideas formed into actual bodies (PA 98). If the intuition of God is human redemption, then Schelling has put inversion to good Baeckian romantic use. Baeck would expect art to function this way for the romantic; the impressing of philosophy to that service might surprise him, though less so as Schellingian philosophy unfolded its true, fantastic colors.

But quite apart from Schelling's own monistic religion of construction, art also stands in intimate relation with what more commonly goes by the name of religion. In what Schelling's son attached as an appendix to *The Philosophy of Art*, Schelling locates religion between philosophy and poesy. Philosophy may be practiced in a purely scientific way, without reference to the world, or with either of two worldly references, namely religion or morality. Poesy, in turn, is always with reference to religion or morality. Within this context, religion is, as already once noted, "speculation that has become an unchangeable objective view of things" (PA 282). The implication is that speculation in pure philosophy is a movement (as are the potences, which move in reverse directions into each other) while religion arrests speculative motion and freezes it. This inversion suggests the Baeckian romantic passage from feeling, through freezing, to dogma. However, the endpoint of this Schellingian reversal is not a mere component of religion, but religion as such.

If religion is morality's counterpart, then within Schelling's construction it would fall in the place of the first potence of the ideal, which is knowledge. Baeckian romantic dogma also presumes to the status of knowledge. But Schellingian religious knowledge is not dogma. It is, alternatively, one of two things, depending on whether the time in which it manifests is ancient or modern—classical mythology in the first case, Christian theology in the second. Neither of these is dogma, simply because neither is mandated by self-preserving institutions, but rather by the unfolding of the absolute itself. The Greek gods are the universal particulars that result from the ancient informing of the infinite into the finite; Christ is the departicularized universal that results from the modern informing of the finite into the infinite. Both the gods and Christ are translations into reality of the ideal movements of universal and particular, which invert across the dividing line between ancient and modern.

If art stands to philosophy as mirror image, its relation to religion is more complex. Art is not the mirror of religion (or mythology), but its objective manifestation (PA 8). The relation here is not inversive, for mythology and art both move in the same direction, from infinite to finite. Rather, art is to mythology as form to content. "Mythology is the necessary condition and the first content of all art" (PA 45). Mythology is an infinite domain (PA 50) that in art is formed into the finite. Schelling's mythological world cannot but express itself in art. The totality of pictures, statues, and stories of the ancient gods are their living reality.

Because the movement of the absolute within antiquity is precisely congruent with mythology's, ancient art can be the perfect expression of religion. For ancient religion, most broadly understood, is ancient myth, and the movements of myth and art are identical. Modern religion effects a breach in this harmony. For the movement of the absolute within modernity, from finite to infinite, is precisely opposite to mythology's. Mythology is fractured in modernity. The modern world has "no self-enclosed mythology" (PA 71). Art, whose movement follows the absolute's, is likewise congruent with mythology. And yet mythology is the necessary condition and content of art. So art, too, is fractured and self-divided. In modernity, the age necessarily fails to provide a comprehensive mythology.

Dante is the paradigmatic response to modernity's lack of a comprehensive mythology. For in modernity, it falls to individuals to create the myths that the age fails to supply (PA 74). This is only in keeping with modernity's beginnings in individuality, but the project of creating myths contradicts itself. For mythology proceeds from the infinite to the finite. It originates with infinity, i.e., the absolute, not human finitude. How can humans effect a movement that begins in the infinite? Art provides a way. For artistic creation is partially unconscious. Among the family of opposites united in the artwork are conscious and unconscious, analogously related as finite to infinite. The artwork, which begins in the unconscious, begins with infinity, and so moves in exact congruence with myth. Dante is not modernity's only artistic myth maker. Shakespeare, too, created a mythic world, as did several other individuals whom Schelling considers. All these figures are necessarily individual in that they resist the movement of the absolute into infinity. They hold the infinite to the finite, as though against its will. They are modernity's inverts.

The distinctive individuality of the modern artist, as opposed to the communal identity of the ancient artist, cannot but affect his work. And at this juncture, the artist begins to imitate the absolute itself. For the whole of known reality and ideality unfolds within the "subject-objectifization" of the absolute. And the modern artist, as opposed to the ancient, who is fundamentally anonymous, imitates this movement exactly. He puts himself into his created object. Across the whole vast array of the modern arts—in novels, drama, poetry (PA 230, 250, 222)—the artist becomes "truly identical with his subject matter" (PA 230). That is part of the self-enclosure of his self-created mythology. He is the absolute in microcosm, who by inverting the absolute's modern return to the infinite, allows myth and art to remain in a movement that would otherwise swallow them up. Schelling concedes about the modern artist what Baeck would insist upon about the romantic, that he cannot really perceive anything outside himself; cannot view nature, for instance, except in a subjective (self-referring) "emotional sense" (PA 92). But these inversive self-projections occur, for modernity, in a way Baeck would not have predicted—in defiance of God, not in passive submission to him.

It is no accident that the greatest exemplars of modern artistry are poets. If sculpture climaxes the ancient informing of the ideal into the real, poetry performs the same service for modernity's informing of the real into the ideal. Language is already more significant to modernity, in this endeavor, than the matter of a sculpted block ever could be. For modernity is determinatively ideal, and of all the expressions of reason, language is the least corporeal (PA 203). "Verbal art is the ideal side of the world of art" (PA 102). But all the potences of ideality are oppositionally real. Language is as high as reality can rise within ideality without ceasing to be real (PA 100, 204). In its indifference of real and ideal, language constitutes in the potence of art a microcosmic repetition of art, is itself "the most perfect work of art" (PA 9).

Within the potence of art, language already accomplishes the movement from infinite to finite that inverts modernity's movement in the opposite direction. Language, like ancient art, moves towards indifference schematically, not allegorically. As Hegel would also observe, language seeks the particular through the universal (PA 46).[38] If for Hegel, it was the "divine nature" of language to lead reason through dialectic towards the final conscious union of the knowing subject with its object, for Schelling it was the "sublime significance" (PA 100) of language that it, like the gods, simultaneously is what it intends. Meaning within language does not owe to any presumed objective reference outside it—it is, itself, already an objective expression of the infinite through its accessibility to the senses (PA 99)—but, as in all works of art, from the position of its parts within the whole of it (PA 101). The self-sufficiency of language seems to obviate the need of verbal artists, except that by the subject-objectifization of all modern art, the artist is projected into the language he uses, and becomes part of its self-sufficiency. That vanished distance between the artist and his medium is a simultaneity of opposites— here, of subject with object—that sets the stage for irony. And Schelling does call irony the form by which self-objectifization occurs (PA 231).

Baeck would only expect as much. Baeckian romantic irony is the means by which the romantic elite enjoys its self-enclosed fantasies. The role of language within Baeckian romanticism is to provide a self-contained space within the real world where fantasy may reign unchecked. A self-contained, self-referential language is the hallmark of Baeckian romantic artistry. This is also Schelling's understanding of language, though the work of fantasy within its bounds is more than play. Modern fantasy, of which *The Philosophy of Art* is an instance, employs language in the hard work of myth-building. The bulk of *The Philosophy of Art* is a strenuous exercise in art criticism, in which Schelling rigorously applies and reapplies the categories of his construction to individual genres and works of art, which become, if Schelling succeeds, gods in their own right. All the instances of inversion we have so far only abstractly encountered, between finite and infinite, real and ideal, free and necessary, subjective and objective, receive concrete esthetic applications. So, the hero of ancient tragedy, by freely accepting his fate "precisely at the moment of greatest suffering . . . enters into the greatest liberation and greatest dispassion" (PA 254). For the harsher the necessity, the greater the triumph of freedom in accepting it. The light in landscape painting, though inseparably bound to the colors on a canvas, "allows a higher kind of truth to manifest itself, . . . the true object, the true idea . . . " (PA 145). Sculpture joins the infinite to the finite (PA 198) and in modern drama "the subjective is portrayed objectively" (PA 250).[39] The picture, the sculpture, the drama, all immediately present in finite reality what they signify, namely an infinite idea. More even than esthetics, *The Philosophy of Art* is about revelation.

If so, Schelling has accomplished the task of the Baeckian romantic elite, to transpose esthetic categories to religious ones. That, too, is inversion. By this means, the Baeckian romantic artist can redeem even the ugliness and evil of life. Schelling notes that natural ugliness, portrayed in art, ceases to be ugly (PA 161) and becomes the occasion for one of art's time-honored expressions, namely comedy (PA 160). Comedy, as the art of reverse ideals (PA 40), is inversion to the second power, for it presupposes the inversive indifference of the real and ideal already effected in tragedy. Even before drama in the hierarchy of arts, architecture already anticipates the comic. It imitates its own real, functional ends nonfunctionally (PA 167), or the purposes of building, nonpurposively (PA 169). That is the first inversion, which it practices on itself. It raises inversion to a second power when it additionally imitates organic natural forms, such as plants or trees. The tree, as organism, is already a relative indifference of real and ideal in nature. The columns of classic art, Doric, Ionic, Corinthian, press organically purposive forms into nonpurposive uses. Natural necessity is freely transposed, so much so that from the Doric column, which merely "in a sense improves" on nature (PA 172), the ancient arts advance to the Corinthian column, whose capital "allows us to forget that it is yet subject to the laws of gravity" (PA 173) and so positively defies its own natural model.

In comedy, the same transposition of necessity to freedom occurs, only reciprocally. The freedom that the tragic hero portrays subjectively is projected outward onto nature, which behaves unpredictably; while necessity is read subjectively into human character, which is consequently deindividualized and raised to the universal level of a predictable type (PA 263). Comedy succeeds only when the ground of the predictable type in true subjectivity is visible to the spectator. For part of the comedy is in precisely this contrast. It is for that reason that ancient comedy at its highest, in Aristophanes, named its heroes after eminent public figures. The known and re-spected name held the place of a true subjectivity, over which was laid the inversely objective type. Here is the true inversion, which Baeck never acknowledged, showing itself however, where Baeck would have predicted, in the unseriousness of romanticism.

Is the result, in Schelling, a private redemption of the soul, in accord with Baeckian romanticism? Unexpectedly, the result is nei-ther private nor preeminently religious, but public and moral. Aristophanes' comedies could only be performed in a free state, for only such a state would permit public parody of its own leaders. The free state, in its very freedom, publicly mirrors the private freedom of antiquity's moral pinnacle, the tragic hero. It freely accepts the damaging critiques that are ever in store for it. But in the end, com-edy is tragic, too, for subjectivity, feigning objectivity, must finally accept the feint, which is no true indifference, and return the names it has borrowed to their true owners; but it is also moral, for the per-sons have in the meantime been subjected, parodisticly, through their names, to a limit-preserving public critique. Schelling's tragic comedy turns the tables on Baeck, and grants ethics the final word.

Completion

The Baeckian romantic elite secure their redemption by means of their ironic and creative arts. But the lesser lights of romanticism fall prey to the confines of a closed, authoritarian system, which Baeck finds typified in the dogmas, sacraments, and priests of the Christian church. Baeck believes romanticism must unfold inex-orably into a self-enclosed system that inverts its origins in un-bounded freedom and the infinite play of emotion. Early on in *The Philosophy of Art*, Schelling registers his ambition to bring his con-struction of art "to its final completion" (PA 19). And the Baeckian ro-mantic ideal of self-enclosure weaves organically throughout the whole system. Self-enclosure is inevitable in any monism, whether Schelling's, Stoicism's, or Spinoza's. The absolute act of affirmation is, after all, a self-affirmation. And the potences embedded within this act reproduce the same self-enclosure. Schelling explicitly en-closes a whole host of potenced determinations within themselves, including the universe itself (PA 34), cosmic bodies (PA 39), nature

(PA 65), the ideal world (PA 271), art and artists (PA 7, 8, 205), mythology and gods (PA 195, 196), language (PA 205), the color system (PA 124), epics (PA 216), and tragedy (PA 261).

What distinguishes Schelling's monistic self-enclosures from Spinoza's, is that they are not modeled after Euclidean geometry but, instead, the natural organism. Appropriately, *The Philosophy of Art*, despite its Spinozistic sequence of numbered propositions, annotations, and elucidations, reads much less like a Euclidean proof than like a messy birth, as indeed it was, having been assembled posthumously, by Schelling's son, many years after its conception. Schelling characterizes the organism as a "self-generated and self-repeating succession" (PA 130). By repeating itself within itself, the organism generates parts that are microcosmic wholes. Each part is, in turn, self-enclosed and knows relation only as its fundamental identity with the whole. By this means, Schelling attains a structured blurring of boundaries, with results highly congenial to the Baeckian romantic. Perhaps first among these is that nature is intellectually animated. There are "mysterious forces in stone and plants" (PA 78) that assimilate them to higher forms. Plant structures anticipate animals' (PA 172); and the whole earth is "completely expressed in human beings" (PA 159). Just as all of determinate existence inhabits the vanished space between opposites, which grounds the absolute identity of God, so is all difference confined to a space just about to vanish, which has in fact already vanished to the discerning eye of the philosopher and the artist. It is just because the distance has ever all but vanished, or just but vanished, that the particular, the organism, the repetition of self-enclosure, exist at all.

But the animism that results in the real world of the self-enclosed organism merely titillates the romantic sensibility; what thrills it to the heights of its hopes are the vanished distances that occur in the ideal world. Here, at last, is tamed that vexing condition of all disruptive change and decay, namely time itself. The taming occurs at the very beginning of the potence of art, in the first art of the first, and formative, sequence of arts, which is music. It is rhythm that subjects time to all rhythmic artworks (PA 205, 206) so that the work possesses its own time, outside what for Kant was so fundamental to any knowing act, namely the forms of sensible intuition. On the one hand, the subjection of time to objects within time is simply another inversion. But on the other, this is the inversion by which art, its creators and observers, attain the redemption of eternity. Rhythm is so significant a part of music that Schelling deems it "the music within music," alongside the other forms of music, namely modulation and melody (PA 112). Music organically repeats itself within itself, but also within the other arts, guaranteeing them all their "subjugation of time" (PA 205). The epic poem, like the perfect portrait, gathers what time has dispersed and shapes it into a unit (PA 146, 238). Music, united with poetry, produces song which, further united with dance—the union of poesy and painting—yields theater. Theater is the "most perfect composition of all the arts" (PA 280) for it reproduces in ideal form what sculpture produced in the real, namely the perfect indifference of reality with its ideal intent. Actors are animated sculptures, in perfect identity with what they represent.

These euphoric heights do not conceal from Baeckian analysis that they are, after all, heights, and so bear, however concealed, hints of authoritarian hierarchy. Schelling does not hide the hierarchical nature of his system. Organisms have centers that are more indispensable than their peripheries. The highest natural organism, the human body, is itself a hierarchy. The digestive and reproductive systems are "subordinated . . . to the highest, whose locale is the head" (PA 185). And within the head, the "most significant features" are the eyes and forehead (PA 187). The arts themselves are hierarchical by virtue of imitating the potences, of which the highest, after the finite and the infinite, is always indifference. Thus music is the art of finitude within the series of formative arts, since its rhythms are finitizations of infinite time that sacrifice time to the concrete, while sculpture indifferently unites the finite and infinite in the symbol, whose intended infinite idea is present in the actual piece of marble.

Schelling's tone is uncompromising at points. His concern is with the "highest manifestations" of art (PA 267), and he does not conceal his contempt for the ancient popular appeal of Euripides (PA 262). He is impatient with the diverse theories of art, and believes his own "absolute view of art," carried out "methodically," must finally banish the "capricious" (PA 7). He might wish to apply to his own system what he says of a good tragedy, that from beginning to end it "unfolds with complete purity without a break" (PA 261). Such stances so unaccommodating of what Kierkegaard might call the exception, may seem authoritarian, especially if the logic behind them, the logic of construction, fails to persuade. Surely Baeck is unpersuaded, and must take Schelling's absolutist views as all too typical of the romantic authoritarian.

But there are breaches in the Schellingian system's seeming perfection of self-enclosure. The unfolding of the potences has surprises in store. First among these is the relation between mythology and art. This is primarily a relation of content to form. But it does not follow the analogy-generating paradigm of real in relation to ideal. Both mythology and art are real indifferences within the ideal. The relation between them most resembles that between ideas and nature in reason's domain of the real. The potences within nature of matter, light, and organism are oppositionally ideal. Ideas are the idealities within nature that provide the content for its concrete forms, just as gods are the realities within the ideal world that provide the content for its particular artworks. Ideas and gods are identical, absolute opposites, after the pattern of the opposition between ideal and real, but this is not true of art and gods.

The form-content relation between art and mythology does not bind the two to necessary, inextricable interdependence. Each is indifferent, self-enclosed, and separately constructable from the other. This is not the only place in *The Philosophy of Art* where a paired form and content, in defiance of Aristotelian and Kantian dicta, are so separable. In his discussion of the plastic arts, Schelling notes that its forms, which are architecture, bas-relief, and sculpture are mutually separable in a way the forms of music, which are rhythm, harmony, and melody are not (PA 163). The relation between mythology and art occupies a position somewhere between the respective internal relations of music and the plastic arts. Like the forms of music, all of which occur in any one musical piece, art—the form of mythology—is always mythic. But unlike the forms of music, which simply repeat the three potences within music and so attain a perfect symbolic indifference only in the third, art, in perfect parallel with myth, is separately indifferent from it. Here art and myth are more like the plastic arts, each of which attains an indifference apart from the others.

But then, why does not art occur apart from myth? Because art, in itself, is contentless. Schelling constructs art as the ideal indifference of necessity and freedom. The mutual interpenetration of freedom and necessity is comprehensible as a pure movement. But the contents of freedom and necessity, augmented by a host of analogous determinations—action and knowledge, goodness and truth, consciousness and unconsciousness—do not, from out of themselves, suggest any new content to fit the new form. It was precisely the absence of such a content that was such a vexing lacuna in Kant. Kantian freedom and necessity inhabited separate parallel realms, so much so that the human being who seemed to join them had to be understood as a citizen of two worlds. Kant allowed for a formal interpenetration of freedom and necessity in human beings, but could supply no single content for the world they inhabited, much as he may have suggested, in the *Critique of Judgment*, that this would be the world of beauty.

It is mythology, in Schelling's system, that fills the Kantian lacuna. Art's need of content is "poetically resolved in mythology" (PA 490. Part of what makes the resolution poetic is that it freely occurs. When Schelling says that "Greek mythology emerged quite automatically as the solution to all those demands" of art (PA 53), he must be taken most literally. The automatic emergence is self-propelled. Philosophical construction does not press mythology into the service of art; it merely constructs a space that both mythology and art may together fill. And so they do. But all that compels their uniting in that common space is their mutual need. That art's need is filled by a determination that perfectly suits it owes less to philosophy than to what Schelling and other early romantics might call magic. And here is the first contingency that blocks any aspirations the Schellingian system might have had to an authoritarian self-enclosure.

Mythology also needs art. Mythology, as real content in the domain of the ideal asks for concrete form, which is what artworks supply. Otherwise, the gods hover above their own realizations. Schelling does suggest a sense in which this occurs, when he alludes to the "hidden" beginnings of mythology prior to its artistic form, in a nonempirical state (PA 52). It is as though the separation between mythology and art inhabits that vanishing space all divisions do, except that this division has always just vanished, so that we can barely conceive it at all. It exists only in what Schelling would later call the eternal past, a domain where things "happened without having really happened."[40]

In *The Philosophy of Art*, Schelling presents no permanent, presuppositional past. But he does begin to interpret time ontologically, in terms of the primal movements of being. Time as sheer movement is pure form (PA 18). Schelling calls it "the form of the informing of the infinite into the finite" (PA 109). This form receives various contents throughout *The Philosophy of Art*. For example, self-consciousness in a subject is simply the informing of its unity into multiplicity (PA 213), that is, its self-division or self-objectifization. However, time receives another characterization, too, as "the difference between possibility and actuality" (PA 213). This formulation, which closely resembles one of Schelling's definitions of freedom, is elaborated in *Bruno*. In the differentiated world, possible and actual are not wholly united. The possibility and actuality of a being that is not wholly indifferent (and this includes everything except artworks and their equivalents) manifest as its future and past, respectively.[41] The two accounts of time are not opposed. They both project a need. Where time is simply the form of the informing of infinite into finite it, like art, needs a content; where time is the difference between possible and actual, the need projected is for their indifference. If possible and actual are in analogy with infinite and finite, then the two definitions are combined when time is the informing of the infinite into the finite without indifference, i.e., with whole or partial loss of one or the other.

On this view, the division that time most significantly marks within *The Philosophy of Art* is between the ancient and the modern. It is not so much that time spans this difference, as that it receives no realization in ancient art, and perfect realization in modern art. This is because the informing of infinite into finite is perfectly realized in all ancient art; while modernity, which is characterized by the opposite movement of finite to infinite, does not yet know their indifference except in discrete, proleptic instances. The unfolding of ancient and modern in their given sequence is determined by construction. There is a sequence of moves in the absolute act of self-affirmation: first the finite is differentiated, then infinitely affirmed, and finally united with infinity in absolute identity. The trace of the finite is the first potence; of the infinite, the second potence; and their union in the differentiated universe, which copies the absolute identity, is the third. It is the trace of the second potence, or infinity, that sets the tone for modernity. And this tone, far from attaining the harmony of perfect self-enclosure, is strident, irrational, open-ended (PA 203).

This is the second break in the systematic nature of Schelling's system. That no "system of art" (PA 192) can characterize modernity, as it does antiquity is, ironically, a necessity of the whole system. This is why Schelling treats modern art through individual instances of it, rather than by genres. Each modern artist is burdened with creating his own system, which amounts to a mythology, and which supplies the content for his art. It is as though the modern artist anticipates the accomplishment of the as yet historically unrealized third potence, which will bring to the whole of its age the longed-for indifference of infinite and finite.

The "Oldest System-Program of German Idealism" heralds the onset of such an age. It believes there lie at hand, in the achievements of science, the makings of a new, epochal mythology that will allow art, now passed through the fires of the infinite, to regain its ancient calm on a higher level. *The Philosophy of Art* might construct such an age as the third in line, after antiquity and modernity. This would be the age of the third potence, or indifference, following the prior hegemonies of finitude and infinite respectively. But as though in imitation of an older Kantian reserve, Schelling refrains from formally constructing the epoch of the third potency. Instead, he offers brief characterizations of the manner in which a new mythology will arise. To the extent that modernity knows artistically renderable gods, they occur in history. History is the domain of moral action, which is ever subsuming the finite under the infinite ethical command. No art can occur unless the infinitized finite is returned to the finite with its infinity intact. This occurs only sporadically, in the work of individual artists. It will occur for the whole age only when modernity's gods of history are transposed to a universal medium of the finitized infinite. And this, within Schelling's construction, is the real world of nature. The "gods of history must take possession of nature in order to appear as gods" (PA 226). This is why the future of modern science seemed so promising in the "Oldest System-Program of German Idealism."[42] The content of science is, after all, nature.

In the meantime, there is within modernity one location of a finitized infinite that is more than merely individual: this is the church. The church must be distinguished from doctrinal Christianity which, a true child of the age, or, better, its parent, has eyes only for the infinite. Christianity aspires to negate the finite and succeeds in the Christ of the logos doctrine. Christian theology is another breach of self-enclosure, in defiance of what Baeck would expect of this, for him, paradigmatically romantic religion. But then, where Christianity fails the Baeckian romantic ideal, the church succeeds in satisfying it. The church secures its origin in the infinite sweep of doctrinal Christianity by grounding itself in a correspondingly universal reality, namely the poor and marginalized (PA 59). If the church can include the most outcast, there are none whom it cannot encompass (PA 67). Inverting the norms of nature (PA 66), which dominated antiquity, the church grows in decay (PA 67), and so instantiates the Christian teaching that the lowest will be the highest (PA 58). But grounding itself so universally, the church insists on particular forms for its daily life. At the center of these is the cult, which itself centers in the sacraments. The sacraments are true symbols because they indifferently unite the ideal with the real. The baptismal water is both water and cleansing spirit. This constitutes them, additionally, as artworks. They differ from the artworks of antiquity in that they are not things but actions.

The whole church unfolds symbolically from its cultic center. The sacramental participants are symbolic too. They are both human actors and the spiritual (ideal) body of Christ. Christ is the head of the church, and the faithful its body, hierarchically arranged from head downwards through the levels of clergy to the laity. For Schelling, the hierarchy of the church is necessary to it (PA 66). If nature was a hierarchy in the realm of the real, constructable upwards from the inorganic through plants and animals to human beings, then the church is the reverse in the realm of the ideal, beginning at its pinnacle in Christ and unfolding downwards to its universal base in all humanity.

The sacramental, hierarchical church was what Baeck took for the final unfolding of modern romantic religion. And Schelling's picture of the church matches Baeck's up to a point. The sacrament is a miracle, and the priest, a hierarchical functionary. But for Schelling, all art, of which the sacraments are merely instances, is miraculous for transposing the infinite to finite without loss of the infinite (PA 5,7). Perhaps the sacrament is even more miraculous for accomplishing this feat in defiance of the infinitizing tenor of the modern age. But, as against Baeck, the sacrament does not convert the miracle to finitude and leave it behind. The miracle remains in the finitized infinite, formed to water or wine. Nor does the priest usurp a former, private experience. He plays just one, albeit necessary, part in a "living work of art . . . in which each member had a part" (PA 65).

The church is a living work of art because it so successfully converts actions to symbols. And here the Schellingian church must in one crucial way disappoint Baeckian romantic expectation. One part of the concretization of the Baeckian romantic church was its dogma, or frozen feeling. But dogma is not part of Schelling's symbolic Christianity. All Christian doctrine is fundamentally allegorical, negating the finite. The doctrines that enable the sacraments are not, themselves, symbolic. And so in Schelling's church, Baeckian romantic feeling receives no permanently instating translation. The connoisseur of feeling must abandon the church for the private subjectivity of the mystic which, though the essence of Christianity, has always been held suspect by the church.

The church is a self-enclosed whole, but one that stands curiously opposed to Christianity. Schelling's account of the church anticipates a later, Dostoevskian reading of it, in which an institution-bursting Christ confronts the Grand Inquisitor. The church purchases its serene self-enclosure at the price of Christianity. This recalls Baeck's ironic church, which confines its true self to the Bible while openly preaching the opposite of biblical teaching. But the cleft between Christianity and the church is not ironic. It does not invert, but perfectly matches the self-divisions that characterize the epoch of the infinite. The church as Christian is more truly modern, in Schelling's sense, than Baeck could ever have predicted. But then, even its modernity is cut on the separating edges of the modern. Schelling lapses into past tense when discussing the church. The church is a drama "in which every member *had* a part." Schelling does not detail the decline of the church through the Reformation and Enlightenment, as Novalis does in "Christendom or Europe," but he hints at it (PA 70). Clearly all strains of inward pietism, as they developed out of Lutheranism, to say nothing of the radically egalitarian iconoclasm of George Fox, would undermine the esthetic nature of the church. What remains of participation in the liturgical church is the only modern counterpart to what the ancients knew in their dramas as esthetic acts of public, moral import (PA 280). The church alone supplies to the limited public of its faithful a universal world that is finitized in the "spiritual drama" (PA 65) of the liturgy. The church is the closing topic of *The Philosophy of Art*. But the closing words about it hardly betray any of the satisfactions of self-enclosure. The verbal arts of antiquity peaked in drama. The public drama of the modern church persists "only in an extremely diminished and reduced form" (PA 280). Schelling's tone is neither exultant nor ironic nor grandly despairing. It is, as one commentator notes, "muted, complex, even skeptical"[43] as befits one who has at hand the construct of a last, perfected age, but from modesty, or doubt, or deference to the incompleteness of the present, refuses to articulate it. Restraint was not an attribute of Baeckian romanticism. But then, how faithful to a genuine romanticism has Baeck been?

Conclusions

It is difficult to test an apologetic work by one that presents itself as scientific in the German sense. The tones of apology and science are so different that ideas in the one that illustrate the other are easily concealed. The subjective effusions Baeck would lead us to expect of romantic writing do not much occur in Schelling's *The Philosophy of Art*. The very ideal of indifference counts against unbridled, reality-usurping subjectivity. The two components of indifference are variously characterized as affirming/affirmed, ideal/real, infinite/finite, but these in turn are all expressions of the subject/object divide. Ever since Kant had set these two in correlative opposition, philosophy seemed itself in need of redemption from the consequences: a world divided between determining and determined, noumenon and phenomenon, action and being. Indifference, an inversive product of an oppositionally identical reason and imagination, comes to heal these splits, but less for the benefit of individual subjectivities than for the benefit of philosophy itself.

To heal philosophy's self-division is to secure God's self-knowledge. Art may be the mirror of philosophy, but philosophy is in turn the mirror of God. This is why philosophy is so all-encompassing. Philosophical construction is God's own self-knowledge, which the philosopher, a true particular within the absolute, absolutely finitizes in his simultaneously philosophical and artistic work. Such a philosopher-artist seems far removed from the Baeckian romantic, who is ever bent of his own self-enclosed redemption. But there are similarities. The creative artist is an idea within the absolute, which is the true first cause of all art (PA 84–85). But the same is surely true of the constructive philosopher, though Schelling does not explicitly say so. Philosopher and artist do attain something like the Baeckian romantic loss of self, that is simultaneously an absolute and self-enclosed self-affirmation. It is simply that Schelling does not present these individual loss-affirmations as the crown of his system.

When Schelling does explicitly consider the individual (*das Individuum*), he holds out for him no immediate prospect of self-enclosed redemption. The individual is a function of modernity's finite beginnings and ambiguous end, either short of infinity, where it longs to be, or embraced by the infinite and lost to itself. Art and authoritarian religion are the Baeckian romantic's cure of the unredeemed individual. For Schelling, the cures are philosophy and art. But these are hardly available to all. The (popular) religion available to the modern individual is simply art expressed as (liturgical) acts. But modern religion appears in Schelling as, if not moribund, at least much reduced from its former vibrant days. The age of the infinite is still waiting for the infinite to turn once more wholly to the finite. But at that point, modernity will have ended and a new age begun.

In the meantime, the models of self-enclosed redemption remain in antiquity, where Baeck, the religious classicist, would not expect to find them. If, for the sake of argument, he grants their presence there, he would expect Schelling, as romantic, to linger longingly among them. But Schelling does not. The classical receives its due, as half the location of the epochally unfolded absolute, but no more. In a striking reversal of Baeckian expectation, the ethics of infinite striving is shifted out of the classical, where, for Schelling it did not significantly exist, and into the modern, where, allied with Christianity, it sets the modern mood. But the mood of infinite striving is, once again, in defiance of Baeckian romanticism, dark, unsettled, and irrational. Darkness is as much a presence in *The Philosophy of Art* as Baeck would predict. But its presence there owes not to adulation of feeling, but to the very ideal of the infinite that Baeck, following Kant, found enshrined in the free response to the infinitely commanding moral law. Baeck correctly notes a romantic discomfort with freedom. But he speaks too hastily for romanticism when, following Luther, he lets freedom transform to grace. No such metamorphosis occurs in Schelling. Modernity suffers honestly in its freedom, while waiting for a future indifference of necessity and freedom not yet epochally realized.

Art functions redemptively in the breach, at least for those few who can create and appreciate it. But art is much less self-enclosedly divorced from ethics than Baeck would predict. Schelling comments early on that "there is . . . no realm of study that is more social than that of art" (PA 10). The social nature of the particular genres of art comes to the fore in ancient comedy, which is art's most explicitly public moral act. If modern art is less explicitly social, that is because it, alongside all modernity, functions under such a heavy burden of individuality. In a sense, all modern art is comic[44] by virtue of inverting the definitive movement of modernity self-effacingly into the infinite; a triumph of inversion that the paradigmatic artwork of the modern age alludes to by its very title: *The Divine Comedy*. Dante's social act, like the social act of all modern artists, is to create an art-enabling mythology where one does not exist. These acts of creation function redemptively for those who are able to receive them until such time as the infinite, having returned to the finite, produces an epochal mythology once more.

CHAPTER 4

A Reading of
The Star of Redemption
through *The Philosophy of Art*

Introduction

In Rosenzweig's commentary on the "Oldest System-Program of German Idealism," the author of which he takes to be Schelling, he staunchly maintains that we may no longer name Schelling "the Proteus of Idealism."[1] This epithet fell to Schelling because of the seeming inconsistency of shapes his philosophy took over the course of his long life. Rosenzweig's point is that if Schelling really is the author of the "Oldest System-Program," then the lifelong unfolding of his three greatest tasks—to construct natural philosophy, philosophy of art, and mythology—is already anticipated there.[2] At the same time, the consensus among Rosenzweig scholars is that Schelling's late work, especially *Ages of the World*, profoundly influenced *The Star of Redemption*.[3] Rosenzweig himself asserts that his own *Star* need never have been written, except perhaps for a Jewish audience, if *Ages of the World*, which is only a fragment of a projected but never completed whole, had been finished,[4] and he additionally notes in the *Star* itself that "we are moving along the lines of the later philosophy of Schelling" (SR 18). But if Rosenzweig's own Schelling scholarship is correct, and the later Schelling is of a piece with the earlier, then traces of early Schelling works, like *The Philosophy of Art*, should show as well in *The Star of Redemption*.

If by Rosenzweig's own admission, *The Star of Redemption* descends most directly from the late Schelling, *Ages of the World* would surely provide the sharper lens for reading Rosenzweig's work. But part of what defines the late Schelling is the extent to which he had left behind the interconnected thought-worlds of romanticism and idealism; so that his late work, applied interpretively to the *Star*, will not directly uncover Rosenzweig's romantic leanings. Even so, of Schelling's early work, *The Philosophy of Art* is hardly the most distinguished. It lacks the rigorously reasoned development of the slightly earlier *System of Transcendental Idealism*, and its critiques of individual genres and works of art owe too much to the late eighteenth century, especially the Schlegels, to translate persuasively or engagingly into the late twentieth. For all that, in the philosophically and religiously climactic role the work assigns to art, it is undeniably romantic, and so may serve the romantic reading of the *Star*, and its forays into art criticism offer more scope than the *System of Transcendental Idealism* does, for interpreting the several pages of attention Rosenzweig lavishes on the theory of art, music, and poetry.

Both *The Philosophy of Art* and *The Star of Redemption* are systematic works. Neither builds linearly, on a progression of static syllogisms, but organically, on analogical movements and perceived correspondences between seemingly disparate things. It is tempting to relate the titles of the works analogously. Both titles are constructs of two nouns, the first in the nominative case, the second in the genitive, as appears more obviously in the German original. The temptation is to draw analogies between philosophy and the star, and between art and redemption. To succumb to temptation is not, in this case, any grave error. Art does function redemptively for Schelling. And the star does work for Rosenzweig somewhat the way philosophy does for Schelling. Rosenzweig presents the completed star as a figure he has "geometrically constructed" (SR 256). And construction is virtually synonomous with Schellingian philosophy. Philosophy, for Schelling, presents within its bounds the whole of the universe, as the star, for Rosenzweig, does the whole of reality. The star is of course a symbol, as Rosenzweig explicitly calls at least its inverted half (SR 256). It is even symbolic in Schelling's sense, for once the points on which it is built are understood, it shows itself as just the movement of meetings that Rosenzweig has been discussing all along. Further, Schelling's philosophy and Rosenzweig's star are both mirrors in which the human sees itself, in the first case indifferently identified with God, and in the second, related to God across a genuine difference.

It is across the difference between difference and indifference that the analogy breaks down. The inverted triangle within Rosenzweig's star symbolizes reality, which is simply the relations of creation, revelation, and redemption. The upright triangle, by contrast, builds on the points of the prereal, protocosmic elements, which can only be called ideal in a sense that, contra Schelling, is definitively distinguished from the real. The star is not an indifference of real and ideal, which is precisely what the climactic nodes of Schellingian construction are, but, in Rosenzweig's own vocabulary, a configuration. A configuration is an oriented joining of differentiable figures. The differentiable figures within the star of redemption are the upright triangle of "ideality" and the inverted triangle of reality. The orientation of the figure is supplied by God who, stationed at the top, dominates.

If the concept of indifference is analogously represented in *The Star of Redemption*, it is by the relation between relation and difference. Difference and relation are logical consequences of the shattered idealist All. Rosenzweig is antimonistic because he believes in the fundamental factuality of three, not one. The three factualities of God, human, and world are both different and, in reality, related. In *Bruno*, Schelling took the highest indifference to efface the distinction between difference and indifference.[5] Rosenzweig might respond that the highest relation relates difference and relation. Perhaps this relation even approaches indifference. Difference without relation closes in on itself and can no longer know itself as different from an other. Relation without difference loses the poles across which it is strung, and collapses into a point or, at best, a circle, precisely the shape idealism takes in the end. Relation can only be between differences, and differences are not knowable as such apart from relation.

If Schellingian indifference plays itself out in a host of analogies, relation in Rosenzweig assumes as many shapes as there are pairs of poles to connect. Such poles occur as the pairs of active and passive within each of the three protocosmic elements; as the emerged halves of each of the elements, each partnered with one of the other emerged halves; and as Judaism and Christianity, which only together figure the truth that God knows. These three sets of relations are represented structurally by the three parts of Rosenzweig's book. Schelling's book, too, breaks into parts: the abstract construction of art in general, and the specific constructions of the individual arts. The difference between three parts and two is significant. The protocosmic first part of the *Star*, philosophy's domain, corresponds to Schelling's construction of art in general. The application of philosophical construction to specific contents occurs in both the third part of the *Star*, and the second of *The Philosophy of Art*. For Judaism and Christianity function for Rosenzweig like

artworks do for Schelling, as both concretions of construction and locations of redemption. But Rosenzweig's intervening second part has
no analog in *The Philosophy of Art*. That was, of course, the book of
experience, a concept that goes unconstructed in Schelling's work.
For Rosenzweig, philosophy is at least formally limited to the first
part of the *Star*. That philosophy, unlike Schelling's, does not offer
up an intuition of the real God, but only a concept of God that, on its
own, fails to reach reality. Rosenzweigian philosophy is, as it stands,
empty of reality, not indifferent with it.

Where reality occurs in the *Star*, philosophy has ended and theology begun; or better, the two are wedded as ground to grounded.
Theology for Schelling is Christian allegory. It is the body of teaching
that follows the effacement of finitude in infinity, which is the definitive Christian movement. Theology, for Rosenzweig, comes much
closer to playing the role that philosophy does for Schelling: it is the
understanding of experience as such, that is later, in the third part
of the book, formed to the specific contents of Judaism and Christianity, just as philosophy, for Schelling, is the understanding of the
universe as such that is, throughout *The Philosophy of Art*, formed
to the specifics of art. If Schelling offers a philosophical religion that
serves to elucidate genres and works of art, then Rosenzweig offers
a theological "religion" that serves to elucidate Judaism and Christianity. The quotes around religion are indispensable: Schellingian
philosophy offers a path to God through sheer ideas as they occur in
nature, independently of mythology and art, and so functions as a
religion, but Rosenzweigian theology, like Schellingian mythology,
offers no path to God apart from what Schelling might call its "objective manifestation" in Judaism and Christianity. Here, the analogy between art and redemption breaks down. It is not just art, but
philosophy also that functions redemptively within Schelling's *The
Philosophy of Art*.

But Rosenzweigian redemption, for its part, also refuses confinement to analogy with Schellingian art. Redemption in one of its
expressions is experiential and so belongs to the real world of the
second part of the *Star*. Schellingian art, as the real potence of indifference within the ideal might, on the basis of a shared orientation
towards reality, join up with this redemption in analogy. But then redemption has another, nonexperiential meaning for Rosenzweig.
And in this meaning, redemption, in utter defiance of all idealist aspirations, refuses to be understood except, in analogy with the protocosmic elements themselves, as a darkness to all human noetic
efforts.

So, much as the respective titles of Schelling's and Rosenzweig's books tempt us to analogize, we would risk what Rosenzweig reproves the fanatic for doing, namely succumbing to the temptation of correlating the as yet uncorrelatable. What Schelling's title may safely do is guide an interpretation of Rosenzweig's star: of first the upright triangle, then the inverted one, and finally the two configured together. These three figures correspond to parts one, two, and three of the *Star* respectively. Rosenzweig himself shows us this, in case we could not easily tell, by illustrating the title page of part one with an upright triangle, the title page of part two with an inverted one, and the title page of part three with the configured star—an unwitting parody, perhaps, of Schellingian architecture, which builds buildings out of newly and freely purposed natural forms, if not books out of geometric ones.

Schelling's title joins two terms, philosophy and art. Though the connective is the so intimate "of" of the genitive, ambiguously assigning both philosophy to art, as art's philosophy, and art to philosophy, as philosophy's art, the very sober Schelling divides the two so sharply as to suggest their intimacy is a paradox. Philosophy's objects are ideas, and art's are sensual realities. If we stop the movement of indifference short of the unity into which it would propel these two, and which would take us outside the relationality of the *Star*, then we would have two useful lenses through which to examine each part of *The Star of Redemption*. These lenses will focus the *Star* quite differently from the way Baeck's five-faceted romanticism did. Baeckian romantic art was the inversive alternative to religious authoritarianism. Read through "Romantic Religion," the *Star* shows the role of art on the Christian's eternal way. But now the *Star*'s esthetics, read through *The Philosophy of Art*, will appear in intimate relation with philosophy, a connection that Baeck's essay could not uncover. Schelling will both fine-tune what Baeck could teach us about Rosenzweig's understanding of art, and educate us, as Baeck could not, in the significance to the *Star* of philosophy.

Let us then read the *Star* through the concepts of philosophy and art, successively applied to each part of the work. We will read Rosenzweig's use of these concepts, and the additional concepts they subsume, against the backdrop of Schelling's use of them in *The Philosophy of Art*. Our concern is not to suggest, much less demonstrate, any historical influence of the one work on the other, but much more, in the spirit of Schellingian magic or Rosenzweigian miracle, to see to what extent the earlier work may serve as elucidating ground to the later.

Philosophy and the Protocosmos

The introductory first page of the first part of the *Star* is super-
scripted, "In philosophos!", literally: To the philosopher! "Down with
Philosophy,"[6] better captures the intent, or, in the spirit of a call to
arms: Into Philosophy! The translations are complementary: one
must enter into philosophy if one wants to pull it down. Rosenzweig
appears to move more deeply into philosophy in the *Star*'s first part
than in either of the other two. The third part will show how Christianity and Judaism figure the reality of revelation. But that part
cannot appear until the pretensions of idealism to, itself, reveal are
exposed in all their errancy; hence, to the extent that philosophy is
idealism, "down with it!"

Rosenzweig does identify philosophy with idealism (SR 4). But
he also deems the postidealist thinkers, Schopenhauer and Nietzsche, philosophers. In Neitzsche, the philosopher does not vanish
into his thoughts, idealistically, but conversely, the thoughts vanish
into the life of the philosopher (SR 9). Nietzsche continues an indi-
vidualizing "philosophical period" that began with Schopenhauer,
and "whose end has not yet arrived" (SR 8). Rosenzweig implicitly
assigns himself and his own thinking to this still incompleted period,
and to that extent he is as much constructing a new philosophy as
deconstructing an old one.

Between idealism and Rosenzweig, Schelling might fall in any
of several places. In light of what, judging from his commentary on
"The Oldest System-Program of German Idealism," was Rosenzweig's own intimate knowledge of the early Schelling, it is striking
that idealism is represented in the *Star*'s first part chiefly by Hegel.
Schelling appears more often as either the romantic philosopher of
nature (SR 45), or as the postidealist nonrationalist (SR 12) who,
like Rosenzweig himself, sought a way of understanding God's existence prior to his being (SR 18). The implication is that the *Star* is
not indebted to the idealist Schelling, the author of *The Philosophy
of Art*, for its understanding of either idealism or the successor philosophy of the new philosophical period. And yet already ideas from
The Philosophy of Art may be visible from behind Rosenzweig's
words. Schelling was much exercised in his late work, *Ages of the
World*, by a sense in which a God eternally past antecedently chose
his own being or nature. But already the much earlier *The Philosophy of Art* sought to construct God's being as the product of an antecedent act of divine self-division. And we have seen what large a

role unresolved irrationality plays in *The Philosophy of Art*'s understanding of modernity. The late Schelling's post-rationalist thinking
is incipient in the irresolutions of the modern.

On the other hand, *The Philosophy of Art* does allow the tension
between thought and being to resolve, idealistically, in the artwork.
And all such resolutions, esthetic or otherwise, are precisely the object of Rosenzweig's deconstructive work in the first part of the *Star*.
When Rosenzweig insists about the "nonidentity of being and reasoning" that "it cannot be harmonized by a third party which is neither being nor reasoning" (SR 12) he could, at least theoretically,
have had indifference in mind. So, contrary to what Rosenzweig's explicit references to Schelling might suggest, *The Philosophy of Art*
may serve to clarify both the idealism Rosenzweig contests in the
first part of the *Star*, and the new philosophy he begins to construct
there.

What, for Rosenzweig, is the problem with idealism? It is that it
is a "compassionate lie" (SR 5). It is a lie because there is no warrant
for the passage idealism makes from self-conscious reason to the
world. When reason takes itself for object, it moves in just the opposite direction of world-generation—it takes itself outside the world
(SR 13). The idealist presupposition is that reason, in itself, is pure
form. So, if reason becomes an object to itself, or content, then it
must project itself outside itself, i.e., generate a world. But, says
Rosenzweig, reason need not be taken to be pure form. If reason admits a content of its own, then the appearance of a content in it need
not be world-generating. That content is precisely itself. Reason that
doubles as subject and object simply wraps around itself (SR 12–13).

Of course, idealism's lie is that reason's self-projections generate
the whole of the world. How is so abstract a lie compassionate?; because it rationalizes what to human beings is the most fearsome
component of the world, namely death. Idealism comprehends
death. Death is the passing of separate selves. But there are no separate selves in monistic idealism. So there is no death.

Schelling's *Bruno* could stand in for idealism here more successfully than *The Philosophy of Art* can. For *Bruno* examines at much
greater length how the world unfolds out of self-conscious consciousness.[7] But the absolute self-affirmation, with which *The Philosophy of
Art* begins, does also generate a world, and so stands, as well, under
Rosenzweig's condemnation. Beautifully personified in the opening
paragraphs of the *Star*, idealism-identified philosophy stands with
"index finger outstretched" while "weaving the blue mist of its idea of
the All" around the human being, trembling in terror of death, at its

feet (SR 3–4). The image sardonically inverts Boethius' much older picture of the savior philosophy, who enters the *Consolation of Philosophy*, also at the start, and in response to thoughts of death.[8] Boethian philosophy is honestly compassionate; Rosenzweig's, only falsely so. It is striking how alluringly philosophy has been portrayed by its informed detractors. Perhaps Rosenzweig's predecessor in this is the medieval Jewish philosopher, Judah Halevi, whose poems he translated, and whose book, *HaKuzari*, also opens with a beautifully presented, but soon to be rejected, account of philosophical salvation. Certainly his predecessor here is not the early Schelling, for whom philosophy "encompasses everything" (PA 13).

The personification of philosophy as a compassionate liar suggests that one who internalizes its claims deceives himself. And here the writer who shows through Rosenzweig's words is Kant, who pondered both theoretical reason's drivenness to self-deception, in the *Critique of Pure Reason*,[9] and, in the more practically minded *Religion within the Limits of Reason Alone*, the "innate guilt" of humans who take their evil dispositions self-deceivingly for good.[10] It was Kierkegaard who, building on the challenge sin posed to Kantian ethics, let sin disrupt ethics and dislodge it from its premier place among the philosophical sciences.[11] And it is in these footsteps that Rosenzweig follows when he lets death disrupt philosophy itself.

But death does not simply disrupt the old philosophy—it begins the new. For *The Philosophy of Art*, death was the completion that, joined to life, yields indifference in sculpture. In the protocosmic *Star*, death is the first among irrationalities. Joined to nothing but itself, death first stimulates honest thought about the human. The limitation of death to one among several irrationalities is significant. Idealism's lie begins back further than its denial of irrationality. It begins in the presumption to have only one irrationality to lie about, or at least only one at a time. Hegel's *Phenomenology of Spirit* generates an abundance of discrepancies between reason and being, but they all follow on the single one, presented at the start, between "this" and its actual object. Hegel's originary irrationality, which ignites the dialectical flame, is epistemological. This is one of Rosenzweig's irrationalities too. We have already begun to consider it. It is the world that remains when reason, taking itself for object, abstracts itself out of the world. Such a world is not necessarily bereft of reason. But the reason that remains to it cannot be generatively active. For reason's activity is focused on its world-removed self. Death is an entirely different kind of irrationality. The humanly significant death is what remains when all subsuming universals, typified by the moral commands of practical reason, are abstracted out of human life. There is a third irrationality, too. Kant unwittingly indicated it with his "ideal of reason," which sought, through a God it mistakenly took for objectively necessary, an objective guarantee that the natural world would finally harmonize with moral humanity. Idealism prematurely harmonizes the two by collapsing the present world into God. So the third irrationality is what remains of God when all worldliness is extracted out of him.

In "The New Thinking," Rosenzweig suggests that his new philosophy builds on the ending of the old.[12] The three "irrational objects" (SR 19)—God, human, world—are abstracted precisely out of the old idealism, and are barely comprehensible apart from it. The protocosmic world denies epistemometaphysical idealism; the protocosmic human denies moral idealism; and the protocosmic God, religious idealism. Except for esthetics, which we consider separately, Rosenzweig's denials span the breadth of what, "nach geheiligtem Brauche"[13] (according to hallowed custom), make up a system of philosophy.

Certainly *The Philosophy of Art*'s identification of God with the universe illustrates just the sort of religious idealism Rosenzweig rejects. Rosenzweig thanks Kant for "showing the way" to the multiplicity of irrationalities (SR 21), as though the rejection of idealism must bypass the idealists themselves for its inspiration. But *The Philosophy of Art* already moves to undermine idealism by dividing ancient and modern up across a real/ideal divide. It is especially moral idealism that suffers by this break. Ancient ethics positively builds on the irrational, on the acceptance of undeserved affliction. And in what amounts to a critique of Kantian practical reason, Schelling shows modern ethics suspended over a chasm between finite and infinite it can never livingly bridge. But then, the modern is precisely the age of the irrational, ever tempted by its own demise in the infinite, which Schelling might well call with Rosenzweig "the gruesome capacity for suicide" (SR 4) and which painfully inverts antiquity's already painful enough inability to grant its heroes the peace of death (SR 79).

But the world, too, is split in two by the divide between ancient and modern. Antiquity's world is an infinite-surpassing nature, and modernity's, a finite-subsuming history. Even God is, for the one age, gods, and for the other, Christ. Schelling, as we saw, refused to construct the third age that would heal these divisions, and left us no consolation but art. Has not *The Philosophy of Art*, too, shown the way to a thinking that takes multiplicity seriously?

But the irrationalities of *The Philosophy of Art* are, like Kant's, endpoints, not origins, of reasoning. Rosenzweig thanks Hermann Cohen for starting to philosophize anew from the point of the "particular Naught" (SR 21). Cohen, idealist that Rosenzweig concedes he was, wanted by his logic of origins to deduce reality from nothing[14]; this is far from Rosenzweig's own project and he senses the confusion that might result from allowing such traditional phrases as "negative theology" to name his reasoning from the particular nothing of God. Negative theology culminates mystically in the vision of an absolutely predicateless God. By contrast, what Rosenzweig calls his metaphysical God is a pure conceptual abstraction, without reality. There is no living relation with it at all, mystical or otherwise. For the purposes of the protocosmos, the metaphysical God is nothing more than "ein methodischer Hilfsbegriff"[15] (a methodological helping-concept).

If reasoning is to proceed from a multiplicity of nothings, then reasoning, too, is multiple, for "he who denies the totality of being, as we do, thus denies the unity of reasoning" (SR 12). Three originary nothings ask for three different reasonings. Rosenzweig coins names for each of the reasonings, based on what they proceed without. Metaethics reasons about the human prior to its ethical nature; metalogic, about the world, prior to its logical nature; metaphysics, about God, prior to his having any nature at all. Together, these reasonings constitute the new philosophy of the first part of the *Star*.

In "The New Thinking," Rosenzweig calls the *Star* a system of philosophy.[16] Obviously, philosophy here cannot mean idealism. What it does mean comes into clearer focus when, in the same essay, he refers to the difficult constructive parts of the three books of the first volume,[17] or, within the body of the *Star* itself, to the "structured" meta-logic world (SR 53), which he has been hypothetically "constructing" by way of grounding our belief in the real world (SR 42). Construction here is opposed to creation, and constructions, to actual beliefs we hold. The connotation within construction of opposition to the actual asks to be paralleled with the connotation of potentiality within Schelling's construction of potences.

In her early commentary on Rosenzweig's *Star*, Elsa Rachel-Freund already noted the similarities between Rosenzweig's protocosmic elements and the potences of Schelling's late work, *The Ages of the World*.[18] Those later potences precede any actual being that they elucidate, but do not rationally necessitate it. The potences of *The Philosophy of Art* are more like mirroring shadows of the movements that cast them. They do not so much elucidate reality as ensure the ultimate identity of real and ideal. Rosenzweig does not put his protocosmic elements to any such purpose. But his constructions of them do bear several formal resemblances to these early Schellingian potences.

The protocosmic reasonings and the Schellingian potences are both movements in consciousness. Further, they are movements comprising dual components of finite and infinite, passive and active, content and form, necessary and free. Finally, they both yield abstractions that are matched to relatively concrete terms from ordinary language. The principal difference occurs at the concluding stage of the movements: Schelling's culminate in indifference, Rosenzweig's in relation. We have already once examined protocosmic reasoning for its role in inversion. Let us now consider it against the backdrop of the potences in *The Philosophy of Art*.

For Schelling who, in Rosenzweig's terms, grants only one element, namely God, a sequence of potences is determined within the absolute act of self-affirmation. There is first the affirmed, then the affirming, and finally their indifference. What corresponds in protocosmic reasoning to the affirmed potence is passive essence, the product of an affirming movement; what corresponds to the affirming potence is active predicate, which negatingly deflects from the essence all that it is not. The protocosmic negating movement depends on, though not by way of issuing from, a prior affirmation, just as the affirmed potence precedes the affirming in Schelling's system.

Rosenzweig's multiplicity of elements complexly reconfigure the dual determinations that are set in simple analogies with Schelling's affirming and affirmed—infinite and finite, form and content, free and necessary—but do not introduce any fundamentally new dualities. The single finite and infinite potences of God multiply into two divine infinities, two human finitudes, and one each of worldly infinity and finitude. The first of each pair is a passive essence: divine fate, human character, worldly kind, all of which are necessities; and the second is an actively negating movement: divine power, human will, worldly particular, all of which are free.

The origins of protocosmic reasoning in a triad of nothings reallocate as well the Schellingian form and content. Form and content have fairly simple applications in Schelling's construction. Forms are movements in consciousness between finite and infinite that yield the various contents—nature, knowledge, art—that Schelling discusses. Form originates in the absolute self-affirmation, where a division between affirmed and affirming is resolved in unity. In protocosmic reasoning, form originates in nothing. There is a logical connection between the originary nothings and form. For a nothing cannot be fruitfully affirmed, but only left (SR 26). One can leave it in two ways: by affirming its negation, or by negating it directly (SR 21). These movements are the protocosmic forms. But one cannot begin by directly negating a nothing. For what results is a chaotic affirmation of everything, which is scarcely an improvement over affirming nothing. So the beginning must be to affirm the negation of the nothing. Such a movement "circumscribes as inner limit the infinity of all that is not Naught" (SR 27). Rosenzweig symbolizes this form by the letter x. Now it is possible to negate the originary nothing. For the non-nothing just affirmed provides a chaos-conquering direction in which the negating action can move. What is negated is everything that is not the non-nothing just affirmed. Rosenzweig symbolizes this form with the letter y. The equation $y=x$, read from left to right, symbolizes the defining action the negating form performs on what the affirming form has affirmed.

Now the values of universal and particular, or infinite and finite, symbolized by A and B respectively, come to fill these variables, and supply content to the purely formal $y=x$. For Schelling, and idealism in general, the affirming form is always infinite, and the affirmed form finite. For a presupposition of idealism is that what is affirmed is bounded, and that whatever affirms surpasses bounds (for otherwise it cannot encompass the affirmed, so as to affirm it). So the definitive equation of idealism is $A=B$, which shows an infinite negating activity affirming a passive finitude, precisely what happens in the absolute act of self-affirmation. A consequence of the multiplication of elements is that form and content now interact in more complex ways. Rosenzweig emphatically excludes the idealist equation $A=B$ from the protocosmos, but he admits the other three possible distributions of contentful A's and B's within the formal $y=x$, namely $A=A$, $B=B$, and $B=A$. These equations, resulting from interpenetrations of form and content, symbolize God, human, and world respectively.

The idealist $A=B$ ultimately becomes $A=A$, for the finite, having emerged from the infinite, is transposed back into it. So $A=A$ might symbolize the Schellingian equation of God with nature, or with the artwork, since both nature and art are absolute particulars that repeat the divine indifference. The equals sign in a Schellingian $A=A$ would stand for indifference. In Rosenzweig's protocosmos, the equals sign stands for a relation between two contentful forms that are equally grounded in the same nothing. Rosenzweig's emphatic denial that either contentful form emerges out of the other (SR 28) is a direct rejection of Hegelian idealism, which phenomenologically traces the dialectical transposition of forms into contents and back into new forms. The grounding of the equated A's and B's in a shared nothing leaves their emerged equality free to take the form of a genuine relation, i.e., the spanning of a division between two separables. And that is just the form they take.

But Rosenzweigian relation, having pointedly distinguished itself from idealist identity, now begins to articulate itself in familiar, idealist terms. The old vanishing movement of idealism is performed once again, only now under the cover of differential calculus. Calculus is the perfect language for protocosmic reasoning because, as Hermann Cohen showed, it offers passage from nothing to something. The concept of the differential spans the divide between nothing and something. It is "the dimension as this loses itself in the immeasurable" and the "infinitesimal [with] all the characteristics of finite magnitude with the sole exception of finite magnitude itself" (SR 20). The differential is a finite nothing that indicates something, rather like a Schellingian potence that emptily occupies a just vacated space. The difference between the potences, and the dimension just about to lose itself in the immeasurable, is that the first merely traces what was, while the second still is. It is as though potency and differential are two different points on the same road of vanishing. The potency occurs after the endpoint of the vanishing, and the differential at any point before. Rosenzweig himself suggests this image when he adjures us to "capture" the negating form "short of the end of the movement" it undergoes (SR 31). Schelling and Rosenzweig are watching the same movement, only Rosenzweig stops it sooner. To some extent, Asian spirituality holds the place of idealism in the protocosmos. The idealists were familiar with the Asian religions which, in "The New Thinking" Rosenzweig dismissively dubs "the darlings of the moderns,"[19] and which in some points their idealism resembles. Within the protocosmos, Rosenzweig locates the Asian religions in the same place idealism would hold there, at the end of the vanishing. But, for Rosenzweig, there is no reason to privilege that place. The unvanishing (*Unvergehendes*) remains just where it was captured.[20]

What remains unvanished within the protocosmos are the contentful products of each component of the protocosmic reasonings. God's essence remains distinguishable from his capricious freedom, the human character from human will, worldly kind from worldly particular. But though the endpoints of the two poles of each of the protocosmic reasonings do not vanish into the other, they do effectively alter each other in reciprocal relation. Each begins to re-semble the other, to such a degree that the space between them takes on a single, determinate character. The relations that hover between their so anti-idealistically separable poles begin to show some familiar Schellingian shapes.

This very manner of presenting a determination recalls Schel-lingian construction, which understood all determination as repro-duction of relations between the points of absolute self-affirmation. But the mutual borrowings between the contentful parts of each pair of protocosmic forms is another instance of inversion. For the two forms, if not always the two contents, that constitute each protocos-mic element are opposed, as negative to positive, or active to passive. The relations between these active and passive poles are passive ac-tivities, or active passivities that are, furthermore, nameable. The passive activity of God is his vitality; of the human, his defiance; of the world, its individuals.

Schelling too constructed new contents out of inversive relations between old forms. Nature was the absolute self-affirmation's af-firmed component, which inversely subsumed its own affirming op-posite as light. The concept of vitality was not, to be sure, central to *The Philosophy of Art*. Schelling does construct the idea of life as "the joining of something infinite in itself with something finite" (PA 197), which would enliven all indifferent things, including God him-self. It is, perhaps, striking that Schelling and Rosenzweig take live-liness for a composite of opposites of finite with infinite, or active with passive, suggesting a common insight between them that true vitality comes from a directed, and so circumscribed, freedom. But any tracing to Schelling of the importance of vitality to Rosenzweig, would have to pass through Schelling's late work.[21]

The defiance of the human has more palpable precedent in *The Philosophy of Art*'s figure of Prometheus. Rosenzweig constructs human defiance as willed finitude. Finitude is the essence of human being; human freedom that affirms it defies the very conditions of finitude, i.e., powers greater than its own, chiefly death. Death is not the power greater than Prometheus; Zeus is. But Prometheus, also, affirms finitude when, in defiance of Zeus, he affirms human beings. Schelling himself asserts that Prometheus represents "the whole human race" (PA 55)—an anticipation of Rosenzweig's own defiance-defined humanity.

But the most extended anticipation within *The Philosophy of Art* of a protocosmic relation pertains to the protocosmic world. For here, Rosenzweig stops the formal movement of negating in three places before it expires in the universals of the world, namely at the point of the particular, the individual, and the category. The particular is the negating emergence from the nothing of the world. Its negativity is in its blind, chaotic directionlessness. It is only by moving towards the worldly essence of universals that it acquires definition. It is just this movement of the particular towards the universal (not from it, as in idealism) that substantiates the worldly equation, read from left to right, of $B=A$. Contra idealism, reason, symbolized in the equation by A, can only construct a world because the particulars it receives are already ensouled (SR 50).

Schelling and Rosenzweig employ the particular (*das Besondere*) to precisely opposite effect. Here they address each other over the divide of idealism. For Schelling's particular is an indifference, and these do not occur in Rosenzweig's system; and Rosenzweig's particular arises out of the world's nothing, which does not occur in Schelling's. But as Schelling's particular descends out of indifference, and as Rosenzweig's rises to receive "the criteria of the universal on its body" (SR 48), the two meet in the concept of the individual (*das Individuum*). In both systems, the individual incorporates the universal, but incompletely; in Rosenzweig's, as a means to self-awareness merely, when it wakens to its own difference from the universal; in Schelling's, by failing to unite indifferently with the universal. The two individuals reflect each other across the idealist divide. Rosenzweig's individual, gazing into Schelling's system, finds himself reflected in the modern artist, that sentimentalist who is so acutely self-aware. But Schelling's individual is reflected in the whole of Rosenzweig's anti-idealist program, whose primal threesome of individual elements has shattered ("zerschlagen"[22]) the indifferent All of idealism.

In "The New Thinking," Rosenzweig responds to what he clearly sensed were difficulties in the protocosmic reasoning. He advises the reader of the *Star*'s first part to let these pass for now; the real significance of the protocosmic elements does not appear until the end of the book, anyway, or, at the earliest, at the close of the book's first part.[23] That short section, entitled "Transition," prepares the way for the protocosmic deductions to unfold their contents into the wider world of reality. What will define that world are relations that are no longer self-enclosed, but that now extend between what were hitherto the separate elemental individuals. The power of that unfolding, the miraculous nature that Rosenzweig will want to claim for it, depends in part on the airtightness of the self-enclosures that precede. And now we can see that, to this end, Rosenzweig has applied a duo of concepts that has already once been aired in *The Philosophy of Art*, namely the self-enclosed and the presupposed.

Idealism had presumed to presuppose nothing. But only the presupposition of thought's identity with being allows passage from self-conscious reason to being. And once that presupposition is exposed, the passage is blocked. If there must be presuppositions, says the new philosophy, then let them be nothings, for out of several nothings something can arise. But by the end of the protocosmic reasonings, it is clear that the nothings serve less to generate our concepts of God, human, and world, than to enclose the concepts of them we already have in on themselves. It is only when the reader takes the protocosmic reasonings for presuppositionless demonstrations, presuming, like idealism, to conjure up contents out of the contentless, that he agonizes over the steps on the way. Let it be granted from the start that something "slumbers in the lap" of the nothing (SR 20), as Rosenzweig concedes when he admits that in reasoning to the completed three elements he was conducted by the belief in their factuality (SR 88), and we do no more than finish where we began. But that is just the point of the seeming reasonings—to separately encircle each of our concepts of God, human, and the world.

Of course, Schelling's system is rife with presuppositions that contain conclusions. The originary act of self-affirmation enfolds the entire universe within itself. But does anything enfold that originary act? With this question, which *The Philosophy of Art* does not ask, we draw nearer the nothings that Rosenzweig presupposes. The *System of Transcendental Idealism* does ask it, in its concluding pages on art, and responds, somewhat hermetically that, prior to that self-divisive act, there is nothing to query.[24] Could this be the early Schelling's anticipation of what Rosenzweig would say about his own nothings, that they are unlocatable unnameables, to be positioned, if anywhere at all, "before every beginning" (SR 26)?

The Philosophy of Art lays out two oppositionally identical self-enclosed worlds of real and ideal. But within the self-enclosures, it allows for fractures that take the form of contingency and incompletion. Rosenzweig systematizes fracture in the form of the three elements, and then encloses each off perfectly within itself. Now it is not just God who is enclosed within his own self-affirmation (as in Schelling), but the world, too, is "inspired within its own spirit" (SR 61), and the human, unable to register anything other to itself (SR 82). Unlike the Schellingian particular within the absolute, the three elements are separate from and oblivious to each other. And yet they mimic the identity that serves as the only relation between Schellingian particular and absolute. For each element claims for itself the definitive characteristic of the other two: human and world claim the divine vitality; human and God, worldly individuality; and God and world, the defiant selfdom of the human (SR 84). The protocosmos begins to resemble a Schellingian comedy. Fractured as it is, its sporting of idealist traits reads like parody. But then, it was Baeck who proposed a superscription for the *Star* of "the poetry which remains."[25] And all modern art is essentially comic.

Art and the Protocosmos

It might surprise first-time readers of Rosenzweig that he discusses art at all; what need of esthetics to a star of redemption? Idealist philosophy blocks a proper figuring of redemption, and so it, as pretender to an office it cannot hold, must be addressed at the start. If art must be addressed as well, the reason owes in part to Schelling. For it was *The Philosophy of Art*, among other works, that helped forge philosophy's link to art and a series of links, constituting a tradition of art-oriented philosophizing, that continues up until today. Apart from that, the tradition is very old, and precedes Schelling. The ideas of beauty and truth have been vying, now amicably, now quarrelsomely, for intellectual preeminence ever since Plato. Rosenzweig was drawn to the arts. His mother, reports Glatzer, "had a lively enthusiasm for art, for music, and poetry,"[26] and, towards the end of his life, Rosenzweig himself was writing reviews of musical recordings.[27]

Art first enters the German edition of the *Star* under the heading, "Aesthetische Grundbegriffe: Aussere Form." The succeeding sections, subtitled "Innere Form" and "Gehalt" complete the protocosmic esthetics, which copies *The Philosophy of Art*'s presentation first of art's general form, then its general content. Curiously, and no doubt due to sheer proofreading error, the first section, on outer form, goes untitled in Notre Dame Press' English version, though a blank space holds the place of the title. Art enters this English version surreptitiously and unannounced. It is not obvious that this is not, in any case, what Rosenzweig might have preferred, at least if we are to take seriously his resistance to naming the most recessed of presuppositions. For this short, highly abstract section on art's outer form is the most outwardly removed from the discussions it helps ground, in the book's next part, on the living arts. But Rosenzweig's express publishing wishes were not always honored.[28]

Outer form may be the outer limit of realized art's presuppositions, but it stands face to face with Schelling and reflects his views precisely. Here, at art's first entry, is the first statement of its link with religion. For Rosenzweig shares Schelling's view that art is essentially mythic. And if mythology was the content of Schellingian art, it is, for Rosenzweig, the protocosmic content of God. That God was a vital self-enclosure, divorced from world and human. But this is just what the ancient Greek gods were: "a life purely unto itself" (SR 34). The gods of ancient Greece live the construction that emerges out of the divine nothing. They personify the suspensions between caprice and necessity that constitute vitality. Because both the mythic and protocosmic god are self-containedly vital, neither is subject to death (SR 34). Schelling's gods too had self-contained vitality. As absolutes in limitation, each was an unrestricted whole among wholes, living out its "particular and free life" (PA 37). They were alive precisely because they were oppositionally absolute and limited, sustaining a self-enclosed tension of contraries. Despite its demise in the protocosmic reasoning, the old Schellingian absolute opposition echoes in the connection Rosenzweig also draws between contradiction and self-enclosure: the enlivened contradictoriness of the gods is a function of their self-enclosure.

But on one crucial point, Rosenzweig differs from Schelling: mythology is not the content of art, but a contributing factor to its form. Forms are movements, and the movement myth performs on art's behalf is precisely to conceal from view all that is not art. Such a formative function resembles the y-symbolized movements of protocosmic reasoning that negate all that differs from their corresponding x's. Outer form negates what is outside the artwork. But just as the negatings within protocosmic reasoning have their own contents, and do not convert, contra Hegel, into the contents of what they implicitly affirm, so mythology, as the outer form of art, fails to become the content of art. Art must mediate "something like a breath of that 'easy life' of the Olympian gods," but need not objectify it. Quite the contrary, the actual existence art mirrors is just as likely "want and tears" (SR 38).

Rosenzweig anticipates the outer form of art in the *Star*'s introductory pages, where he compares the contentful world of multiplicity to a painting hanging on a blank wall (SR 13). In that context, the wall is self-enclosed reason. Both the wall and reason support without generating the things they bear. The painting, for its part, excludes from itself the wall that bears it. As complete within itself, the painting becomes, with respect to the wall, "an excluding All." Mythology, as art's outward form, holds the place of the wall: it is the blank space within which the artwork may show as exclusive and self-enclosed. Mythology is another nothing. It stands to art as the protocosmic nothings of the elements to their realized relations. The gods of art do not wait upon it for their realizations—they exist, rather, to die in the twilight Rosenzweig assigns them to, so that in the emptiness they leave behind, actual artworks can hang.

The works themselves have an inner form that Rosenzweig discusses in the next esthetics section. Schelling did not distinguish between outer and inner form. For him, the universal form of art was uniform: the real indifference of real and ideal within the ideal. But Rosenzweig's dual artistic form mirrors the duality of each of the protocosmic reasonings. If outer form does the work of the y-symbolized components of protocosmic reasoning, inner form does the work of the x-symbolized components. And if the universally negating movement of the divine freedom set the tone for outer form, the affirming passivities of the metalogic universals set the tone for inner form. These were the universals into which the world's particulars moved for definition. The individual was the particular that a universal had begun to define. If each universally defined individual makes a distinct figure, then all the world's individuals, individually defined by the universals that exclude, intersect, and subsume each other, make a configuration. This is the inner form of art: "the thoroughgoing interconnection of every part with the whole, of every individual detail with every other" (SR 60).

If ancient mythology supplied a content for the protocosmic God, the ancient polis supplies one for the protocosmic world. The member of the ancient Greek city-state was also subsumed by a complex of universals, which took the form of powers, classes, or castes. Like the particular within the metalogic world, his meaning ended in a universal that located him within the whole, without reproducing the whole within him. Such a universalized individual, who failed to repeat the whole and who was indeed prone to "disappear" (SR 55) within his community caste, resembles, for all his antiquity, the modern Schellingian individual. And it is this individual that Rosenzweig takes in analogy with art, not the Schellingian particular. The ancient polis has "evoked the comparison with a work of art" (SR 55).

It has done so because the inner form of art configures individuals as the polis did, in subordination to wholes that surpass and even swallow them, rather than wholistically instating them. The details of the artwork vanish in their interconnections, just as the exterior of the artwork had vanished on account of outer form. And so it now appears that if outer form creates an emptiness without, inner form creates one within.

It is tempting to relate the dual emptiness of protocosmic esthetic form to indifference, as Schelling relates identical opposites. Indifference was, after all, an emptiness to the understanding. But Rosenzweig would remind us that by succumbing to the temptation of indifference, we forfeit the content that emptiness already holds in store. If we ask after the content of art's formal emptiness, we will not at first receive much help from Schelling, since his own candidate for that office, namely mythology, has already been left behind. But the use Rosenzweig has made in his esthetics, of ideas previously developed in metaphysical and metalogical reasoning, leaves the metaethical to supply the final component of art, its content, namely the defiant self.

The individual of the world was a stage in the development of a previously undefined particular. It is the B of the equation $B=A$. But the individual reappears in the metaethical equation of humanity, $B=B$, as the right-sided B, i.e., as a passive stasis. And this stasis undergoes a development of its own. It begins like a worldly individuality, as a member of a universal, here, the human species. As a member of the species, its point is to reproduce the species. So, at the onset of eros, and the completion of that function, individuality begins to die. If the human were merely worldly individual, this would begin the end of its life, as it does indeed do in so many animal lives. But the human persists beyond reproductive function. It persists in the service of nothing but itself. It is just this persistence that defines the self, as distinct from the individual.

Rosenzweig further defines the self as the relation between defiance and character. Character is what the individual becomes after it has succeeded the significance of itself to the universal, and has transformed to "Eigenheit,"[29] which Hallo translates "peculiarity" (SR 68), but which might be better rendered "ownness" (unbeholdenness to any other, including the species). Defiance is what emerged from the finite human will's affirmation of its finite individuality. The defiance that persists in affirming what succeeds the individual, as character, creates the relation of the self. Now the affirmation is no longer simply in defiance of finitude; it is additionally in defiance of meaninglessness. For it was the species that endowed the individual with meaning.

Rosenzweig's specific notion of character may echo what Schelling wrote about this idea with respect to Shakespeare, that "greatest creator of character" (PA 270). The Shakespearean character is also an individual who fails to carry the imprint of the whole. But what produces a so much more striking congruence when overlaid the Rosenzweigian self, is the whole idealist notion of self-constituting self-reference. For, as already once noted, the Rosenzweigian self *is* its self-consciousness (SR 68).

And now it appears that precisely this self, hovering between character and defiance, is the content of art. Rosenzweig defines content in this context as "something immediately equal, something which men do not share with one another like the common world, but rather something which is equal in all" (SR 80). It is as though a shared esthetic content, like the world, would produce a mediated equality, rather than an immediate one. And the forms of art have created a space that precludes mediation. A mediator connects separable units. But the outer form of art has blocked the path the artwork might have had to its exterior, and the inner form has swallowed up the artwork's units of separate detail into relation. So the content of art must present itself immediately, through nothing but itself.

But then, an absolute incomparable is incomprehensible. If art is to be humanly comprehended, its immediate content must be communicable across distances; but not through a mediator; which is to say it must somehow already exist in whomever is receiving the communication. Not only the artworks themselves, but human beings must bear the content of art within them. But the only content all human beings equally bear is their own self, honed to an ownness that precludes all others. If art is to have an unmediated, communicable content, it can only be this. The human self, as content of art, suspended between two forms of nothing is indeed, as Rosenzweig calls it, "a straight line leading from one unknown to another" (SR 72), an image that recalls the two chance points of beginning and end, between which Schelling locates all epic narratives (PA 215).

Rosenzweig's concept of a self that is "condemned to silence in man and yet is everywhere and at once understood" (SR 80) has deeper roots in Kierkegaard and Kant, than in the early Schelling. Kierkegaard had described human knowledge of original sin in similar terms, as something that "each man understands solely by himself."[30] And Kant characterized religious mystery as that "which may indeed be known by each individual but cannot be made known publicly, that is, shared universally."[31] Such similar phrasings apply to such disparate objects—mystery, sin, and self. Art is eerily illumined by such darkly lit companions as these.

The contentful precedent of Rosenzweig's artistic content is the hero of ancient tragedy, whose self was the self-enclosed content of art (SR 73). It was this self, depicted on stage, that woke the spectator to his own self-awareness, by stimulating feelings that drew attention inward. But the dramatic actor addresses only himself, not the spectator. And the spectator is alone with his own feelings. "Everyone remains by himself, everyone remains self" (SR 81). And so the understanding that occurs "at once" is occasioned but not mediated by the artwork of the drama.

For Schelling, all artworks are, by their indifference, self-enclosures. But the hero of ancient tragedy further enclosed the action of the drama within his own character (PA 258), as occurs, too, in Rosenzweig's account. Ancient drama occupies a middle ground between the contentful realizations of art's form—Greek mythology and the ancient polis. For, from Rosenzweig's standpoint, as against Schelling's, in no sense did the gods ever really exist, while the polis was peopled by real living beings. Drama, on the other hand, realistically represented what Rosenzweig would consider unreality. Reality is relation, and it was precisely the aim of ancient tragedy to depict its absence. This it accomplished superbly, or at least the works of Aeschylus did. Rosenzweig shares Schelling's lower opinion of the later dramatists, especially Euripides, though not, with Schelling, because they depicted character feelingly, but because they depicted it relationally (SR 77). But these playwrights and the actors who performed their plays, as well as the spectators who in watching them knew self-enclosed selfhood, were all members of the polis, too. They had a real life of relations outside the world of art. At this point, Rosenzweig's rejection of Schelling's idealism shows up most importantly. For in Schelling's scheme, ancient art was precisely real world. It was the unique assignment of all antiquity to realize the ideal realistically, but mediated through the ideal, and this it accomplished by its artworks. These artworks, in their congruence with the ancient movement of being, expressed that world perfectly. Monism obstructs Rosenzweig's quite different definition of reality as relation; within monism, ideality is as much relation as reality is—or as little, since both are swallowed up in the single absolute act of self-affirmation.

When the Schellingian actor of antiquity removed his mask, he stepped out of a perfectly realized relationlessness into an imperfect one. If anything, the drama he momentarily lived was realer. But the same actor, through Rosenzweig's eyes, stepped from perfectly relationless unreality into relational reality. Antiquity is not the realized real, confronting an oppositionally modern ideal. Modernity crossing backward to antiquity does not cross any boundary of the real at all. Modernity and antiquity are equally and uniformly real. The ancients knew the reality of relation; for example, the relation with God when they tremblingly approached him "on the trails skirting Olympus."[32] All that they lacked was an adequate construct or figure of relation. The pagan rites were truly "nothing but stupendous error."[33] But what paganism did have, in its mythology, was part of a construct that effectively predicts reality. For reality is grounded in self-enclosure. And all the ancient Greek expressions of the forms and content of art—myth, polis, drama—perfectly figured self-enclosure, that bifurcating equality of two separables in one.

It is not only the protocosmic nothing whose significance is first revealed only after it has been introduced, but art's too. Art, like the three unreal elements, takes the prefix "proto-". By the unmediated understandings it occasions, it is protolanguage. If the protocosmic elements become relational in reality, then art becomes the language through which they relate. Art predicts the language of reality.

But from what vantage point does art predict? Art's vantage point is unreality. And that location, prior to the real, is only visible as such from the standpoint of the real. The inhabitants of reality, Rosenzweig and his readers, project back from reality to an antecedent. Rosenzweig names this antecedent the protocosmos, but this says no more of it than that it precedes the cosmos. Here Schelling's movements of potences may help illumine the world of art. For though Rosenzweig cannot relate the ancient to the modern across a divide between the real and ideal, he can relate reality to philosophy across a divide between the relational and nonrelational. The manner of relating across the divide is the same for both, namely inversion. Art belongs to the world of philosophy, or ideality, as Rosenzweig might admit in agreement with Schelling, but from this vantage point it simply predicts the real, by its inversive relation to it. Once again Rosenzweig stops the same movement Schelling follows earlier than Schelling does. One half of a divide moves towards the other by the same inversive track, but is arrested before the point of identity is reached. This Schelling might say yields an "unchangeable objective view of things," or even, in Baeck's words, a "frozen" view, for it stops philosophy's natural course short of its natural end. It yields what Schelling would call, descriptively—but which Rosenzweig would call, pejoratively—religion. In fact, says Rosenzweig, the halt to philosophy preserves reality. A freezing does occur, but precisely in the place where it belongs, in the place of presupposition to reality. Philosophy and art, considered for themselves, are both frozen in permanent states of presupposition. The climactic peaks of Schelling's system are presuppositions in Rosenzweig's. Philosophy and art are potences to the real, and can themselves become real only by groundfully vanishing into it. Everyone should once philosophize, says Rosenzweig.[34] But having done so, they must realize that the product of their thinking is at best merely ("bloss") a system of philosophy.[35] If Baeck's superscript to the *Star* fits—"the poetry which remains"—then Rosenzweig might equally have said, the product is merely a work of art. What dwarfs these achievements into merenesses? Simply, the real world of the cosmos.

Philosophy and the Cosmos

Though the inversive passage from protocosmos to cosmos is not necessitated, it does not go unheralded. For all its abstractness, or perhaps, because of it, the whole of the protocosmos evokes in those whom Rosenzweig has brought to see it, the terror and compassion generally reserved for observers of its dramatized metaethical element. It is not simply the imagery of death and darkness that has this effect. "Protocosmos" is perhaps not so innocent a name after all. The German "Vorwelt" may also be translated as primeval or antediluvian world, a setting that has sometimes served the horror genre of art. Rosenzweig evidently aims for this effect when he shows his metaethical hero confronted by a strange, Munchlike world in which screams alternate with silences (SR 77). Part of what troubles about the protocosmos is its ambiguous status. Rosenzweig somewhat airily allows that we may take it either for a world of "mysterious . . . occult powers" or as a context for "stages on the road of . . . cognitive construction" (SR 88). Prior to the presentation of the cosmos that it grounds, the protocosmos is open to being taken in any of several ways.

But it is not just the obscurity of the protocosmos that asks for a complementing and clarifying cosmos. Rosenzweig virtually animates his protocosmic elements with the psychology of a self-defeating megalomania. "Each part posits itself monistically as the whole" (SR 84). But none are in fact the whole, so all the positings fail. The elements seem to know this. The world set free from reason's all-generating domination, for instance, suddenly finds its body exposed "to whatever may have happened to it," without "protection" against the God who, it transpires, will providentially create it (SR 15). The elements are vulnerable, and here the terror felt on their behalf becomes compassion. They affect a self-sufficiency they do not really have. It is as though each of the elements, disemboweled of the aspects of the other two it had once unhealthily consumed, and closed over its own true shape, recalls a former largeness, and wants to find some, now, healthy way back to it. But separated now in their own spheres, they do not know how to relate to each other. Rosenzweig paints a frightful picture of chaotic vyings for "the gigantic proportions of the All" (SR 87), of bloated and blurred boundaries (SR 84), of rotating wheels (SR 85) that never come to rest, as if the protocosmos were a supernatural game of chance that holds its players in a warped eternity of unresolved suspense.

Not only do the elements not relate to each other; they do not understand the concept of relation at all. How could they, when the philosophical masters of their fate, from Thales to Hegel, had forced each, alternately, to know the other only by consuming it? The terrors of the protocosmos effect a necessary purge. The passage from protocosmos to cosmos is a passage to relation.

The Schelling who lies behind this dramatic picture of primeval striving is several years older than the author of *The Philosophy of Art*. Schelling's late work, *Ages of the World*, describes a chaos of potences much like Rosenzweig's chaos of elements, even down to the image of the "rotating wheel" of possibility (SR 85).[36] Rosenzweig uses Schelling's image, but sparingly, for Schelling's chaos presumed to more ontological status than it deserved (SR 26). The late Schelling's location of the competing potences in God's eternal past evokes a theosophical tradition that does not directly serve Rosenzweig's purpose. That purpose, in part two of the *Star*, is to do for relation what the early Schelling did for indifference in *The Philosophy of Art*: explicate and apply it. But where Schelling's explication is philosophy, Rosenzweig's merely presupposes it.

Rosenzweig states explicitly that "the science we are practicing" (SR 140) in part two of the *Star* is theology, not philosophy. In time, some thinkers would use the phrase "dialogical philosophy." But Rosenzweig is still too close to the old philosophy, namely idealism, to be able to regard genuine relation as anything but nonphilosophical. He does not title his commentary on the *Star*, The New Philosophy, but, more boldly, "The New Thinking," as though all philosophy belongs irrevocably to the old. Perhaps he is bolder still to deem the new thinking a theology. God is after all only one of the partners in the relations that part two narrates. But it is not because of God's part in relation that part two is theology: it is because all genuine relation is miraculous, and miracle is theology's, not philosophy's, "favorite child" (SR 93).

Philosophy is not thereby banished from the cosmos. The new philosophy had reasoned three ways to separation. Philosophy passes into part two as the presupposition of theology. For the relations of theology presuppose an unsubsumable (but bridgeable) separation. Against the backdrop of idealism, the logical problem of relation reverses that of change. It was a philosophical conundrum how sameness could occur over difference; while relation presupposes difference across the sameness of connection, a difference that the idealism of indifference (but also of Hegelian dialectic) ultimately sacrifices to monism. But if, behind the connections theology articulates between the elements, the separations philosophy constructed are still visible, then the problem of relation is solved.

The separate elements remain visible beneath their relations because the relations are themselves composed of the elements' own components. Those components were oppositional movements of passive affirmation and active negation, that met in parity some distance short of identity. The same components constitute the relations, only inverted and reconfigured. What was passively affirmed in God by his own negating movement, now actively seeks affirmation from outside. What within the human element actively affirmed the human's own passive character, now passively affirms an object outside. The active need of God matches what the human passively supplies. But beneath God's need, his self-contained essence is visible. For the need is the essence, turned inside out. The same is true of the human. Beneath the face it passively turns to God, its active denial of all outside itself is visible. For the turning is the denial in reverse. The inversion of the affirmed divine and the negating human, reconfigured together in a parity that stops short of identity, is the relation of revelation. The distance between the protocosmic components of God, that previously allowed for an encircled self-enclosure of God, now repeats as the distance between the divine need and human supply that, brought together, constitute revelation.

Creation and redemption are similarly reconfigured inversions. What negated in God, on behalf of himself, now affirms on behalf of another. What was affirmed in the world, by its own negating movement, now seeks affirmation from outside. That meeting of need and supply is creation. What was affirmed in the human by its own negating movement, now seeks affirmation from outside. What negated in the world, on behalf of itself, now affirms on behalf of another. And that meeting is redemption. As before, what was given within now seeks to be supplied from without. What supplied itself, now supplies another. What was positively valenced within, by the rest it enjoyed, is negatively valenced without, by the need it has. What was negatively valenced within, by its self-distinguishing from all otherness, is positively valenced without, by affirming the other. Through each relation, one component from each of two of the former self-enclosures is visible. Relation is the joint product of inversion and reconfiguration. The remapping of the component movements of the elements outward creates connection. The identity through inversion of each remapped movement with its protocosmic predecessor reveals the separate elements beneath the connections. And the connecting of the visibly distinct is relation.

The star of redemption is the climactic presentation of the elements beneath their relations. The points of the upright triangle are the protocosmic elements. The relations between them are figured by the inverted triangle whose corners occur between the protocosmic points. The inverted triangle of relations is superimposed over the upright one of the elements, but the elements are clearly visible beneath.

Rosenzweig's tripartite construction of relation might draw from the Baeckian observer the same forthright "Fantastic!" that Schelling's construction of art did. Evidently, Rosenzweig himself continues even after the end of part one to hear enough echoes of idealism in his work to pointedly distinguish the two. The most important of these differentiations is surely between relation and Hegelian synthesis, which makes of two relata a thesis of subsequent synthesis, and so continuously undercuts the separation within relation (SR 230). But "no dialectical process is arrived at" within the new thinking (SR 230). In another contrast, Rosenzweig notes that idealism's only content is its own form (SR 105); while for the new philosophy, content, which is differentiably finite and infinite, is fashioned to differentiably positive and negative forms. Finally, for idealism, the world is "rationally comparable to its origin" (SR 136) while for the new philosophy, a gap unnegotiable by sheer reason separates the real world from its protocosmic origin. Though it is Hegel whom Rosenzweig overtly distances, Schelling's idealism falls equally within range of these critiques. Indifference undercuts relation as much as Hegelian dialectic does, albeit less elegantly and persuasively. Form and content name, for Schelling as for Hegel, two sides of the same ultimately reunited absolute act; and the world is, simply, the rationally comparable, indeed rationally identical, content of that act.

But Rosenzweig, who understood the impact of perspective on the appearance of truth, might well grant that outside his own anti-idealist perspective, his differences from idealism are overshadowed by the similarities. *The Philosophy of Art* and *The Star of Redemption* both build on tripartite inversive movements. Inversion functions the same way for both, to found difference in sameness. It is simply that in one case, the difference is taken seriously, and in the other case not. Both systems offer up structured placements that receive, hopefully illuminatingly, a host of imprecise but humanly important ideas. Where these placements are analogously situated within the system, the ideas that fill them are set in analogy, too. For example, natural organisms and artworks are analogously related in Schelling by their placements at nodes of indifference. And these placements speak to the puzzle of art's provocative similarity to nature. Rosenzweig's divine and human love are both momentary externalizations of a passive self-containment that, externalized, must fall without the support it inwardly enjoyed, but that, successively whole in each moment of falling, never ceases to fall, whether or not received by an other and borne. That both loves proceed by retraction, supporting through the act of seeking support, may point up an essential feature of love.

Schelling's system is closest to Rosenzweig's, however, in the place it assigns to unsubsumed contingency, that is, contingency that is not converted to necessity. Schelling's concern with freedom does not burst unannounced into his late work. *The Philosophy of Art* already anticipates that turn. The anticipation does not occur in the place Schelling specifically constructs for freedom, as the potence of the real within the ideal. For this freedom is ultimately sacrificed in the artwork. It occurs in the unnecessitated but perfect matching of need and supply between mythology and art.

Rosenzweig considered it an idealist ploy that "in the process of being thought about, the contingent changes itself into something necessary" (SR 12). He especially guarded against it in his own system, insisting that, though the shape of relation is grounded in the protocosmos, the fact of relation is not (SR 255). Relation itself is groundless. That it occurs at all is miracle. Once the miracle has occurred, it shows itself as the fulfillment of a promise. The components of the protocosmic elements bore the promise in their self-enclosed relations of divine vitality, human defiance, and worldly individual. But the promise the components carry is not revealed as promise until they reappear, inverted and reconfigured, in the relations of reality. Before then, the protocosmos is enigma. This is why, before the revelation of part two, Rosenzweig could indifferently allow for different viewings of the protocosmos.

Schelling, too, allows for miracle. But for him, the meaning was different. Indifference itself was miraculous for uniting opposites in one. But indifference effaced all contingency in its neither/nor of freedom and necessity. And it seems to occur almost in defiance of prediction, rather than fulfillment of it. That certainly holds true for the sacramental miracles of Christianity, which unexpectedly preserve the finite in the infinite, when Christianity itself would sacrifice all finitude to infinity. It is not Schelling's miracle that anticipates Rosenzweig's, but his magic. The meeting of art and mythology in the real potence of indifference within the ideal owes to the magic of the system, which erects a place for both to fill together, without compelling either to enter it. Magic is the unnecessitated meeting of need with supply in a space constructed by concepts. A reciprocally matched need and supply is something like a fulfilled promise. The shape of the need predicts the supply that will meet it. That the meeting occurs is fulfillment.

Rosenzweig disparages the idea of magic. But what he means by magic is much closer to Schelling's miracle. Islam affirms magic when it exults in the inexplicability of the Koran (SR 116). So magic is inexplicable, just as indifference is, at least to the understanding. Insofar as explanation situates effects within chains of causes, indifference cannot be explained. It can only be intellectually intuited. So indifference may well stand with Islamic magic outside Rosenzweig's cosmos. But Schellingian magic may be at least partially admitted. For its matchings of need to supply resemble the miraculous, because unforcedly predicted, matchings of divine need to human supply, human need to worldly supply, worldly need to divine supply in Rosenzweig's system.

A curious feature of Rosenzweigian miracle is that it cannot be hoped for. It could be hoped for only if its prediction were known before its fulfillment. But the fulfillment shows its predictive ground only after it has occurred. Thus we begin within the miracle and only retrospectively project back its ground. The protocosmos is enigmatic only to those who linger there. In philosophical books, especially, earlier sentences depend on later ones for their meanings.[37] This is why Rosenzweig encourages his readers to rush, uncomprehendingly if need be, through the *Star*'s first part.[38]

But the impregnability of the protocosmos from a standpoint within it, and the clarity it attains from a standpoint without, points up another anti-idealist feature of the new thinking: it is unsublatedly perspectival. Hegel initiated humans to the one absolute viewpoint or, what amounts to the same thing, a single absolute finally knows itself. For Rosenzweig, there are not only three vantage points on cosmic reality—the divine, the human, the worldly—but three tenses in which it occurs—past, present, future. Thus each participant in the three relations of reality perceives them differently. A striking instance is the case of worldly redemption. God as creator endowed the world with laws of growth. These are the universal categories of the protocosmic world, turned outward and supported by God's now other-directed care. But it is only the kinds of things that receive the divine assurance of growth, not the individuals within them. The human act of love towards the worldly individual is, for the world, the "great surprise" that, once experienced, constitutes a law of growth in its own right: to "move towards man's act of love" (SR 240). What the world receives as surprise and incorporates as law, the loving human offers spontaneously on command—God's command to "Love me!"—and unconscious of its effects. It is as though the relation of redemption is pieced together from its two poles which, looking down the line of the same relation from opposite ends, see different views. The human soul cannot see the law of growth it inspires and that moves the world its way, and yet it must unconsciously presuppose it. For the soul "demands" that its love ensoul, for which purpose the world supplies a body. If love, which is all self-denial, demands, it must be from channeling the divine love that occasioned it. It is only God, whose creative provision for the world includes the human love he revealingly commands, who sees the redemptive relation whole, from the middle outward to the poles. But then, he does so by virtue of not directly participating in it.

We, Rosenzweig's readers, are ourselves assigned a place in the construct of the star that fixes our perspective. We are beloved souls, stationed, opposite God, at a pole of revelation but, as instances of the human kind, also components of the very creation we are directed, through revelation, to redeem. We experience the fullness of revelation in the divine command to love, but only parts of creation and redemption. These whole and partial experiences constitute our experience of time. They can do so because they unfold for us in a sequence. Rosenzweig pointedly distinguishes creation, revelation, and redemption as sequence from the same relations as categories (SR 189). The category, at least in its descent from Kant, presumes a schematic connection to experience by which to order it. But creation, revelation, and redemption already *are* experience. The event of ordering is no imposition on experience from without, but a necessary unfolding from within as experience emerges from its protocosmic moorings. Once revelation has occurred, creation necessarily falls into place before it and redemption after, as we saw in chapter two.

Revelation defines the present, which is the vanished distance between love and its expression that occurs in God's love command. Creation defines the past, which is the presupposition philosophy takes for its task to construct retrospectively out of the present. Redemption defines the future, that hovering-over-the-present of creation's anticipated completion. The past, like prediction, only comes to be from the perspective of the present. The protocosmos cannot know itself as past. Part of the chaos of the protocosmos was that, from within it, there was no temporal orientation. The protocosmos becomes past in light of the present that succeeds (SR 133). From within the present, it would be positively wrong to take the elements of the protocosmos for mere "conceptual elements." They are rather "immanent reality" (SR 108), that is, conceptual presuppositions of reality. The elements themselves change appearance in passing from protocosmos to cosmos. From a protocosmic standpoint, God is simply one among three self-contained elements, with as much, or little, right as the others have to claim the whole for itself. From a pagan's point of view, which is as protocosmic as a human viewpoint gets, God's self-enclosure is not fundamentally different from his own and so is, in a sense, "visible" through his own (SR 158). But from within the cosmos, a self-contained god is simply unknown. The protocosmic construct now appears in precisely the opposite light, as a construct of the invisible, the unknown. What is known to the beloved soul, namely the revealed God, is concealed from the tragic hero. What is known to the tragic hero, namely the self-enclosed god, is concealed from the beloved soul (SR 158). And that does indeed match fairly well how the God of Judaism and Christianity has been portrayed: knowable in act, but not in essence.

As against idealism, it is not thought that effects the most important change, but temporal crossings. Schelling anticipated as much. Christ marks the boundary between modernity and antiquity across which the picture of reality changes, from gods to Christ, nature to history, particular human to individual. Across this boundary, the revealed and concealed switch contents. In antiquity, under nature's dominion, nature was immediately visible and history concealed. In modernity, under morality's sway, history is visible and nature concealed. Modernity combs nature for secrets (PA 77) that it would not have occurred to antiquity to seek.

Schelling's perspectivism serves the interests of his monism. It owes to different perspectives on the absolute act of self-affirmation that antiquity and modernity exist at all. Schelling's perspectivism is a way of discounting difference, while Rosenzweig's is a means of instating it. Rosenzweig is so committed to multiplicity, he pays perspectivism as the price for it, rather than marshaling it as a solution. The problem is not to efface perspectives, but to fix them in a single structure. And this is precisely the role that philosophy plays to theology in part two of the *Star*. It was the experiential theology of Schleiermacher that rested content with the private, subjective perspective, and renounced all grounding in objectivity. Philosophy comes to show that experience is a structure of perspectives, grounded objectively in a knowable past. For the lines of relation that constitute experience lead back to the self-enclosed protocosmic objects that, having successfully predicted experience, now appear as both past-constituting and knowledge-conferring.

At the end of part two, in a difficult section entitled "The Eternal God," Rosenzweig considers God's perspective on creation, revelation and redemption. For God, these do not define tenses, for they do not sequentially unfold for him, but he knows them all at once. Further, unlike human and world, God perceives these relations as identical with his role in them—"for him, the creation of the world means becoming the creator" (SR 258)—as though to undermine the very partnership of two on which relationship depends. Finally, God both processively becomes creator, revealer, and redeemer, for there is a sense in which the work of these relations is incomplete and ongoing, and occupies the point of completion at their end. That divine straddling of becoming and being underlies the paradoxical claim that "this Becoming of God is, for him, not a changing, growing, augmenting" (SR 258).

With these paradoxical assertions, Rosenzweig moves back towards the definitively idealist space, where two vanish into one. And Schelling's own articulation of that space, as the trace of two movements that have just vanished into absolute identity, may helpfully illumine Rosenzweig's intent. The three lines of creation, revelation, and redemption may be set in analogy with the two lines of the potences, the affirming and affirmed, that vanish into absolute self-affirmation. The vanishing is the mirroring divide, through which the absolute act of self-affirmation, itself wholly one, casts a reflection of two. The inversive identity across the divide, of two with one, enables a host of paradoxical assertions, such as that the potence of affirming, or of the affirmed, both relations, are simply the absolute identity itself; that these unipolar relations are unique to God, who simultaneously becomes by affirming and already is wholly and restfully affirmed. Humans largely inhabit the world of the potences, and see them from within them. But God, who is the absolute identity, always sees them as the trace of something just vanished. They are, to build on Rosenzweig's use of "proto-", a protodivinity, through which divinity understands itself.

This Schellingian overlay on Rosenzweig must not be pressed too far. For Schelling, the divine perspective on multiplicity is available to humans through philosophy and art. For Rosenzweig, the human perspective irremediably colors human assertion. Any human attempt to speak from God's perspective strains language to the breaking point and ultimately reduces to silence. But the mere fact of a divine perspective tempts to speculation about it, to which Rosenzweig partially succumbs. Perhaps it is not so surprising that Rosenzweig sounds so idealist here. He himself allows that the philosopher's error was simply one of placement: the All is not presupposition but result, "indeed the result of a result" (SR 258). And he thereby invites a Schellingian interpretation of God's perspective, in which all three lines of relation vanish into God. The vanishing occurs hypercosmically, beyond human experience, in what from the human perspective is always future. But we can only speak from out of the present. To speak from out of the future requires a mode of communication that stands to language as language does to art. And this Rosenzweig finds in what Schelling deemed a living work of art, namely the liturgy.

Art and the Cosmos

Within part two of the *Star*, Rosenzweig's reflections on art take the form of a theory. The three subsections on art, dispersed over the three books on creation, revelation and redemption, are all titled

"Theorie der Kunst." And yet such a title, which might suitably name a full-length treatise on art, such as Schelling's own *The Philosophy of Art*, names within the context of part two of the *Star*, in Rosenzweig's words, "a mere episode" (SR 198). If the casual reader asked why art was introduced at all in part one, he might wonder even more why these openly episodic insertions occur in part two; and Rosenzweig responds, precisely to identify art as mere episode (SR 249).

If art must be explicitly identified as episode, it must presume to much more. In the first part of the theory of art, under the subsection "Idealist Esthetics," Rosenzweig states art's presumption to be

at once confirmation of the method of reasoning—"organon", that is—and visible manifestation of an "absolute" (SR 147).

The second presumption, to manifest the absolute, is central to *The Philosophy of Art*; but the first, to be organon, surely alludes to the sixth part of the *System of Transcendental Idealism*, where Schelling calls art, "the only true and eternal organ and document of philosophy."[39] In the works of Aristotle, the organon comprises the treatises on logic.[40] These construct the repeatable forms of reasoning, that is, of moving from premise to conclusion. In the *System of Transcendental Idealism*, art is organon because by means of it philosophy passes from the protracted premise of its subject-object divide, the necessary premise of all knowledge, to its desired conclusion in divisionless knowledge. Schelling explains that consciousness, in its capacity as knowing subject, repeatedly outstrips itself as known object, so that part of it is always unconscious. What philosophy "cannot depict in external form" is "the unconscious element in acting and producing."[41] It cannot make the unconscious fully conscious. But this is just what happens in artistic activity. The artist consciously produces an unconscious product that wholly reflects or externalizes his conscious activity. Consciousness and unconsciousness attain what in *The Philosophy of Art* would be called indifference.

For Hegel, art was not the organon of philosophy, but a station on the way of the organon, which was dialectic. But the Schelling of the *System of Transcendental Idealism* fits Rosenzweig's account of idealist esthetics perfectly. By the time of *The Philosophy of Art*, Schelling had somewhat modified his claims for art. By the identity philosophy of that time, natural philosophy and art constituted parallel, oppositionally identical avenues of indifference. But Rosenzweig's critique applies just as well to both of Schelling's works. For they both understood the universal as the product of a movement of infinite and finite, or free and necessary, forms towards each other. And yet idealism could doubt its own pretension to generate reality out of these movements. Art reassured it that the meeting of freedom and necessity did indeed generate something real. For it was just in the undeniable reality of art that the meeting most patently occurred. The trouble with this assurance was that it rested on a self-deception. For the human had to double as both generator of the art product and appreciator of its "nature-like reality" (SR 147). Though, for Rosenzweig, language, like art, offered a vanished distance between opposites, it was not, as art was, a generatable product. And so idealism could not properly assimilate it. For Rosenzweig, the price of an idealist assimilation of language would be the end of idealism. For language culminates in a very different "conclusion"—not subject-object unity, but an expression of love across distance.

Rosenzweig allows that Kantian idealism stood on the brink of acknowledging genuine separation. Kant did so when he took the *Ding-an-Sich*, or noumenon, for the outer limit of reason's reach, and further understood a noumenal human character to share with it a "'common obscure root'" (SR 142). For the equation of these two particulars, by means of the common root, would have yielded the idea of a self-enclosed, rationally unassimilable particular. In Rosenzweig's philosophic algebra, it would be symbolized $B=B$, precisely the symbol of one of the pre-real, protocosmic elements. If post-Kantian idealism had taken the common obscure root seriously, instead of attempting to generate it out of self-consciousness, as Schelling himself did in the *System of Transcendental Idealism*,[42] the concept of genuine relation might have surfaced all the sooner.

And yet, for all the magnitude of idealism's oversight, "the idealist mode of thinking" (SR 189) is still partially applicable. Its application is precisely to the theory of art. From within the context of the *Star*, it is just because art does not serve as organon that it can be theorized about (SR 150). If art were organon in the *Star*, then it would lead to one of the desired conclusions of that work. Within the context of part two, it would lead to relational reality. And reality is not theoretically explicable. By its miraculous nature, it surpasses theory. Reality shows in narrative, imperative and choral forms of language, not in the theoretical language, that bypasses experience, of idealism. But the artwork truly is what idealism would make of all reality, namely a product. It appears during the course of a genuinely self-enclosed process, which subsumes, in addition to art, the creator-artist and the appreciative spectator. These are not three self-enclosures between which meetings occur, as in genuine reality, but "segments" or "members" of a continuous movement, as in idealist thinking.

But it is not idealist dialectic that can any longer construct a theory of art. Rosenzweig has already rejected the linchpin of both Schellingian and Hegelian idealism, that subject and object are indifferently subsumed under the relation that connects them, to create a differentiably new subject-object. But the generative powers of idealism do in any case stop short at the miracle that conditions, indeed constitutes, Rosenzweigian reality. Now, unexpectedly, it is just this reality that obliges the nonreal world of art with the constitutent parts of a theory. For reality has at hand just the set of categories by which a theory of art might be constructed, namely creation, revelation, and redemption. These constitute the sequence of reality. But they are prefigured in the prerelational world of the protocosmos, where art also dwelt. It dwelt there as the occasion of a common understanding that arose, unmediated, among separate and uncommunicating individuals. In that capacity, art prefigured language, which miraculously appears in the real world as the sign to art's prediction. But language is the organon of reality, the medium through which creation, revelation, and redemption occur. So art, in predicting language, must contain some prefigurements of these as well. At least these three reality-constituting movements may be abstracted out of their living world and refashioned as categories. As categories, they do not accompany reality on its miraculous emergence, but assert "something that already is 'in existence'" (SR 189). The quotation marks imply that the existence available to be asserted prior to the emergence of the real is not real existence. Rosenzweig might call it preexistence. From the perspective of the *Star*, all the categorial thinking of idealism is preexistential. But art is a preexistence that genuinely remains even after idealism has passed. And so "the idealist mode of thinking" may model the application of the categories of creation, revelation, and redemption to a preexistential theory of art.

Rosenzweig distributes these three categories over the three stages in the genesis of an artwork. He applies the creation category to the creator-artist, revelation to the artwork itself, and redemption to the appreciative awareness of the spectator. Beneath these applications are visible both Rosenzweig's own observations on the unfolding of these categories in the real world, and Schelling's much earlier reflections on genius, the universal and particular, and the forms of art. Certainly Rosenzweig follows Schelling's division of the arts into music and fine art on the one hand, and poetry on the other.

The first two constitute the real arts for Schelling, the sensual arts for Rosenzweig; the second is Schelling's ideal art, Rosenzweig's conceptual art. But let us begin at the beginning.

Art begins in genius. Rosenzweig characterizes genius as "an inner diversity, a world of creatures, insights, ideas, which nevertheless are held together in an intrinsically harmonious juxtaposition by the personal style, the internal way, of the artist" (SR 149). The characterization recalls the creation of the world, wherein God's providential caring meets the creaturely world's own need of provendure. And genius is indeed created, "does not fall ready-made from heaven" (SR 149). Genius is a sudden and unexpected surprise. Rosenzweig sees it conditioned by the emergence of the self, that personality-succeeding defiance that endures in growing isolation after the needs of the species have been satisfied. That self, too, appears in the course of human development as a surprise, an "assault" (SR 71) not to be predicted by the laws of the world. Rosenzweig also calls the human self a *daimon*, as though to register its supraworldly status, taking the human out of the world and constituting it a separate element on its own. If genius is conditioned by the self, then it must be born in solitude. Romantic visions of the solitary artist aside, self-enclosure seems a necessary condition of genius. The artist needs self-enclosure to nurture the world of creations within him. For the world of real relations cannot be trusted to harmonize with his own inner harmonies.

Rosenzweig quite openly invites idealism into this discussion. For the artwork's creation "takes place in the author," quite apart from any authorial effort. The creation of the work is its location in the artist's inner world. The artist simply receives it there. It is the sheer givenness of creation, prior to conscious effort, that constitutes its unconscious component, so "rightly emphasized by idealism" (SR 148). Certainly Schelling would insist on the unconscious component of artistry. Its indifference with the conscious is just the miracle of art. Schelling would also applaud Rosenzweig for the central role he assigns genius and the daemon, only he identifies the two, and puts the daemon to different use. The daemon of genius connotes not its supraworldly nature—a God-identified world is after all exhaustive—but its divine provenance. Genius is the "eternal concept of the human being in God as the immediate cause of his productions" (PA 84). Rosenzweig could never reduce the human to a concept in God. Such attempts simply underscore how much the self was a "matter of indifference" to idealism (SR 145). But across the two different views of genius, it remains a matter of "harmoniously juxtaposed" concepts or ideas. Here, Kant's infinitely interpretable esthetic idea is the not so obscure common root. For both Schelling and Rosenzweig, genius must draw from an inexhaustible well. Within the confines of his "personal style" or particular concept of himself in God, the artist must be able to draw on an infinity of ideas. If not, says Schelling, he will be less productive (PA 84); never "more than a 'frustrated' genius at best" (SR 150) says Rosenzweig.

There is some correspondence between artistic creation and what Rosenzweig introduced as the outer form of art in part one. The outer form of a work locates it in a larger world by differentiating the two, the work from the world. Artistic creation assigns a work its artist's inner world, "the common character and the family resemblance" (SR 192) it shares with all the works born of that world. As bearer of his own created world, the artist in Rosenzweig's account receives a distinctive name: poet. It is the poet whose artistry moves out of an inexhaustible world of creatures, insights, and ideas. As "mere" artist, the poet simply executes his ideas. Both Schelling's and Rosenzweig's discussions of genius are followed by accounts of the relation between poetry and artist, or poesy and art. Here, too, Rosenzweig follows Schelling. Schellingian poesy is also a movement from infinite world to finite, executed work (PA 85). But perhaps the most striking parallel between the two is what Baeck might identify as both the presuppositional and passive nature of their accounts of poetic genius. The artist does not create his world, but receives it preconsciously or divinely. For Rosenzweig, the poet is simply the first stage of a creative process that subsumes him. For Schelling, it is actually the concept of the poet in God that produces. Schelling might well regard Rosenzweig as a companion theorist of modern esthetics. For Rosenzweig's poet, like Schelling's modern artist, must create out of his self-contained world. There is no overarching mythology to supply the content; there cannot be, after the shattering of the All, and the restriction of God to one of three. Rosenzweig identified the self as the condition of genius; but it is also, from part one, the content of art. Under the circumstance of the shattered All, this might not sound so strange to Schelling. For the poet's inwardly diverse world reads a little like the mythology Schelling's artist creates. If so, the modern artist might step back and forth quite comfortably between Schelling's and Rosenzweig's pages; for he is equally well shielded in both from their very different outside worlds. The outside world is in Schelling's case a vexed oscillation between infinite self-loss and loss of the infinite, and in Rosenzweig's case, the real world of creation, revelation, and redemption. It is true that the artist is closed off from the first to his salvation, and from the second to his destruction, but self-enclosed he remains in both.

It might seem that the category of revelation, which actually opens up the real world of relations would, applied to art, redeem the artist from his self-enclosure. But it does not. It simply replaces one enclosure with another. Even so, it is in revelational terms that Rosenzweig describes the passage from creative genius to artistic execution. The analogy is explicit. So, for example, what harmony does for rhythm in the musical work is "quite like revelation which endows the mute self with speech and soul at once" (SR 198). Rosenzweig develops the revelational passage from genius to executed work over three ever narrowing stages: first from genius to artist, then within the artwork, over its epic and lyric qualities, and finally between fine art and music, over their specific differences.

What defined real revelation was love. And love was the repeated outpouring of the whole into each successive moment, heedless of consequence and of the demise it suffered over and over again. Love was one of Rosenzweig's translations of Baeckian romantic self-sacrifice. And now this love repeats within the self-enclosure of art, as genius giving way to artistry (SR 193). To begin with, the genius has already sacrificed his humanity. For his self-enclosure already separates him from human life in its God- and world-related richness. This sacrifice was indeed necessary for the benefit of the rest of humanity. For if there was no art, there would be no prediction of language, which could not then be received as the miracle it is. And humanity could not appreciate how much the "Love me!" it receives from God attests to the love of God, which allows itself to be truthfully foretold. The artist lives ongoingly in the prediction of language, at the cost of his own real involvement with language, like Moses who, having led the way to the Promised Land, is denied entry into it. Already the artist begins to take on tragic hues. The Rosenzweigian artist, like the Schellingian tragic hero, willingly accepts the affliction of genius. But now, as though the affliction of his self-enclosure is too great to bear, he pours it out into his artwork. In artistry, a piece of nature is formed esthetically. Each detail of esthetically unformed nature that will constitute the executed work is stamped with the idea of the whole work that precedes in genius. If genius corresponds to the outer form of art, artistry corresponds to the inner. For each of the details, so enlarged by the whole, assumes the status of the whole, without relation to the others (SR 194). The details vanish into the whole, in conformity with the detail-subsuming work of inner form. The details of the artwork are also like the objects of real, revelatory love, which "passionately unmindful of self . . . immerse[s] itself into whatever detail confronts it" (SR 193). The artist's informing of his genius into the detail is an act of love. But the love is not relational. It moves not by connecting the separate, but by reconstituting the whole in the part. The whole sacrifices itself to the part, "into complete oblivion" (SR 194). And now the part enjoys the same self-enclosure within the whole that was formerly confined to genius. But then, there is no real sacrifice after all. The creative genius has, for the duration of his artistry, sacrificed his genius. But he gains it back in the details that have absorbed his genius. In them, he sees himself. Far from losing himself in his artistry, "his self-revelation takes place [there] for him" (SR 193).

The creative genius is in a sense one with his work. The passage from genius to artistry is a relation that, monistically and idealistically, subsumes its poles. It is an extension of self-enclosure, not a bursting of it. Schelling's esthetics resounds throughout what Rosenzweig has described. Artistry proceeds from the infinity of genius to the finite detail of the artwork. The detail is only seemingly separate from the genius that confronts it. Genius "does not consider [the detail] to have proceeded from within it" (SR 192), any more than the Schellingian infinite, in affirming the finite, knew itself, prior to indifference, to be affirming itself. The work of artistry proves to be just as much a self-affirmation as Schellingian indifference is. The detail serves the genial whole as self-reflective mirror. Rosenzweig's detail is a Schellingian particular.

Rosenzweig has described an informing of the infinite into the finite without loss of the infinite. And this is Schelling's definition of art. But there is a small discrepancy. For Schelling, it is by one continuous movement that the infinite informs the finite. But Rosenzweig distinguishes between the outward movement of genius, and the detail-inspiriting work of artistry. The first is genial inspiration proper; the second is diligence. And genius cannot generate diligence. When Rosenzweig says that genius sacrifices itself to diligence (SR 193) he suggests the one movement picks up where the other leaves off. If the two movements are distinct, then the diligently executed detail need not mirror the genially inspired whole, and whatever mirroring occurs takes on the flavor of miracle. Schelling had of course called all art miraculous for unaccountably finitizing a perduring infinite. But Rosenzweig's separation of diligent from genial movement allows him to construct within the domain of art a categorical copy of his own understanding of miracle. And this indeed he does. For he pointedly ascribes to the genial whole that attribute so redolent of actual miracle, namely prediction (SR 196, 197). But he will not complete the image. The executed detail is not "sign." For the prediction occurs within a self-enclosure after all. The detail does not answer the whole over a genuine distance. Genius and diligence simply name two segments of a unified process, as Rosenzweig indicates when he concedes that genius "must become diligence, must turn itself into diligence" (SR 193). The contingency of the mirroring is illusory, "there is simply no such thing as a 'frustrated genius'" (SR 192), and merely foretells the real contingency that occurs outside art in the genuine miracle. But miracle is virtually synonymous with revelation in the larger sense. If "revelation as esthetic category" (SR 191) unfolds a prediction of miracle, this might have been predicted, as perhaps Rosenzweig himself does in part one of the *Star* when he exclaims that "only the magic flute of art could bring off the miracle of making the unison of human content resound in discrete selves" (SR 82).

If in the creative process, the wholeness of the artwork genially precedes the executed detail, then in the completed artwork the wholeness only follows. Each detail is a microcosmic whole. But only the sum of executed details reconstitutes the whole macrocosmically. The whole of the realized artwork Rosenzweig designates its epic attribute. The repetition of the whole within each detail is its lyric attribute. The epic and lyric as attributive content of art simply repeat the constitutive forms of genius and artistry. The mirroring that occurred between the genius and the executed detail of his creation now repeats within the artwork itself, between whole and part. The self-reflective self-enclosure of the artistic genius now animates the artwork too, which Rosenzweig invests with a soul of its own (SR 195). Schelling had done the same, more dramatically. His "completely self-enclosed" (PA 206) artworks were nothing less than realized gods. The lyric and epic as universal contents of all art follow on the division Rosenzweig made, and Schelling did not, between the two segments of the movement from genial infinity to finite detail. Schelling took the lyric and epic for "individual poetic genres" (PA 201) within the verbal arts alone. Over their differences, Rosenzweig and Schelling contrast the lyrical and epical in similar ways. Rosenzweig's contrast between epic whole and lyric part resembles Schelling's between lyric particularity or difference and epic absoluteness or unity (PA 208, 212). Both contrasts point to the dramatic as conjunctive third. If Rosenzweig fashions two distinct

Schellingian genres as attributes of all art, he is only exploiting the suggestive interchangability of parts within Schelling's monistic whole.

Rosenzweig takes quantitative differences in the relative proportion of epic and lyric components within the arts to explain qualitative difference between them. Thus epic dominance yields the visual arts which, extended in space, show their wholeness at a glance, while lyric dominance results in music which, extended in time, shows each of its detailed parts in succession. Schelling too associated the lyric with music, the epic with painting (PA 208, 214). But Rosenzweig's reductive proportionalism follows more closely on Schelling's explanation, in *Bruno*, of difference as such. There Schelling states that what distinguishes determinate individuals from each other is the difference in the way they establish "the opposition of the real and ideal."[43] A series of analogies might well connect *Bruno* through *The Philosophy of Art* to the *Star*: real is to ideal, as particular to universal, as lyric to epic. The very attempt to explain qualitative difference quantitatively is idealist. All difference in *Bruno* is fundamentally a product of long division; Rosenzweig's spatio-temporal expressions within the arts of different lyric-epic proportionalities is a kindred piece of thinking.

To complete his discussion of the artwork, Rosenzweig examines the different ways the fine arts and music realize ideas of genius. In fine art, the genial idea precedes the executed detail as a vision of the whole. The vision may be stimulated by natural impressions, but ultimately removes itself from nature entirely. From that purely ideal height, it pours the whole of itself, successively, into each natural detail of the material it confronts. The vision cannot serve to guide the self-pouring, for it, itself, is poured out in it. And so the pouring is as unpremeditated and blind as love, that sacrifices itself to its object. The movement of the vision into the detail occurs feelingly, without vision, like the blind, feeling movement of actual love. When it has finally come to rest, the natural detail has been rendered as ideal and natureless as the original vision. It has been vitalized with the protospeech of the art that magically effects a common understanding across silence. Music, as extension through time, cannot be previewed in a single moment of vision. But the rhythm of a musical piece does function like the artistic vision to predict the completed whole. Harmony fills the role in music that the vitalizing detail does in fine art. Where rhythm fashions a succession of differently extended moments, harmony makes them resound. The rhythmic moments are the details that harmony, blindly accepting whatever durations it confronts, inspires with pitch. And now comes the analogy with revelation already cited, of harmony to rhythm as soul to self (SR 198).

The sharp contrast Rosenzweig draws between the artistic vision and nature recalls Schelling's oppositional identity between real and ideal. The two cannot be identified until each has been isolated in its own exclusive purity. This occurs for Schelling in the original act of absolute self-affirmation. But Rosenzweig, who has banished all such acts, must first purify the ideal of the real with which it is originally given in experience. The product of the purifying division is projected backwards to the creation of the artwork, which occurs in the genial mind, prior to execution. So purified of nature, the vision's inversive transformation into nature foretells all the more powerfully the miracle to come. Rhythm, too, predicts. And here the tie to Schelling is closer. For rhythm also served Schelling as the beginning of music, its first potence of the finitized infinite. In Schelling's monism of multiple embeddings, rhythm microcosmically encompassed the whole of music, and constituted "the music within music" (PA 111). For music as such is the formative art in which the infinite informs the finite and, within its own potences of rhythm, modulation and melody, it is rhythm that microcosmically repeats that movement. But then rhythm, for Schelling, was the universalizable esthetic potence that assured not only music but all the verbal arts their temporal self-enclosures.

For Schelling, the artwork constitutes a climactic completion of embedded self-enclosure. There at the node of indifference within the ideal potence occurs that redemptive rest from movement that reproduces the inner quiet of the natural organism and of the absolute identity itself. But for Rosenzweig, the creative process shifts self-enclosure to one last location, where it must occur before the artwork concludes, namely the place of the appreciative audience. Here is the last application of reality to art: "redemption as esthetic category" (SR 242).

Like the Schellingian artwork, the completed artwork in Rosenzweig stands enclosed within its own vitality. But unlike Schelling's artwork, Rosenzweig's stands on an outskirts. There are no outskirts in monism, or true empty spaces in which to hover. But in Rosenzweig's prereal world of three, there are bounds that might be crossed. The finite self-enclosure of the human establishes potentially crossable bounds around every human. The completed artwork has absorbed the genius of the creator. But then it has been reflected back to him and left the artwork bereft. The creator has no more eyes for this work; he has moved onto the next, to which he once more offers himself a sacrifice. The artwork has been empowered with speech but, exiled to the outskirts of the creator's self-enclosure, like art itself from the Platonic state, it has no one to address.

Only Rosenzweig's artistic world, not Schelling's, allows for a space across which art can project an unfulfilled need. Here the artwork resembles a beloved soul who, empowered with love, turns to express it to a space bereft of world. But in reality, the world is there to receive the love. And in the prereality of art, a receptor stands there too. It is the spectator. The spectator fills the creator's role in reverse. The life of the creator poured into his work now animates the viewer. If the idea of the work emerged a distinct whole out of the infinity of genius, and passed into the details, it now reemerges in an appreciative consciousness, where it once again assumes a place among an infinity of like ideas, all "collected and lovingly arranged in the course of a long life" (SR 48). The viewer who studies the work's detail is mirrored there, a connoisseur, just as, in the fashioning of the same detail, the creator had first known himself an artist. The two self-reflections reflect each other without bridging any distances. They serve rather to augment the traveling self-enclosure, now enclosing the viewer with the work at the end of the creative process. The work which was the creator, externalized, is now internalized in the connoisseur. The line from creator to connoisseur extends continuously over the segments that successively bear the self-enclosure. It is no real miracle that a spectator stands at the finish of the work, to receive it. If there were no viewer, there would be not frustrated, needy art but, no art at all.

There is no real redemption in self-enclosure. But across the mock distance of the artwork from the spectator, a mock redemption occurs. The reaching of the artwork for an audience is like the cry of redemptive love for the world. The viewer who supplies the audience is like the world that grows towards love, its store of lovingly ensouled detail organically expanding. The mock redemption predicts the reality. The connoisseur, "inwardly full of form" (SR 48), stands on the brink of that other fullness, the beloved soul's, which passes into redemptive love. But before the world of art is edged over the brink, and takes on the work of the real world, it must complete the dangling ends of its own prereal redemption.

Under the aegis of revelation as esthetic category, epic and lyric emerged as attributes of art; and fine art and music, as their respective exemplars. Now the dramatic effects a balance between the epic attribute, that would rest in its wholeness, and the lyric attribute, that impulsively presses forward each detail, one after the other, as equal to the whole. The dramatic is the third attribute. It distributes the lyric immediacy simultaneously over the whole epic scope of the work, rather like what redemptive love has accomplished after wending its way through the whole world. The art that exemplifies the dramatic is poetry. Poetry is dramatic by uniting in itself the epic scope of fine art with the lyric immediacy of music. For it is both visionary, or pictorial, and rhythmic. It is not that fine art and music do not possess a drama of their own. Fine art's dramatic attribute is its structure, which emerges after each of its details has been successively imprinted with the visionary whole; and music's is melody, which, superimposed over rhythm and harmony, unites the encompassing of the first with the individual sounding of the second. What distinguishes poetry from these is that it begins in the conjunctive work of drama, not in the epical vision of the artist, or the lyrically anticipatory rhythm of the composer. It does so by taking for its medium neither space, like art, nor time, like music, but "conceptual thought" (SR 245). Thought is the medium of drama because only thought subsumes both the epic scope of space and lyric immediacy of time. For thought is "the common inner source of both" (SR 245).

Here, at its climactic finish, the theory of art confirms the impression of its idealist base, if this were not sufficiently confirmed already. For who but an idealist would locate the common source of space and time in thought? Kant had already pointed this way when he presented space and time as the forms of sensible intuition, the first of outer sense, the second of inner. But Schelling, in the *System of Transcendental Idealism* quite boldly deduces them, transcendentally, from the absolute act of self-positing,[44] and in *The Philosophy of Art* they are assigned locations related to the absolute act of self-affirmation: space to the real or finite potence, time to the infinite as it moves towards the finite (PA 109, 119). Thought is the conjunction between space and time but, more idealist still, it is ideas. Poetry is the only art that turns on ideas which, transcending the wholeness of poetic tone and the particularity of poetic diction, "infuse the poem with life" (SR 247). The idea of a poem is virtually sensible. Feuerbach too had taken ideas for sensible.[45] The poem's idea corresponds to the visible structure of a painting, and the audible melody of a musical composition (SR 248). It is "the effective and affective reality of the work" (SR 247).

Layers of idealist thought underlie these few remarks on poetry. Under the canopy of this single art, Rosenzweig has arrayed the

whole Kantian sequence of representations as they appear in the
Critique of Pure Reason, from sensible intuition to conceptual
thought to climactic idea. The Kantian sequence moves from least to
greatest universality. But, though the ideas crown the sequence for
generality, they do not do so for reality. Kantian ideas have no objects. At best, they guide the understanding in exploration of its own
objects. Rosenzweig has marshaled the Kantian idea for its perfection of universality, just as earlier, in connection with artistic vision,
he had purged the ideal of all naturalness, but he will not deprive it
of an object. The idea within the artwork *is* the reality of the artwork
as much as for Schelling the ideal *is* the real (PA 35). Kant had anticipated this move in his *Critique of Judgment*, when he defined the
esthetic idea as a noncognitive reference to an intuition.[46] But both
Schelling and Rosenzweig indicate by their language more than a
mere reference of idea to intuition. The idea is actually "within" the
poem, not "somewhere behind it" (SR 248). Rosenzweig comes as
close here as anywhere to speaking in Schelling's voice.

But then, the whole theory of art could pass for a Schellingian
construction. It is a continuous passage in thought through repetition of the same tripartite construction of concepts. This is why
Rosenzweig can construct his theory "on the analogy of a family tree"
(SR 198). The same relations between endpoints repeat, and so relate the endpoints analogously. The theory turns on the distinction
between the universal whole of a work and its inspired particular.
By a three-step movement, the whole becomes the particular and
then whole again. The agents of each step are, respectively, the poetic genius, the diligent artist, and the appreciative spectator. The
work itself reflects the contribution of each agent through its epic,
lyric, and dramatic qualities. Finally, the genres of art divide by
which of the qualities is definitive for them: epic for art, lyric for
music, dramatic for poetry. The overarching movement of the theory,
from whole to part to whole, mirrors the same act that inaugurates
Schelling's system, the absolute act of self-affirmation. For this, too,
proceeds by dividing a presupposed whole, and reuniting.

The Schellingian system had fissures. One occurred at the point
of the modern; and at the same point a fissure occurs in Rosenzweig's theory. For if a discussion of modern tragedy is to occur in the
Star, it ought to fall at the point of the theory's climax, where the
spectator, the dramatic, and poetry converge. Instead, modern
tragedy escapes the confines of the prereal theory and precedes it,
headed by the reality-defining section title, "The Act of Love." Here,
Rosenzweig presents the modern tragic hero, so definitively distinct

from the ancient one, by his vexed enmeshment in relations, including those with the spectators. Having turned toward relation, the modern hero, like the beloved soul, escapes self-enclosure. But he does so at this price: others turn to him as well, and so generate with him a cacophony of perspectival readings of reality. The modern hero's perspective is ever only one of many. The monologue form, so essential to the ancient hero's self-enclosure, reappears in modern drama as a context for the hero's approach of a perspectiveless or absolute view of his world. And indeed the modern dramatist bends all his efforts to guide his hero there, and sometimes succeeds, as Shakespeare with Hamlet, or Goethe with Faust. But it is not enough merely to be guided to the absolute view. The ancient hero dwelt from start to finish in the absolute, albeit the enclosed one of himself. Correspondingly, the high point of modern tragedy would be a relational hero who overcomes perspective and "lives within the absolute" (SR 211). But at this high point, tragedy would outdo itself and produce a saint. For the saint is "the perfect human being, the one, that is, who lives absolutely in the Absolute" (SR 211)—not his own absolute, but God's. The tragedy is outdone because at this point there is no character to move the definitively modern tragedy of character. Character has been converted to absolute love. This is why modern tragedy falls under a section headed by love; but it is also why it falls outside the theory of art. A modern tragedy that attained its goal would cease to be tragic, would cease to be art at all. For the goal that is the saint "lies at a distance that tragedy cannot traverse" (SR 211) and remain within the bounds of art.

Rosenzweig's discussion recalls the critical studies of Dostoevsky's *The Idiot*, and of the extent to which this work succeeds in artistically portraying the tragic saint.[47] But it recalls much more immediately the whole plight of the Schellingian modern who cannot humanly reach the goal of infinity without dissolving as human. Of course, it is only Rosenzweig's dramatic artist who is tempted by his own demise, not the human as such. At this juncture, Rosenzweig inverts the redemptive power of Schellingian art. Schelling's modern artist saves the human from dissolving in the infinite, where religion would lead him. Rosenzweig's artist is saved by the absolute when it takes him outside art and into the human, under the aegis of revelation. But salvation is not the artist's lot. Instead, he launches a course of self-enclosures, that proceed from himself through the artwork to the connoisseur, and that all along the way foretell a redemption others are to know. The artist is a kind of living fossil; he inhabits the real world of relations like a Schellingian potence, a trace of what has always just vanished. But without the potences there would be no world; and without the artist, there would be no miracle of reality.

Philosophy and the Hypercosmos

By the time of the *Star*'s third part, the explicit challenge of philosophy, in the form of erring idealism, has largely spent itself. There are no section headings that name idealism here, as there are in the second part. In the last book of part three, the ghost of idealism is explicitly raised once more in order to receive one last, overt banishing—"to reject here for the last time the blasphemy of philosophy" (SR 392). The blasphemy of philosophy was that no truths lay outside itself (this had been Schelling's claim for philosophy) so that whoever philosophizes finds truth within himself. It is rather the reverse, that we find ourselves in the truth, which we cannot encompassingly live. We behold truth. But what we behold is outside us. If we find ourselves in the truth, it can only be by way of reflection, pointing us back to our own necessarily perspectival, and so only partially true lives.

But before the final banishing of idealism, it performs some constructive reflecting on its own. It reflects an erring incompleteness in the second, epochal form of Christianity, namely the Pauline (SR 281). Petrine Christianity was all outward conquest. The early and medieval church of St. Peter turned in love towards the conversion of the whole pagan world. It wanted the outward, bodily signs of obeisance to Christ. In its zeal for the outward, it ignored the inward. It even devised a means of protecting itself from the awareness of the danger posed by the inward pagan. By its doctrine of the two truths—one for faith, one for reason—it clothed the inward pagan in a veil of respectability. Pagan reason did, after all, know a truth of its own, however limited. But pagan reason was never so tame as to rest content with second place, as the Reformation would reveal. For the Reformation church, which inaugurates the Pauline era, now abandons the outer Christian and looks solely to the inner. It takes upon itself the work of conquering the inward pagan. Its *sola fides* makes spirit, which hitherto was nothing, virtually all. The world and all Christian forms indebted to it are banished. Idealism now arrives as the reductio ad adsurdum of Protestant Christianity. For idealism, not satisfied to banish the world, insists on consuming it and disgorging it whole. It is an unattractive office but an instructive one. For, by mirroring the excess of Pauline Christianity in its worst light, idealism turns Christianity off that track and onto a new one that sanely links what Peter and Paul had jointly sundered. In the new, Johannine Christianity, an inwardly Christian soul lives its bodily life within the world and so accomplishes the world-loving movement of faith that unfolds out of revelation into redemption.

The trouble with revelation passing into redemption is that it is blind. The Johannine Christian needs eyes to guide his worldly way. And this is what prayer supplies. If love only reaches as far as it can touch, which is always only so far as the nearest neighbor, prayer extends to a vision of what lies at the end of love's groping way. In fact, the world is already pushing forward to receive the human work of redemption. The Johannine Christian prays for the completion of his meeting with the world, for that portion of the world that he will have ensouled by the end of his course. But this prayer is strangely dual. It enfolds a bridge over genuine distance, between human and world, in self-enclosure. For the face of the world the human meets in this prayer is his own, enworlded.

Rosenzweig anticipated Johannine prayer in his account of artistic genius. For the genius ensouls his artwork with a whole-embracing part of himself. But unlike the artist, the Johannine Christian reaches across a distance that remains, despite the self-enclosure that is constructed over it. In effect, the Johannine Christian inverts the movement from protocosmos to cosmos. That movement constructed relation over enclosure; this one constructs enclosure over relation.

The prayer of the human to his own enworlded self courses through the relation revelation opened up between soul and world; but he who prays this prayer, unconscious of the revelation that grounds it, prays in unbelief. The Johannine prayer is essentially individual; it is of the individual and to the individual, that is, to his individual embedding in the world. The individuality and unbelief of the prayer are related. Belief was the province of the theologian. His was the belief in the miraculous acts of creation, revelation and redemption. What distinguishes these acts from the protocosmic thought courses is that they were acts of genuine relation. The theologian prays, in belief, from a stance that is self-consciously relational. And, correspondingly, the prayer prayed, in unbelief, from the stance of individuality falls precisely to the philosopher.

If the prayer of unbelief were not oxymoronic enough, the praying philosopher is even more so. Philosophy comes in answer to Boethius' "quiet thinking,"[48] not his prayers; and even the thinking is directed more toward death than toward philosophy (though the distinction is fine in Rosenzweig's eyes). But philosophers do pray. Socrates' prayer at the close of *Phaedrus* succinctly seals what philosophy has led him to believe about beauty:

> Socrates: Beloved Pan, all ye other gods who haunt this place, give me beauty in the inward soul; and may the outward and inward man be one. May I reckon the wise to be the wealthy, and may I have such a quantity of gold as a temperate man and he only can bear and carry. Anything more? The prayer I think is enough for me.
>
> Phaedrus: Ask the same for me, for friends should have all things in common.
>
> Socrates: Let us go.[49]

Socrates' prayer is peculiar, in part, because his self-conscious reflection on the prayer, at the end, is barely distinguishable from the prayer itself; as though, for philosophers, prayer and self-examination are the same. Socrates' prayer is a paradigm of philosophical prayer as Rosenzweig understands it. Socrates prays for individual unity. He asks for a particular station in the context of the world. And he prays in the exclusive first person singular. The very last line of the dialogue is almost comically heedless of Phaedrus' request. But that only shows how much philosophical prayer fails to include the friend, much less the community.

The self-enclosure of philosophical prayer walls it up within unbelief. But in a more conventional sense of unbelief, it is unbelieving for bypassing God and passing directly to the world. Pan is, after all, a god of nature. He who prays to his self-objectification in the world prays to part of a genuine other. The world offers itself to receive the human's imprint. And from the world's viewpoint, this is no loss of itself to the human, but its own growth in essence or redemption. Creation and revelation condition the mutual approach between human and world, but they are not the channels along which philosophical prayer passes. It is the prayer of belief, which the theologian prays, that follows the paths of all three relations. The grounding role that philosophy plays to theology appears once more, but in the context of prayer. For Rosenzweig insists that believing prayer is a "supplement to the prayer of the nonbeliever . . . and is effective only as such a supplementation" (SR 289). It is as though Rosenzweig is formulating, in a very abstract way, one interpretation of the injunction from Leviticus 19:18, or Matthew 19:19, to love the neighbor as oneself, namely that no one can love his neighbor without antecedently loving himself. But his thought here is much more definitively and exclusively Christian. The Christian must pass through the Petrine conversion of the outwardly other and Pauline conversion of the inwardly same, i.e., he must become the object of his own conversion, before he can truly pray the Christian prayers of creation, revelation, and redemption—the prayers that link him to the whole of reality and not just to his own part in it. Christianity is definitively conversive. It always addresses the pagan. But in a world from which official, institutional paganism has long been banished, the pagan must be individually created anew. The prior Christian ages work paradoxically to that end. They create the conditions for the prayer of unbelief, of the individual to himself. It is just that self-enclosure of confirmed individuality that Christian teaching presupposes, addresses, and opens to relational life. All Christians must be philosophers first.

In a provocatively inverted anticipation of this view, eight years before publication of the *Star*, Rosenzweig wrote to Rudolf Ehrenberg, explaining his disavowed decision to become a Christian: "I could turn Christian only qua Jew—not through the intermediate stage of paganism."[50] It is as though Christianity is only accessible through some opposition to it, whether pagan (and philosophical) or Jewish. The same might be said of the new philosophy, which is so very long in rejecting the blasphemies of the old. The new philosophy, whose portion was to reason a rationally unsubsumable separation of elements, lays methodological ground for the definitive role of opposition. Each element included a negating movement that, acting on behalf of the affirming one, raised all opposition for the sheer sake of denying it. Negation shaped the affirmed essence more definitively. It was the later Schelling who, especially in his *Inquiries into the Nature of Human Freedom*, understood freedom as the overcoming of a prior resistance. And this idea surfaces again in Rosenzweig's understanding of temptation's role in prayer life, the introductory topic of part three. But theological prayer is not to overcome philosophical prayer. The two are to unite in one individual, who prays with both hands, one philosophical, one theological, entreatingly extended.

The author of *The Philosophy of Art* is not among the small company of praying philosophers. There is hardly need for prayer when the absolute already shows itself finitely in a myriad of accessible artworks. Prayer is of much less interest than liturgical rites, which are less important for the prayers they contain than for the public artistry they constitute. In one passage, where Schelling does consider individual prayer, he identifies it with mysticism. For the inward prayer that takes no outward form foregoes all grounding in the finite, and bears its speaker, sacrificially, into the infinite (PA 65). Self-affirmation is surrendered to self-loss. It is art that, by holding the finite to finitude even as it attains the infinite, repeats the absolute self-affirmation that inaugurates the whole *The Philosophy of Art*. And here a harmony with Rosenzweig sounds. For the philosopher's prayer is also a self-affirmation. The absolute self-affirmation might be taken for prayer, too, if the distance across which it reached were not so short-lived, having always just vanished, rather than an enduring distance of the kind that separates the praying philosopher from his worldly image.

But even if the absolute self-affirmation were taken for prayer, it would have to share pride of place with theological prayer, a caveat from Rosenzweig that, however acceptable to the rabbinic mind, which pictured God studying Talmud, is simply inadmissible to philosophical science. Ultimately, philosophical prayer must remain an absurdity to the early Schelling who, in turn, must illustrate for Rosenzweig philosophy at its blasphemous worst. It is perhaps all the more surprising, then, that as Rosenzweig moves beyond philosophical prayer, to its theological mate, he sounds still closer to a philosopher with whom the early Schelling was, in his time, sometimes explicitly identified, namely Plato. If the so inescapably theological concept of miracle offered passage out of the philosophical protocosmos into the theological cosmos, the corresponding passage out of the cosmos is offered by a concept definitively shaped by the works of Voltaire and Kant, namely Enlightenment (SR 261). Only Hallo's translation conveys this suggestion, for it renders both *Aufklaerung*, which Rosenzweig discusses in the early pages of part two, and *Erleuchtung*, which begins the passage to part three, "enlightenment." It is a happy accident of translation. All the *Aufklaerungen* Rosenzweig discusses in the section named for them "represent . . . that knowledge with which it [belief] must contend" (SR 97). And the *Erleuchtung* of part three is about nothing if not truth, for which all the knowledge-hungry *Aufklaerungen* labored. Plato, who critiqued the mythology of his own culture, belonged to the first *Aufklaerung*. But surely no philosopher is more identifiable with *Erleuchtung* than he, whose image for reason was the sun. The star, whose light is only visible in darkness, is a more suitable image for Rosenzweig's truth, which is so explicitly wedded to images of darkness and to language that, in the third book of part three, is scarcely pellucid. But Rosenzweig leaves no doubt that the hypercosmos is an "ocean of light" (SR 80) that, like those by now oft-cited waves of Baeckian romanticism, engulfs all life. Like the Platonic soul, one perceives (SR 394) this light, but does not continuously dwell within it. The "mysterious-miraculous light of the divine sanctuary" (SR 424) does not support human life. We descend from this light back into life, just as Socrates descends from the summit to which he has guided Glaucon in book seven of the *Republic*. Human life transpires in part two of the *Star*, which is the world of revelation, whose organon was language. The return to life and language is a return from silence. Silence is the extended accompaniment, through part three, of the vision presented there. Vision supplants language (SR 295) in the hypercosmic "leap beyond the world of words" (SR 385). In this "redeemed world above-and-beyond" (SR 418), revelation ceases. That the revealed name of God is so bounded by strictures on its pronunciation, at least within Jewish tradition, already anticipates the final end when it is altogether rescinded (SR 383–384). The points of climactic silence within the Jewish and Christian liturgical cycles—at Yom Kippur (SR 323–324)[51] or during the mass (SR 370)—are further anticipations.

A contrast sometimes heard of the ancient Jews with the Greeks is that the first were foremost aural, and the second visual. The one was naturally attentive to language, the other to vision. Certainly Plato located his highest visions of goodness, beauty, and truth in a world beyond words. Socrates seems to plead for silence when he "recalls," with Phaedrus, the pre-ensouled vision of ideal beauty.[52] In a striking parallel with Rosenzweig's claim about eternal truth, that it assumes an imagable configuration (the star) (SR 422), which is beyond, but related to, the real world, Socrates tells Glaucon, in the *Republic*, that at the height of dialectic he would "behold not an image only but the absolute truth . . . [which] would have been something like reality."[53] Socrates is skeptical that words could ever express what is seen there for, "I want to know whether ideals are ever fully realized in language? Does not the word express more than the

fact, and must not the actual . . . fall short of the truth?"[54] Rosenzweig also devalues language before vision, since language gives itself away in speech: "a word forgets itself and is to be forgotten" (SR
372); while light, as neoplatonists have always observed, is not reduced by shining but "is visible by remaining wholly in itself" (SR
295). Even the ascending Platonic sequence of fact, actual/language,
truth, could be taken in parallel with the protocosmic, cosmic, and
hypercosmic sections of the *Star*. Truth is the climactic height for
both.[55] Both describe the dangers of scaling these heights—the "nox-
ious weeds" of improperly applied dialectic,[56] the excess of emotion
and self-enclosure that threaten Christianity and Judaism, respectively, at their farthest outward and inward reaches; so much so that
Rosenzweig is prompted to warn his readers, in one of his few direct
addresses to them, to "be very careful for the sake of your souls" (SR
418), an admonition that raises the tremors associated in rabbinic
Judaism with the study of esoteric lore.

The comparison with Plato cannot be pressed too far. Socrates
was after all a major contributor to the philosophical cult of death,[57]
which Rosenzweig takes such pains to undermine. But Plato proves
a suggestive meeting ground for *The Philosophy of Art* and the Pla-
tonically resonant sections of part three of the *Star*. One contemporary of the early Schelling called him "this second Plato."[58] Plato
appears very early in *The Philosophy of Art* as "the divine Plato" (PA
4), whose banishment of poetry from the ideal state is a serious challenge indeed. Schelling explains that troubling exile, decreed in book
ten of the *Republic*, on grounds that ancient art necessarily privileged the finite, or real, towards which the infinite moved, while
Plato instated the infinite as determinative goal centuries before its
time. If Plato had lived to see the aspiring infinity of Christian art,
just finite enough for the sake of art, he would never have banished
poetry from his state. Plato, the idealist, was a modern, as are all who
pine for the infinite. This is already an affinity with Schelling. For
both, the infinite is disclosed in vision. For neither, is the vision primarily sensual. It is no accident, surely, that Schelling's reflections on
Plato follow immediately on a paragraph in which "the sensual eye"
is deemed wholly useless to philosophy (PA 4). The Schellingian vision is an intuition in the Kantian sense, of an immediate representation; but, as against Kant, it is not confined to sense, and is not
determined by universal concepts. Purely sensible intuition is only
comprehensible through the mediation of concepts. So the conceptually unmediated must be nonsensuous. Kant would restrict these
representations to the pure forms of sensual intuition, space and

time, and to the ideas, the objectless ones of theoretical reason and the esthetic ones of judgment. But for Schelling, there is one conceptually unmediated representation that is neither objectless nor exclusively esthetic, and this is indifference. As formulated in *Bruno*, indifference is precisely the identification of objective sensations with subjectively imposed concepts. In the collapse of that separation there is no longer a distinction between givenness (of sense) and determining (by concepts), or between known and knower. The knower, become knowing, is simply knowing knowing.[59] That is his intellectual vision.

But at this juncture, Schellingian and Platonic vision part ways. They part over a division within vision itself, which can be either the act of seeing or the object seen. Schellingian vision subsumes the object under the act. But Platonic vision does not. Plato sets up a correspondence between knowing and known: the act of knowing can only be of being, which are the ideas.[60] Socrates describes a "drawing near and mingling and becoming incorporate with being,"[61] but the movement of this subsumption is, if anything, of the act under the object, the direction neoplatonism would follow and that German idealism would reverse. But certainly two of the most memorable metaphors from the *Republic*, the cave and the divided line, work to accentuate the distance between subjective act and object. "In the world of knowledge the idea of the good appears last of all and is seen only with an effort."[62] It is "the fragility of goodness"[63] that drives the threefold Platonic denial—of the world, for the sake of knowledge of the good; of the body, for the sake of the happiness of the good; of tragic literature, for the sake of the beauty of the good. The vision of the good is never assured; it hovers above the highest act philosophy can commend, namely dialectic. The vision begins where dialectic, so inseparably bound to language, ends. Part of the poignancy of the Platonic dialogues is that, by committing Socrates to so much dialectical discourse, they allow him so few occasions for actual vision. Only the silences that sporadically occur, in fits of solitary abstraction, in the places where Glaucon cannot follow, in "memory of scenes which have passed away"[64], open a space for it.

Here Rosenzweig is the truer Platonist. For the truth perceived in part three of the *Star* is emphatically only perceived, and not incorporated under any vital human act. All that is vital and active is confined to part two. If anything, Rosenzweig's drift in part three follows Plato's towards an act-encompassing truth, except that the truth points back to acts, like the vision from which philosophers descend back down into the cave. Both Plato and Rosenzweig deny the unfigured immediacy of truth. Rosenzweig shifts immediacy to divine love (SR 392), which is one with its linguistic expression. But truth, transcending language, must be mediated by figures. Socrates, too, has recourse to these—the winged horses of the soul,[65] the sun of reason—for the highest truths are "a theme of large and more than mortal discourse."[66] Rosenzweig's figure for the truth is, of course, the star of redemption. The content of the star is not new. Its content is the inversive meetings of part two, overlaid the protocosmic points of part one. What is new is the form of the presentation. The new form is signaled by the changes in the titles of the three major parts of the book, from Elements to Course to Structure (*Gestalt*) (SR 295). The elements were a chaos of self-enclosures competing for the position of the whole. The courses were the avenues of directed movement over which the externalized elements met in shared constitution of the whole. Directed movement succeeds chaos. In structure, rest succeeds movement. The structure is an end in which all coursing ceases, including life itself (SR 380). It is as though to see the whole of the course, which is identified with life, one must step outside it. The light of the hypercosmos ends revealed life in the double sense in which death ends created life. Just as death intensifies the direction towards individuality in which created human life moves, and so, in a sense, fulfills it in the very act of ending it, so the light of truth intensifies the direction towards truth in which the only partially true lives of revelation move, ending them in the very act of completing them. This is why the hypercosmos is simultaneously life and a "view beyond life" (SR 384, 416), a paradox that follows the idealist logic of vanishing, by which two sides of a vanished space can take the same, or opposing, predicates. So Rosenzweig can say, in addition, that the life of revelation is transformed into hypercosmic light (SR 380).

If life moves upward, vanishingly, into the figure of the star, God moves downward, revealingly, into it. God "gives himself figure" (SR 422) in the truth of the star. God is doubly related to the star. He constitutes one of its three points, and from that station coursingly meets both human and world. This is how human and world know God in their own life courses. But the revelation of God in the course is simultaneously a self-concealment. The revelation of God projects, backwards, a veil of concealment over the protocosmic God. That God now shows itself for a construct of nonknowledge, that predicts the creating, revealing God of the cosmos. The hypercosmos is a complementary presentation of divine concealment, projected forward from the present, instead of backward. The end it shows of the coursings is concealed from us who livingly inhabit them. It shows what from within life defies presentation, namely our own ends. The difference between God and us is that he experiences the star, as we do the course, while we only catch it in a vision. It is the culmination of our moment of philosophizing, which Rosenzweig says everyone should do just once. The "millennial secret of philosophy" is, after all, that death is its "musaget" (SR 5), the conductor of its multiple voices not only from "Iona to Jena" (SR 12) but beyond also, to Frankfurt and the new philosophy, which once again teaches the fulfillment of ends; except that now, philosophy should bare its secret and retire. We are not to long for our deaths, but return to our lives, and leave the vision of the star to a future that is always just ahead.

It was the burden of the Schellingian modern to long for an infinite he could not livingly attain. Only modern art, which miraculously infinitizes the finite, could offer moments of fulfillment. Rosenzweig, too, will accommodate the visionary moment. But the figure of the star wakens no longing to dwell in it. Rosenzweig imposes upon the figure of the star the secondary figure of a face. Because the star is fixed by God's position at the top, it exhibits a hierarchy that can be interpreted after the model of a human face. The upright triangle of protocosmic points provides structure for the face: God, the forehead; human and world, the cheeks. The inverted triangle of coursings provides the two active organs: creation and revelation, the eyes; redemption, the mouth. Schelling had also singled out eyes and forehead as "the most significant features" of the head (PA 187). The human form is "an image of the universe" and the eyes, the organ through which "the innermost light of nature looks out" (PA 187). If Rosenzweig's imagistic face is superimposed on Schelling's, then the eyes of creation and revelation do not so much see as mediate a light that looks out through them. Rosenzweig does indeed build on this image: the eyes shine, the one evenly, the other flashingly—the one continuously, in support of the world's need, the other discontinuously, in need of human support. Rosenzweig differs from Schelling in drawing attention to the mouth. If the mouth is redemption, it speaks no words. For God does not directly address either the human or world in redemption. But like the prophetic images of the word that is not heard but seen (Amos 1:1, Isaiah 2:1), a visible but wordless communication shapes itself on the mouth: it is a kiss. An image of love is seen in the mouth. And this is the moment that the visible face vanishes into the audible word of the command to "Love me!" The light of the hypercosmos turns back into the life of the cosmos and the lived course of creation, revelation, and redemption.

Towards the end of part two, in a section entitled "Relationship to the Protocosmos," Rosenzweig considers the relation of the cosmic coursings to the protocosmic points. The paths that connect the emerged points to the cosmos are the same as those that meet within the confines of each of the self-enclosed points of the protocosmos. It is on this basis that Rosenzweig connected philosophy to theology as the latter's predictor. If the hypercosmos, in turn, refers back to the cosmos, then it marks an area of inquiry that likewise stands to theology as philosophy does, only inverted, referring back to theology instead of forward to it. And this would suggest that philosophy, whose proper province is the protocosmos, is nonetheless precisely mirrored in the hypercosmos. Rosenzweig himself suggests the mirror when he names three major sections of the third book of part three after the sections of each book of part one. "God (Theology)," "Truth (Cosmology)," and "Spirit (Psychology)" in part three mirror "Negative Theology," "Negative Cosmology," and "Negative Psychology," in part one. This could explain the peculiarly philosophical tenor of the hypercosmic sections, harking back to Plato at his most visionary and to all who, like Schelling, follow in his train. An object and its mirror image reverse the sides of a common axis. From the vantage point of a line drawn down the middle of the object, what is rightward from there is leftward from the standpoint of the same line repeated in the image. And so if the hypercosmos mirrors the protocosmos, they must reverse each other over a common axis. But this is just what they appear to do. The common axis is a concept that applies to both the protocosmic elements and the structured star, namely factuality. The reversals are developed over a host of analogous oppositions: truth and nonknowledge, lightness and dark, wholeness and part, prayer and logic.

Both the protocosmos and the hypercosmos culminate in facts: the facts of the three self-enclosed elements, the fact of the star. Rosenzweig contrasts the factuality of the elements to the paths of reasoning that culminate in them (SR 63), and the fact of the star to multiple points of view (SR 422). It is as though factuality stands opposed to movement and possibility, which are, themselves, interrelated. Movement presupposes possibility. Both concepts are integral to the idea of change. Facts are contents at rest, as opposed to the realities of creation, revelation, and redemption, which are meetings of movements. So, for example, the reality of human nature exhibited in revelation and redemption cannot be said to be "in fact at all" (SR 282); rather, it becomes.

Among the idealists, it was Fichte who elaborated the concept of facticity. In *The Science of Knowledge*, that "the self posits itself as determined by the notself" is both the result of a deduction and "a primordial fact occurring in our mind."[67] That is, the paradoxical act of self-determination through limitation by an other occurs both unconsciously and, in philosophy, as the conclusion of a conscious process of thought. The fact is both the unconscious (primordial) occurrence and the deduced thought that corresponds to it.[68] In philosophy, the primordial fact, "elevated by reflection into the consciousness"[69] becomes a proved fact that excludes all other possibilities. The Fichtean circle of facticity is fundamentally the same as the Schellingian circle of self-affirmation. For Schellingian self-affirmation is also an identification of unconscious and conscious activity. What affirms itself has transformed a noncognized beginning into a cognized ending. Both Fichte and Schelling are tracing the genesis of knowledge within monism. By employing the language of facticity, Rosenzweig situates himself in this heritage. But by breaking with idealism, he also fractures the concept of facticity. The identified unconscious and consciously deduced fact breaks in two along the seam of the meeting between conscious and unconscious, and all of reality intervenes between them. The unconscious fact falls back into a permanent presupposition of reality, incomprehensible apart from reality, while the conscious fact falls forward into a vision of reality that can never be vitally known (at least by us). Rosenzweig alludes in passing to the idealist backdrop of his discussion when he observes that "factuality is completed only in contemplation; now no more is heard of object and act" (SR 295). Rosenzweig retains from idealism the fixity of facts. By the completion of factuality, he means the transformation of the chaotically unrelated protocosmic elements into their unalterably fixed positions within the star. He also retains from idealism the culminating station of facts, at the conclusion of a movement, but it is no longer a movement of pure reasoning. The old idealist completion of factuality passed from unconscious identity of act and object, through conscious act, to conscious identity of act and object. But now a vast expanse of reality blocks these passages, and no more is heard of act and object. The three protocosmic facts are transposed to the one hypercosmic fact, not by way of the self-conscious play of object and act, but by the cosmic courses of revelation. The courses, exited and then contemplated as a unified fact in hypercosmic vision show the

protocosmic facts beneath them. The enigmatic facts of the protocosmos, which figure in reality as largely unconscious presuppositions, are mirrored in the consciously contemplated fact of the
hypercosmos. It is the idealist heritage of factuality, lying beneath
Rosenzweig's split application of this term to both protocosmic elements and hypercosmic star, that points to the axial role facts can
play between the two nonreal cosmoses.

The oppositions that arrange themselves around this axis have
already begun to show. The protocosmic elements are culminations
of nonknowledge, products of reasoning from contentful nothings.
The star is a vision of truth. Rosenzweig explicitly arranges the opposition of *das Nichts* and the truth around a common factuality:
"The Nought, exactly like the truth, is not an independent subject
at all. It is a mere fact . . . seeking the ground on which it stands"
(SR 390). Here, factuality is what lacks subjectivity. Unlike idealist
factuality, Rosenzweig's cannot produce itself as a product of an authenticating movement. It must seek its ground outside itself. The
Nichts finds its ground in the cosmos, i.e., it becomes comprehensible as predictor (not producer) of the cosmos. When Rosenzweig applies the same lack of subjectivity to the truth, he undermines in a
single step the whole idealist program. For what fuels idealism's
conviction that self-authenticating truth may be found (SR 386) is
the belief that truth may function as active subject, indeed, as subject of the sentence "Truth is God." By inverting this sentence, and
locking it into its reversal, "God is truth," Rosenzweig reduces truth
once more to the place of a mere factual object. It, like *das Nichts*,
requires grounding outside itself. And this, says Rosenzweig, is
God. If truth stands to God as protocosmic *Nichts* to cosmos, then
God would seem shifted forward to a place beyond truth, like the
cosmos that, from its place beyond the protocosmos, projects back
onto it a meaning. And Rosenzweig does affirm that God is "'more'
than the truth" (SR 386). But then, in an unexpected reversal, the
position from which God authenticates the truth is shifted back to
before the first appearance of truth, into the cosmos. For the star of
truth is generated by the cosmic coursings. And, from a human perspective, these begin in the revelatory command to love, unfolding
from there backward into creation, and forward into redemption. It
is because God pronounces "Love me!" that the cosmic course, on
which the star is built, exists at all. And so God does authenticate
the truth; "God is its origin" (SR 388). But that hypercosmic stance
of God towards truth precisely reverses his protocosmic stance towards *das Nichts*. The protocosmic God is nothing's product; the hy-

percosmic God is truth's origin. These two opposing locations of God exhaust the positions from which the question "What is God?" may be sensibly posed and answered: "God is the Naught" and "God is the truth" (SR 390).

That opposite answers may come with equal justice to the same question evokes shades of Schelling's indifference. But indifference would draw the two answers into a single truth, while Rosenzweig separates them over the divide of reality. The question of "what God is" cannot even be posed from within reality. For the question presupposes God's isolatability, a fact that reality denies. God is an isolatable fact only in his protocosmic capacity as nothing, or his hypercosmic capacity as truth. Even to ask what God is, one must have fallen backward into the protocosmos, or forward into the hypercosmos. Because protocosmic nothing predicts reality, and hypercosmic truth has its origin there, passage does lead forward from the fact of nothing and backward from the fact of truth into a common reality. But far from uniting these facts in a single affirmation, reality negates them, for it does not deal in the stasis of facts at all, but only in the reality of movement, and preserves them within itself only as separable traces, the one of a permanent past, the other of the future. Rosenzweig has turned indifference inside out. It was indifference that left behind the trace of reality. Now it is reality that conceals traces of a broken indifference.

The broken indifference extends over two other, familiar Schellingian oppositions: light and dark, whole and part. In the light of the hypercosmos there occurs "a direct view of the whole truth" (SR 416). In the dark of the protocosmos, the whole has been shattered into three unrelated parts. The parts are not particulars in Schelling's sense. None of them reproduces the whole within itself, but each remains separately by its own self. And yet, here again, through the shared axis of factuality, the unrealities of light and dark, whole and part, seem to mirror each other. The protocosmic elements, chaotically arranged, reappear permanently fixed in the hypercosmic star. Reciprocally, the light of the hypercosmos takes on some features of darkness. The God who originates truth does reveal himself in the love command, but simultaneously withdraws beyond the truth he shows, like the cosmos beyond the protocosmos, to a station "beyond all that can be imparted . . . above even the whole" (SR 417). And suddenly the hypercosmos is as much about concealment as the protocosmos, so much so that the light of the one "is the same as that which spent the night in God's bosom prior to all existence" (SR 417), i.e., in the protocosmos. Alternatively, from the standpoint of the cosmos, the three elements constitute a "glowing tripod" (SR 257) in the protocosmic night, that lights the way in two opposite directions: toward their own origin in nothing, and toward the origin of their mirrored, hypercosmic projections in God. Over the separation of reality, the light reflects the darkness, and the darkness, the light, much like the Schellingian potences that subsume their opposites within them. In the end, both proto- and hypercosmos darken the view of God by offering walls behind which his essence may retire, and lighten it at the same time by the mirrored pointings they make to his cosmic reality.

In another redounding to philosophical origins beyond Schelling, in Plato, Rosenzweig casts mathematics as the organon of the protocosmos. For arithmetic was the first stage of education towards Platonic dialectic. In a highly unlikely pairing, prayer occupies the corresponding role or organon in the hypercosmos. It is hard to see how any mirroring can occur here; but it does, through silence. From the standpoint of spoken (dialogic) language, the organon of reality, the communal prayers of the Jewish and Christian hypercosmos are as silent as the algebraic equations of the protocosmos. Here again, the commonality is mirrored or inverted across the divide of the two nonreal cosmoses. Algebra is mute from lacking words; communal prayer, from surpassing them (SR 385). Words obstruct communal immediacy. Ultimately, prayer culminates in gestures that silently communicate the whole of their speakable content. Now it is no longer a private language of command that connects two, immediately, in dialogue, but a shared silence that connects many, immediately, in community. The communal prayer extends beyond the individual enworlding of philosophical prayer, to a vision of absolute completion. The object of prayer having expanded, the praying subject does too.

The premise of the hypercosmos is the six-part course of the cosmos. The desired conclusion of the hypercosmos is a vision of the truth, single and whole. Communal prayer is the organon of the hypercosmos because it is the means by which passage is offered from premise to conclusion. Part of the difficulty of the *Star*'s last part may owe to a mixing of genres it imposes on itself. Just as, if art is the organon of philosophy, Schelling's *System of Transcendental Idealism* must eventually convert from philosophical exposition to art, so, if prayer is the organon of absolute truth, must the last part of the *Star* ultimately convert to prayer. It does take on the tone of prayer, especially in the final section entitled "Gate," where there erupts that singular admonition to take care for our souls, followed by a passage from one of the most famous prayers of Jewish ritual, the priestly blessing of Numbers 6:25. But mostly, what part three offers is an interpretive exposition of prayer, culminating in expository remove, at second hand, in the desired vision. We have already considered the opening sections of part three, on philosophical prayer. These function as prelude to the two lengthy books on Jewish and Christian prayer. For, as Rosenzweig explains, "life . . . must first become wholly temporal, wholly alive [as it does in the self-affirming individuality of philosophical prayer] before it can become eternal life" (SR 288). Rosenzweig speaks loosely here, since it is only Christians who must first be enlivened to philosophical individuality, and only Jews who know eternal life. Still, between them, and their respective liturgical cycles, they exhaust all the truly communal prayer the *Star* acknowledges.

We have seen philosophy play the presuppositional handmaid to theology, as it does in the introduction to part three of the *Star*, on philosophical prayer, and we have seen philosophy mirrored in the final climactic approach to truth, as occurs in book three of part three, on truth. With regard to Judaism and Christianity, which are treated in the two intervening books, philosophy plays these roles again in different guises. Philosophy as dualistic paganism is the presupposition of Christianity; philosophy as monistic self-enclosure of opposites is the protocosmic mirror of Judaism.

Like the philosophy of art, which according to Schelling unites opposites in one, Judaism and Christianity are inherent self-contradictions. They are courses of liturgical acts that are nonetheless hypercosmically instated beyond the reality of courses. Alternatively, they realize the unlivable star in two alternatively livable ways, one facing inward towards the star, the other facing outward, and each is blind in the other's direction. The figure that allows for these living contradictions is the hour, which temporally translates a circle. The hour marks a passage with a distinct beginning and end, but it is stationary, since the end comes back to the beginning and recommences (SR 290). The repetition of hours, a concept that already evokes the monastic prayer day, is a figure of eternity. Eternity is the inversion of time, the end that precedes the beginning or, as Rosenzweig puts it, the moment whose perishing is a beginning (SR 289), and this is just what occurs at the boundary between hours. It is because the Jewish and Christian liturgies are built on the hour—on days, weeks, months, years patterned after it—that they can move those who practice them towards a vision of the eternal, perspectiveless truth. As it happens, only Jews, who face inside their own liturgical cycles, attain the vision, while Christians, ever facing outside their sacred hours, to the inhabitants of profane, merely successive time, miss it.

If the common form of Christianity and Judaism, a static movement, is paradoxical, their contents too embrace explicit oppositions. The divisions within Judaism and Christianity owe to their respective inward and outward facings. Judaism is a religion of one, particular people who claim to bear an exhaustive religious significance for all peoples. Judaism oscillates between the poles of this particular and universal status. Christianity discounts the divisions of peoples entirely. The church, which a portion of the world's individuals have joined, claims to bear a message of exhaustive religious significance to all individuals. It is here that Christianity confronts philosophy in the form of protocosmic paganism. For philosophy had enclosed each of the protocosmic elements within an equation of its passive essence and active, negating movement. And these equations are the philosophical constructions of pagan divinity, humanity, and worldliness, whose historical paradigms are ancient Greek mythology, tragedy, and polis. It is the bearer of these protocosmic thought structures that Christianity confronts as it faces outward from its sacred hours.

But Greek mythology, tragedy, and polis belong to the ancient world. No one vitally inhabits these ancient protocosmic expressions anymore. Still, if Christianity is to operate as revelation, it must provide routes for self-enclosures to open towards each other in meeting. For this is what revelation, most broadly understood, is. And that presupposes self-enclosures to address. Since these self-enclosures are no longer given in vital paganism, Christianity, as we have seen, must recreate them, and does so, paradoxically, within the very confines of the church. The church carries within its embrace those who have been converted to its liturgical forms, but not its inward beliefs, and conversely, those converted to the beliefs, but not the liturgical forms. It is by the tolerant catholicity of the church, which is both Petrine and Pauline, that it admits so broad a spectrum. Christianity itself is much less tolerant. It counts for its own only those who know inwardly (experientially) the courses of revelation; and these it presents to be known only through the liturgy. So only the souls in which outward and inward conversion meet can claim to be true Christians. But it is just here that the paradoxical figure of the praying philosopher appears. For the soul may ride on the movements that converge within itself, of the outwardly and inwardly churched, but reject their churchly contents, and know their meeting

as a self-affirmation, rather than as affirmation of Christianity. This occurs when, as is almost proper, the merely churched individual wakens to the Christian inadequacy of the merely outward or inward turns and, abandoning the profession of either, takes their union within himself as a meeting of his own outward and inward self. This is what Goethe does when he prays to his own enworlded fate. And so a portion of the flock the church has nurtured becomes pagan, i.e., self-enclosed.

It was Maimonides who understood God's prolonged and seemingly pointless preparations of the Jewish people to receive his law to exemplify the divine category of the "gracious ruse."[70] But surely Christianity's use of the church to prepare its own true Christians surpasses in complexity all other instances of the divine use of ruse. For all their outward professions and inward confessions, the Christians of the Pauline and Petrine churches are pre-Christians at best. Unknown to themselves, they are trodding a long, slow path through Christian forms to a vibrant paganism. It would seem that the convergence of the outward and inward halves of pre-Christian life would culminate in the first full Christian. And, in a sense, they do. "Goethe," who for Rosenzweig typifies the praying philosopher, "is truly the great heathen and the great Christian at one and the same time" (SR 283). But his was a Christianity in form only, composed of the joint outward and inward movements, but not the contents, of Christian conversion. Now, however, at the Goethean summit of philosophical prayer, paganism is revived in its formal and contentful wholeness. The three self-enclosed dualities of the protocosmos repeat in his person and perspective. Rosenzweig explicitly presents only the human duality, which Goethe's prayer to his own fate illustrates. The fate, or enworlded completion of himself, is constructable as protocosmic human character; the prayer to it, as the protocosmically willed affirmation of character. Both together effect a human self-enclosure. But in any even superficial reading of Goethe's *Faust*, the divine and worldly self-enclosures of paganism may be read as well. Pagan divinity enclosed within itself anything of human or world it touched, and so inclined to pantheism. Pagan worldliness enclosed over the divide it suffered between ideal form and concrete reality. Faust exhibits both tendencies when in his first long speech of Goethe's play, he rejects his books (ideal form) for "nature's hidden powers," which encompass even him in their divinity ("Am I a god?").[71]

The church culminates in Goethe. And now, to complete the ruse, Christianity finally has its say. Goethe was exceptional in his capacity to negotiate self-enclosure. It is a dangerous undertaking, bordered by abysses. Few can sustain the balanced tension of a vital self-enclosure, perfectly poised between an incompleted fate and the hope to complete it. The temptations are too great rashly and violently to force the fate, before its time, or abandon it altogether, on account of the anxious waiting it imposes, and presume oneself, falsely and capriciously, "free to entreat everything" (SR 286). By the title of the section that presents these dangers, "Goethe and Nietzsche," Rosenzweig indicates who he takes to warn us, by his example, against following Goethe. But there is no need to follow him. For once Christianity, via the church, has created self-enclosure, it was never its intention to linger there. Goethe, who did linger, is a worthy sacrifice to pay for all the others who, in his self-enclosed wake, are to be opened up to genuine relation.

Goethe functions as the modern protocosmos. Now that pagan pantheism, heroism, and worldly duality have been revived in him, Christianity comes with its threefold bifurcation: of God, between Father and Son; of human, between priest and saint; of world, between sacred and secular, to confront and eclipse the self-enclosed pagan dualisms. We have already seen, in chapter two, how this occurs. What remains to note is how explicitly Rosenzweig refers the Christian dualities back to those of the protocosmos. The "rays" of Christianity "burst visibly and divisibly into the night of the pagan proto- and hypocosmos" (SR 415). Christianity purchases its eclipse of paganism at the price of its own division into the Petrine, Pauline, and Johannine churches. The church can unite only "beyond the outer space of the protocosmos" (SR 398) when, as St. Paul says, "the full number of the Gentiles [have] come in" (Romans 11:25).

Of the three Christian churches, it is the Pauline one, or Protestantism, that Rosenzweig discusses under the headings "Modern Man" and "Modern Life in the Split Reality" (SR 280–281). The modern human is inward, fixed on the actions of his inner soul. The life he leads splits on the divide of the inner from the outward, which becomes the explicitly disparaged worldly. This is the sensibility for which church and world are opposites. But it is not as though division stops here, or even with the distinction from the two other churches, the Petrine and Johannine. Rosenzweig's analysis of Goethe, who culminates the Petrine and Pauline church, suggests that Christianity is to be further distinguished from these. Christianity merely builds on the self-enclosure jointly effected by Peter, Paul, and Goethe. Under the long section "Sanctification of the Soul: the Clerical Year," Rosenzweig traces the liturgical figurings of creation, revelation, and redemption that all completed Christians know experientially. These are the Johannine Christians who, grounded in the sacred hours of the clerical year, are the first Christians capable of redemptive love, always spontaneously and self-sacrificially whole, that Rosenzweig described in book three, part two of the *Star*.

Rosenzweig suggests that, if Pauline Christianity is modern, Johannine Christianity is the future church that succeeds modernity. It has already come into being. Indeed, all three churches, Petrine, Pauline, and Johannine, mark a succession more logical than temporal, present since the beginning of Christianity. Here, Rosenzweig is more sanguine than Schelling. For Schelling, too, intertwined Christianity with modernity. For him all Christianity was essentially modern (in Rosenzweig's terms, Pauline) by virtue of its divisive longing for the infinite. The Christian is divided not so much over inner and outer as over his paradoxical longing for what would efface him. The Schellingian Christian, like all moderns of nonmystical stamp, is divided from the whole by his own individuality on which, like the Pauline Christian of Rosenzweig's analysis, he is self-consciously (sentimentally) fixated. What corresponds in Schelling to the Petrine church is the church entire. The Schellingian church is what, by its concrete extension in history, its institutional and liturgical forms, guarantees a Christian art. A common division between Christianity and church runs through Schelling and Rosenzweig. Schelling's self-enclosed church saves an infinite Christianity for art. Rosenzweig's self-enclosed churches of Peter and Paul enable the salvation that occurs in John's, the final church of a genuinely relational Christianity. In *The Philosophy of Art*, Schelling offers no realized Christian analog to the Johannine church. If the Schellingian church is to offer any salvation other than the mystic's, it must be taken as art.

Rosenzweig will not take Christianity as art. However, he will allow Christianity to apply the arts to its liturgical figurings of creation, revelation, and redemption. Strangely and unexpectedly, it is Judaism that will go furthest to mirror the Schellingian self-enclosures of art. By the same token, it is Judaism that mirrors, rather than overcomes, the protocosmic self-enclosures. Judaism generates its own sets of balanced contradictions and these, says Rosenzweig, are "mirror-like" reflections of "all possible contradictions" (SR 402). The Jewish people, as the one people that claims to stand in for all peoples before God and world, microcosmically reproduces within Judaism the universal relations between God, human, and world, that are the subject of the *Star*'s second part. The God who creates and reveals becomes the creator God of the biblical book of Genesis, the most universalistic of the five books of the Jewish Pentateuch, and the revealer God of Exodus, the book in which the Jews are constituted the people who particularly receive God's love. The universal human who receives revelation and redeems the world becomes the elected Jewish people and the expected messiah who will reconcile the nations. The world that receives creation and redemption becomes what the rabbinic literature divides up between this world, *olam haze*, and the world-to-come, *olam haba*. In the liturgical sequence of Judaism which, like that of Christianity, figures creation, revelation, and redemption in organically repeated successions, these oppositions are not felt in tension. Each aspect of the Jewish God, human, and world receives its liturgical focus. But considered in stationary isolation, as constituting the "Jewish essence" (SR 305), the bipolar God, human, and world are each suspended between a contradiction: God, between the justice of his creating and the mercy of his revealing; human, between the private relation with God and the charge to redeem the world; world, between Israel and the rest of the peoples. Like the protocosmic elements, each of which differently envalues the variables of the equation $y=x$, each of the Jewish contradictions particularizes a universal contradiction between the particular and the universal. Unlike Christianity, Judaism does not take its contradictions outside itself, but resolves them within itself. It is mysticism that, from within Judaism, bridges the universal-particular polarities. Mystical correspondences connect Jewish world to all the world; Israel to all the peoples; revealed God to transcendent God (SR 408–411).

From cosmic coursings to Jewish essence to mystical exegesis, Rosenzweig traces a movement from universal to particular and back again to universal. The freezings of the courses in which revealed God, human, and world flow, so as to extract out of these elements a static Jewish essence for each, is already a return to protocosmic factuality. As self-contradictions, Jewish God, human, and world lend themselves to mirroring the old protocosmic elements, for these were also self-enclosed polarities. A factuality is both a given and a conclusion of an authenticating movement. In the protocosmos, the nothing of each of the elements was both given and the result of a unique reasoning process. But the God, human, and world of the Jewish essence start and conclude a different movement, namely that which courses back and forth between universal and particular. Mystical exegesis is the movement by which the given, particular world of the Jewish essence becomes, in conclusion, the universal world of nature. But the universal conclusions of the exegesis are still markedly Jewish. It is aspects of the distinctly Jewish world that show beneath the seemingly a-Judaic qualities of nature. In Judaism, the particular becomes the universal while retaining its particularity.

But this formula is already familiar from Schelling. It is the formula for indifference, applied outside the absolute act of self-affirmation to the determinations within the potences of real and ideal. The particular, as opposed to the individual, was the microcosmic repetition of the whole. The Schellingian idea, a paradigmatic indifference, anticipates the relation between Jewish essence and cosmic whole:

> Every idea has two unities: the one through which it exists within itself and is absolute—hence the one through which the absolute is formed into the particularity of the idea—and the one through which it is taken up as a particular into the absolute as into its own center (PA 35).

One could easily substitute "element of Jewish essence" for "idea" in this passage. God and Jewish God are the absolute and the particular. Mystical exegesis effects the forming of each into the other.

Overlaid the relation between the elements of the protocosmos and those of the Jewish essence, Schellingian indifference points up the mirroring between them. The protocosmic elements are parts that unsuccessfully strive for the whole of being. Protocosmic God, world, and human are constructed in complete separation from each other. From the point of view of any one of them, nothing else exists. But we who see the protocosmos in retrospect, from within revelation, know that each is only a third of the whole. As opposed to the protocosmic elements, none of the elements of Jewish essence presumes to exhaust the whole of being, but only the whole of its own part in the whole. The constriction of God, world, and human into Jewish God, world, and human opens a space that separates the universal God, human, and world from their particularizations. A kind of Schellingian indifference occurs across this space. The common axis of the mirror between protocosmic and Jewish God, for example, is their factuality. The opposition between them, which creates the reflection, is the location of the separating space they presume to span: unnegotiably outside the protocosmic God, negotiably within the Jewish one. Alternatively, the opposition is over indifference: the one attains it, the other does not.

If excavations in the *Star*'s third part uncover indifference in one place, namely at the center of Jewish essence, the curious seeker may well wonder whether this quintessentially idealist idea is not lurking beneath other surfaces there. This is especially so in light of the intimate oppositional parallels Rosenzweig draws between Judaism and Christianity. In the German edition of the *Star*, published by Suhrkamp, all the section headings of the book are gathered together in a long list at the end. Major section headings are capitalized, minor ones lowercased. So presented, the parallel development of books one and two of part three, on Judaism and Christianity respectively, is very plain to see. Especially revealing are the parallel, inverse headings of the opening and closing sections of each book. Sequentially presented, these are: "The Promise of Eternity," and "Eternity of the Promise," for Judaism; "The Eternity of Realization," and "Realization of Eternity," for Christianity. The promise of eternity is the election of the Jews as eternal people. The eternity of the promise is the persistence of the people's witness, against all who would tempt fate, that eternity is still to come. The eternity of realization is the Johannine Christian bearing of livable figures for creation, revelation, and redemption to all the rest of the world. The realization of eternity is the completion of that work. The sequence of headings effects a double mirror image. Each pair of headings is a self-contained mirror-image, but the pairs, juxtaposed, also mirror each other. This is, by now, a familiar device, from the mirroring across which the components of each protocosmic element (except the world's) emerge into revelation, or from the complex enfolding of mirror images within Schelling's absolute act of self-affirmation. We have already once encountered the multiple mirroring between Judaism and Christianity.[72] They are prime candidates for the absolute opposition that underlies indifference. For they do oppose each other. There is an "enmity between the two for all time" (SR 415), based on the opposing stations they take up on either side of eternity, the one heralding, the other realizing, its unfulfilled promise. Yet God "withal has most intimately bound each to each" (SR 415).

Rosenzweig states the intimacy most strongly over the two sections "Eternity of the Promise" and "Realization of Eternity." He follows an image of Judah Halevi's, whose concept of God's "secret plan for us" (SR 379) anticipates the Maimonidean God's gracious ruse. Halevi likened the Jewish people to a seed whose growth into a fruit tree both transforms it, unrecognizably, and prepares for its recognizable reappearance in the fruit. Halevi likens Christianity to the tree, and the reappeared seed to the messiah awaited by the Jews.[73] By retelling the parable, Rosenzweig suggests that Christianity is more than the mirror image of Judaism, but its outwardly distinct transformation. In time, Christianity will unfold from within itself the very Judaism that gave it birth. The parable tempts the title of Hermann Cohen's book *Religion of Reason out of the Sources of Judaism* to subtitle the *Star*, only altered to: "Idealism out of the Sources of Judaism." For what is Christianity, then, but a self-objectifization of Judaism, a lengthy course away from Judaism, whose final return to it mimics the self-affirmation of the absolute. Rosenzweig's phrase for the Christian return to Judaism, "das Be-waehren der Wahrheit,"[74] the confirmation of truth, actually invites this comparison. Once the truth is confirmed, the confirming movement may vanish. Rosenzweig cannot resist a final inversion: because the end of Christianity's way is in eternity, "sein Ende in der Ewigkeit ist," it is indeed eternal. But because eternity is its end, "die Ewigkeit ist sein Ende," it vanishes there.[75]

In all fairness to this seeming subordination of Christianity to Judaism, the claim of St. Paul, who does after all define the modern church, must be recalled, that, at the end of time "the Son himself will also be subjected to him who put all things under him, that God may be everything to everyone" (I Cor. 15:28). But subordination is not indifference. And if Christianity is simply the course of Judaism's self-affirmation, the two are scarcely indifferent. But then, the Jewish people, who live the eternal life against Christianity's eternal way, also ends in eternity. "For not the way alone ends here, but life too" (SR 380). It is not so much that Judaism and Christianity attain indifference with each other as that they submerge in a larger indifference. Proto- and hypercosmos are divided by the great span of reality, which blocks their indifference. But now Judaism and Christianity, having instated reality beyond itself, appear to connect the two nonreal cosmoses across the real one, rather like the sacrament of baptism which "vouchsafes him [who is] in the minority of his life, the consummation of life" (SR 373), or even more, like Hegelian dialectic, which courses between the so outwardly similar but really oppositional worlds of sense certainty and absolute knowledge.[76] Judaism and Christianity jointly figure as the course that verges on uniting proto- and hypercosmos in indifference. For the two parallel section titles, "The Eternal People: Jewish Fate," and "The Way through Time: Christian History" (SR 298, 337) point back to either side of the universal protocosmic equation $y=x$, where x was fatedness and y was movement. On that analogy, the hypercosmos simply repeats in unified sequence what the protocosmos accomplished in unordered and mutually exclusive simultaneity: the negating instatement of essence. Christianity is the active "y" that equates with the essential "x" of Judaism by negating all pagan-philosophical challenges to it. Now the common axis is "$y=x$." The opposition over proto- and hypercosmos is that the first can only instantiate the variables over a triad of mutually unrelated equations of A's and B's, while the second does so simply and singly with Judaism and Christianity. The three become one in the mirror. And then the components of the one vanish in the all-embracing scope of the equals sign.

Judaism and Christianity could easily pass for Schellingian moderns who are finally empowered to vanish in their own completions. And then the question arises of whether and to what extent the final vanishing instates the old idealist All. Rosenzweig himself invites such speculation. The dismembered totality of idealism, which he hoped at the very beginning of the *Star* to recover (SR 22) has by the end of the book "now grown back together again" (SR 390). The choice of words is revealing. Rosenzweig has not himself reassembled the All. He has simply followed a course along which the All reassembles itself. For all that he pointedly abandons the Asian religions early on the in the *Star*, Rosenzweig exhibits a paradoxical ideal at their center, to goallessly attain a goal. It is rather like the idealist passage through unconsciousness to consciousness. The difficulty with all explicit purposes is that they tracelessly disappear on attaining their ends (SR 269). It was love, which hoped to redeem the world, but which so wholly externalized itself in each successive moment that there was no distance through which to espy a goal, that remained even at the attainment of its goal. But the projected completion of love's work is not to be taken for fulfillment of a goal in any case, but for an existence "beyond any desire for or joy in realization" (SR 384). Love's work is a succession of ends that collapse the distinction between the sighting of a goal and its realization. In that, redemptive love prefigures eternity which, liturgically figured by the "boundary between two years," is the point where "all purposes become vain" (SR 325). Love at its end in eternity is what it has been all along. It vanishes as it has always vanished, but not tracelessly. The existence "beyond joy in realization," "where everything is sacrosanct" (SR 384) is its trace. Certainly Rosenzweig at this juncture is very close to the Schellingian absolute All, into which all determinations likewise goallessly vanish, but not without leaving the trace of the potences.

Rosenzweig distinguishes the All of the cosmos from idealism's All (SR 254–255). The cosmic All is the three relations that connect the three elements in a pattern that can be figured as a star. The passage from protocosmic All to cosmic All passes through experience, revelation, or miracle, all denials of idealist passage. But Rosenzweig does not distinguish the hypercosmic All from idealism's, except on the matter of placing. For the cosmic All becomes hypercosmic not through miracle, but through that term already so charged with incipient idealism, namely enlightenment. It is simply that this final All must be placed quite finally, not initiatingly. We do not force its being from the start, but only spy it at the end. Idealism is right, but only in the end.

Art and the Hypercosmos

"The shadow realm of art . . . it longs for life itself" (SR 249). Art inhabits the living world, but lifelessly. Art traces life to its origin in prediction, is itself the ongoing prediction of life in the midst of life, and so testifies to life's status as miracle. But if nothing else, Schellingian idealism testifies to how much art would play a grander role, would itself be life or the life beyond life. By confining art to the role of herald, Rosenzweig awakens longings in it for the heights it knew under idealism's patronage.

Rosenzweig knows art's allure for the human being. "Whatever he may desire he can, after all, find in museums and concert halls" (SR 360). The "whatever" here is not carelessly exhaustive. Stephane Moses observes that, for Rosenzweig, "art is for the individual a quest for salvation."[77] Creation, revelation, and redemption are repeated in the sequence of acts that produce art, from genial vision to appreciative viewing, only here they name not relations but stages in a continuum of self-enclosures. An artwork redeems by incorporating the appreciative viewer in the self-enclosure of the creative sequence, and by contributing to the growth of his own, self-enclosed store of esthetic ideas. But it does not redeem in the real sense of connecting him with the world. Moses' observation continues: art offers "a profane salvation, that is, a solitary one that does not care for communion with other humans."[78] Rosenzweig himself calls art the pagan god of the individualists (SR 421). He anticipates the pagan god of art very early on in part three of the *Star*, when, in connection with the

Petrine, medieval church, he likens the antique paganism that the church must, for conversive purposes, revive, to a mural, "at once uncannily elusive and most colorfully visible" (SR 280). Rosenzweig also suggests that the pagan god of art will "live on to the eternal end" (SR 421). He thereby implies that, despite all his efforts on art's behalf, it will not accept the merely predictive role he has conceived for it, but will continue, until the end of all viewpoints, to offer itself as end.

Art's view of the end of viewpoints translates, figuratively, as a rotation in the star of redemption, so that the human occupies "the supreme place in the All" (SR 421). For art is after all an individually human product. In art's vision of the end, it is a star of creation that appears. For it is now creation that holds the position opposite the reigning point of the star, and that indicates, as redemption once did, the climactic relation into which the other two move. Revelation, the movement from God to human must appear as inward and passive inspiration; redemption, the movement from human to world, as active and outward artistry. And creation is the climactic consequence of the two movements. If we would set the star of creation in analogy with its redemptive cousin, then we must also speak of human self-creation, just as we did of God's self-redemption. And that surely confirms the power of this star to figure the view of the esthetic pagan; for what higher act of pagan self-enclosure is there than self-creation? That is, after all, what the artist does when he recovers himself in the work to which he has sacrificed himself.

Schelling's own focus on creation seemed a challenge to Baeckian romanticism, until it appeared how much the very distinction between creation and redemption pales in the construction of art. Rosenzweig does not name the individuals who idolize art, but Schelling might be one. For Schelling, art constitutes the end of viewpoints, since as the perfect representative of philosophical monism, art is ultimately one. All the individual artworks of antiquity "were merely the different branches of one, universal, objective and living work of art" (PA 9). Schelling presents again the paradoxical pairing that so often appears in the history of philosophy, of universality with individuality. For though art is universal, it "can express itself only with the individual" (PA 94), for otherwise there would be no location for the indifference art attains between the universal and particular. If in addition all artworks are objective and self-enclosed manifestations of gods, and if all self-enclosure is pagan, then we have construed Schellingian art as, in Rosenzweig's terms, the pagan god of the individualists.

Schelling would deny that the star of creation, patterned after the star of redemption, could figure his esthetic theory. For the human is not, to begin with, an isolable element of the All that can be raised over the rest. Insofar as it is constructed out of genuine relations, no star is monistically admissible. But Rosenzweig might offer the star of creation as the reductio ad absurdum of idealist esthetics, just as idealism itself played that role to Protestant Christianity. Of course the star of creation is inadmissible. But this is not because of any fault with relationality, but because experience shows that humans are not ascendant. Redemption is the end of creation. The world experiences the beginning of creation but not its end; the human experiences both the beginning and revelatory midpoint of creation, but not its end. Only God experiences all three points along creation's way: beginning, middle, and end. It was for this reason, as we saw in chapter two, that the star of redemption is immovably fixed under God's ascendancy.

At the same time, Rosenzweig might agree with Schelling that creation's completion in redemption occurs only in art; it is just that, since art is prior to living reality, the redemption known there is unreal. But this does not disqualify art from playing out its reality-predicting role one more time. Insofar as art is pagan, it constitutes one more challenge to Christianity on its world-converting way. Since Christianity converts paganism by shaping itself to its self-enclosed structures, and then bursting these open in relation, it must shape itself, too, to the forms of art. But this it does at its very foundation. If Judaism is the particular religion of a universal people, Christianity is the universal religion of many individuals. Christianity's address to the individual is a function of its converting mission. It builds relation out of self-enclosed individuality. Where it cannot find self-enclosure, it fashions it itself. But art has been self-enclosed from long before Christianity began. Art is a ready-made candidate for Christian mission.

And now one of those mutual meetings of need occurs that Schelling called magic and that Rosenzweig, in other contexts, called miracle. Self-enclosed art longs for life. Relational Christianity longs for self-enclosures to instate in living relations. The two meet in liturgical art.

The Christian ritual, like its Jewish counterpart, instates the living reality of creation, revelation, and redemption in liturgical acts. These are the acts that burst the self-enclosures of pagan individuality and found relations. Thus they are decidedly not artworks in Schelling's sense. The liturgy founds relation in two ways: by affording a performable vocabulary for the relational acts of creation, revelation, and redemption, and by uniting the individual performers in relation with each other, i.e., in community. But the passage from individuality to community does not necessarily come easily. Goethe, after all, held back from it, as do all who prefer the private redemption of the arts. But it is just these same arts that, by occasioning a common understanding of themselves without explicit communication, begin to forge a link between individual and community. And if the arts can be persuaded to sacrifice their purity of self-enclosed purposelessness, they can be applied to the task of founding community. In return, the arts receive a portion of that real life for which they have longed.

The Christian liturgy draws the individual practitioner of Christianity into community by incremental stages. The stages follow both the theory of art as presented in parts one and two of the *Star*, and the overall structure of the tripartite church. Just as art in general is first specified by outward form, and the first of the arts are the spatial ones; and just as the first Christian church is the outwardly and spatially expanding one of St. Peter, so the first community into which the individual Christian is initiated is a spatial one. It is the community of the assembled congregation. But the congregation is assembled in a specific place, namely a church. The applied art that serves this level of community-building is church architecture. Church buildings foster community by creating within themselves a single orientation: forward towards the altar, upwards to heaven (SR 356). Out of the univocally fixed spatial orientation of a church, only one room can arise. And so all those who enter find themselves placed in a common, divisionless space. Church music adds to the outward presentiment of community an inward dimension. Music functions here in analogy with the second or inward form of art, with the purely temporal expression of art, and with the inwardly turned church of St. Paul. The pairing of time with inward sense has, of course, Kantian precedent, but here Rosenzweig is interested in the inwardness of feeling. Music "arouses the assembled ones, each for himself, to the same feelings" (SR 362). Finally, just as poetry united the outward spatiality of the fine arts with the inward temporality of music, and just as the Johannine church sent inwardly converted Christians into the merely outwardly converted world, so does the liturgical expression of poetry, namely dance, combine space and time, body and rhythm, in gestures that silently evoke for the inner and outer Christian the deepest intimacy with his fellow worshippers.

Rosenzweig's interpretation of dance as an expression of poetry will win the ready assent of any balletomane. But for others, Schelling's *The Philosophy of Art* provides a helpful backdrop. Schelling understood dance as part of the reverse movement, back to the formative arts, that the verbal arts make after they have attained their highest expression. Drama, which unites the verbal forms of lyric and epic in indifference, completes the series of the verbal arts. If the artistic impulse would press further than drama, it must make new combinations with old antecedents. Song is the form of poesy that has recovered music, the first of the formative arts; theater, the form that has recovered the plastic arts; and dance is the form that poesy takes when it has recovered painting (PA 372). Rosenzweig's passage from poetry to dance omits the intermediate step of painting; what is more, by setting dance as the climax of a discussion titled "Sociology of the Dramatic Arts: Miracle Play," he conflates two art forms that Schelling pointedly distinguished, namely theater and dance, precisely by their different references in the antecedent arts. But even this blurring of esthetic categories is instructive. For ultimately, it is neither dance nor theater in their respective fullnesses that Rosenzweig wishes to marshal for service in perfecting community, but a small shared piece of them that indifferently reproduces each of them whole, namely gesture.

Rosenzweig does not explicitly claim for gesture what Schelling might call the reproduction in particular of the universal wholes of dance and theater. But the explicit claims he does make for it imply that it can bear within itself the whole power of these two arts to structure community around themselves. It is gesture that "perfects man for his full humanity," by reducing "the space separating man from man" to the space traversed by a single, even very slight motion (SR 322); so slight, perhaps, that the space itself no longer separates at all but is all connection, like the "Love me!" command that hones language to so narrow and concentrated a space, the words are converted by the sheer pressure of their confinement into the very act they command. Rosenzweig offers several examples of the power of gesture: the army salute between soldiers of equal rank, which evokes for them the whole history of "working and suffering together . . . and the danger common to both" (SR 322); or the "power of the glance," wholly unforgettable, of the goddess of love, who "danced at last only with her eyes" (SR 372).

But now it is no longer just balletomanes who understand what Rosenzweig means by the poetry of dance. All lovers of literature will, in response to Rosenzweig's discussion, recall their favorite descriptions of sometimes very minute gestures that conjure whole worlds of connective feeling. There is, to build on Rosenzweig's example, the transvestite dancer whose artistic brilliance consists of "hardly moving at all" except for "very subtle movements, loose, relaxed, of the shoulder and hips";[79] the lost lady whose "glance . . . made one's blood tingle," whose charm was "in the quick recognition of the eyes," and who "had always the power of suggesting things much lovelier than herself";[80] and the sleepless little boy who prepares for the "volatile essence" of the nightly maternal kiss with the "punctiliousness which madmen use who compel themselves to exclude all other thoughts from their minds while they are shutting a door, so that when sickness of uncertainty sweeps over them again they can triumphantly face and overcome it with the recollection of the precise moment in which the door was shut."[81] The dance, the glance, the kiss may all transpire in that by now familiar infinitesimally small space where all distance vanishes.

But Rosenzweig weights the dancelike gesture with still heavier philosophical content. The glance, unlike the word, survives as vividly in memory as it was at performance. The break between performance and memory is a mirror in which the reflection shows as powerfully as the reflected. The reflective power of gesture that expands to dance may mirror a whole people in itself. This is precisely what occurs in "festival processions and parades" (SR 372) when, as spectators join the procession, the distinction between performer and reflective audience breaks down. The unity of performance and reflection is the old idealist self-consciousness revisited. By means of the dancelike liturgical gesture, church-going observance becomes church-constituting people of God.

This is most literally true for the part of the Christian liturgical calendar that the applied art of dance serves, namely the festivals of redemption. Redemption for Christianity is the conversion of the nearest neighbor to its livable figures of creation, revelation, and redemption. The figures of redemption are the secular festivals, like Corpus Christi, that spill outside the church building into its worldly confines. This figure of redemption merges with creation when the first pagan observer of the procession is moved to join in. The figure of redemption culminates for Christianity in the sacramental figure of its own creation and constitution, namely baptism. Ultimately, redemption is for the church what Schelling might call an act of self-affirmation.

Rosenzweig understands the incremental incorporation of the Christian into community as a continuum of rising self-consciousness. The applied arts contribute supportively along the way. Thus the first awareness of belonging to one community reaches the Christian through the service of the word. This service unites the congregants in a silent space of communal attentiveness to scriptural reading or preaching. It was architecture that foretold this space. Next, the service of the Eucharist unites the congregants in a community of inward feeling, most literally figured by the ingested host. It was music that foretold this community of feeling, "but which now, in the partaking of the sacrament [which figures the body of both Christ and the church] becomes fully conscious" (SR 363). Architecture foretold community but did not create it, since the occupants of a church building could ignore each other, as they would if they were different groups of visiting tourists. If the tourists were persuaded to participate in the music that culminates in the Eucharist, then architecture's unfulfilled promise of community would begin to be realized (SR 361). Finally, if the tourists, now practicing Christians, accompany the congregation on its redemptive festivals out into the world, they participate in the church's own expansive self-affirmation.

Rosenzweig calls music, in its application to Christian liturgy, "the guide of souls" (SR 371). But all the arts are guides into the stages of the liturgical cycle they respectively serve. Perhaps part of the reason the individual must be guided into the liturgy is that, from outside it, it represents a loss of freedom. Between directives from the prayerbook and the clergy to rise, to bow, to sit, to listen, or to speak prescribed words, the individual who, before entering the course of completed Christianity is already a self-contained whole, must regard this sustained context of commanded gesture a confinement indeed. On a Baeckian reading, it is a confinement; on a Schellingian reading, it is not. Rather, the prescriptions provide the structure on the basis of which freedom can differentiate itself from caprice. Architecture already inaugurates this freedom by its ironic, nonpurposive imitation of purposeful spatial structure. Architecture, which begins Rosenzweig's sequence of the applied Christian arts, predicts a future freedom. The participant in choral song sacrifices the whim to speak what he will, in exchange for prescribed words that are, from the standpoint of language's living, dialogical use, "entirely free of purpose" (SR 362). It is just the structured purposelessness of liturgical acts that constitutes the freedom of which their performers partake. The height of freedom is reached in the applied liturgical art of dance, which Rosenzweig calls a "self-exposition" (SR 372). Prescription and performance merge, just as in the "Love me!" command. It is another vanishing of distance, such as Schelling saw in intellectual intuition or, more appropriately in the context of this discussion, as the poet Yeats saw when he wrote:

> O body swayed to music, o brightening glance,
> How can we know the dancer from the dance?[82]

The liturgy is a structure with which one can merge, and emerge free. Certainly this is also how Rosenzweig understood the body of the Jewish commandments. But from what does the liturgy free us? The transcendence of purpose was a characteristic mark of eternity. The freedom liturgical observance confers is, in part, from time. This was also the freedom known in the Schellingian artwork, which mastered time. But the freedom is also from suffering. Both art and the Christian liturgy overcome suffering by structuring it. By giving figures for the contradictions on which the pagan soul is wracked—the fated and free God, the perduringly finite human, the incompletely reasoned world—the Christian liturgy consoles. But so does art. Rosenzweig's account of art's tragic content follows Schelling's depiction of the tragic hero, who freely accepts the affliction that is not his due. For Rosenzweig, as for Schelling, Prometheus is prototypical (SR 376). The artist is already tragic by accepting the self-enclosure that is imposed on him, not as any due punishment, but because the logic of miracle demands it. But his consolation are his artworks that, while he is creating them, figure for him his own self-enclosed world. "In the depiction he reconciles the contradiction that he himself exists and that suffering too exists at the same time" (SR 376). The appreciative viewer knows the same consolation, in reverse, as connoisseur. The same art that serves the liturgy, also declares its own self-sufficiency, and offers an alternative to Christian redemption. Rosenzweig does not consider the possibility that art, in a rebellious mood, might declare its own purposeless self-sufficiency within the very context of the liturgy, and inversely subordinate the liturgical forms to itself. Kant, that great depreciator of positive religion, pointed the way to art's rebellion against religion when he inadvertently linked esthetic ideas to ceremonies in analogy: esthetic ideas "quicken" and "animate the soul"[83] just as religious ceremonies "quicken truly practical dispositions."[84] The quickening is, in religion's case, an intensification of devotion to the moral law; and in art's, of the imagination as it searches the Understanding, unsuccessfully, for concepts that might be adequate to the infinitely interpretable esthetic idea. If religious and esthetic signals were ever crossed, the liturgy might quicken in the manner of an esthetic idea, and invite the connoisseur's self-absorbed appreciation of it. Then the liturgy would be a stage in the self-enclosedly redemptive course of art. This would hardly disturb Schelling, for whom the liturgy already redeems precisely in its capacity as art. But Rosenzweig would have to concede, with Baeck, that the price Christianity pays for converting paganism is the ever present possibility of succumbing to paganism itself.

The heart of the enmity between Christianity and Judaism is over Judaism's unrelenting witness to Christianity against all self-enclosed paganisms of completed redemption. For Christianity is tempted to take the endpoints of its trifurcated way—wholly spiritual God, perfected human, completed world[85]—for self-enclosed achievements in the present instead of as, in the spirit of the Kantian ideas of reason, spurs to its work in the world. Judaism can stand guard against this for Christians, even over the church's protest, just because Judaism has no connection to paganism at all. The Jew is not the converted individual, who must first be a philosopher; he is converted before his birth by his incipient location in a community that already lives in and for redemption. Not individuality, but peoplehood pertains to the Jewish essence. And the people is a "self-contained whole into which the individuals have dissolved" (SR 343). The secular category that challenges the spiritual hegemony of a people is not art which, as Schelling said, is always of and for individuals, but the state (SR 332). The state, it is true, has esthetic pretensions, as Rosenzweig admits when he acknowledges the comparisons that have been made between art and the ancient polis. But within the context of the *Star*, the state is pointedly distinguished from art as both the opponent of art, and Judaism's particular challenge.

Art neither challenges Judaism nor serves significantly in its liturgical cycles as "guide of souls." Since Judaism addresses the Jewish people, and the people already constitutes a community, there is no need of a helping agent to negotiate the distance between the individual and community. It is precisely the givenness of the Jew's communal sense, which, howsoever unconscious, requires only a "gentle push"[86] to be restored to consciousness, that permits the "conspicuous lack of attention" (SR 358) of congregated Jews to scriptural readings or sermons, so essential to building Christian community. Nonetheless, Judaism does bear a relation to art very like its relation to philosophy. Judaism mirrors the self-enclosures of art. This already appears in the challenge the state poses to Judaism, to the extent that the state is comparable to a work of art. Certainly the ethnic whole of the Jewish people, into which individuals may be seen to have dissolved, resembles the esthetic whole of the artwork, into which the details of inner form are dissolved (SR 55, 60). Judaism's liturgical structures figure the relations of creation, revelation, and redemption, just as Christianity's do, only not outwardly towards the non-Jewish world, but inwardly towards its own. The church stands in an ultimately all-encompassing expansion of brotherliness. The festivals of redemption carry redemptive love out into the world. But Jews stand in a self-enclosed temporal line of propagation (SR 305). Their world does not expand (SR 329). Instead, the universal is figured in liturgical acts that occur within the confines of the people, a particular that in Schelling's sense of the term reproduces the universal within itself.

If Judaism were the perfect mirror of art, it would not be relational. As against art, Judaism encloses genuine relations that expand, in figures, to the whole of humanity. But Judaism breaks with art in another way. Art is never hated, not even by Christianity, its spiritual rival. And yet Rosenzweig titles the section on the Jewish witness to Christianity, "The Eternal Hatred for the Jew" (SR 415). Perhaps the hatred the Jew receives can be read as an affliction that falls to him, as self-enclosure to the artist, or punishment to the ancient hero, by necessity's decree, rather than by any freely willed fault. As the artist must endure self-enclosure for the sake of miracle, and the hero, unmerited affliction for the sake of his freedom, so must the Jew endure hatred for the sake of the truth that the creation of the world is not yet complete.

In a section entitled "Modern Tragedy" within part two of the *Star*, Rosenzweig considers "the tragedy of the saint" (SR 211). The phrase may be read in two ways, as implying that saints are tragic, or that tragic dramas may have saints for heroes. The ambiguity suits Rosenzweig's remarks. For the saint, as we saw, is a border-figure, hovering between the end of modern drama and the beginning of modern life. Drama that attains the saint produces the saint, and ends. Perhaps the modern movie, "Jesus of Montreal," about an actor who, by playing Christ, becomes Christlike, illustrates.[87] Rosenzweig's suggestive title for the ensuing section is, "The Servant of God." It is God's servant who suffers so famously in Isaiah 49–53. On traditional Jewish readings, the Suffering Servant is Israel. The saint, like the servant, is "resolved on the sublime" (SR 211). If he is resolved, then he does not suffer inwardly, and can only "become the

hero of a tragedy by virtue of his earthly residue of profane ingredi-
ents" (SR 211), i.e., by outward impositions of physical and social
degradation that leave the soul untouched. Certainly this hero is
"the exact antithesis of the hero of classical tragedy" (SR 211) who,
as Schelling observed, attains his tragic heights precisely by accepting into his inward self-enclosure outwardly imposed afflictions. The
modern tragic hero is anticipated by that ancient precursor of the
modern, with whom Rosenzweig has already shown much affinity,
namely Plato, whose Socratic hero is so resolved on the sublime that
he dies inwardly unmoved by outward events. But if, as Schelling
writes, "an entire people can be constituted an individual" (PA 215),
then Rosenzweig comes within a hairsbreadth of suggesting that Israel is the art-ending hero of modern drama.

In that case, Judaism has its encounter with paganism after all,
not as its rival, but as the barely visible end of the pagan's own deepest aspiration. "In the eternal people the nations experience that
closed eternity for which they themselves reach out helplessly," not
suspecting that in that people "they are presented with a picture of
their universal future" (SR 378). Life imitates art here as closely as
it ever could. For the peoples follow art into the end-fulfillment of Israel which, itself ever just vanishing, vanishes finally into the hypercosmic All.

Conclusions

It would simplify the romantic reading of Rosenzweig through
Schelling if the philosophy of *The Philosophy of Art* could be identified with idealism, the art with romanticism, and the two separated
over an irreconcilable divide. Then all Rosenzweig's explicit rejections of idealism, and all his overt acceptances of art, could be taken
for at least implicit affirmations of romanticism. We could read the
Star's relation to idealism and romanticism along the lines of a protocosmic equation, where x was the passive affirmation of romantic
essence, and y the active negation of idealist otherness. But idealism and romanticism are not so separable. The harnessing of idealist philosophy to the interpretation of art is a definitive mark of
early German romanticism. The Schelling who inverts is as much
idealist as romantic. *The Philosophy of Art*, though conceding the

oppositional nature of philosophy and art, argues for their ultimate indifference, not their separate locations on either side of an idealist/romantic divide.

But then, must the resounding sounds of idealism's rejection, which echo so loudly up until the last sections of the *Star*, be taken for a rejection of romanticism, too? They might have been, if we had not been able to uncover in the *Star* so many explicit and implicit congruences with Schelling's romantic idealism: the protocosmic elements, so like the Schellingian potences; the inversive passages across mirroring divides; the particular that is indifferently its universal (true of the Jewish people in Rosenzweig); the concessions to contingency and magic, and to fracture, over the issue of the infinite All; the perspectivism; the Platonism; the vanishing of separations; the idealism of art; the art of Christianity; and, perhaps most importantly, the shared testimony to the irresistible attraction of the All, even if all vanishings before it are postponed to the final end.

Rosenzweig's principal departure from Schelling is on the issue of indifference. Indifference is banished from the *Star*'s middle part, on reality, where relation functions in its stead. The central location of reality in the unfolding of the *Star* is not coincidental. It figures there the human perspective of the beloved soul, which must begin philosophizing, if philosophize it must, *in medias res*. It is only from the perspective of reality that protocosmic philosophy and its mirror image, hypercosmic prayer, can be understood. Schellingian romanticism figures in Rosenzweig's reality as presupposition, at least to the extent that the protocosmic thought courses copy the movements of the potences, and as prolepsis, insofar as in prayerful vision the All reinstates itself. But Rosenzweig explicitly subordinates these presuppositions and prolepses to the reality that gives them meaning.

Art's office in the *Star* repeats philosophy's. Art is either presupposition to reality, as in the first and second parts, or accompanist to a vision that succeeds reality, as in the third, but never, itself, wholly real. Philosophy and art preserve their intimacy across the passage from Schelling to Rosenzweig, but jointly surrender their pinnacle position for one subordinate to reality.

In a brief section of the esthetics component of the second part of the *Star*, Rosenzweig discusses the tone of poetry (SR 246–247). The tone of a poetic work, if not its diction, is always plain to the attentive reader (SR 249). *The Star of Redemption* and *The Philosophy of Art* may illustrate. Both are systematic works. In their evident comfort with system, both demote the merely "empirical" (PA 280,

SR 190). And yet both are self-consciously aware that they are en-meshed in the empirical, and so are negotiating a contradiction. Schelling registers this very early on when he deems the very idea of *The Philosophy of Art* a contradiction (PA 13), and Rosenzweig, when in the extension of the *Star* into his own commentary on it, he names its philosophy, in the late Schelling's words, an "absolute empiri-cism."[88] For empiricism's tone is usually experimental and open-ended, not absolute. If the contradiction between system and sense restates an older opposition between ideal and real, then the affinity between the "idealist" Schelling and the "realist" Rosenzweig comes into clearer focus. For then as sensible systematizers both, they are both trying to negotiate the same real-ideal divide.

The tones of their negotiations are in several ways inverse. Schelling speaks out of what by his own reckoning is the age of the ideal. If he is himself an idealist, he ought to like his age. But life under the ideal is self-contradictory and self-divided. No wonder the tone of *The Philosophy of Art* is "muted and skeptical."[89] By contrast, the tone of the *Star* is, at least by the third part, after the rigors of the first part and the pathos of the second, unrestrainedly exuber-ant. Especially as it approaches its end, it increasingly exhorts, ad-monishes, and prayerfully exclaims. Rosenzweig can barely contain his enthusiasm for reality. He seems scarcely content merely to priv-ilege the reality-defining relations of creation, revelation, and re-demption within part two, but wants to send his readers off into the lived and *nichtmehrbuchlich*[90] experience of them. Rosenzweig's vengeance on the ideal, which as early as *The Philosophy of Art* had already begun to show a depressive affect, was to banish it from re-ality into the forward and rearward wings of the book.

But the banishing is reminiscent of the older Platonic banish-ment of poetry. Plato's own poetic gifts are too much in evidence for the exile to be taken very seriously. Rosenzweig does not so much de-mote the partnership of art and philosophy as leave them to their own unreal height, and diminish the importance of scaling it, or, if it must be scaled, let it be only once. The tone of Rosenzweig's, every-one should philosophize once,[91] is concessive, not hortatory. The trouble is that Rosenzweig's own scaling of the height is enthusiastic and triumphant, not concessive or resigned. It is true that the flag he plants on the hypercosmic peak of vision, where philosophy and art stand watching, claims it and them for the real world of the cos-mos. But is it really back into the cosmos that Rosenzweig sends us when, in exclamatory capitals, at the close of his book, he bids us turn off the hypercosmic heights *"into life"*? We have been in life all along; even the ancient pagans, who worshipped according to all the wrong figures were, unbeknownst to themselves, situated in relations of creation, revelation, and redemption. Our sole advance over them is that now, and even ever since the beginning of the second millennium BCE, there are habitable, performable figures that raise these relations to consciousness. These are the liturgical cycles of Judaism and Christianity. But these cycles belong to the hypercosmos. They inhabit the same rearward, unreal, height-scaling wing of the *Star* that philosophy and art find so congenial. Rosenzweig does not banish us from the heights; he instates us in a livable continuity of them.

Rosenzweig's enthusiasm for the real is not for the open-ended, unstructured love of part two, but for its Jewish and Christian instatings in part three. In his pioneering work on Rosenzweig, *Franz Rosenzweig: His Life and Thought*,[92] Nahum Glatzer portrays himself not as editor or author, but merely as presenter, as though the life and thought are already so organically intertwined, they have accomplished in advance, by themselves, all the connective work that usually falls to biographic authors and editors. Rosenzweig would appreciate this testament to his life's influence on his thought, for it locates him with Kierkegaard, Schopenhauer, and Nietzsche squarely within the tradition of the new philosophy. Rosenzweig's own life turned ever more deeply into the Jewish liturgical cycles, so much so that, across the broad spectrum of Jewish observance in the late twentieth century, he is still taken by many for the model *ba'al teshuvah* (returnee to Judaism). It is not as though Rosenzweig would have all his readers take up Judaism, or even choose between Judaism and Christianity. In "The New Thinking," he observes, with regard to the Jewish tone of the *Star*, that a Christian would have expressed the same ideas differently, and even a pagan, though he could not have used the relation-denying thought forms of any historical paganism, might have his own words for creation, revelation, and redemption.[93] What is important to Rosenzweig is that what he has expressed be somehow expressed, that is, that real life be faithfully figured.

But what is the point of figuring the real? Why not rest unconsciously in its embrace?; Why not, if not because the ideal itself compels? In the ideal the real is mirrored and knows itself for the first time. That, in simple sum, is the message of idealism. The idealist is a little like the music-lover who, untrained in musical notation and theory, exerts himself painstakingly to learn this, as Rosenzweig puts it, most difficult of the arts (SR 249). All who suffer over the intimations of chaos lying on the other side of consciousness, find comfort in idealism which, with the single axiom that a known limit is ipso facto surpassed, overcomes all limits. Indifference was the perfect expression of limit-banishing idealism. No enduringly unconscious reality can surpass the conscious ideal, since real and ideal are one. The trouble with indifference is that it does not sustain: the real and ideal come unraveled as, by the very admission of indifference's own theorist, Friedrich Schelling, they do in modernity, and leave even him prone to a muted and skeptical tone.[94]

The Jewish and Christian liturgical cycles are, for Rosenzweig, a more reliable idealizing of the real. It is just because reality is sustainedly idealizable that Rosenzweig is so enthusiastic for it. And now Baeckian romantic critique swells the stream of Schellingian idealism that feeds Rosenzweig's enthusiasm for reality. For the instatement of eternity was a Baeckian romantic goal. The realized ideality of the Baeckian romantic and the idealized reality of the Schellingian idealist mirror each across their common meeting ground in Rosenzweig's *The Star of Redemption*.

CHAPTER 5

Conclusions

In large measure, Baeck's theory of romanticism fails the test of Schelling's *The Philosophy of Art*. Redemption is not clearly the determinative category of Schelling's *Kunstreligion*, nor is it unambiguously subsumable under experience, feeling, or passivity. Ethics is not dismissed from *The Philosophy of Art*, but receives two articulations there, one ancient, one modern. Darkness does not go unbalanced by light, and the seeming completion of the system is disrupted. Only Baeckian romantic inversion passes the test, though with two qualifications: what is inverted is not, as Baeck asserts, lost in the inversion; and the subject on whose behalf the inversion occurs is not us, but God.

This is not to say that Baeck has not offered a viable picture of romanticism; but simply that the romantic amalgam he constructs must draw from a broader range of sources. Schelling belongs to the early period of German romanticism. Later romanticism did indeed advance more deeply into darkness, so much so that in popular literature today, the romantic is identified with, among other things, despondency, insanity, and the occult. In these permutations of darkness, the reaching may well be for a redemption that bypasses moral considerations, and the hope, for a completion that excludes all fissure. Indeed, if St. Paul is admitted to the ranks of the romantics, as Baeck proposes, then we can just as easily turn backward from *die Fruehromantiker* eighteen hundred years, as forward two hundred years, to find aching in abundance for a completed redemption.[1]

Baeck offers a broad, generally unnuanced picture of romanticism that answers to some popular conceptions of it. It is as though Baeck and Schelling stand at opposite ends of the spectrum along which romanticism has been conceived. Schelling, together with the other early German romantics, exemplifies the romanticism that is taken to continue, not disrupt, the rationalist projects of the Enlightenment. Irrationality, darkness, and feeling do not simply complete, but themselves take on the aspects of the opposites that ineluctably ground them, namely reason, thought, and light. Early romanticism longs for the very system it denies itself, and in the longing is the tribute to older Enlightenment ideals. Baeck, by contrast, has articulated some features of the romanticism that is taken to reject the Enlightenment sensibility in toto. The usefulness of the dichotomy between Baeck and Schelling is in the space between the poles they constitute, where the *Star*, so situated, may show its own romantic shades.

As Baeck would predict of a romantic work, the *Star* is a star of redemption, and not of the revelation that centers the book; ethics in the Kantian sense, *is* set aside; darkness *does* frame the experiential center, in the form of chaos on one side and blinding light on the other; and inversion is the means by which redemption is secured. Of course, the distortion in the fit is over the meaning of redemption itself. What Baeck calls redemption is closer to what Rosenzweig means by revelation. For Rosenzweig's revelation participates with Baeck's redemption in the same family of ideas: experience, feeling, miracle, and passivity. The Baeckian romantic relation with God, cut off from the rest of the world, translates into the *Star* as the presupposition of redemption, not its defining content.

But against Baeckian romantic ideals of self-enclosed remove, the *Star* does not present itself as a system in which the reader is invited to rest. Rather, Rosenzweig all too eagerly pushes the reader out of his book: he rushes us through a first part we can barely understand, past descriptions of experience he would rather we knew, firsthand, for ourselves, and on to a climactic vision from which we are summarily dismissed. Unlike the *Phenomenology of Spirit*, which progressively absorbs us, the *Star* behaves like what Lacoue-Labarthe and Nancy call an exergue: a structure that exists to deconstruct, in testament to something else.

In that, the *Star* fails to meet the Baeckian romantic criterion of completion. But here is where Rosenzweig shows an affinity with the alternative romanticism that Schelling represents. In its movement toward self-destruction, the *Star* exemplifies the self-divisions that Schelling understood as definitively romantic or modern. In a characteristically romantic movement, the whole of *The Philosophy of Art* illustrates the modernity that part of it describes. Divided between ancient and modern, the work denies itself the construction of a future reconciliation. *The Philosophy of Art* comes at the end of the first period of German romanticism. Its very form, of the lecture series, may itself attest to decline, like Hegel's owl of Minerva, and partially explain the tone of the book.

Rosenzweig took upon himself the inheritance of Schelling's incompleted task to systematize the relation between being and becoming. The systematic form of Rosenzweig's work, and its attention to philosophy and to a philosophically explicated art, are as close to Schelling's romanticism as they are removed from Baeck's. Even the buoyancy of tone that marks parts of *The Star of Redemption* may be read in inverse continuum with Schelling's maturing darkness. And yet, there is a point at which all three thinkers converge, namely at the concept of liturgy. This institutional structure that, for Baeck, typifies romantic authoritarianism, and for Schelling, the communally livable artwork, is at least one point that the otherwise so discordant Baeck and Schelling agree to take seriously. But if the authoritarianism of the liturgy feeds Baeck's polemical tone, and its status as a mere remnant feeds Schelling's skepticism, it is precisely the combination of sustainable structure, which Baeck takes for authoritarian, and communal livability, which Schelling takes for diminished remnant, that accounts for the enthusiasm it inspires in Rosenzweig. Liturgy is a romantic endpoint for all three thinkers. It is part of the final pieces that close the Baeckian romantic system in on itself; of the heritage of ancient, public drama that has, otherwise, largely disappeared for Schelling; and of the hypercosmic vision that Rosenzweig postponed to the end of the *Star*.

It is just the livability of the structured liturgy that resists the movement of "religion" to encase it. Among the many ways Rosenzweig descends from the early romantics are his suspicions of institutional authority. It is not self-perpetuating institutions, but the system of the *Star* that raises the liturgy to its high, hypercosmic office. But this must not conceal from less romantically attuned eyes that what Rosenzweig has crowned with the role of ending his system is more commonly understood as: religion, and that by taking time for explicit subordinations of philosophy and art, which nonetheless function in grounding ways, Rosenzweig has taken up, after the philosophy-privileging *Phenomenology of Spirit* and the art-privileging *System of Transcendental Idealism*, the third way of hierarchically arranging these three expressions of the highest-reaching German *Geist*.

The romantic reading of the *Star* is complicated by its in some ways so much more obvious debt to philosophical idealism. The relation between idealism and romanticism, of at least the early German variety, is a little like that between two very similar, close, and competitive siblings. Idealist systems like Hegel's can, by closing in on themselves so perfectly, close off the characteristically *fruehromantische* postponement of closure; or they can, like Schelling's, repeatedly miss the closure they seek or even systematize indefinitely enduring places of nonclosure.

The third book of part three of the *Star* presents a vision of final closure. But it is a vision ineluctably future, vitally God's alone. What is vitally accessible to us, now, from out of the vision is multiply divided: first between Judaism and Christianity, which are inimical, and then, within Judaism and Christianity themselves, between their respective self-divisions and bifurcations. Like the Schellingian modern, the Rosenzweigian Jew and Christian are suspended over contradictions which do not, now, resolve except, in imitation of the sporadic momentariness of Schelling's esthetic redemption, once annually, and for Jews alone, on Yom Kippur. Closure is otherwise future; the present is unresolved.

In this regard, a remark of Baeck's about Rosenzweig, and of Rosenzweig's about Schelling, may be instructively compared. Rosenzweig on Schelling:

> Vor lauter Programm kam er nie zum vollendeten Werk, vor lauter "Ideen" und "Entwuerfen", "Darstellungen" und "Nachrichten", Verheissungen und halben Erfuellungen nie zur ganzen Tat. "Ich werde" blieb sein letztes Wort, wie es sein erstes war.[2] (From nothing but program he never came to the complete work, from nothing but ideas and sketches, representations and reports, promises and half-fulfillments, never to the full act. "I will" remained his last word, as it was his first.)

Baeck on Rosenzweig:

> He had found his task: he had been able to begin a work. And he knew that no man can bring a work to an end; it is given him only to begin a work.[3]

Baeck may have had in mind a passage from Pirkei Avoth in the Mishnah: "You are not required to complete the work, but neither are you at liberty to abstain from it."[4] By applying this saying to Rosenzweig, Baeck means to claim him for the open-ended striving

of classical religion. But of course it is just the beckoning of the unfinished or infinite that differentiates *fruehromantische* sensibility
from its idealist counterpart, that subsumes Schelling's esthetic idealism under the rubric of romanticism, and that invites a philosophical descendant, some one hundred years later, to take up the task
again. The specific task to which Baeck alludes is the Bible translation Rosenzweig undertook with Buber. Rosenzweig died before it
was complete. But one might claim just as much that he predeceased
the completion of the *Star*. The *Star* itself hovers between the proleptic completion of Yom Kippur and the postponed completion for
which the rest of the world pines. The hypercosmic vision of the end-
completion exists to vanish in the incomplete reality of the present, a
passage poignantly symbolized by Jewish ritual when it allows the
fragile habitations of Sukkot to follow so closely on the day-long syn-
agogue-enclosure of Yom Kippur. The ceasing of hypercosmic unreality serves to refocus attention on the incompletion of the real. The
Star, too, left Rosenzweig with a feeling of incompletion. In later
years, he observed that he would have written the book differently,[5]
did indeed attempt a more accessible rewriting, but, unsatisfied with
the results, withdrew it from publication.[6] If Schelling passed an incompleted work onto Rosenzweig, Rosenzweig in turn bequeathed to
later generations the unfinished task of the *Star* to be interpreted.[7]
We have attempted a contribution to that end.

Notes

Chapter 1: Introduction

1. Gershom Scholem, "Rosenzweig and his book *The Star of Redemption*," in *The Philosophy of Franz Rosenzweig*, ed. Paul Mendes-Flohr (Hanover, New Hampshire: University Press of New England for Brandeis University Press, 1987), 23.

2. Moshe Schwarcz, *Safah, Mitos, 'Omanut* (Jerusalem: Schocken Books, 1966), 333.

3. *Encyclopedia Judaica*, s.v. "Schelling, Friedrich Wilhelm Joseph."

4. Hannah Arendt, *Rahel Varnhagen: The Life of a Jewish Woman*, trans. Richard and Clara Winston (San Deigo and New York: Harcourt, Brace, Javanovich, 1974), xvii.

5. Siegbert Prawer, introduction to *The Romantic Period in Germany: Essays by Members of the London University Institute of Germanic Studies*, ed. Siegbert Prawer (London: Weidenfeld and Nicolson, 1970), 4.

6. Hermann Cohen, "Deutschtum und Judentum," in *Juedische Schriften* (Berlin: C.A. Schwetschke & Sohn, 1924), vol. 2. Partially translated in Hermann Cohen, *Reason and Hope*, trans. Eva Jospe (Cincinnati, Ohio: Hebrew Union College Press, 1993).

7. Jacques Derrida, "Interpretations at War: Kant, the Jew, the German," *New Literary History* 13 (1991): 51–52.

8. Gershom Scholem, "On the Social Psychology of the Jews in Germany: 1900–1933," in *Jews and Germans from 1860 to 1933: The Problematic Symbiosis*, ed. David Bronsen (Heidelberg: Carl Winter Universitaetsverlag, 1979), 15, 27.

9. Raymond Immerwahr, "The Word 'Romantisch' and Its History," in *The Romantic Period in Germany*, 36.

10. Henry Chadwick, "Romanticism and Religion," in *The Future of Modern Humanity*, ed. J. C. Laidlaw (Cambridge, England: Modern Humanities Research Association, 1969), 18.

11. Anatole Broyard, "Can Art Make the World Safe for Romanticism," *New York Times Book Review*, 7 February 1988, p. 13; Jamie James, "Though This Were Madness, Was There Method in't?" *New York Times*, 7 August 1994, sec. 2, pp. 27–28; Jim Koch, "Transforming a Ghoul into a Leading Man," *New York Times*, 6 November 1994, sec. 1, pp. 59, 62; James Oestreich, "A Hit 1,000 Years in the Making: Atop of the Pop Charts Gregorian Chants," *New York Times*, 8 May 1994, sec. 2, p. 32.

12. Prawer, introduction to *Romantic Period in Germany*, 1–3.

13. Philippe Lacoue-Labarthe and Jean-Luc Nancy, *The Literary Absolute*, trans. Philip Barnard and Cheryl Lester (Albany: State University of New York Press, 1988), 8.

14. Wilhelm Wackenroder, *Outpourings of an Art-Loving Friar*, trans. Edward Mornin (New York: Ungar, 1975).

15. Philippe Lacoue-Labarthe and Jean-Luc Nancy, *Literary Absolute*, 155–164.

16. Immerwahr, "The Word 'Romantisch,'" 44.

17. Novalis, *Henry von Ofterdingen*, trans. Palmer Hilty (Prospect Heights, Illinois: Waveland Press, 1964).

18. For example, Jean Paul, "Vorschule der Aesthetik," in *Werke*, ed. Norbert Miller (1967), 5:86, quoted in Ernst Behler, "Romantik, das Romantische," *Historische Woerterbuch der Philosophie*, 1976.

19. Novalis, "Christendom or Europe," in *Hymns to the Night and other Selected Writings*, trans. Charles E. Passage (Indianapolis: Bobbs-Merrill Educational Publishing, 1960).

20. Prawer, introduction to *Romantic Period in Germany*, 4; Paul Roubiczek, "Some Aspects of German Philosophy in the Romantic Period," in *The Romantic Period in Germany*, 320; William Arctander O'Brien, *Novalis: Signs of Revolution* (Durham, North Carolina: Duke University Press, 1995), 216–271.

21. Chadwick, "Romanticism and Religion," 28.

22. Arthur Lovejoy, "The Meaning of Romanticism for the Historian of Ideas," *Journal of the History of Ideas* 2 (1941): 262–264.

23. Immerwahr, "The Word 'Romantisch,'" 35.

24. Ibid, 47; Prawer, introduction to *Romantic Period in Germany*, 6.

25. Novalis, *Henry von Ofterdingen*, 108, 110, 111, 156.

26. Lovejoy, "Meaning of Romanticism," 272.

27. Friedrich Schlegel, "Atheneum Fragments," in *Philosophical Fragments*, trans. Peter Firchow (Minneapolis: University of Minnesota Press, 1991), 24.

28. Friedrich Schlegel, "Brief ueber den Roman," in *Kritische Ausgabe*, ed. Ernst Behler (Munich: F. Schoeningh, 1958), 2:333, quoted in Behler, "Romantik, das Romantische."

29. Schlegel, "Atheneum Fragments," 32.

30. Theodore Ziolkowski, *German Romanticism and Its Institutions* (Princeton, New Jersey: Princeton University Press, 1990), 329–333.

31. Library of Congress Subject Cataloging Division, *Library of Congress Subject Headings* (Washington, D.C.: Cataloging Distribution Service, 1988), 2:1961.

32. Henry A. Lea, "Mahler: German Romantic or Jewish Satirist?" in *Jews and Germans from 1860 to 1933*, 288, 299.

33. Arthur Lovejoy, "On the Discrimination of Romanticisms," *PMLA* 39 (June 1924): 235.

34. For example, Jacob Neusner, "Judaism," in *Our Religions*, ed. Arvind Sharma (San Francisco: Harper San Francisco, 1993), 304.

35. Gershom Scholem, "Three Types of Jewish Piety," in *Sinn und Wandlungen des Menschenbildes*, ed. A. Portmann, Eranos Jahrbuch, vol. 38 (Zurich: Rhein-Verlag, 1972), 331–347.

36. Eveline Goodman-Thau and Christoph Schulte, "Kabbala und Romantik: die juedische Mystik in der deutschen Geistesgeschichte von Schelling zu Scholem," *Athenaum: Jahrbuch fuer deutsche Romantik* 2 (1992), 243–249; Scholem comments on affinities between Lurianic kabbalah and Schelling in *Major Trends in Jewish Mysticism* (New York: Schocken Books, 1941), 409, 412; see also Novalis, *Werke, Tagebuecher und Briefe Friedrich von Hardenbergs*, ed. Hans-Joachim Maehl and Richard Samuel (Munich: Carl Hanser Verlag, 1978–1987), 2:499.

37. The rise of mysticism "coincides with what may be called the romantic period of religion." Scholem, *Major Trends in Jewish Mysticism*, 8.

38. Ralph Marcus, "The Hellenistic Age," in *Great Ages and Ideas of the Jewish People*, ed. Leo W. Schwarz (New York: Random House, 1956), 98, 102.

39. Abraham Sachar, *The Course of Modern Jewish History* (New York: Vintage Books, 1990), 161; also, David Rudavsky, *Modern Jewish Religious Movements* (New York: Behrman House, 1967), 190.

40. Rudavsky, *Modern Jewish Religious Movements*, 142, 220; Hans Liebeschuetz, *Von Georg Simmel zu Franz Rosenzweig: Studien zum Juedischen Denken in deutschen Kulturbereich* (Tuebingen: J.C.B. Mohr (Paul Siebeck), 1970), 180–184; David Sorkin, *The Transformation of German Jewry, 1780–1840* (New York: Oxford University Press, 1987), 164–171.

41. Sorkin, *Transformation of German Jewry*, 96.

42. George L. Mosse, *The Crisis of German Ideology: Intellectual Origins of the Third Reich* (New York: Schocken Books, 1981), 124, 183.

43. From Heine's notebooks, quoted in Michael Hamburger, *Contraries: Studies in German Literature* (New York: E.P. Dutton & Co., 1970), 146.

44. Guenter Oesterle, "Juden, Philister und romantische Intellektuelle: Ueberlegungen zum Antisemitismus in der Romantik," *Athenaum: Jahrbuch fuer deutsche Romantik* 2 (1992), 55–89.

45. Ibid., 71.

46. Schlegel, "Atheneum Fragments," 31.

47. Michael A. Meyer, "Reform Jewish Thinkers and their German Context," in *The Jewish Response to German Culture*, ed. Jehuda Reinharz (Hanover, New Hampshire: Published by University Press of New England for Clark University, 1985), 70; Novalis, *Werke, Tagebuecher und Briefe*, 2:427, 2:764; Schelling, *The Philosophy of Art*, trans. Douglas W. Stott (Minneapolis: University of Minnesota Press, 1989), 58.

48. Schelling, *Ages of the World*, trans. Frederick de Wolfe Bolman (New York: AMS Press, 1967), 159; Novalis, *Werke, Tagebuecher und Briefe*, 2:776; Werner J. Cahnman, "Friedrich Wilhelm Schelling and the New Thinking of Judaism," in *German Jewry: Its History and Sociology*, ed. Joseph B. Maier, Judith Marcus and Zoltan Tarr (New Brunswick, New Jersey.: Transaction Publishers, 1989), 222.

49. Cahnman, "Friedrich Wilhelm Schelling," 215.

50. Otto Poeggeler, "Between Enlightenment and Romanticism: Rosenzweig and Hegel," in *The Philosophy of Franz Rosenzweig*, 122.

51. Dorit Orgad, "Jehuda Halevi ve-Rosenzweig: Re'ionot Choffim ve-Mishnoteihem," *Da'at: A Journal of Jewish Philosophy and Kabbalah* 21 (1988), 115.

52. "Das juedische Denken hat in Rosenzweig seinen Pascal und Kierkegaard kongenialen Ausdruck gefunden." (Jewish thought found in Rosenzweig its equivalent of Pascal and Kierkegaard.) Albino Babolin, "Der Begriff der Erloesung bei Franz Rosenzweig," in *Der Philosoph Franz Rosenzweig*, ed. W. Schmeid-Kowarzik (Kassel: Verlag Karl Alber, 1988), 2:608.

53. Franz Rosenzweig, "Stefan Georg," in *Kleinere Schriften* (Berlin: Schocken Verlag, 1937), 503.

54. Scholem, "Franz Rosenzweig and His Book *The Star of Redemption*," 21.

55. Lacoue-Labarthe and Nancy, *Literary Absolute*, 49.

56. Ibid., 11.

57. Franz Rosenzweig, *The Star of Redemption*, trans. William Hallo (Notre Dame, Indiana: Notre Dame Press, 1985), 143. Further page references to *The Star of Redemption* are prefixed with the abbreviation, SR, and given, parenthetically, in the body of the text.

58. Paul Tillich, *The Construction of the History of Religion in Schelling's Positive Philosophy*, trans. Victor Nuovo (Lewisburg, Penn.: Bucknell University Press, 1974), 40.

59. Hegel, *Phenomenology of Spirit*, trans. A.V. Miller (Oxford and New York: Oxford University Press, 1977), 13, 26, 66.

60. Immanuel Kant, "What is Enlightenment?," in *Critique of Practical Reason and Other Writings in Moral Philosophy*, trans. Lewis White Beck (Chicago: University of Chicago Press, 1949), 286.

61. Friedrich Schelling, *System of Transcendental Idealism*, trans. Peter Heath (Charlottesville, Va.: University Press of Virginia, 1978), 231.

62. Lacoue-Labarthe and Nancy, *Literary Absolute*, 122.

63. Hegel, *Phenomenology of Spirit*, 51.

64. Lacoue-Labarthe and Nancy, *Literary Absolute*, 67.

65. Ibid, 48.

66. "The existentialists most of all seem perennially entangled with idealism." Robert Gibbs, *Correlations in Rosenzweig and Levinas* (Princeton, New Jersey: Princeton University Press, 1992), 34. "The Romantics make it even more difficult to include feeling in philosophy. The task is left to the existentialists . . . ." Roubiczek, "German Philosophy in the Romantic Period," 318.

67. Franz Rosenzweig, *Franz Rosenzweig: His Life and Thought*, presented by Nahum Glatzer (New York: Schocken Books, 1961), 130, 174.

68. Leo Baeck, "Types of Jewish Understanding from Moses Mendelssohn to Franz Rosenzweig," *Judaism* 9 (Spring 1960): 163–168. Albert Friedlander, "Leo Baeck and Franz Rosenzweig," in *Der Philosoph Franz Rosenzweig*, 1:248.

69. Friedlander comments on the lack of "personal closeness" between Baeck and Rosenzweig. Friedlander, "Leo Baeck and Franz Rosenzweig," 248.

70. Rosenzweig, *Franz Rosenzweig: His Life and Thought*, 117.

71. Glatzer, "The Frankfurt Lehrhaus," in *Essays in Jewish Thought*, 256, 264.

72. Albert Friedlander has compared them in "Die messianische Dimension bei Franz Rosenzweig und Leo Baeck," in *Aus zweier Zeugen Mund: Festschrift fuer Pnina Nave Levinson und Nathan Peter Levinson*, ed. J. H. Schoeps (Gerlingen: Bleicher, 1992), 167–176; also in Friedlander, "Leo Baeck and Franz Rosenzweig."

73. Friedlander, *Leo Baeck: Teacher of Theresienstadt*, 141.

74. Franz Rosenzweig, "Ein Rabbinerbuch," in *Kleinere Schriften*, 43–49; partially translated in Rosenzweig, *Franz Rosenzweig: His Life and Thought*, 120.

75. Franz Rosenzweig, "Apologetic Thinking," in *The Jew: Essays from Martin Buber's Journal "Der Jude," 1916–1924*, trans. Joachim Neugroschel, ed. Arthur A. Cohen (University, Alabama: University of Alabama Press, 1980), 265–266.

76. Ibid., 266.

77. Ibid., 272; cf. Hegel, *Phenomenology of Spirit*, 66.

78. Rosenzweig, "Apologetic Thinking," 272.

79. Franz Rosenzweig, *Briefe und Tagebuecher*, II: 1918–1929 in *Der Mensch und sein Werk: Gesammelte Schriften*, I, ed. Rachel Rosenzweig and Edith Rosenzweig-Scheinman (The Hague: Martinus Nijhoff, 1979), 918, 919.

80. Ibid, 919.

81. Glatzer, "The Frankfurt Lehrhaus," 259.

82. Hermann Cohen, *Religion of Reason out of the Sources of Judaism*, trans. Simon Kaplan (New York: Frederick Unger, 1972), 20–22, 202.

83. Lacoue-Labarthe and Nancy, *Literary Absolute*, 40.

84. Friedlander, *Leo Baeck: Teacher of Theresienstadt*, 120.

85. The following summary account is abstracted from Ernst Behler, "Romantik, das Romantische," in *Historisches Woerterbuch der Philosophie*, 1976.

86. Carl Schmitt, *Political Romanticism*, trans. Guy Oakes (Cambridge, Massachusetts: MIT Press, 1986), 29–30.

87. Friedlander, *Leo Baeck: Teacher of Theresienstadt*, 37.

88. Leo Baeck, "Romantic Religion," in *Judaism and Christianity*, trans. Walter Kaufmann (Cleveland and New York: World Publishing Co.,

1958; Philadelphia: Jewish Publication Society of America, 1958), 232–233, 251–152. Further page references to "Romantic Religion" are prefixed with the abbrevation, RR, and given, parenthetically, in the body of the text.

89. Schmitt, *Political Romanticism*, 56.

90. Fritz Strich, *Deutsche Klassik und Romantik; oder Vollendung und Unendlichkeit*, 4th ed. (Bern: A. Francke Ag. Verlag, 1949), 19–30.

91. Rosenzweig, *Briefe und Tagebuecher*, II, 1918–1919, p. 903.

92. Friedrich Schelling, *The Philosophy of Art*, trans. Douglas Stott (Minneapolis: University of Minnesota Press, 1989), xxvii–xxviii. Further references to *The Philosophy of Art* are prefixed by the abbreviation, PA, and given, parenthetically, in the body of the text.

93. Michael Ovsjannikov, "Die aesthetische Konzeption Schellings und die deutsche Romantik," in *Natur, Kunst, Mythos: Beitraege zur Philosophie F. W. J. Schellings*, Schriften zur Philosophie und ihrer Geschichte, 13 (Berlin: Akademie:Verlag, 1978), 130; Jochen Schulte-Sasse, "The Concept of Literary Criticism in German Romanticism 1795–1810," in *A History of German Literary Criticism 1730–1980*, ed. Peter Uwe Hohendahl, trans. Franz Blaha and others (Lincoln, Nebraska: University of Nebraska Press, 1988), 157.

94. Richard Crouter, introduction to Friedrich Schleiermacher, *On Religion: Speeches to Its Cultured Despisers*, trans. Richard Crouter (Cambridge, England and New York: Cambridge University Press, 1988), 30.

95. Lacoue-Labarthe and Nancy, *Literary Absolute*, 28.

96. Azade Seyhan, *Representation and Its Discontents: The Critical Legacy of German Romanticism* (Berkeley: University of California Press, 1992), 18, 48.

97. Schmitt, *Political Romanticism*, 55–57.

98. Franz Rosenzweig, "Das Aelteste Systemprogramm des deutschen Idealismus," in *Kleinere Schriften*, 249.

99. Ibid., 272–273.

100. Lacoue-Labarthe and Nancy, *Literary Absolute*, 79.

101. Roubiczek, "Some Aspects of German Philosophy in the Romantic Period," 305.

102. A. R. Caponigri, "Romanticism, Philosophical," in *New Catholic Encyclopedia*.

103. Edmund Husserl, "Philosophy as a Rigorous Science," in *Shorter Works*, trans. Peter McCormick and Frederick Elliston (Notre Dame, Indiana: University of Notre Dame Press, 1981), 168.

104. Friedrich Schlegel, "Atheneum Fragments," 24.

105. Elsa Rachel-Freund, *Franz Rosenzweig's Philosophy of Existence*, trans. S. L. Weinstein and R. Israel (The Hague: Martinus Nijhoff, 1979); Robert Gibbs, *Correlations in Rosenzweig and Levinas* (Princeton: Princeton University Press, 1992); Stephane Moses, *System and Revelation*, trans. Catherine Tihanyi (Detroit: Wayne State University Press, 1992); Xavier Tilliette, "Rosenzweig et Schelling," *Archivio di Filosofia* 53, no. 2/3 (1985).

106. Franz Rosenzweig, *Briefe*, ed. Edith Rosenzweig (Berlin, 1935), 299, quoted in Werner J. Cahnman, "Friedrich Wilhelm Schelling and the New Thinking in Judaism," 236.

107. Tilliette, "Rosenzweig et Schelling," 145–146.

108. Rosenzweig, "Das Aelteste Systemprogramm," 275.

109. Ibid., 263.

110. For a history of the interpretations, see Frank-Peter Hansen, *Das Aelteste Systemprogramm des deutschen Idealismus: Rezeptionslehre und Interpretation* (Berlin: De Gruyter, 1989).

111. Ibid.; also, Franz Rosenzweig, "Das Aelteste Systemprogramm." For English translation, see Friedrich Hoelderlin, "The Oldest System-Program of German Idealism," in *Essays and Letters on Theory*, trans. Thomas Pfau (Albany: State University of New York Press, 1988), 154–156.

112. Hoelderlin, "Oldest System-Program," 154.

113. Rosenzweig, "Das Aelteste Systemprogramm," 240.

114. Hoelderlin, "Oldest System-Program," 154.

115. Rosenzweig, "Das Aelteste Systemprogramm," 245.

116. Ibid., 244.

117. Schelling, *System of Transcendental Idealism*, 231.

118. Ibid., 232–233.

119. Rosenzweig's interpretation is faulted here by Frank-Peter Hansen, *Das Aelteste Systemprogramm*, 20–44.

120. Rosenzweig, "Das Aelteste Systemprogramm," 267, 269.

121. Ibid., 273–277.

122. Rosenzweig, "Vertauschte Fronten," in *Kleinere Schriften*, 354–356.

123. Rosenzweig, "Das Aelteste Systemprogramm," 277.

124. Norbert Samuelson, *An Introduction to Modern Jewish Philosophy* (Albany: State University of New York Press, 1989); Shmuel Bergman, *Dialogical Philosophy from Kierkegaard to Buber*, trans. Arnold A. Gerstein (Albany: State University of New York Press, 1991); Julius Guttman, *Philosophies of Judaism*, trans. David W. Silverman (New York: Schocken Books, 1973); Nathan Rotenstreich, *Jewish Philosophy in Modern Times* (New York: Holt, Reinhart & Winston, 1968).

125. Robert Gibbs, *Correlations in Rosenzweig and Levinas*, 9. Gibbs comments on Rosenzweig's "idiolect" of German.

126. Samuelson, *Introduction to Modern Jewish Philosophy*, 216–217.

127. As Walter Benjamin appears to have done. Stephane Moses, "Walter Benjamin and Franz Rosenzweig," *The Philosophical Forum* 15 (Fall–Winter 1983–1984): 190–195.

128. Franz Rosenzweig, "Das neue Denken," in *Kleinere Schriften*, 374.

129. R. Horowitz, "Kavim le-be'aioth ha-safa ve-ha-dibur be-hagut Rosenzweig," *Da'at* 6:25, quoted in Dorit Orgad, "R. Yehuda Halevi ve-Rosenzweig," 115.

130. Rosenzweig, "Das neue Denken," 391.

Chapter 2: A Reading of The Star of Redemption *through Romantic Religion*

1. Franz Rosenzweig, "Apologetic Thinking," 272; Franz Rosenzweig, "The New Thinking," in *Franz Rosenzweig: His Life and Thought*, 201, 204.

2. Franz Rosenzweig, *Briefe und Tagebuecher*, II: 1918–1929, p. 903.

3. Franz Rosenzweig, "Apologetic Thinking," 271.

4. Franz Rosenzweig, "Apologetic Thinking," 267.

5. Uriel Tal calls it, "perhaps one of his [Baeck's] most important efforts" in *Religious and Anti-Religious Roots of Modern Anti-Semitism*, Leo Baeck Memorial Lectures, no. 14 (New York: Leo Baeck Institute, 1971), 3. Alexander Altmann calls it a "great essay" in *Leo Baeck and the Jewish Mystical Tradition*, Leo Baeck Memorial Lectures, no. 17 (New York: Leo Baeck Institute, 1973), 10. Samuel Sandmel notes that it is "among the best known of Baeck's essays" in *Leo Baeck on Christianity*, Leo Baeck Memorial Lectures, no. 19 (New York: Leo Baeck Institute, 1975), 12.

6. Rosenzweig, "Apologetic Thinking," 271.

7. Franz Rosenzweig, "Das neue Denken," 382.

8. Rosenzweig, "Apologetic Thinking," 271.

9. Rosenzweig, "Das Aelteste Systemprogramm," 276.

10. Spinoza, *Spinoza's Ethic's*, trans. Andrew Boyle (New York: Dutton, 1959), 224.

11. Rosenzweig, "The New Thinking", 205.

12. Immanuel Kant, *Critique of Judgment*, trans. Werner S. Pluhar (Indianapolis: Hackett Publishing Company, 1987), 29.

13. Immanuel Kant, *Critique of Pure Reason*, trans. Norman Kemp Smith (New York: St. Martin's Press, 1965), 608.

14. Leo Baeck, "Romantische Religion," in *Aus drei Jahrtausenden* (Berlin: Schocken Verlag, 1933), 54. "Man does not live but is lived, and what remains to him is merely . . . experience" (RR 204).

15. Hegel, *Phenomenology of Spirit*, 46.

16. Experience is so identified on p. 220 of "Romantic Religion"; feeling, on p. 195; passivity, on p. 192; miracle, on p. 227.

17. Rosenzweig, "Das Neue Denken," 374.

18. Actually, Rosenzweig's claim is that "only the singular can die" (SR, 4). A particular universal, e.g., a species of animal, is more sustainable than a concrete singularity, e.g., an individual animal, but is still prey to extinction, as environmentalists are concerned to note.

19. The transition from ethics to religion occurs, according to Cohen, just because moral universals cannot speak to the moral and physical suffering of private individuals. Hermann Cohen, *Religion of Reason out of the Sources of Judaism*, 165–168.

20. In this regard, Stefan Meineke's comments on Rosenzweig's idealization of Bethmann Hollweg, German chancellor from 1909 to 1917, are perhaps telling. Meineke, "Franz Rosenzweig in History and Politics," in *Leo Baeck Institute Yearbook* 36 (1991): 472–475.

21. Rosenzweig, "Das Neue Denken," 383.

22. Rosenzweig, "The New Thinking", 205.

23. Ibid., 198.

24. Ibid., 207.

25. Reiner Wiehl, "Experience in Rosenzweig's New Thinking," in *The Philosophy of Franz Rosenzweig*, 62.

26. Rosenzweig, "The New Thinking," 207.

27. Wiehl, "Experience in Rosenzweig's New Thinking," 57, 60.

28. "Revelation means the experience of a present which . . . rests on the presence of a past" (SR 157).

29. Rosenzweig explains that historical theology was enlisted to protect the subjectivity of present experience from any challenges to its validity from the past. This instance of theology functioning defensively provides Rosenzweig with another context for differentiating the true grounding of theology he seeks, from the poor substitute of apologetics (SR 108).

30. Ludwig Feuerbach, "Towards a Critique of Hegelian Philosophy," in *The Young Hegelians*, ed. L. Stepelevich (Cambridge, England: Cambridge University Press, 1983), 116.

31. Franz Rosenzweig, "'Urzelle' des *Stern der Erloesung*," in *Kleinere Schriften*, 362.

32. In *Philosophical Inquiries into the Nature of Human Freedom*, Schelling presents his own early idealism, which took the form of "identity philosophy," as an enlivened or ensouled Spinozism. Schelling, *Philosophical Inquiries into the Nature of Human Freedom*, trans. James Gutmann (LaSalle, Illinois: Open Court, 1936), 22–24.

33. Rosenzweig, "The New Thinking," 200.

34. Feuerbach, "Towards a Critique of Hegelian Philosophy," 105.

35. Ludwig Feuerbach, "Provisional Theses for the Reformation of Philosophy," in *The Young Hegelians*, 161.

36. Ludwig Feuerbach, *Principles of the Philosophy of the Future*, trans. Manfred Vogel (Indianapolis: Hackett Publishing Company, 1986), 54.

37. Passivity at the level of sheer belovedness also conditions knowledge. It is just when it acknowledges being loved that the soul becomes certain of God who loves it (SR 182).

38. Schlegel, "Athenaeum Fragments," 75.

39. Franz Rosenzweig, "Atheistische Theologie," in *Kleinere Schriften*, 279.

40. Cf. Kant: "Personality is the capacity for respect for the moral law." Immanuel Kant, *Religion within the Limits of Reason Alone*, trans. Theodore Greene and Hoyt Hudson (New York: Harper & Row, 1960), 23.

41. Hermann Cohen, *Religion of Reason out of the Sources of Judaism*, 165–168.

42. Though nonethical in the Kantian sense, the relations of revelation that Rosenzweig describes in part two of the *Star*, between God, human, and

world, might well be judged ethical by other criteria. Emmanuel Levinas, who deeply admired Rosenzweig, traces the roots of his own overtly ethical theory back to the concepts of revelation and relationality in the *Star*. Recent commentators have explored the connections between ethics in Levinas and relationality in Rosenzweig. See Robert Gibbs, *Correlations in Rosenzweig and Levinas* (Princeton, New Jersey: Princeton University Press, 1992) and Richard A. Cohen, *Elevations: the Height of the Good in Rosenzweig and Levinas* (Chicago: University of Chicago Press, 1994). But just as Rosenzweig's understanding of philosophy was too tied to the Hegelian past to serve as the subsuming category of his new thinking—Rosenzweig preferred to call the new thinking a theology—so his understanding of ethics was too rooted in the Kantian past to serve as the subsuming category of the relations of creation, revelation, and redemption he presents in the *Star*. Later thinkers might find in the *Star* a dialogical philosophy and a relational theory of ethics. But more distance from Kant and Hegel than Rosenzweig himself knew had to intervene before dialogue (rather than dialectic) could appear as philosophy, and relationality (rather than subsumption under the law) as ethics.

43. L. P. Hartley, *Eustace and Hilda* (New York: Putnam, 1958), 365.

44. Friedrich Meinecke, *Historicism: The Rise of the New Historical Outlook*, trans. J. E. Anderson (London: Routledge and K. Paul, 1972), 415.

45. Ibid., 297–298.

46. Ibid., 489.

47. Isaiah Berlin, foreword to Meinecke, *Historicism*, p. l [i.e. 50].

48. Stefan Meineke, "Franz Rosenzweig in history and politics," 464. Meineke cites a diary entry from Rosenzweig, dated November 20, 1906, which is published in Franz Rosenzweig, *Briefe und Tagebuecher*, I, 1900–1918, p. 65.

49. Shlomo Avineri, "Rosenzweig's Hegel Interpretation," in *Der Philosoph Franz Rosenzweig (1886–1929): Internationaler Kongress*, 2:832–834.

50. Rosenzweig, *Hegel und der Staat* (Munich and Berlin: Oldenburg, 1920), 2:246, quoted in Avineri, "Rosenzweig's Hegel Interpretation," 834.

51. Avineri, "Rosenzweig's Hegel Interpretation," 833.

52. Baeck, "Romantische Religion," 119.

53. Franz Rosenzweig, *Der Stern der Erloesung* (Frankfurt am Main: Suhrkamp Verlag, 1990), 436.

54. Rosenzweig, *Stern der Erloesung*, 467.

55. Paul Mendes-Flohr, "Franz Rosenzweig and the Crisis of Historicism," in *The Philosophy of Franz Rosenzweig*, 160.

56. Gershom Scholem, "On the 1930 Edition of Franz Rosenzweig's *Star of Redemption*," in *The Messianic Idea in Judaism* (New York: Schocken Books, 1971), 320.

57. Scholem, "On the 1930 Edition of Franz Rosenzweig's *The Star of Redemption*," 320.

58. Baeck, "Mystery and Commandment," in *Judaism and Christianity*.

59. Baeck sets the ethical lives both Paul and Luther led in opposition to the doctrines they taught (RR 254).

60. Christian romanticism is "the religion of pure egoism" (RR 281).

61. See also: "night of the Nought" (SR 46); "darkness of the Aught" (SR 87).

62. There is also the darkness of the tragic hero's world (SR 78).

63. Scholem, "On the 1930 Edition of Franz Rosenzweig's *The Star of Redemption*, 323.

64. Friedrich Schelling, *Ages of the World*, trans. F. de Wolfe Bolman, Jr. (New York: AMS, 1967), 144.

65. Baeck quotes a poem by Nietzsche. The image of the waves of the world also occurs in Feuerbach, but there they refresh and enliven rather than drown. Feuerbach, *Principles of the Philosophy of the Future*, 67.

66. Rosenzweig also mentions Hermann Cohen in this connection (SR 21).

67. "Not life but death perfects the created thing into individual solitary thing" (SR 274).

68. Hegel, *Phenomenology of Spirit*, 9.

69. Rosenzweig, "'Urzelle' des Stern," 364.

70. Ibid., 372.

71. For Hegel's discussion of force, see Hegel, *Phenomenology of Spirit*, 79–103.

72. Hegel, *Phenomenology of Spirit*, 83.

73. Plato *Phaedrus* (trans. Jowett) 249–250.

74. Hegel, *Phenomenology of Spirit*, 56.

75. "The soul . . . attains being, a being visible to itself, only when it is loved" (SR 182).

76. Rosenzweig refers to the "difficult constructive parts" of the *Star* in "Das Neue Denken," 379.

77. Thanks to Peter Fenves for calling attention to this feature of the *Star*.

78. Fichte, *Science of Knowledge*, trans. P. Health and J. Lachs (New York: Cambridge University Press, 1982), 94ff.

79. Nathan Rotenstreich, "Rosenzweig's Notion of Metaethics," in *The Philosophy of Franz Rosenzweig*, 85.

80. Rosenzweig, "Das Neue Denken," 384.

81. Rosenzweig states this case in terms of philosophy and theology (SR 108).

82. Paul Nathanson, *Over the Rainbow: the Wizard of Oz as a Secular Myth of America* (Albany: State University of New York Press, 1991).

83. Rosenzweig, "Aelteste Systemprogramm," 269.

84. Rosenzweig, "Das neue Denken," 396–397. Once life has begun out of the book, the book becomes *"Nichtmehrbuch"*.

85. Rosenzweig, "The New Thinking," 200.

86. Hegel, *Phenomenology of Spirit*, 66.

87. Feuerbach, *Principles of the Philosophy of the Future*, 58.

88. Kant, *Critique of Judgment*, 165–170.

89. Ibid., 168.

90. Nietzsche, *Genealogy of Morals*, trans. Walter Kaufmann and R. J. Hollingdale, and *Ecce Homo*, trans. Walter Kaufmann (New York: Vintage Books, 1989), 284.

91. "Every romanticism demands the sacrifice of the intellect" (RR 207).

92. "What is good here is characterized by repose" (RR 219).

93. Nietzsche, *Beyond Good and Evil*, trans. Walter Kaufmann (New York: Vintage Books, 1989), 9–32.

94. These are the Genesis account of creation, the Song of Songs, and Psalm 115.

95. See Elsa Rachel-Freund, *Franz Rosenzweig's Philosophy of Existence*, trans. S. Weinstein and R. Israel (the Hague: Martinus Nijhoff, 1977), 29. Rachel-Freund was one of the first to study the influence of Schelling on Rosenzweig.

96. Rosenzweig, *The Star of Redemption*, 257.

97. Stephane Moses, *System and Revelation*, trans. by C. Tihanyi (Detroit: Wayne State University Press, 1992), 267.

98. Rosenzweig, *The Star of Redemption*, 259.

99. Rosenzweig, "The New Thinking," 206.

100. Richard Siegel, Michael Strassfeld, Sharon Strassfeld, *The First Jewish Catalog* (Philadelphia: Jewish Publication Society of America, 1973). The *Catalog* cites Rosenzweig's *The Star of Redemption* on p. 114, within its chapter on the meaning and observance of the Sabbath.

101. George Mosse, *The Crisis of German Ideology* (New York: Schocken Books, 1964), 88–107.

102. Rosenzweig, "Atheistische Theologie," 284.

103. Rosenzweig, "Apologetic Thinking," 265.

104. Alexander Altmann observes that Rosenzweig took this name from Schelling. Alexander Altmann, "About the Correspondence," in *Judaism and Christianity: The Letters on Christianity and Judaism between Eugen Rosenstock-Huessy and Franz Rosenzweig*, ed. Eugen Rosenstock-Huessy (New York: Schocken Books, 1971), 35.

105. Victor Turner, *Ritual Process* (Chicago: Aldine, 1969), 95.

106. Ibid., 138.

107. Ibid., 107.

108. Hegel, *Phenomenology of Spirit*, 46.

109. Franz Rosenzweig, *Franz Rosenzweig: His Life and Thought*, presented by Nahum N. Glatzer (New York: Schocken Books, 1961), 75, 77.

110. Schelling, *Ages of the World*, trans. F. de Wolfe Bolman (New York: AMS, 1967).

Chapter 3: A Reading of The Philosophy of Art *against Romantic Religion*

1. Friedrich Schleiermacher, *On Religion: Speeches to its Cultured Despisers*, trans. John Oman (Louisville, Kentucky: Westminster/John Knox Press, 1994), 138–141; Novalis, *Pollen and Fragments: Selected Poetry and Prose of Novalis*, trans. Arthur Versluis (Grand Rapids, Michigan: Phanes Press, 1989), 125. See also, W. F. Otto, "Kunstreligion," *Historisches Woerterbuch der Philosophie*, 1976.

2. Ibid., 282. This appendix, entitled "Ueber das Verhaeltnis der Naturphilosophie zur Philosophie ueberhaupt," appears with four other

supplementary additions at the back of the Wissenschaftliche Buchgesellschaft's 1960 reprint edition of *Die Philosophie der Kunst*. These appen-
dices, though part of Schelling's manuscript of *The Philosophy of Art*, had
already been published elsewhere as separate pieces before Schelling's son,
Karl, in 1859, prepared the whole manuscript for publication. They are separate but clearly related parts of Schelling's thought world in *The Philosophy of Art*.

3. Schelling, *Saemtliche Werke*, ed. Karl F. A. Schelling (Stuttgart and
Augsburg, 1856), 7:301, quoted in Michael F. Ousjannikov, "Die aesthetische
Konzeption Schellings und die deutsche Romantik," in *Natur, Kunst,
Mythos: Beitraege zur Philosophe F.W.J. Schellings*, Schriften zur Philoso-
phie und ihrer Geschichte, 13 (Berlin: Akademie-Verlag, 1978), 137.

4. Nature's harmonies are visible "more in the whole than in the individual, and in that individual only for certain moments" (PA 108).

5. Friedrich Schelling, *Bruno*, trans. Michael G. Vater (Albany: State
University of New York Press, 1984), 171.

6. Friedrich Schelling, *Philosophie der Kunst* (Darmstadt: Wissenschaftliche Buchgesellschaft, 1960), 8.

7. Schelling, *Philosophie der Kunst*, 192.

8. David Simpson notes that, for Schelling, "neither modern nor ancient culture is in absolute terms superior to the other." David Simpson,
foreword to Schelling, *The Philosophy of Art*, xix.

9. Hegel, *Phenomenology of Spirit*, trans. A.V. Miller (Oxford: Oxford
University Press, 1950), 8–9; also, Ousjannikov, "Aesthetische Konzeption
Schellings,"130.

10. Fichte, *Science of Knowledge*, trans. Peter Heath and John Lachs
(Cambridge: Cambridge University Press, 1982), 228–229, 237–238.

11. Baruch Spinoza, *Spinoza's Ethics*, trans. Andrew Boyle (London:
Dent, 1959; New York: Dutton, 1959), 7.

12. I substitute the Spinozan infinite for the Schellingian universe on
grounds that they both illustrate the idea of a bounded unboundedness.

13. Schelling, *The Philosophy of Art*, 35.

14. The gods illustrate pure limitation because they are "always com-
mensurate with their limitations" (PA 55), i.e., they are never frustrated by
a desire it is not already in their nature to have fulfilled.

15. In Baeck's scheme of romantic inversion, the miracle becomes
sacrament (RR 221). Schelling implies that the Eucharist is miraculous
when he refers to miracles as "direct intervention of the supersensible into
concrete reality" (PA 77), since that is what happens in Transubstantiation.

16. Schelling, *Bruno*, 159.

17. Ibid., 158–159.

18. Friedrich Schelling, *System of Transcendental Idealism*, trans. Peter Heath (Charlottesville, Virginia: University Press of Virginia, 1978), 46.

19. Schelling, *Philosophie der Kunst*, 26.

20. Hegel, *Phenomenology of Spirit*, 9.

21. Simone Weil, *Gravity and Grace*, trans. Arthur Wills (New York: Octagon Books, 1983), 131–136.

22. Schelling, *Bruno*, 139.

23. Novalis, "Christendom or Europe," in *Hymns to the Night and other Selected Writings*, trans. Charles E. Passage (Indianapolis: Bobbs-Merrill Educational Publishing, 1960), 54–57.

24. Construction "anticipates with reason that to which a correctly executed explication will finally lead" (PA 54).

25. Construction was "a boring show of diversity." Hegel, *Phenomenology of Spirit*, 8.

26. Bernhard Barth, *Schellings Philosophie der Kunst* (Freiburg: Karl Alber, 1991), 16.

27. Schelling, *Bruno*, 137.

28. Schelling, *The Philosophy of Art*, 28.

29. Tennessee Williams, *Night of the Iguana* (New York: New Directions, 1962). No less a theological eminence than Karl Barth was struck by the use of the word "fantastic" in this play. Karl Barth, *Evangelical Theology: An Introduction* (New York: Holt, Rinehart and Winston, 1963), vi.

30. Schelling, *System of Transcendental Idealism*, p. [1].

31. Schelling, *Bruno*, 171.

32. The fountain image appears in the title of the classic work by the medieval Jewish neoplatonist, Ibn Gabirol: *Fons Vitae* (originally in Arabic).

33. Schelling, *System of Transcendental Idealism*, 222.

34. Spinoza, *Ethics*, 2.

35. Michael Vater calls part six an epilogue, thus distinguishing it from the rest of the system. Michael Vater, introduction to Schelling, *System of Transcendental Idealism*, xv.

36. A fact particulary noted in Michael Hamburger, *Contraries: Studies in German Literature* (New York: E.P. Dutton & Co., 1970), 66.

37. Peter Fenves, "Kantian Critical Tradition II," seminar lectures at Northwestern University, Winter 1992.

38. Hegel, *Phenomenology of Spirit*, 66.

39. Drama "does not merely mean or signify its objects, but rather places them before our very eyes" (PA 261).

40. Schelling, *Ages of the World*, trans. Frederick de Wolfe Bolman (New York: AMS Press, 1967), 142, 192.

41. Schelling, *Bruno*, 151.

42. Friedrich Hoelderlin, "Oldest System-Program," 154.

43. David Simpson, foreword to Schelling, *The Philosophy of Art*, xxiv.

44. Schelling implies that all modern art is comic when, in one passage, he defines modern drama as the "combination of opposites," i.e., of tragic and comic elements, in which "both are definitely differentiated," and then, in another, suggests that the "mixed nature" of *The Divine Comedy* is what entitles it to be called a comedy (PA 267–268, 240).

Chapter 4: *A Reading of* The Star of Redemption *through* The Philosophy of Art

1. Franz Rosenzweig, "Das aelteste Systemprogramm," 264.

2. Ibid., 265.

3. Robert Gibbs, *Correlations in Rosenzweig and Levinas* (Princeton, New Jersey: Princeton University Press, 1992); Xavier Tilliette, "Rosenzweig et Schelling," *Archivio di filosofia* 53:2–3 (1985); Stephane Moses, *System and Revelation*, trans. Catherine Tihanyi (Detroit: Wayne State University Press, 1992).

4. Rosenzweig, *Briefe und Tagebuecher*, I, 1909–1918, p. 701.

5. Schelling, *Bruno*, 138–140.

6. Shmuel Hugo Bergman, *Dialogical Philosophy from Kierkegaard to Buber*, trans. Arnold A. Gerstein (Albany: State University of New York Press, 1991), 201.

7. Schelling, *Bruno*, 158ff.

8. Boethius, *Consolation of Philosophy*, trans. V. E. Watts (New York: Penguin Books, 1969), 35.

9. Immanuel Kant, *Critique of Pure Reason*, trans. Norman Kemp Smith (New York: St. Martin's Press, 1965), 327–328.

10. Immanuel Kant, *Religion within the Limits of Reason Alone*, trans. Theodore M. Greene and Hoyt H. Hudson (New York: Harper Torchbooks, 1960), 33.

11. "If ethics is to include sin, its ideality comes to an end," i.e., it cannot be generated out of pure practical reason, but must presuppose something prior to reason. Soren Kierkegaard, *The Concept of Anxiety*, trans. Reidar Thomte (Princeton, New Jersey: Princeton University Press, 1980), 17–18.

12. Rosenzweig, "The New Thinking," 192.

13. Rosenzweig, "Das neue Denken," 375.

14. Gibbs, *Correlations in Rosenzweig and Levinas*, 46–54.

15. Rosenzweig, "Das neue Denken," 377.

16. Ibid., 374.

17. Ibid., 379.

18. Elsa Rachel-Freund, *Franz Rosenzweig's Philosophy of Existence*, 103.

19. Rosenzweig, "Das neue Denken," 382.

20. Ibid., 391.

21. Friedrich Schelling, *Philosophical Inquiries into the Nature of Human Freedom*, trans. James Gutmann (La Salle, Illinois: Open Court, 1936).

22. Rosenzweig, *Der Stern der Erloesung*, 91.

23. Rosenzweig, "Das neue Denken," 377.

24. Schelling, *System of Transcendental Idealism*, 233–234.

25. Leo Baeck, "Types of Jewish Self-Understanding," 116.

26. Nahum Glatzer, introduction to Franz Rosenzweig, *Franz Rosenzweig: His Life and Thought*, xxxvi.

27. Franz Rosenzweig, "Der Konzertsaal auf der Schallplatte," in *Kleinere Schriften*.

28. For example, Rosenzweig would have preferred the first edition of the *Star* to be published in three separate volumes, instead of in the single volume in which it appeared ("Das neue Denken," p. 375). Also, he did not wish his short work, *Understanding the Sick and the Healthy*, to be published at all, and it was, posthumously.

29. Rosenzweig, *Der Stern der Erloesung*, 72.

30. Kierkegaard, *Concept of Anxiety*, 51.

31. Immanuel Kant, *Religion Within the Limits of Reason Alone*, 129.

32. Rosenzweig, "The New Thinking," 202.

33. Ibid.

34. "Jeder soll einmal philosophieren." Rosenzweig, "Das neue Denken," 397.

35. Ibid., 374.

36. cf. Schelling, *Ages of the World*, 119.

37. Rosenzweig, "Das neue Denken," 376.

38. Ibid, 377.

39. Schelling, *System of Transcendental Idealism*, 231.

40. Richard McKeon, introduction to "Logic," in Aristotle, *Introduction to Aristotle*, ed. Richard McKeon (New York: Modern Library, 1947), 2.

41. Schelling, *System of Transcendental Idealism*, 231.

42. Ibid., 68.

43. Schelling, *Bruno*, 161.

44. Schelling, *System of Transcendental Idealism*, 140–145.

45. Feuerbach, *Principles of the Philosophy of the Future*, 58.

46. Immanuel Kant, *Critique of Judgment*, trans. Werner S. Pluhar (Indianapolis: Hackett Publishing Co., 1987), 215.

47. "Saints and martyrs have frequently been regarded as impossible subjects for true tragedy." Louis L. Martz, "The Saint as Tragic Hero: *Saint Joan* and *Murder in the Cathedral*," in *Tragic Themes in Western Literature*, ed. Cleanth Brooks (New Haven: Yale University Press, 1960), 150.

48. Boethius, *Consolation of Philosophy*, 35.

49. Plato *Phaedrus* (trans. Jowett) 279. Karl Jaspers also links philosophy to prayer. But prayer for him stands not at the end of philosophy, sealing it, but before it, on the "frontier" of it. Karl Jaspers, *The Perennial Scope of Philosophy*, trans. Karl Manheim (New York: Philosophical Library, 1949), 82.

50. Rosenzweig, *Franz Rosenzweig: His Life and Thought*, 25.

51. For Rosenzweig, the whole Jewish year is a "curriculum of communal silence" (SR 353).

52. Plato *Phaedrus* (trans. Jowett) 250.

53. Plato *Republic* (trans. Jowett) 533.

54. Ibid., 473.

55. "The view on the height of the redeemed hypercosmos" (SR 424).

56. Plato *Republic* (trans. Jowett) 492, 538–539.

57. Plato *Republic* (trans. Jowett) 387.

58. Johann Jacob Wagner to Andreas Adam, January 6, 1803, quoted in Schelling, *Bruno*, 100.

59. Schelling, *Bruno*, 140–143.

60. Plato *Republic* (trans. Jowett) 477.

61. Ibid., 490.

62. Ibid., 517.

63. From the title of a book by Martha Nussbaum, *The Fragility of Goodness: Luck and Ethics in Greek Tragedy and Philosophy* (New York: Cambridge University Press, 1986).

64. Plato *Symposium* (trans. Jowett) 174; Plato *Republic* (trans. Jowett) 533; Plato *Phaedrus* (trans. Jowett) 250.

65. Plato *Phaedrus* (trans. Jowett) 246.

66. Ibid.

67. Fichte, *Science of Knowledge*, 196.

68. Ibid., 197.

69. Ibid.

70. Maimonides, *Guide of the Perplexed*, trans. Shlomo Pines (Chicago: University of Chicago Press, 1963), 528.

71. Goethe, *Faust*, trans. Walter Kaufman (New York: Anchor Books, 1963), line 439, p. 99.

72. See the section "Romantic Completion" in Chapter 2.

73. Judah Halevi, *The Kuzari*, trans. Hartwig Hirschfeld (New York: Schocken Books, 1964), 226–227.

74. Rosenzweig, *Der Stern der Erloesung*, 422.

75. Ibid.

76. Hegel, *Phenomenology of Spirit*, 58. Sense-certainty, which is actually the poorest kind of knowledge, gives the appearance of being the richest.

77. Stephane Moses, "Rosenzweig in Perspective: Reflections on His Last Diaries," in *The Philosophy of Franz Rosenzweig*, 198.

78. Ibid.

79. Andrew Holleran, *Dancer from the Dance* (New York: New American Library, 1978), 110.

80. Willa Cather, *A Lost Lady* (New York: Grosset and Dunlap, 1923), 41, 70, 172.

81. Marcel Proust, *Swann's Way*, trans. C. K. Scott Moncrieff (New York: Modern Library, 1956), 31–32.

82. William Butler Yeats, "Among School Children," *The Norton Anthology of Poetry*, 3d ed. (New York: W. W. Norton & Company, 1983), lines 63–64.

83. Kant, *Critique of Judgment*, 182.

84. Kant, *Religion within the Limits of Reason Alone*, 189.

85. See the section "Romantic Redemption, in Chapter 2.

86. Franz Rosenzweig, "Towards a Renaissance of Jewish Learning," in *On Jewish Learning*, ed. N. N. Glatzer (New York: Schocken Books, 1965), 65.

87. "Jesus of Montreal," directed by Denys Armand, was released in 1990. For a collection of reviews, see "Jesus of Montreal," *Film Review Annual* (1991): 776ff. David Denby is quoted as saying, "By the end of the movie, Daniel *is* Christ," *New York* (6 June 1990). Daniel Colombe, played by Lothaire Bluteau, is the actor in the story who plays Christ in a passion play.

88. Rosenzweig, "The New Thinking," 207.

89. David Simpson, foreword to Schelling, *The Philosophy of Art*, xxiv.

90. Rosenzweig, "Das neue Denken," 397.

91. Ibid.

92. Franz Rosenzweig, *Franz Rosenzweig: His Life and Thought*, presented by Nahum Glatzer (New York: Schocken Books, 1961).

93. Rosenzweig, "Das neue Denken," 391.

94. Ibid. See the sections, "Ethics," "Darkness," and Conclusions," in Chapter 3.

Chapter 5: Conclusions

1. For ancient anxiety and redemptive longings, see the short book by E. R. Dodds, *Pagan and Christian in an Age of Anxiety* (New York: W. W. Norton & Co., 1965).

2. Rosenzweig, "Das aelteste Systemprogramm," 238.

3. Leo Baeck, "Types of Jewish Self-Understanding from Moses Mendelssohn to Franz Rosenzweig," 167.

4. Aboth 2:16. Translation from *Gates of Prayer: the New Union Prayerbook* (New York: Central Conference of American Rabbis, 1975), 20.

5. Rosenzweig, *Franz Rosenzweig: His Life and Thought*, 161.

6. Nahum Glatzer, "Introduction to Rosenzweig's *Little Book of Common Sense and Sick Reason*," in *Essays in Jewish Thought* (University, Alabama: University of Alabama Pr., 1978), 244.

7. Scholem offers specific reasons why the Star did not, in Rosenzweig's lifetime, receive the interpretation it deserved. Gershom Scholem, "On the 1930 Edition of Rosenzweig's *The Star of Redemption*," in *The Messianic Idea in Judaism* (New York: Schocken Books, 1971), 320–324.

Index